The Rudolf L. Baumfeld Collection of

LANDSCAPE DRAWINGS & PRINTS

The Rudolf L. Baumfeld Collection of

Landscape

Drawings & Prints

GRUNWALD CENTER FOR THE GRAPHIC ARTS

UNIVERSITY OF CALIFORNIA, LOS ANGELES

UCLA Art Council Annual Exhibition

GRUNWALD CENTER
• UCLA •

Published by the Grunwald Center for the Graphic Arts,
University of California, Los Angeles.

Distributed by University of Washington Press,
P.O. Box 50096, Seattle, Washington 98145.

Printed in the United States.

This catalogue has been published in conjunction with an exhibition held at the Wight Art Gallery, University of California, Los Angeles, October 10–December 17, 1989, and at the Spencer Museum of Art, University of Kansas, January 13–March 10, 1991.

Editor: Karen Jacobson
Photography: Larry DuPont

Library of Congress Cataloging-in-Publication Data
Grunwald Center for the Graphic Arts.
The Rudolf L. Baumfeld collection of landscape drawings and prints / Grunwald Center for the Graphic Arts. University of California, Los Angeles.
p. cm.
"UCLA Art Council annual exhibition."
"This catalogue has been published in conjunction with an exhibition held at the Wight Art Gallery, University of California, Los Angeles, October 10–December 17, 1989, and the Spencer Museum of Art, University of Kansas, January 13–March 10, 1991"—T.p. verso.
Includes bibliographical references.
ISBN 0-943739-13-6.—ISBN 0-943739-12-8 (pbk.)
1. Art, Modern—Exhibitions. 2. Landscape in art—Exhibitions. 3. Baumfeld, Rudolf L., d. 1988—Art collections—Exhibitions. 4. Art—Private Collections—California—Los Angeles—Exhibitions. 5. Grunwald Center for the Graphic Arts—Exhibitions. I. UCLA Art Council. II. Frederick S. Wight Art Gallery. III. Helen Foresman Spencer Museum of Art. IV. Title.
N8213.G78 1989
760'.04436'090307479494—dc20 89-23550
CIP

ISBN 0-943739-13-6 (cloth)
0-943739-12-8 (paper)

Cover: Graham Sutherland, *St. Mary's Hatch* (cat. no. 105)

CONTENTS

Foreword · *7*

Acknowledgments · *9*

A Remembrance *Konrad Oberhuber* · *13*

A Tribute *Norman Katkov* · *15*

Fine Prints and Fine Printing:
Rudi Baumfeld and Jake Zeitlin *James Cuno* · *21*

About Landscape *Henri Zerner* · *29*

The Rudolf L. Baumfeld Collection *Cynthia Burlingham* · *35*

Color Plates · *41*

CATALOGUE OF THE EXHIBITION

Holly Barnet-Sanchez · Danuta Batorska · Cynthia Burlingham · James Cuno · Lee Hendrix
Nadine Orenstein · Barbara Sabatine

American · *57*

Austrian · *67*

Dutch and Flemish · *73*

English and Scottish · *123*

French · *159*

German · *191*

Italian · *201*

Selected Bibliography · *213*

Index of Artists · *219*

FOREWORD

WITH THIS CATALOGUE WE acknowledge the legacy of Rudolf L. Baumfeld. At the time of his death, in February 1988, we had been preparing this exhibition for more than a year. Cynthia Burlingham, curator of the Grunwald Center, and I had been introduced to Rudi and his collection by Konrad Oberhuber in December 1986. One month later, again in the company of Professor Oberhuber, now director of the Graphische Sammlung Albertina in Vienna, Cindy and I spent a lovely day with Rudi and concluded that the Grunwald Center must exhibit his collection. We suggested this to Rudi, and he agreed without hesitation and without proscription. When upon his death we learned that he had bequeathed his collection to the Grunwald Center, we felt honored and more determined than ever to acknowledge the generosity and intelligence of the man we had only just come to know.

Although we had known Rudi for just two years, he had long been associated with the Grunwald Center. He was one of the original members of the Committee of the Grunwald Graphic Arts Foundation, as the center was then called, joining E. Maurice Bloch, the first curator of the foundation and later director of the center; Fred Grunwald; and others in 1961 as counsels to the foundation. He served on the committee for more than ten years and then was a founding member of the Friends of the Graphic Arts at UCLA, remaining a member until his death. He and Maurice Bloch worked together very closely in the early years of the center, and Professor Bloch and his students mounted an initial exhibition from Rudi's collection in 1968.

We are grateful that the UCLA Art Council agreed to support this enlarged, scholarly showing of the Baumfeld collection as its annual exhibition for 1989. It is the council's exhibition as much as it is ours. The council has provided necessary funding for the catalogue and accompanying symposium and has generously funded the center's UCLA Art Council Graduate Curatorial Fellowship, which brought Nadine Orenstein of the Institute of Fine Arts at New York University and Barbara Sabatine of UCLA to work on the exhibition and the collection from which it was drawn.

I am especially grateful to Cynthia Burlingham, who, as curator of the exhibition, has worked tirelessly to bring it to a successful and most impressive conclusion. She selected the objects and directed the preparation of this catalogue, all the while writing the introduction and researching and writing many of the entries. She has been the guiding force behind the exhibition, working closely with our many authors and consultants, as well as with the catalogue's designer and photographer and the Wight Art Gallery staff responsible for designing and mounting the exhibition and organizing its educational programs. Cindy joins me in thanking all of them and in acknowledging the Spencer Museum of Art of the University of Kansas, with whom we are sharing this important exhibition.

JAMES CUNO, *Director*
Grunwald Center for the Graphic Arts

Acknowledgments

THIS EXHIBITION and catalogue are a tribute to the extraordinary generosity of Rudi Baumfeld, whose bequest of 857 prints and drawings to the Grunwald Center constitutes one of the most significant gifts in the center's history. Though he did not live to see its execution, the exhibition was in the planning stages prior to Rudi's death in February 1988, and we were fortunate to have had the benefit of his valuable insights and knowledge. The exhibition and catalogue serve to document not only the collection and the history of landscape art but also the rich cultural milieu in Los Angeles in which the collection was formed. I hope that both properly represent his legacy, which has provided UCLA with such an invaluable resource for furthering the goals of education and scholarship.

I am grateful to the UCLA Art Council for agreeing to support this project as its annual exhibition and for its continuing support of all the center's programs. In particular I would like to thank Connie Nagler, president; Lois McLane, chairman, Program and Lectureship Committee; and Kirby Atinsky, docent chairman, for their personal dedication. I also thank O. P. Reed for his generous support.

This catalogue and exhibition have profited from advice and information supplied by the following scholars, and I thank them for their assistance: Shelley Bennett, Timothy Benson, E. Maurice Bloch, Jaap Bolten, Barbara Butts, Françoise Cachin, Marco Chiarini, Richard Field, John Hayes, Anne-Marie Logan, Patrick Noon, Ronald Paulson, Bruce Robertson, David Rodes, Diane Russell, Nesta Spink, Robert Wark, and Andrew Wilton. One of the most enjoyable aspects of preparing this exhibition has been the opportunity to meet many people in Rudi's wide circle of friends, especially Betty and Norman Katkov, Elsie Crawford, David Edberg, and Gere Kavanaugh.

At the Grunwald Center, Susan Melton, registrar, ably supervised the inventory of the entire collection and the travel of the exhibition, and Midori Shigetani, curatorial assistant, provided much-needed help with numerous aspects of the preparation of the catalogue. Maureen McGee, conservation technician, and Mark Watters, consulting conservator, skillfully performed the necessary treatment of works in the exhibition. The staff at the Wight Art Gallery, especially Elizabeth Shepherd, Patricia Capps, Cindi Dale, Lynne Blaikie, and Thomas Hartman, have lent their many skills and talents and provided greatly appreciated advice. I would also like to express my gratitude to Jim Whitney and Gregory Ross for their invaluable contributions.

The writing of this catalogue has been a truly collaborative effort and has benefited from the contributions of many individuals. I thank Konrad Oberhuber for his sensitive memoir of Rudi, and Norman Katkov for allowing us to reprint his delightful tribute. Henri Zerner of Harvard University contributed a thoughtful essay on the nature of landscape, which is an important addition both to the catalogue and to the study of landscape art. Nadine Orenstein, the 1987 UCLA Art Council Fellow, wrote all the Dutch and Flemish entries, and her successor in 1988, Barbara Sabatine, contributed the majority of the French entries as well as many Italian and British entries. Graduate assistant Holly Barnet-Sanchez researched and wrote the entries on the eighteenth-century British works and the German expressionist works. Lee Hendrix, associate curator of drawings at the J. Paul Getty Museum, wrote the entries on the sixteenth-century German works, and Danuta Batorska of the University of Houston wrote about the Grimaldi drawing. I thank all the authors for their diligence and consideration in the face of deadlines. A special acknowledgment is reserved for the late Mary Stansbury Ruiz, who did much of the initial research on the Italian prints. All of us who were privileged to have known her greatly miss her warmth, intelligence, and friendship.

James Cuno, director of the Grunwald Center, has provided, as always, unfailing enthusiasm, friendship, and support and has contributed substantially to the concept of the exhibition in addition to writing an essay and catalogue entries. I have enjoyed working with designer Doyald Young, whose consistently elegant sense of design and dedication to perfection are reflected in this handsome catalogue. It has been extremely rewarding to work with editor Karen Jacobson, and I am grateful for her good judgment and skill in refining a work composed of many voices. Lastly, a special note of thanks to my husband, Leon Kenyon, for his patience and support throughout this project.

CYNTHIA BURLINGHAM, *Curator*
Grunwald Center for the Graphic Arts

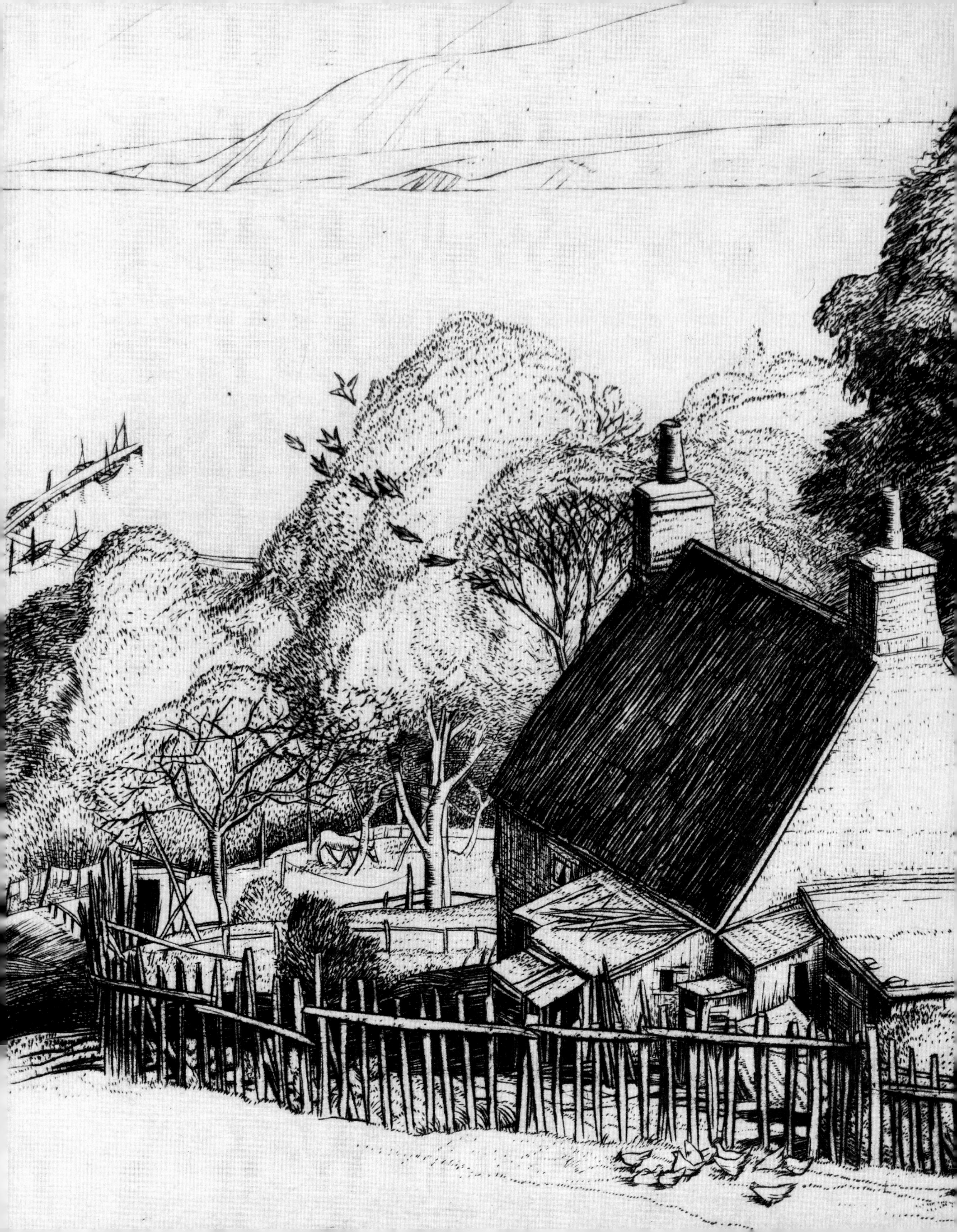

The Rudolf L. Baumfeld Collection of

Landscape Drawings & Prints

Detail of cat. no. 101

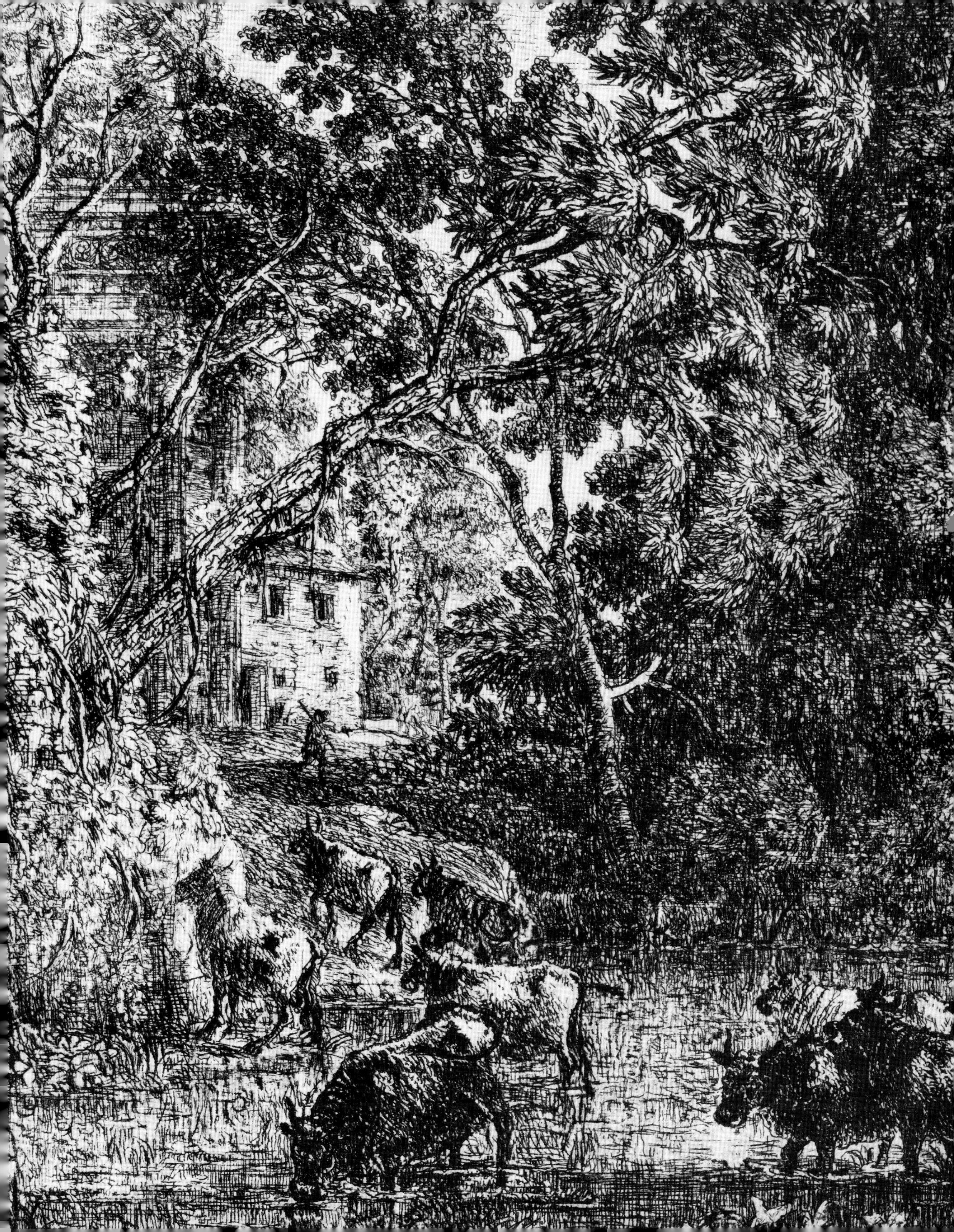

A Remembrance

Konrad Oberhuber

I FIRST MET RUDI BAUMFELD in the early 1970s, when I was a curator at the National Gallery of Art in Washington, D.C. I became a member of the Print Council of America and gave a talk at the group's California meeting. Rudi was one of the National Gallery's patrons. He had given a large group of prints by Jacques Callot to its print collection, which was then still mostly in Jenkintown in the hands of Lessing Rosenwald. Rudi invited me to his quiet, unimposing home and showed me the rest of his collection. I was astonished by his refined taste and the love with which he had pursued his special hobby, the collecting of landscape prints, drawings, and watercolors from many places and periods.

As it turned out, Rudi was a close friend of Nelly Liebmann, a Viennese lady who over the years had become a kind of second mother to my wife and me. I sensed that there was an unfulfilled love affair behind his admiration and subtle criticism of this wonderful woman, whose impeccable taste in furniture, books, and art objects we had always admired. This friendship led us to a circle of cultivated people involved in banking, architecture, philosophy, and art history, centered around this lady of extraordinary charm, who had come to Vienna from a small provincial city and there married Leo Liebmann, a banker, and befriended the others. The Nazis brought tragedy to this circle. The husband died in exile; the friends dispersed. Some came back to Vienna, among them the philosopher Viktor Brod and the art historian Fritz Novotny, who later became the director of a well-known Viennese museum, the Austrian Museum at the Belvedere. They still met regularly at Mrs. Liebmann's apartment near the opera. Rudi appeared there only once a year from America but was always especially welcome and showed his appreciation through extremely considerate gifts.

The members of this small circle were all in some way eccentrics. They were loners who pursued their own affairs quietly but with great determination. They were not at the center of Viennese society but were people of a much more attractive kind, in whom the heart forces prevail and who emanate a loving yet extremely unassuming calm to whomever they meet yet who stand at a critical distance from society. Needless to say, they were all politically left-wing. Nelly Liebmann even tended toward communism but was by far the most radical in her political views. Novotny took pride in his proletarian ancestry and sported a certain roughness through his otherwise extreme aesthetic refinement.

For me, having known all these people only in their later days, it is impossible to imagine them together when they were young and to reconstruct their rela-

Detail of cat. no. 106

tionships and rivalries. I have no doubt, however, that Rudi's taste for art was nurtured by this circle and that his art collection was an expression of his longing for the aesthetic atmosphere of Vienna, which he carried into the New World, where it was fostered by friends such as Jake Zeitlin and Fred Grunwald.

After all, landscape is one of the great loves of the Viennese. Here every Sunday young and old people tramp through the woods surrounding the city. When I recently mounted a show of Italian Renaissance prints at the Albertina, one of the guards approached me and said: "I see only people, mostly nudes, and no landscape. This show is not going to be a popular success." Right he was. Landscape, especially by the Austrian artists of the nineteenth century, is what people here love. They can extend this love to Pieter Bruegel, who has become almost Viennese. Rudi's collection started from that base but grew to encompass all European countries. America gave him a larger view.

In Rudi's light-filled home time always seemed to stand still for a while to allow contemplation and amiable exchange. I am extremely happy that this collection has come to the Grunwald Center for the Graphic Arts. I sincerely hope that it will inspire students and public alike to experience some of that mood of enjoyment and intellectual stimulation that emanated from that small, refined circle of Viennese before World War II and that so bravely continued in the warmth of California.

A Tribute

Norman Katkov*

DEAR RUDI. DEAR FRIENDS. I have lived all my life with a horror of facing an audience. The thought threatens paralysis. I am well into my sixth decade, and this occasion marks only the third time I have risen to speak publicly.

The first occurred early in 1942 when I stood with my right hand upheld and repeated the oath which made me a private in the Army of the United States. The second was a dolorous and anguished event. In both instances my appearance was commanded. So this is my first *voluntary* public appearance, and I think it is no small tribute to the guest of honor.

You shall have to indulge my need to read what I have to say. If I were to try speaking extemporaneously, we would all be inflicted with several moments of increasingly embarrassed silence.

I think most of you have been Rudi's friends longer than my family and I. We are Johnny-come-latelies in the Baumfeld circle. And from the beginning we recognized our chronological liability. We did not retreat from it any more than the prospector retreats from a strike. We were determined to make up in volume what we had lost in time. It has been an easy assignment, even though we have had to share him with all of you. We have persevered. It continues to be one of the most pleasant conditions of our lives.

While all biography is personal, it should of course be tempered with research in the field. I have not avoided that scholarly requirement even though I have taken my own findings over those which might have been contributed by any of you. I am an old reporter, and I believe it is a revealing index of my diligence and affection that I went so far, literally, as to visit Vienna, and not, as you must concede, to pay homage to the Hapsburgs.

I have known Rudi only since his middle years. So what knowledge I possess of the preceding part of his life comes mainly from him. It is not much, and it is not because I lack curiosity. Your individual experiences may differ from mine, but I have always found him to be a particularly private person. I can buttress this proposition by telling you that Jake Zeitlin, a dear and valued friend, learned only last year, quite inadvertently, a fact of Rudi's life that for the rest of us is no more intimate than the color of our cars. I can hear Rudi's reaction to that without

---

*This essay was originally published on the occasion of Rudolf Baumfeld's seventieth birthday on January 1, 1974, and is reprinted by permission of the author.

having consulted him; Jake didn't ask the question, so Rudi did not volunteer the answer.

I cannot remember Rudi avoiding an answer. He is always honest and he is always candid, and not infrequently, his candor does not wait for the question, as many of you ladies who have heard his unsolicited comments about anything, from your coiffures to your clothes, will attest.

I *have* asked questions . . . endlessly. Early on, I learned to my astonishment that the then Gruen partner in charge of design, the architect at the very top of his profession, had been the Peck's Bad Boy of Vienna.

I use the phrase in an educational reference. He was an awful student. By the time he was ready to study architecture, he had no more chance of being admitted to a first-rate university than an Eskimo. I do not have the details at hand, but I am approximating the facts when I tell you that he managed barely to attend a glorified trade school.

I realize that when I said "Peck's Bad Boy" a moment ago I should have used the plural instead of the singular. Because there were two rapscallions hopscotching through the corridors of the Imperial City: Rudi and his ally, Victor Gruen.

I'm not certain who influenced whom, but the liaison was permanent, personally and professionally. Since Victor Gruen is six months older, and since he is not here to protest, let us bestow the onus on him.

Rudi has set a terrible scholastic example for my sons, and I would warn them now against the risk of using him as an archetype. The road to Rudi's eminence is rarely marked with flunks. He is a model to marvel at, not to emulate.

From that picaresque beginning, however, followed a successful career. He was a flourishing architect; he lived in the city of his birth and choice. His future was secure, and then Hitler took Austria.

Rudi was well past thirty-five when he reached America, forced to start all over again.

Happily, his academic sidekick had preceded him. Victor Gruen was in California. Of what followed in that salutary entente you are all aware.

By the time Rudi's path crossed mine he was a decisive element in one of the most successful architectural firms in the country. I was instantly aware of a personality I wanted to cultivate. He was modest, he was civilized, he was cultured. His effect on my family and me was immediate, it was profound, and it was lasting. My sons were barely out of play pens when they could identify "Rudi's blue," a particular shade of that color being apparent somewhere on any building he designed.

By the time we bought a house we had our color consultant. We had our interior decorator. We had our exterior decorator. I carry a festering wound because I didn't have the common sense to take the outside lamps he designed when we sold that house.

I cannot remember an occasion when he did not surprise and delight us. If he appeared with a present, the paper he chose to wrap it in blended with the twine, and both complemented the initials of the recipient, which he had cut out and pasted to the container. The container was always so artfully presented that it became in itself a gift.

It is always an honor to have him in our house and a privilege to face him at our table. What he says is always informative and always instructive. I am always amazed at the breadth of his knowledge. It is encyclopedic.

We learned quickly that his candor was complemented by his reliability. If one of the boys brought him a drawing, and I am talking about a little boy, Rudi was as frank in reaction as though he was dealing with an established artist. He never talked down to the boys, and he never deceived them.

All of us were eager students of the Baumfeld conditioning process. Betty rapidly learned to cook without eggs. We all collaborated to keep Frank, the cat, out of the house. We all agreed Frank would have no successor.

Accepting the Baumfeld critique took a little more doing. For one thing, as I've already mentioned, it was delivered regardless of whether it was solicited. We discovered that it was not uncommon for him to cross the threshold, stop in his tracks, stare, and ask, "*Vat* is *dat*?"

"*Dat*" could be Betty's dress, my suit, Dick's shirt, Billy's hair. "*Vat* is *dat*? " meant disapproval. "*Ach*" meant disapproval . . . a shake of the head meant disapproval.

There was and is, blessedly, surcease from his censure . . . food. Baumfeld's idea of a grand dinner table conversation is a spirited discussion of what his hostess is cooking tomorrow. He may very well be unavailable. The *thought* is sufficient.

He doesn't have to be eating to talk about food. He just has to be awake. He identifies hostesses by the specialties he favors: ice cream, chestnuts, fruit dumplings.

I think he only uses the calendar to note the crop harvests.

If you show him food, he tastes it. Then and there. Display a jar of unique and expensive strawberry jam, and he takes a spoonful. Occasionally, after he swallows, you may be privileged to hear, "Tsall right."

Not good, or great, but "tsall right." That means it isn't from Vienna, and therefore couldn't benefit from the water.

All beer, beef, veal, lamb, pork, grain, fruit, bread, butter, can only reach excellence with Viennese water.

You would think a man with a palate so sophisticated that it can distinguish between waters would belong to a master of cuisine. After all, he has eaten at every three-star restaurant in France. He has dined in every fine café from here to Tokyo. Such a man surely is a successor to Brillat-Savarin.

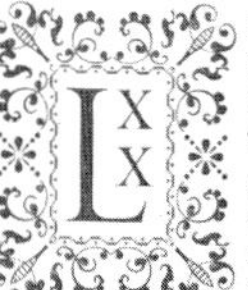

DEAR RUDI. Dear friends. I have lived all my life with a horror of facing an audience. The thought threatens paralysis. I am well into my sixth decade, and this occasion marks only the third time I have risen to speak publicly.

The first occured early in 1942 when I stood with my right hand upheld and repeated the oath which made me a private in the Army of the United States. The second was a dolorous and anguished event. In both instances my appearance was com- ... *voluntary* public ap- ... small tribute to the ... y need to read what ... peaking extempora- ... flicted with several ... arrassed silence. ... been Rudi's friends ... e are Johnny Come ... And from the begin- ... ological liability. We

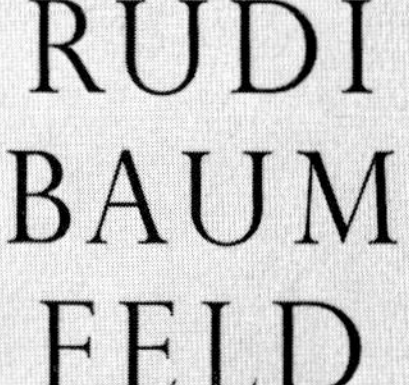

RUDI
BAUM
FELD

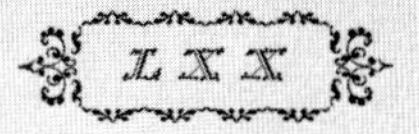

RUDI BAUMFELD'S
70th Birthday
1 JANUARY 1974

A TRIBUTE BY NORMAN KATKOV

Well, I have sampled some of his favorite dishes. Noodles . . . just noodles. Sausage mashed into potatoes. And goulash. And goulash. And goulash.

As for Vienna, I have eaten in that gastronomic citadel . . . "tsall right."

He once told Betty that he should have been a librarian. I shudder at the thought. To have shut himself up in some sequestered hall would have been a crime against society.

He is hardly flamboyant. He remains among the shyest of men. Still, however circumscribed his world, those who have rubbed shoulders with him have been blessed. I use the word advisedly because I cannot believe that my family's experience is unique among his friends, and for us, there is not a facet of our lives that he has not influenced and always and without exception positively.

Years ago Herman Guttman told me that Rudi could not set his watch atop his chest of drawers without creating an artistic configuration. Victor Gruen added a definitive footnote to Herman's comment. Speaking once with no more than his usual urbane mischievousness, Victor complained that he had to maintain a house in Los Angeles because it was the only place available to the firm for entertaining. Of his partners he said that one lived in a mountainous hideout. Another was addicted to air conditioning, freezing the clients. A third thrust his guests into a tepid swimming pool in which they could not swim; some aberration had driven this partner to specify a three-foot depth for his tank. So it went until Victor reached Rudi, who, he commented, inhabited a museum.

Well, it *is* a museum, and it is like no other. For one thing, it is slightly less accessible than the Hermitage. It began as a railroad flat. Of it Rudi has fashioned the most eye-pleasing, the most tranquil, the most elegant and fastidious and functional home I have ever seen.

His study invites reflection. His pipes, set seemingly haphazardly in a bowl, become a bouquet. The long hall which is a trademark of the railroad flat has become a gallery on whose walls there is never a permanent exhibition.

If there is candy on the coffee table, you may be sure the bowl is a collector's item. You may be sure the *color* of the candy is a soothing color. As for the coffee table, it is like a bird in flight, and it *does* belong in a museum.

The apartment is hardly an accident. Rudi has been all his life a patron of the arts, indeed, a relentless pursuer of the arts, particularly the painter's art. He is a collector who has achieved his own reputation among other collectors.

When I began to put down these words, I was reminded of a story. You may be familiar with it: Nathaniel Hawthorne's "The Great Stone Face."

The story is set in New England when the country was young. The great stone face is a juxtaposition of giant rocks left upon a mountainside a millennium ago by a glacial upheaval. They do resemble a man's face. The legend, handed down by the Indians, is that one day a man would appear in the valley below who looked like the great stone face. He would be a man for the ages: noble, regal, a man of high purpose and matching deeds.

The story begins with the boy, Ernest, who is enraptured by the great stone face. He learns the legend. And he starts to wait for the bearer of the face to appear.

Ernest grows to manhood. His life is humble. He is a good man; he does good. Time and again word comes that a stranger is on the way who resembles the great stone face, someone of enormous accomplishment. Time and again Ernest is disappointed.

The years pass. Ernest grows old. He despairs of ever seeing the man he has waited for all of his life.

Until the day when his neighbors stand aside in reverence. Because they see the bearer of the great stone face. It is Ernest.

When I thought of the story, I thought of Rudi. He has devoted seven decades to standing before the work of great artists, unaware that in the process he was creating his own work of art: his life.

We are here to honor him on his seventieth birthday. He has reached the proverbial threescore and ten. He has earned his repose.

The thought of Rudi withdrawing into deserved tranquility brings to mind his favorite painting. It is by Vermeer.

It is a portrait. The subject is a young girl, in or just out of her teens. She is looking over her shoulder at the viewer . . . and at the world. She is surprised, as though you have come upon her without warning. And indeed you have, you and the world, for suddenly she is a woman. She has left her childhood behind, and she is aware of a great mystery which lies ahead. She is a little frightened. She is hesitant and tremulous. But she is, despite her pounding heart, ready for adventure.

Whenever I think of that picture, of that child, anxious and eager, I think of Rudi. Because his curiosity has never waned. His interests have never been sated. His passport is in order. He remains on the wing. God grant him long flight.

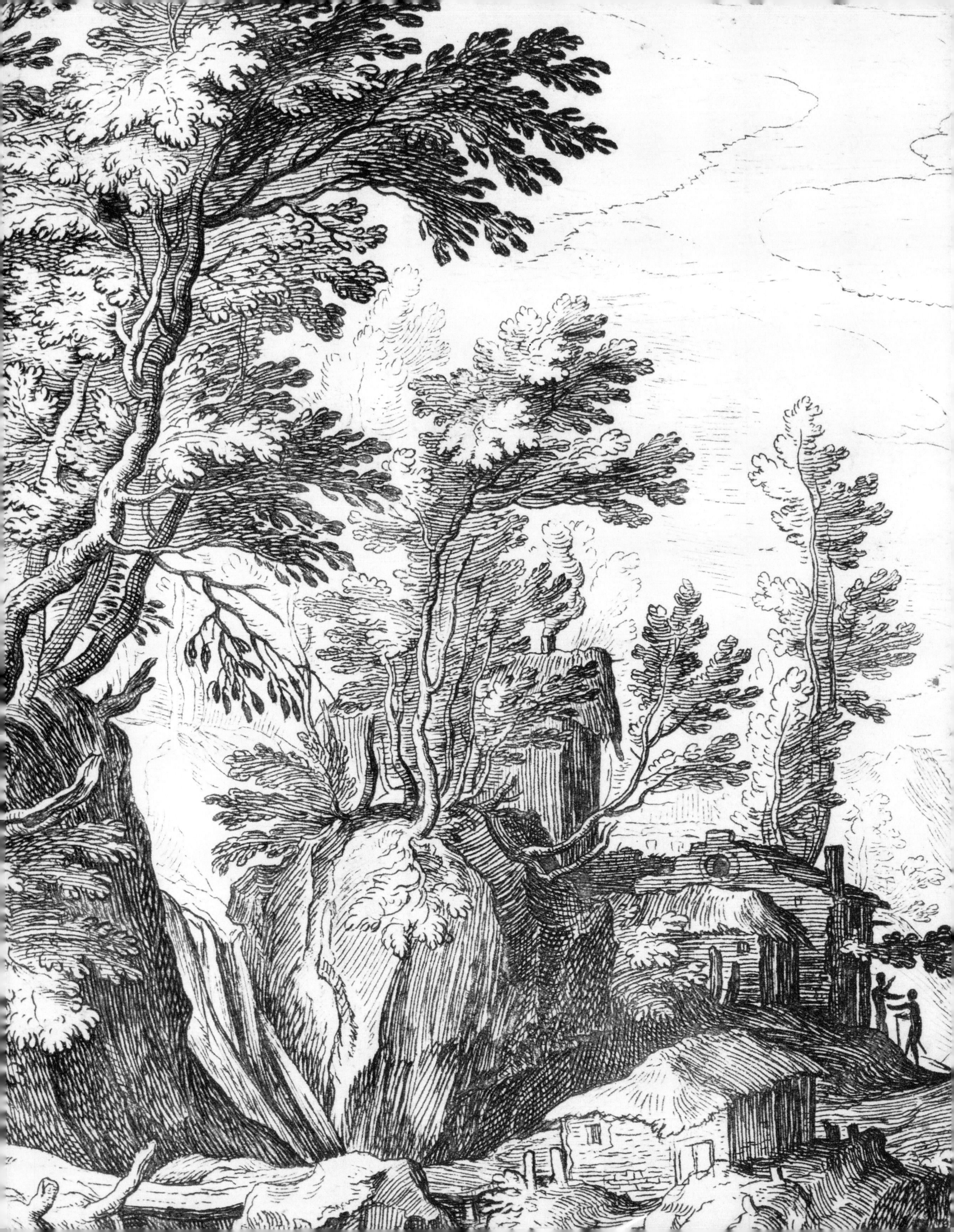

Fine Prints and Fine Printing

Rudi Baumfeld and Jake Zeitlin

James Cuno

"The sources of aesthetic elation are surely nothing if not aristocratic. Nature, the body, the many moods which sometimes momentarily lift us, these are sordid, common, mean." These words were spoken by Merle Armitage in a lecture entitled "The Aristocracy of Art," delivered before the California Art Club open forum at Aline Barnsdall's Frank Lloyd Wright–designed Hollyhock House on March 4, 1929.[1]

Armitage was a New York impresario who had recently settled in Los Angeles to manage the Los Angeles Opera Company and the Philharmonic Auditorium, then the city's music center. By all accounts he was a flamboyant character—a combination of genius and con man, as Jake Zeitlin later described him[2]—who collected prints and drawings and moved in the circle of intellectuals associated with the iconoclastic monthly journal *Opinion*; they included Arthur Millier, the art critic of the *Los Angeles Times*; Lloyd Wright, the architect and son of Frank Lloyd Wright; Jake Zeitlin; Will Connell; Paul Jordan-Smith; and Carey McWilliams. Above all, Armitage was a man of considerable style and arrogance who argued passionately in defense of "the aristocracy of the mind and spirit" as it informed the highest achievements of modernist culture.

Undoubtedly it was Armitage's incessant defense of quality that attracted Zeitlin. For although he disagreed with Armitage's elitist attitudes, Zeitlin published the California Art Club lecture shortly after it was delivered in 1929. Indeed the two men talked frequently at Zeitlin's bookshop on Sixth Street, and it was Armitage who first encouraged the bookseller to exhibit modern prints and drawings on a wall in his small shop. He convinced Zeitlin to write to Carl Zigrosser, then manager of the print department at Weyhe's bookshop and gallery in New York and later one of America's foremost authorities on the history of prints, and ask him for works that could be exhibited in Los Angeles. Zeitlin did, and Zigrosser sent him enough prints for several exhibitions, including shows of the work of Käthe Kollwitz, Marie Laurencin, and Rockwell Kent. Soon Zeitlin began to exhibit the work of local artists as well, including the lithographs of Peter Krasnow, the wood engravings of Paul Landacre, and the photographs of Edward Weston. With these exhibitions, Zeitlin's bookshop soon became as well known for its inventory of fine prints as for its holdings of rare books of fine printing.

Fine prints and fine printing form much of Jake Zeitlin's rich and revered

Detail of cat. no. 23

legacy as Los Angeles's great man of letters. They are certainly what attracted Rudi Baumfeld to Zeitlin's shop in the spring of 1958 to buy a woodcut by Kollwitz; by then the shop was a partnership between Jake and his wife, Josephine Ver Brugge, and was located on La Cienega Boulevard. And they are what kept Rudi returning to Zeitlin and Ver Brugge over the next twenty-seven years, as he built the extraordinary collection of prints and drawings that we acknowledge by this catalogue and the exhibition it accompanies.

Fine Prints and Fine Printing

I wish to address the friendship between Jake and Rudi as I came to know of it from the few conversations I had with Rudi before he died. Perforce my efforts will be modest. I mean them only as observations about the two men's mutual love of fine prints and fine printing, a love that was shared by all who moved in Zeitlin's circle, including Lawrence Clark Powell, Dr. Franklin D. Murphy, and E. Maurice Bloch, who, with Rudi, are responsible for the extraordinary riches that constitute UCLA's great collections of graphic art.

I began with remarks about Merle Armitage not only because they recall the origins of Zeitlin's exhibitions of prints and drawings but also because I suspect there was much of Merle Armitage in Rudi Baumfeld and that this is why we find the two so closely linked to Jake Zeitlin. Armitage collected prints and drawings by Paul Cézanne, Marc Chagall, Paul Gauguin, Wassily Kandinsky, Paul Klee, Henri Matisse, Joan Miró, and Pablo Picasso and was fascinated with modern book design. The publication of his California Art Club lecture was designed by Grace Marion Brown in bold black type with an abstracted palm frontispiece, graphic running heads, and black wrappers over black boards. The severity of its look was coincident with the rigorous tone of the lecture: "Bring a thing down to the level of popular understanding, and you bring it down below the timber line of aesthetic worth," Armitage intoned with oracular authority. It was his first experience with book production, and he was instantly taken by it. By 1932 he was producing books about artists he knew, such as Rockwell Kent and Edward Weston, and in the following years he wrote and designed books about Jean Charlot, Millard Sheets, Picasso, Igor Stravinsky, Martha Graham, and Arnold Schönberg. He was so captivated by the look of a book that once he told Henry Miller, "I write books so that I can design them."[3]

Not everyone approved of Armitage's books. Zeitlin called *The Aristocracy of Art* "funereal-looking," and Bruce McCallister, a highly regarded printer, said of Armitage that his ideal would be a book in the shape of a perfect cube, dense and hard-edged.[4] Discussions about book design and printing were common among Zeitlin's friends. In 1929 Zeitlin and the fine printers he patronized—Gregg Anderson, Ward Ritchie, and Grant Dahlstrom—formed the Thistle Club as an opportunity to meet over dinner and discuss interesting specimens of printing that each admired. Later the club's name was changed to the Rounce and Coffin Club, and the wood engraver Paul Landacre and the printer Saul Marks, as well as Armitage, were added to its membership.

Marks was a recent arrival in Los Angeles. He had been born in Warsaw and had emigrated to this country following World War I. He went first to New York and Detroit and then settled in Los Angeles, where he founded the Plantin Press, named after the sixteenth-century printer Christophe Plantin.[5] In 1933 he was commissioned by Zeitlin's publishing firm, the Primavera Press, to print *A Gil Blas in California*, a translation of Alexandre Dumas's work, designed by Ritchie with wood engravings by Landacre.[6] Although the task nearly finished him—Marks had promised the book for delivery in May, but problems with the press kept him from completing it until late December—it was selected as one of the American Institute of Graphic Arts's Fifty Books of the Year for 1935. Revived, he printed books and catalogues for the Huntington Library, and then, much later, after his original partners withdrew from the unprofitable Plantin Press and Marks and his wife, Lillian, began working out of the basement of their house, he printed books for Dawson's Book Shop.These included monographs on the Nuremberg Chronicle and the King James Bible; *The Malibu* by W. W. Robinson and Lawrence Clark Powell; *Maps of Los Angeles*, from Ord's Survey of 1849 to the 1880s; and *The Life and Works of Eric Gill*, a collection of papers read at UCLA's William Andrews Clark Library.

One of the more interesting projects undertaken by Saul and Lillian Marks was the *Novum Psalterium Pii XII*, which the printer-poet William Everson, then Brother Antoninus, wished printed on a hand press in a folio edition to commemorate the five hundredth anniversary of the psalter's first printing in 1457. After struggling with the project for some time, Everson realized the book could not be completed as intended and sold the printed sheets to Estelle Doheny, the great book collector and papal countess. He then wrote a long introduction, which was printed by the Markses in 1955 and included in the forty-eight completed copies of the psalter printed by Everson and bound in full blue morocco by the Lakeside Press in Chicago.[7]

By Zeitlin's recollection, Saul Marks was a very sensitive man of high ideals and good taste who could be very stubborn. "At times, also," Zeitlin recalled, "if he had an idea that a certain thing was right in the way of typographic format, no matter how much it violated the rules of bibliographic style, he insisted on doing it the way he felt it would look best to the printer's eye."[8] This insistence on the right look of the book is evident in all of the Markses' publications, from the large-format *A Garland for Jake Zeitlin*, published in 1967, to the much smaller *Jake & Jo*, published in 1984. Each has an elegant look that belies the complexity of its design. And each is fully distinguished in materials, typography, and layout, even when quite modest in scale. In his introduction to the checklist of the exhibition of the Markses' work at the Grolier Club in New York, Zeitlin identified the distinctive character of their work as purity. "They have been unwilling to release anything from their shop that does not fulfill their own standards. They have refused to be hurried or bullied by impatient patrons and they have on many occasions, and at great expense, discarded the product of long hours of labor rather than send something forth into the world that was less than their best."[9]

I began this essay with remarks about Merle Armitage because I believe he and Rudi shared certain qualities to which Jake Zeitlin was attracted: an insistence upon the highest achievement in every endeavor, a defense of modern culture, and a knowledge of its roots in earlier traditions, and perhaps even a certain elitism, a kind of aristocratic remove from the commonplace that was, as Armitage insisted, an aristocracy of the mind and spirit rather than of financial means or social class. I could just as easily have begun with remarks about Saul Marks, however. For there was much that Rudi shared with the exacting printer of fine books. Like Marks, Rudi strove for perfection in design. As principal designer of Victor Gruen Associates, he was responsible for all designs produced for the firm's major projects, including the elegant interior of the Century City Joseph Magnin store and much of the exclusive South Coast Plaza in Costa Mesa, for which he remained design consultant long after Victor Gruen Associates had completed its work there.

Fine Prints and Fine Printing

Rudi's friends and colleagues are quick to recall the aesthetic demands he made upon the architects in the firm. Frank Gehry remembers how Rudi would walk up behind him at the drafting table and, like the taskmaster he was, demand in few, very stern words that a drawing be corrected again and again and again. Rudi was as candid as he was demanding. His secretary recalled at the memorial gathering following his death how one day he directed her to follow him into his office as he wanted to dictate a letter. When she did, he looked at her and pronounced, in his clipped Austrian accent, "You look like hell." She thought he meant that her dress or makeup was in disarray, so she withdrew to repair herself. When she returned, he looked up and pronounced, "You still look like hell," and then went on to recommend that she see a doctor because he was sure she was ill. She was in fact quite ill, and she now tells the story to illustrate not only how candid Rudi was but also what a good eye he had for the ill appearance of both people and things.

The novelist Norman Katkov, in the tribute to Rudi reprinted in this catalogue (see pp. 15–19), recalls with fondness "the Baumfeld critique." It was delivered, even if not solicited, with a simple and characteristic frankness. "We discovered that it was not uncommon for him to cross the threshold, stop in his tracks, stare, and ask, '*Vat is dat?*' '*Dat*' could be Betty's dress, my suit, Dick's shirt, Billy's hair. '*Vat is dat?*' meant disapproval. '*Ach*' meant disapproval . . . a shake of the head meant disapproval." Equally, "Tsall right" meant something was good, not great, and certainly not from Vienna, Rudi's home city.

Rudi was a shy man, as demanding of himself as he was of others. He lived in an efficient, modern apartment that he decorated with furniture of his own design: lamps that looked like rigorously simplified and abstracted flowers; a dining table, sideboard, bookshelves, and stereo unit of straightforward design in elegant proportions; and a print cabinet that was unassuming in its economical use of space but that kept in logical order and to hand the nearly one thousand prints that made up his collection. Everything was conceived and executed in the simplest, most elegant manner, not to call attention to itself, but to elicit the response from the visitor, "Just right!" which Rudi would accept matter-of-factly before changing the subject from himself and his work to anything else.

Indeed Rudi's taste was so highly regarded that Herman Guttman once told Katkov that Rudi could not set his watch atop his chest of drawers without creating an artistic configuration. He wore the neatest of suits: simple, functional, "just right!" And he drove the nattiest of small, exceptionally clean, and well-tuned BMWs; a car to match his suits, to complement his apartment, to equal in its efficient and modern design the quality of his architectural work as well as the quality and order of his great print collection.

If Merle Armitage was like the Packard roadster Jake Zeitlin recalled him driving, Rudi was like his BMW: respected for the precision of his quality equipment and the modesty of his proportions. Rudi was also like the designs of Saul Marks: learned, tasteful, appropriate to the task, and treasured by all who knew him. It is thus no surprise to learn that the design and printing of Katkov's tribute to Rudi was entrusted to Saul and Lillian Marks.[10] It was set in a late eighteenth-century typeface named Fournier, with Perpetua headings and title page and dropped initials with fleuron borders (see p. 17). In this respect it is not unlike *Jake & Jo*, a lecture delivered by Bernard Rosenthal on November 6, 1982, designed by Lillian Marks and printed in 1984.[11] Both bear witness to the love of fine things and to the command of craft that gives presence and permanence to that love.

That is how the Markses' work recalls Rudi and why it is important to place him—and all that he was—in the circle of Jake Zeitlin. Rudi left Vienna in 1938, fleeing the Nazis (going first to Prague, then to two prison camps in Italy, then finally to New York), but did not arrive in Los Angeles until 1941. Almost immediately he began working for the Bureau of Yards and Docks of the United States Navy. He lived successively in Hollywood, Corona, and Long Beach before returning to Los Angeles in 1944, where he remained until his death forty-four years later. He joined Victor Gruen, with whom he had gone to architecture school in Vienna, in 1943 and became a partner in Victor Gruen Associates when it was formed in 1951. Finally restoring order to a life that was so violently disrupted by the war, Rudi must have begun thinking about collecting prints and drawings as he once had in Vienna.

The first evidence we have of Rudi's collecting is a simple receipt from Landau Gallery dated January 27, 1956. An inventory put together for insurance purposes, dated three years later, includes—besides numerous African, pre-Columbian, and Native American figures and baskets—an Egon Schiele lithograph of 1918, *Die Tafelrunde*, and a Gustav Klimt drawing, *Standing Woman Reading a Letter*, both of which were bought from the Galerie St. Etienne in New York and remained in Rudi's collection until his death, when the collection was bequeathed to the Grunwald Center. Not listed in the inventory were the prints Rudi purchased from Jake Zeitlin in 1958, which included the Kollwitz woodcut mentioned earlier and plate 10 from Giovanni Battista Piranesi's Carceri d'invenzione. The latter is a second state of three and is still in the collection. The following year Rudi bought from Zeitlin and Ver Brugge prints by Bruegel (from The Seven Vices), Jacques Callot (*The Fair at Impruneta*, third state), and Rembrandt (*The Small Lion Hunt*). Then, on May 27, 1960, only four years after the first record of his resuming print collecting, Rudi bought from Zeitlin and Ver Brugge two folios in parchment binding that contained nearly all of Callot's prints and that instantly made him a print collector of great importance. A few years later he gave his Callot prints to the National Gallery of Art, Washington, D.C., where they joined those given by Lessing Rosenwald to form the museum's great Callot collection, documented in its monographic exhibition of 1975.[12]

Of course, during these early years Rudi bought from dealers other than Zeitlin and Ver Brugge; there are receipts from the Galerie St. Etienne, Frederick Schab, Walter Schatzki, Lucien Goldschmidt, and Kennedy Galleries of New York; Esther Robles, Sabersky, and O. P. Reed of Los Angeles; R. E. Lewis of San Francisco; and a few from diverse European dealers. But by far, Rudi bought from and conferred with Jake Zeitlin. So much so that he kept a separate file of correspondence with Zeitlin and Ver Brugge, while putting correspondence with all other dealers together in another file.

Fine Prints and Fine Printing

During this period Zeitlin was busy selling books, prints, and drawings while still publishing finely printed books.[13] One such book was Kate Steinitz's study of the eighteenth-century collectors of prints and drawings, Pierre-Jean Mariette and the Comte de Caylus.[14] Masterfully designed and printed by Saul and Lillian Marks at the Plantin Press, the book addressed the two men as great amateurs of the arts, letters, and science, who had a special regard for Leonardo da Vinci's art and scientific theories. It is no coincidence that Kate Steinitz, Pierre-Jean Mariette, the Comte de Caylus, Saul and Lillian Marks, and Jake Zeitlin should come together in this publication and that it should be in the library of Rudi Baumfeld. For it was the particular character of the circle around Zeitlin—from Merle Armitage in the late 1920s and '30s to Rudi Baumfeld in the '60s, '70s, and '80s—that each person had a wide range of intellectual interests that were brought to bear on matters related to fine prints and fine printing.

In this respect, and at the risk of being too sentimental, I note that in 1717 Pierre-Jean Mariette went to Vienna to take care of the collection of engravings that his father, Jean Mariette, the great Parisian print and book dealer, had sold to Prince Eugène of Savoy. There, in the library of the palace, Mariette catalogued the prince's collection, described its books and prints, and took care of its many elaborate bindings. Two hundred years later Rudi Baumfeld was a young boy in Vienna about to embark on the architectural studies that would eventually lead him to a successful career in Los Angeles and that would provide him the means to amass a collection of prints that was, although not of the scale of Prince Eugène's collection, comparable to it in taste and discernment. Important to each collector was the counsel of an intelligent book and print dealer. The prince had Jean Mariette, and Rudi had Jake Zeitlin. To both men and their dealers, fine prints and fine printing were intimately linked.

---

1. Merle Armitage, *The Aristocracy of Art* (Los Angeles: Jake Zeitlin, 1929), unpaginated. The California Art Club met once a month at Barnsdall's house. There people such as Stanton MacDonald-Wright and Arthur Millier would debate issues relating to the contemporary arts. See Jake Zeitlin, *Books and the Imagination: Fifty*

Years of Rare Books, interview by Joel Gardner, vol. 1 (Los Angeles: Oral History Program, University of California, 1980), p. 107.

2. Zeitlin, *Books and the Imagination*, vol. 1, p. 67.

3. Ward Ritchie, *Fine Printing: The Los Angeles Tradition* (Washington, D.C.: Library of Congress, 1987), pp. 52–53.

4. Zeitlin, *Books and the Imagination*, vol. 1, p. 112.

5. Ritchie, *Fine Printing*, pp. 46–50.

6. *The Plantin Press, Los Angeles: Check List of an Exhibition: Books, Catalogues, Etc., Printed by Saul and Lillian Marks*, intro. by Jake Zeitlin (New York: Grolier Club, 1971).

7. Ritchie, *Fine Printing*, pp. 49–50.

8. Zeitlin, *Books and the Imagination*, p. 113.

9. *The Plantin Press*, unpaginated.

10. *Rudi Baumfeld's Seventieth Birthday, 1 January 1974: A Tribute by Norman Katkov* (Los Angeles, 1974). Two hundred copies were printed by the Markses at the Plantin Press for friends of Rudi and with the compliments of Victor Gruen Associates and Josephine and Jake Zeitlin.

11. Bernard Rosenthal, *Jake & Jo: Remarks on the Occasion of the Celebration of Jake Zeitlin's Eightieth Birthday at the Tower Restaurant, Los Angeles, November 6, 1982* (Los Angeles: Zeitlin and Ver Brugge, 1984). An edition of 275 copies was published by Zeitlin, planned by his fellow booksellers Muir and Agnes Dawson, with typography by Lillian Marks, presswork by Bonnie Thompson Norman, and photo prints by Michael Dawson.

12. H. Diane Russell, *Jacques Callot: Prints and Related Drawings*, exh. cat. (Washington, D.C.: National Gallery of Art, 1975).

13. Zeitlin's Primavera Press printed books from only 1929 to 1936, twenty-nine books in all, but he continued to publish books under the imprimatur of Zeitlin and Ver Brugge into the 1980s. See J. M. Edelstein, "A Bibliography of Books Published by the Primavera Press," in *A Garland for Jake Zeitlin on the Occasion of His Sixty-fifth Birthday and the Anniversary of His Fortieth Year in the Book Trade*, ed. J. M. Edelstein (Los Angeles: Grant Dahlstrom and Saul Marks, 1967), pp. 113–31.

14. Kate T. Steinitz, *Pierre-Jean Mariette and Le Comte de Caylus and Their Concept of Leonardo da Vinci in the Eighteenth Century* (Los Angeles: Zeitlin and Ver Brugge, 1974).

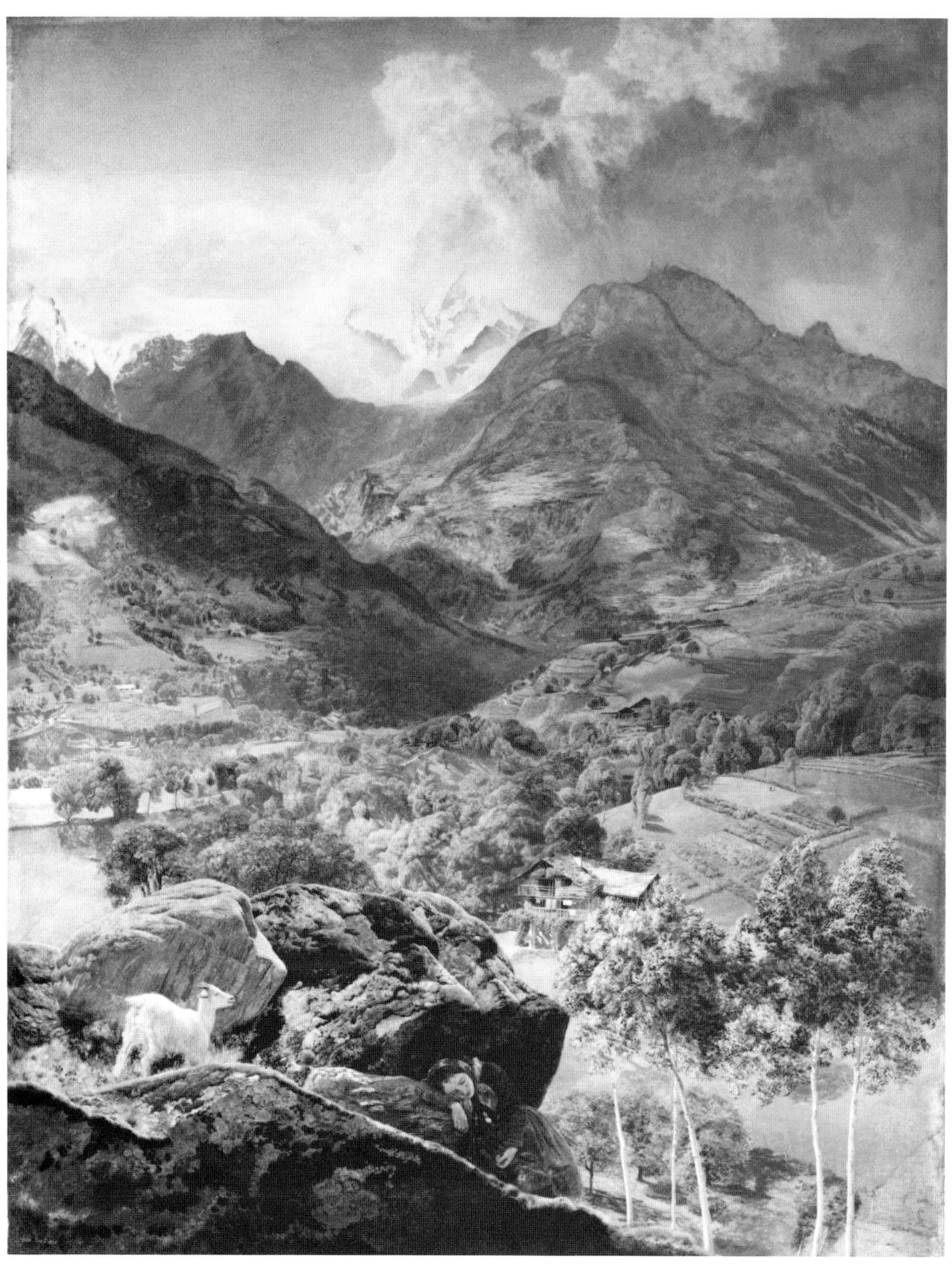

JOHN BRETT (English, 1831–1902)
VAL D'AOSTA, 1858; oil on canvas; 87.6 x 68.3 cm
Photograph courtesy of Sotheby's

About Landscape

Henri Zerner

"A beautiful landscape," I say, and you do not know whether I mean a picture or an actual view. This linguistic ambiguity between a work of art and what it represents does not occur in other instances—between the person and the portrait, the still life and the objects that the artist has staged in it—and it exists not just in English but in all the major Western languages. This may seen innocuous enough, but it does imply something peculiar about landscape, as though our reaction to the image was exchangeable with our experience of the world in a way it is not with other kinds of pictures.

In the summer of 1858 John Brett traveled to the Italian Alps and painted the imposing landscape of Val d'Aosta.[1] John Ruskin, who had admired the young artist's *The Stone Breaker* at the Royal Academy exhibition that year, encouraged the expedition and followed Brett's progress closely. He toured the same region that summer and kept in close touch with the painter. On August 26 Ruskin wrote his father:

> I mentioned that Mr. Brett was with me at La Tour; he has been a week here today. I sent for him to Villeneuve, Val d'Aosta, because I didn't like what he said in his letter about his present work, and thought he wanted some lecturing, like Inchbold: besides that he could give me some useful hints. He is much tougher and stronger than Inchbold, and takes more hammering—but I think he looks more miserable every day; and I have good hope of making him completely wretched in a day or two more—and then I shall send him back to his castle. He is living *in* that castle which I sketched so long ago in Val d'Aosta—Chateau St Pierre.[2]

The humor of the account does not obliterate the sadism, nor the genuine excitement. At last someone would produce just the kind of landscape the author of *Modern Painters* had been dreaming of. The resulting picture is amazing: intense light, crystalline atmosphere, each minute detail fully visible and distinct.

"And here," Ruskin exclaimed in his review of 1859, ". . . for the first time in history, we have, by help of art, the power of visiting a place, reasoning about it, and knowing it, just as if we were there, except only that we cannot stir from our place, nor look behind us." He went on at length about this unprecedented feat of veristic rendering, "every leaf a study." The vividness of the image, the geological exactitude, the unsparing attention to atmospheric effects were all he had been looking forward to. "White poplars on the roadside, shaking silvery in the

wind: I regret to say the wind is apt to come up the Val d'Aosta in an ill-tempered and rude manner, turning leaves thus the wrong side out; but it will be over in a moment." Yet in the end, in spite of his ostensible enthusiasm, Ruskin was deeply disappointed. He found no emotion in the picture, no poetry. "I never saw the mirror so held up to Nature; but it is Mirror's work, not Man's."[3] No mere sadistic onslaught on the poor, misguided painter here, for after all the indictment is also of the guiding hand, of Ruskin's own system and expectations.

The fact is, the extreme superfluity of visual information in Brett's painting does not, as claimed by Ruskin—with how much conviction one wonders—provide an experience identical to being there and equivalent to the physical encounter of nature, but it produces instead the effect of a hallucination.

Ruskin, who was a great writer, also struggled to master painting—therefore the "useful hints" he hoped to pick up from Brett—but was not good enough, in his own eyes, to test the possibilities of pictorial representation. Clearly he did not think that a written description, no matter how great, no matter how detailed, could give us "the power of visiting a place . . . just as if we were there," at least not in the strict sense he intended here. Pictures can give a sense of presence to the representation that made him—and many others—believe that the emotional impact of a landscape painting should be or could be that of the view represented, that of nature itself, giving full force to the equivalence suggested by the peculiar linguistic usage noted above. And the conclusion he drew from this was that the physical barrier of the painting should in so far as possible disappear and that the viewer should be allowed directly into the view.[4] The experiment, however, did not turn out as expected: the painting lacked the anticipated emotion, because the emotions produced by nature and by art are of different kinds, and also—Ruskin does not acknowledge this, but we feel it intensely—the precision and evenness of focus elicit a sense of pure, disembodied appearance, of unreality.

Théophile Thoré, the great critic and friend of Théodore Rousseau, understood this "fantasmagory" very well. In 1862, at the end of a withering review of Pre-Raphaelite landscape, he wrote: "Photography which, I believe, is of great use to English landscapists, sometimes produces images of this kind that seem to be perceived in a dream, although they are traced on reality." On the contrary: "In front of a landscape by Ruisdael,—and perhaps by Rousseau,—one experiences just what one would experience in front of nature, what the author has experienced himself."[5] But how is this possible? Is Thoré justified in posing this equation between what *we* would feel in front of nature and what the painter did? Is he not the toy of visual rhetorics?

William Gilpin, the theorist of the picturesque, at the end of the eighteenth century already understood the roots of the problem and anticipated the dynamics of modern landscape:

> If indeed, either in literary, or in picturesque composition you endeavour to draw the reader, or the spectator from the *subject* to the *mode of executing* it, your affectation* disgusts. At the same time, if some care, and pains be

not bestowed on the *execution*, your slovenliness disgusts as much. Tho perhaps the artist has more to say, than the man of letters, for paying attention to his *execution.* A truth is a truth, whether delivered in the language of a philosopher, or a peasant: and the *intellect* receives it as such. But the artist, who deals in lines, surfaces, and colours, which are an immediate address to the *eye*, conceives the *very truth itself* concerned in his *mode* of representing it.

*Language, like light, is a medium; and the true philosophic style, like light from a north-window, exhibits objects clearly, and distinctly, without soliciting attention to itself. In painting subjects of amusement indeed, language may gild somewhat more, and colour with dies of fancy: but where information is of more importance, than entertainment, tho you cannot throw too *strong* a light, you should carefully avoid a *coloured* one. The stile of some writers resembles a bright light placed between the eye, and the thing to be looked at. The light shews itself; and hides the object: and, it must be allowed, the execution of some painters is as impertinent, as the stile of such writers.[6]

The Enlightenment thinker in Gilpin strongly believed in the transparency of the sign. The words, the pigments should draw no attention to themselves, pose no resistance between us and what they mean, the content, the reality *behind* them. But the man of experience in him, the modest but intelligent practitioner, knew better. He relegated therefore this perfect but never fully realized model of the representation of meaning to language, while pictorial art belonged to a different realm where the distance between the image and its significance was largely collapsed. This gave a particular power to images in a rather unexpected way. For if we believe there is such a difference between images and texts, it must be this resilience of "lines, surfaces and colours," the opacity of the medium, and not the transparency of the signs, that makes the visual representation capable of substituting itself for the actual world in a way discourse can't. This is what Gilpin must have meant when he wrote that "lines, surfaces, and colours . . . are an immediate appeal to the eye." This was also, however clumsily expressed, the argument offered by the government of Louis-Philippe in France when the censorship of caricatures was reestablished in 1835, forcing Honoré Daumier and other cartoonists to abandon their virulent political attacks. The text of the law, both comical and brutal, states: "Article 7 of the Charter proclaims that Frenchmen have the right to circulate their opinions in published form. But when opinions are converted into actions by the circulation of drawings, it is a question of speaking to the eyes. That is something more than the expression of an opinion, it is an incitement to action not covered by article 7."

"Affectation" is what Gilpin calls the fact of drawing attention to the "mode of execution"—"your affectation." For the artist to draw attention to the means of art is to draw attention to himself, and although Gilpin finds this offensive, indeed "disgusting," he considers it more allowable in landscape, where "informa-

tion," that is, the traditional didactic purpose of serious art, is not the issue. (Incidentally, one could think of few pictures more stylized and mannered than his own illustrations.) But we can go farther than Gilpin: it is in fact this dramatization of the "mode of execution" that carries the emotional and expressive weight of landscape art. There is a paradox: on the one hand, landscape seems, more than any other kind of picture, to be a substitute for the outside world, and on the other, it is the most abstract, the most purely pictorial, the most comparable to music in the way it affects us.[7] Above all, it is the apparent confusion between the two, between objective account and subjective experience, that has put landscape at the very center of modern art.

Gilpin's most striking idea, and his most prophetic, is that light is a medium, an aspect of the artistic idiom, rather than, as we might have expected him to think, a part of what is represented. And indeed light will become a dominant preoccupation of landscapists. J. M. W. Turner above all, and after him the impressionists, will make light, often a colored light, so obtrusive that it can at times almost obliterate the view; what Gilpin condemns is just what we admire particularly. Through visible execution and the manipulation of light, the artist conveys a specific, emotionally determined experience of landscape. In accord with Gilpin's prescription, a strong, even, uncolored light is what Brett, and presumably Ruskin, chose for *Val d'Aosta*, the best light for a factual, impartial landscape. The result, however, is not that we react to the represented view as if we were there, but that we see the landscape as devoid of affective impact and even insubstantial, although dazzling to the eye. A sense of materiality and presence seems to depend not so much on physical description as on the artist's ability to convey the affective specificity of an experience.

Finally, the striking equivocation between art and nature peculiar to landscape induces a reverse action. Nature, as Oscar Wilde would have it, imitates art. One would certainly not want to doubt that our encounter with the natural environment can elicit powerful and genuine emotions in us and give shape to our feelings, but it is hard to appreciate how much our perceptions are informed by our pictorial culture and to what extent the art of landscape is responsible for the way we experience the spectacle of nature.

---

1. On this painting, exhibited at the Royal Academy in 1859, see the excellent notice by Allen Staley in *Romantic Art in Britain: Paintings and Drawings, 1760–1860*, exh. cat. (Detroit and Philadelphia: Falcon Press, 1968), no. 234.

2. John Ruskin, *Letters from the Continent, 1858*, ed. John Hayman (Toronto: University of Toronto Press, 1982), p. 147.

3. Ruskin's review is in *Academy Notes*, vol. 14 of the Library Edition (London: Chatto and Windus, 1904), pp. 234–38.

4. Ruskin did not always hold this view, and his analysis of Turner's works shows a keen understanding of the importance of execution. His awareness makes this particular Pre-Raphaelite phase of his attitude to landscape all the more interesting.

5. Théophile Thoré, "Exposition Internationale de Londres en 1862," in *Salons de W. Burger, 1861 à 1868*, vol. 1 (Paris, 1870), pp. 283, 293.

6. William Gilpin, *Three Essays on Picturesque Beauty; etc.* (London, 1792), p. 18.

7. In 1794 Schiller published a most important essay, "Über Matthissons Gedichte," in which he discusses at length the relationship between music and the art of landscape not only in poetry but also in pictures.

Detail of cat. no. 125

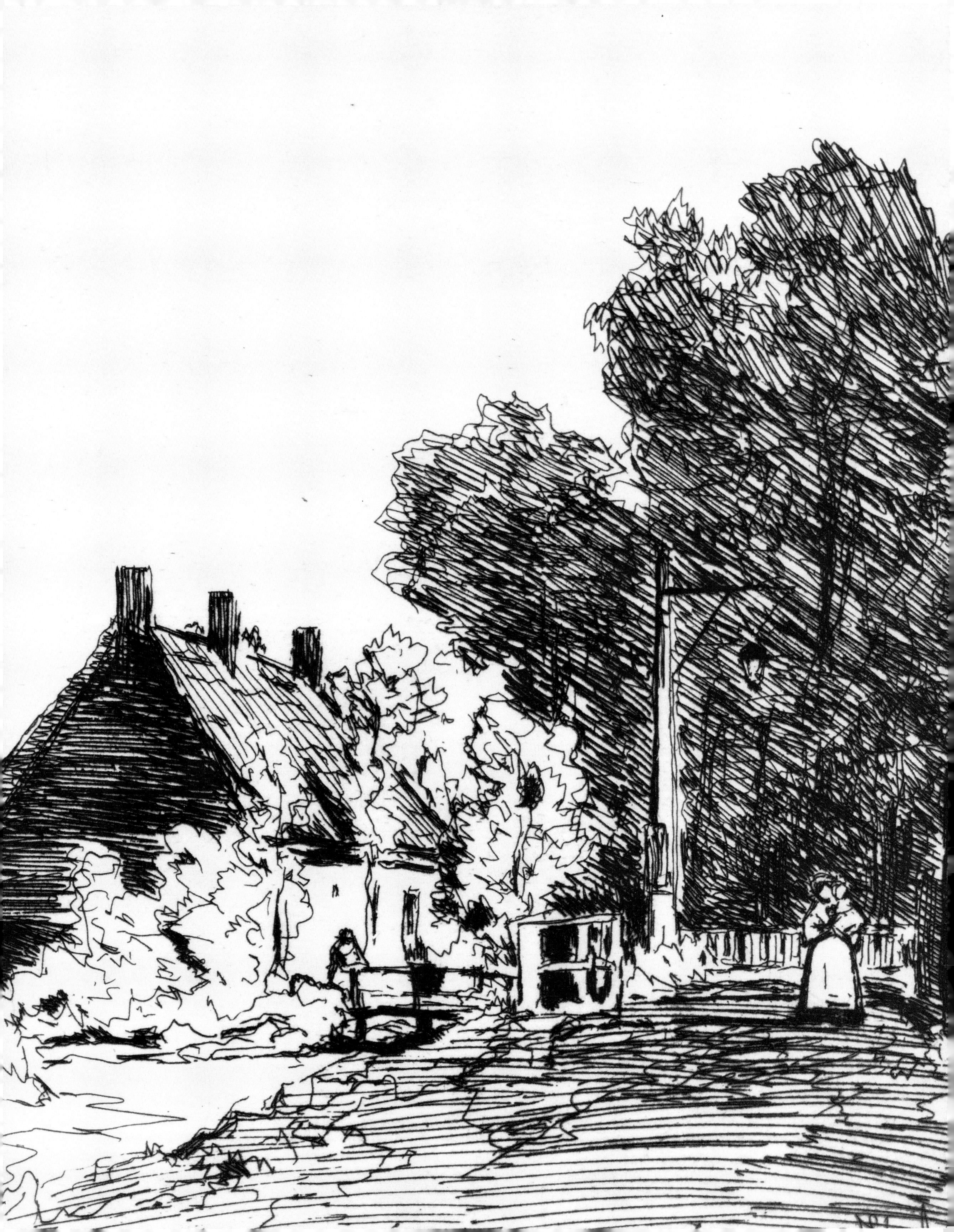

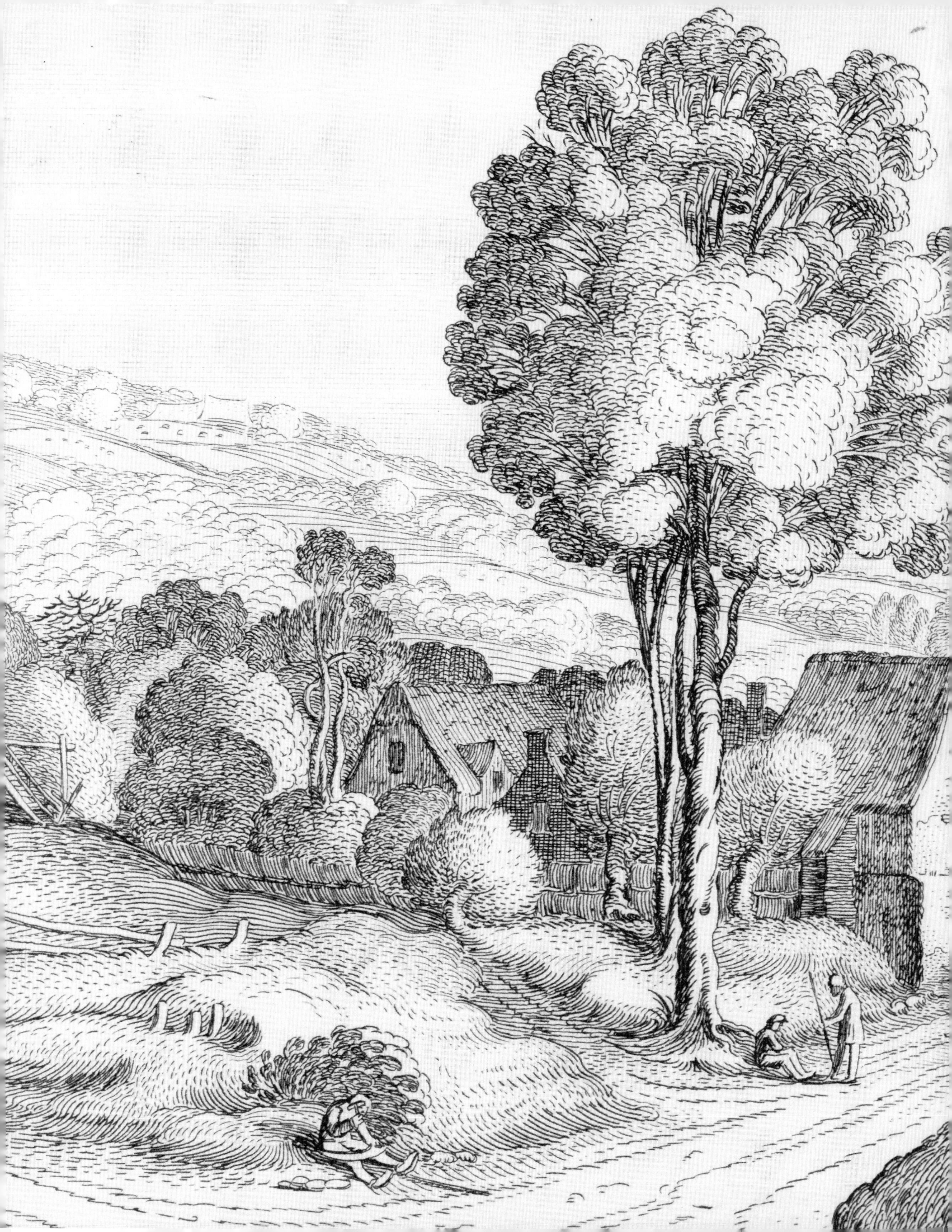

The Rudolf L. Baumfeld Collection

Cynthia Burlingham

The prints and drawings in this exhibition were chosen as they best represent the high quality and historical range of the 857 works of art on paper that make up the Rudolf L. Baumfeld collection of Western landscape art. Baumfeld began forming his collection in the early 1950s and continued to acquire works until a few weeks before his death in February 1988. From the beginning he was interested principally in the representation of landscape, although he occasionally collected in other areas that caught his interest, the most notable being the extensive holding of prints by Jacques Callot that he gave to the National Gallery in the late 1960s (D. Russell 1975, p. xii).

As might be expected, the major strengths of the collection lie within the most fertile periods of landscape art, particularly the seventeenth century in the Netherlands, the eighteenth to early twentieth century in Britain, and the nineteenth century in France. There are strengths in the work of several artists, including Claude Lorrain, Rembrandt van Rijn, Canaletto, Samuel Palmer, Edward Lear, Charles Méryon, James McNeill Whistler, and Graham Sutherland. In general, however, Baumfeld's acquisitions were consistently varied, and during any given month his records reveal purchases representing widely disparate historical periods and regional schools, including those in which the landscape genre is considered incidental.

Throughout all periods represented, most works are pure landscapes or feature architectural ruins or urban views, suggesting that Baumfeld's primary interest was in landscape representation as the subject of a work of art, not as a background setting for narrative subjects. One is tempted to look for a particular orientation on the part of the collector, and certainly the omission of certain types of landscapes that depict nature at its most spectacular—the works of Salvator Rosa and John Martin, for example—might lead one to suggest that the collection is oriented toward a more rational and harmonious view of nature, an idea supported by its numerous cityscapes, the ultimate expression of a civilized landscape. This suggestion is dispelled by the breadth of the collection, however, which indicates that the collector's intention was to develop a comprehensive view of landscape representation, showing how artists of diverse periods and nationalities expressed their experience of nature.

A brief overview of the history of landscape art, as represented by the prints and drawings in the Baumfeld collection, begins during the early sixteenth century,

Detail of cat. no. 42

The Rudolf L. Baumfeld Collection

when a group of artists in southern Germany became the first to make landscape the primary subject of a work of art. Wolf Huber and Albrecht Altdorfer were the most important artists of the Danube school, whose prints and drawings feature expansive vistas of the region's mountains, rivers, and forests. A rare drawing by an anonymous artist in the circle of Huber (cat. no. 138) uses landscape to represent the presence of God in nature itself, rather than as a setting for a traditional religious narrative. The landscape prints of the next generation of artists, such as Augustin Hirschvogel and Hanns Lautensack, show the influence of Altdorfer and Huber in their technique and choice of subject if not in their pantheistic vision.

In Flanders during the mid-sixteenth century at the Antwerp print publishing house Aux Quatre Vents, the publisher Hieronymus Cock played a crucial role in the dissemination of landscape prints. Between 1555 and 1563 he published numerous sets of prints after the designs of the Master of the Small Landscapes, Matthys Cock, Pieter Bruegel the Elder, and Hans Bol. Though they generally feature a more conventional mythological or religious subject, it was the prominence of landscape in these prints that made them innovative. Indeed Cock turned what had been a minor genre within print publishing into a major one, thus laying the foundation for succeeding generations of Dutch and Flemish printmakers (Riggs 1977, p. 184).

At the beginning of the seventeenth century a different style of landscape emerged in the Netherlands, one that featured realistic scenes of local villages and countryside as the primary subject. An important stimulus to this more naturalistic style was the art of Hendrik Goltzius of Haarlem, the foremost printmaker in the northern Netherlands. Around 1600 he made a series of topographically accurate drawings of the low-lying countryside around Haarlem that mark the first step in the adoption of the native Dutch countryside as a suitable subject for landscape. Goltzius's vision was disseminated through prints after his drawings as well as by prints of his own making.

During the first decade of the seventeenth century, print publishing became increasingly dominated by realistic topographical prints. Claes Jansz. Visscher, one of the most important publishers in Amsterdam, published several series of landscape etchings depicting local rural scenes with farmhouses and village streets (see cat. nos. 30–38). He also published prints by proponents of this new style of landscape from Haarlem, such as Esaias van de Velde, his cousin Jan van de Velde II, and Willem Buytewech. These artists produced landscape prints that, though carefully composed, give the impression of topographical accuracy, providing a familiar, if not exact, view of the Dutch countryside. The culmination of this naturalistic tradition came in Amsterdam during the 1640s and 1650s, when Rembrandt van Rijn produced numerous etchings based on his observations of the local countryside, in which he integrated natural phenomena with ideal, monumental landscape motifs, thus transforming the native Dutch landscape "into art of the highest order" (Freedberg 1980, p. 53).

After midcentury, landscape printmakers expanded the vocabulary and range of subjects of Dutch landscape, combining foreign motifs with those of the local landscape. Roeland Roghman's etchings include spectacular Alpine views that recall Bruegel's prints and drawings. Herman Naiwincx's rocky landscapes evoke a foreign wilderness rather than local Dutch scenery, while Allart van Everdingen's Scandinavian motifs include mountainous forests and waterfalls.

By far the most popular foreign subjects among Dutch artists were the ruins and countryside of Italy. Paintings and etchings by Italianate artists such as Bartholomeus Breenbergh, Jan Both, and Karel Dujardin enjoyed tremendous popularity in the Netherlands from the second quarter of the seventeenth century. Their views of the Roman Campagna, like those of Dutch artists who portrayed their native landscape, were based on observations of reality but were not bound by topographical accuracy. Italianate prints remained popular into the eighteenth century, outlasting the indigenous landscape type that had dominated Dutch landscape art during the early seventeenth century.

Until the late sixteenth century Italian landscape painting in Rome was dominated by the northern mannerist landscape tradition brought to Rome by Paul Bril. Around the turn of the seventeenth century, however, Annibale Carracci led an important indigenous school of landscape, based on the observation of natural phenomena yet imbued with "a clarity of organization and a nobility of form that belong to the ideal world of the imagination" (Posner 1971, p. 118). Though landscape was not Annibale's primary subject, his few landscape paintings and numerous drawings formed the basis of a school of classical Roman landscape painting that was influential for painters and etchers such as Claude Lorrain, Gaspard Dughet, and Giovanni Francesco Grimaldi.

While the character of Roman baroque landscape painting led toward a classical style, a significant school of landscape art that flourished concurrently in Florence around the court of Duke Cosimo II still relied heavily upon the northern mannerist school. A small "academy" led by Giulio Parigi included a number of artists such as Remigio Cantagallina and Ercole Bazicaluva, who produced landscapes influenced by scenographic designs executed for pageants and festivals. Their prints, produced in relatively small numbers, were influential for artists such as Callot (D. Russell 1975, p. 274ff.).

Despite this increased activity in Rome and Florence, landscape art did not dominate Italian printmaking until the eighteenth century, when the growth of tourism in Venice and Rome led to increased demand for prints of regional topographical townscapes, or *vedute*. The best of these, executed by Canaletto and Giovanni Battista Piranesi, introduced into Italian landscape prints a new technical brilliance and greater originality in concept and execution. Combining the straightforward topographical view with the capriccio, or architectural fantasy, Canaletto's etchings idealized the splendors of Venice, at the same time conveying an appearance of startling reality. Similarly, in Rome Piranesi turned a tradition of documentary ruinscapes, which had been established in the sixteenth century with the prints of Cock, into grand evocations of an antique past.

The popularity of the topographical views produced by Canaletto during his residence in England from 1746 to 1753 indicate the endurance of a topographical tradition that had been established in England during the seventeenth century with the prints of Wenzel Hollar, another foreign artist who achieved great success

THE RUDOLF L. BAUMFELD COLLECTION

with his prints of local and foreign scenery (see cat. nos. 72–73). Eighteenth-century English watercolorists and printmakers such as Paul Sandby expanded this tradition, combining topographical interests with an eighteenth-century preoccupation with idealized form inspired by the Italian-French tradition of Annibale Carracci and Claude Lorrain. An idealized landscape watercolor by Sandby in the Baumfeld collection (cat. no. 74) shows the prevailing influence of the compositional principles of the classical tradition in its clear order and structure.

During the second half of the eighteenth century, influenced by the growing popularity of the picturesque movement, a shift away from the classical tradition led to the development of a more naturalistic style that would dominate British landscape art throughout the ensuing century. The eighteenth-century roots of this aesthetic can best be seen in the rustic landscapes of Thomas Gainsborough, which were inspired by the countryside of rural England. An appreciation of the picturesque roughness of natural scenery also characterizes the works of his nephew Gainsborough Dupont and Dr. Thomas Monro.

The landscapes of the Norwich school also exemplify the taste for rural landscape, here inspired by seventeenth-century Dutch landscape art. Well represented in the Baumfeld bequest by the etchings of John Crome and Joseph Stannard, the Norwich Society was also the first group of English artists to promote etching as a medium in its own right.

During the early decades of the nineteenth century a new emphasis on the artist's individual response to and experience of nature inspired a more immediate approach to landscape watercolor painting characterized by the direct application of color and increased concern with atmosphere and natural phenomena. Concurrently the watercolor medium gained greater acceptance, as indicated by the founding of the Old Water-Colour Society in 1804. One of its sixteen original members was John Varley, whose teachings and writings emphasized the direct study of nature. Varley's influence can be seen in the direct and unaffected approach to natural observation in an unfinished watercolor by his student Peter De Wint (cat. no. 86). This work, along with others by William Delamotte and David Cox, represents the culmination of the nineteenth-century romantic landscape watercolor tradition in England.

A nostalgia for rural England infused with a profoundly spiritual vision characterizes the art of Samuel Palmer. His pastoral landscapes, usually depicted at daybreak or sunset, resound with sympathy toward human endeavor as well as religious sentiment. Palmer's romanticism is echoed in the landscape prints of twentieth-century etchers Frederick Landseer Griggs, Robert Austin, and Graham Sutherland.

The topographical and picturesque traditions flourished together during the first half of the nineteenth century with a number of publications that featured views of European cities and rural areas. Using the innovative medium of lithography, which became the preferred printmaking technique for romantic landscapes, these publications presented the work of a new generation of English and French landscape artists and topographers who collaborated with lithographic printmakers. English artists in particular expanded the notion of the picturesque to include foreign scenery, encouraged in part by the opening of the Continent following the defeat of Napoléon in 1815.

Richard Parkes Bonington was recruited for the most ambitious of these topographical series, the French publication Voyages pittoresques et romantiques dans l'ancienne France, a series of lithographic albums published between 1820 and 1878, which documented architectural monuments and remote scenery in provincial France. Remaining within the conventions of chalk lithography and the English topographical tradition, Bonington's prints for Voyages pittoresques (see cat. no. 89) combine outline with subtle ranges of tone, more reminiscent of the drawings of eighteenth-century English topographers such as Sandby than of the more recent generation of watercolorists that included De Wint.

In contrast, French artist Eugène Isabey's designs for an 1832 suite of lithographs depicting views of Normandy and Brittany (see cat. no. 119) betray his more painterly and experimental approach to lithography, distinct from the English topographical drawing tradition. Isabey's prints are characterized by dramatic contrasts of light and shade enhanced by scraping away the lithographic crayon to suggest the wear of age.

While French topographical publications such as Voyages pittoresques and Souvenirs d'Eugène Isabey generally featured remote areas of the French countryside, many English publications, such as Thomas Shotter Boys's 1839 Picturesque Architecture in Paris, Ghent, Antwerp, and Rouen (see cat. no. 90) were concerned with the depiction of romantic Paris. Boys's album is also an example of the taste for color printing that dominated artistic lithography after 1835. English publications, particularly after 1840, also indicate a fascination with exotic foreign locales, as seen in the Middle Eastern scenes of David Roberts (see cat. no. 87) and the Italian views of Edward Lear (see cat. no. 93). They also mark the end of the era of English topographical lithography, which declined in popularity after midcentury with the invention of photography.

Like the depictions of provincial ruins in Voyages pittoresques, Charles Méryon's urban views (see cat. nos. 127–29) documented a Paris that was rapidly vanishing in the wake of Baron Georges-Eugène Haussmann's radical transformations of the city in the 1840s. Rather than engendering a romantic nostalgia for a "lost" France, however, Méryon's views of urban life are ominous reflections of the increasingly depersonalized city.

Around midcentury in France, coincident with the growth and renovation of Paris and the industrial revolution, artists of the Barbizon school left the city and retreated to villages in a countryside as yet unaltered by encroaching modernization, portraying these pristine settings in a highly detailed, realistic manner. Camille Corot's *Souvenir de Toscane* (cat. no. 118) recalls the pastoral Campagna scenes of Claude, while Théodore Rousseau's *Chênes de roche* (cat. no. 120) harbors vestiges of romanticism in its portrayal of the rugged Fontainebleau Forest. Additionally Charles-François Daubigny's etching of the Seine at Bezons (cat. no. 121) and Henri-Joseph Harpignies's *Marécage* (cat. no. 123) portray a more serene pastoral oasis.

In contrast to the Barbizon artists, who ignored the onset of the industrial

The Rudolf L. Baumfeld Collection

age, impressionist artists of the last quarter of the nineteenth century portrayed a suburban landscape that incorporated the changes brought on by the industrial revolution. Paul Signac's *Les Andelys* (cat. no. 132) reveals how industrialization has altered the riverside, a subject that had existed in such natural purity in the prints of Daubigny. Factory towers coexist with the washerwomen at the shore, and the realistic detail of the Barbizon school has been replaced by a regular network of impressionistic patches of color. Signac's watercolor of a domesticated garden at Saint-Tropez (cat. no. 133), with its mechanized fountain, contrasts with the rustic simplicity of Barbizon landscapes, in which the primary purpose of a garden is to provide sustenance rather than pleasure.

Daubigny and other French etchers influenced the mid-nineteenth-century etching revival in England and America, represented in the Baumfeld bequest by Francis Seymour Haden and James McNeill Whistler. Whistler's Venetian cityscapes (see cat. nos. 2–3) recall the great eighteenth-century topographical views of the city by Canaletto, but here the etched line is evocative rather than descriptive, suggesting the landscape with a minimum of means rather than detailed rendering. The influence of Whistler's explorations of the etching medium is evident in the works of a generation of American printmakers that includes Joseph Pennell, Childe Hassam, and John Marin.

During the twentieth century landscape assumed equal importance among other subjects of pictorial representation, becoming less a depiction of objective reality than a reflection of a subjective experience of nature or a medium for formal problem solving. Artists associated with the Vienna Secession, including Carl Moll, Broncia Koller-Pinnell, Leopold Forstner, and Franz von Zülow, reacted against the nineteenth-century plein-air tradition of landscape painting, making landscape subject to an emphasis on pattern and decoration that blurred the distinction between fine and applied art. Reacting against this overarching stylization, German expressionist artists such as Emil Nolde, Ernst Ludwig Kirchner, and Erich Heckel imbued their works with powerful emotion. This emphasis on the personal experience of nature characterizes many twentieth-century representations of landscape and indeed can be seen as one of the major preoccupations of landscape art since the romantic era.

Throughout its history, landscape art has encompassed diverse documentary, emotional, and aesthetic responses to nature, recording perhaps more clearly than any other genre of the visual arts the relationship between society and the environment. The works in the Baumfeld collection, because they represent this genre in such depth, also reflect the constantly changing perception of the nature and purpose of landscape art itself.

Color Plates

John Marin

Autumn on the Road to Deblois, Maine, No. 2
(cat. no. 7)

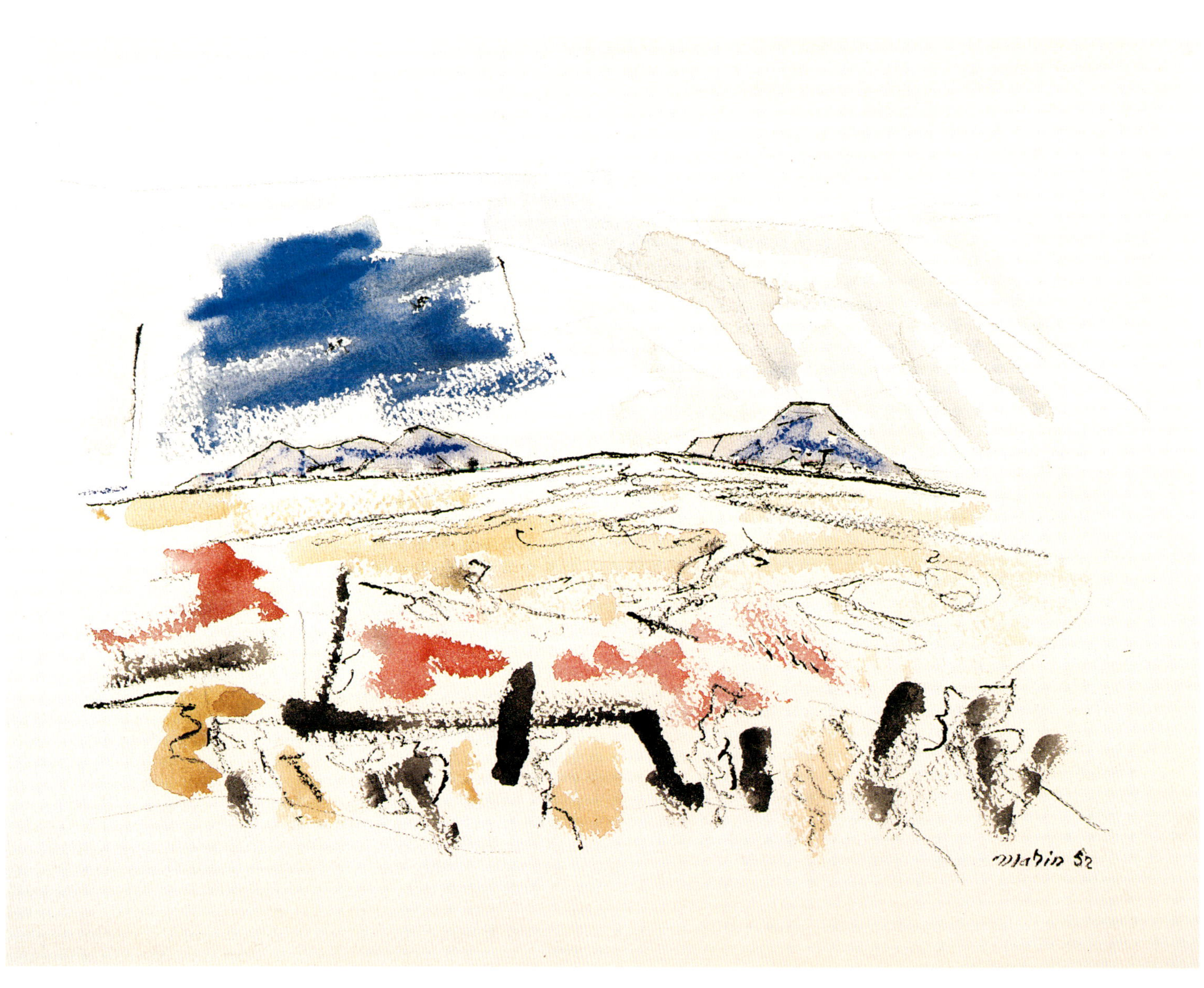

LEOPOLD FORSTNER

Oberösterreichische Landschaft

(cat. no. 10)

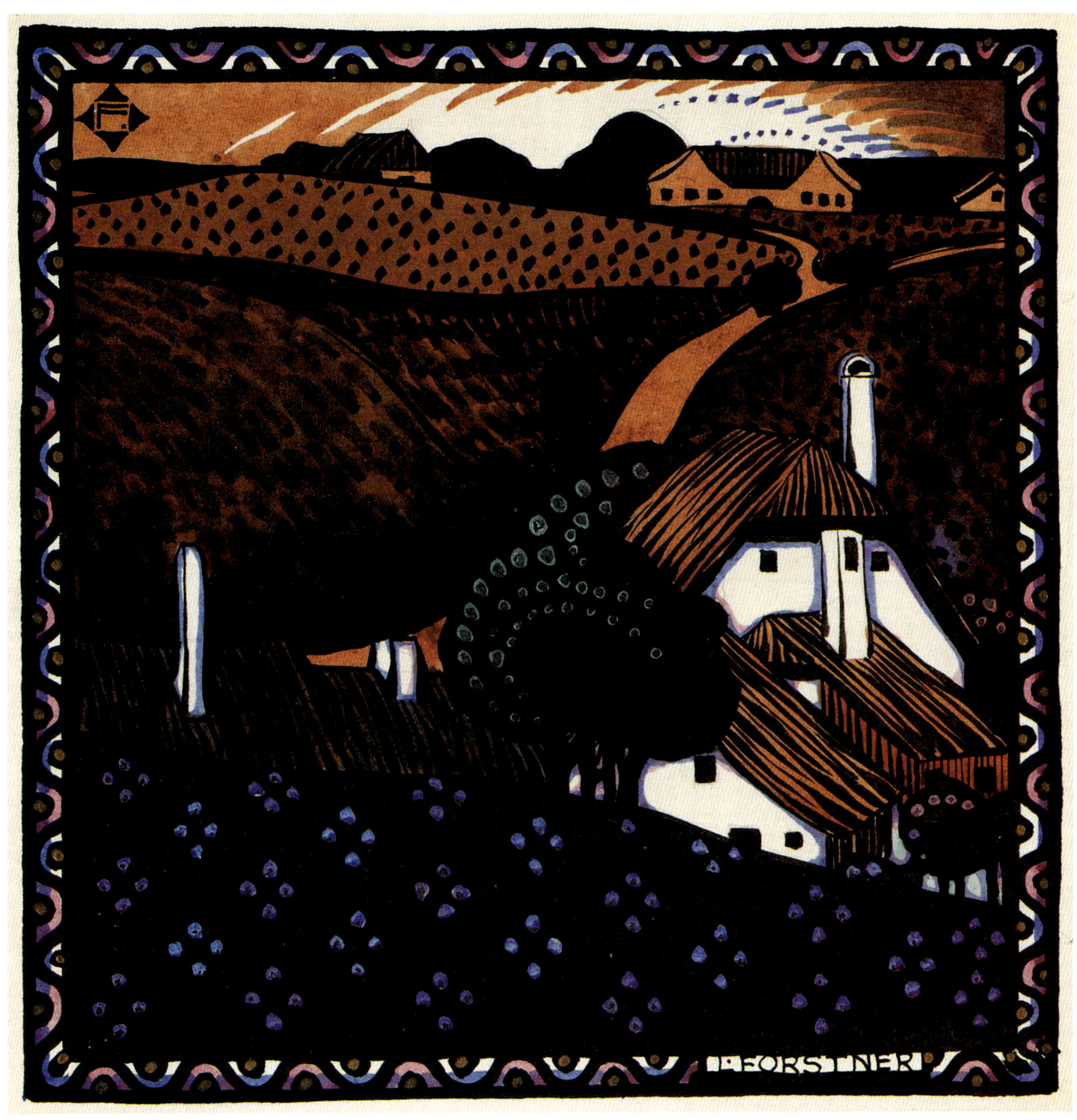

PAUL SANDBY

Hilly Landscape

(cat. no. 74)

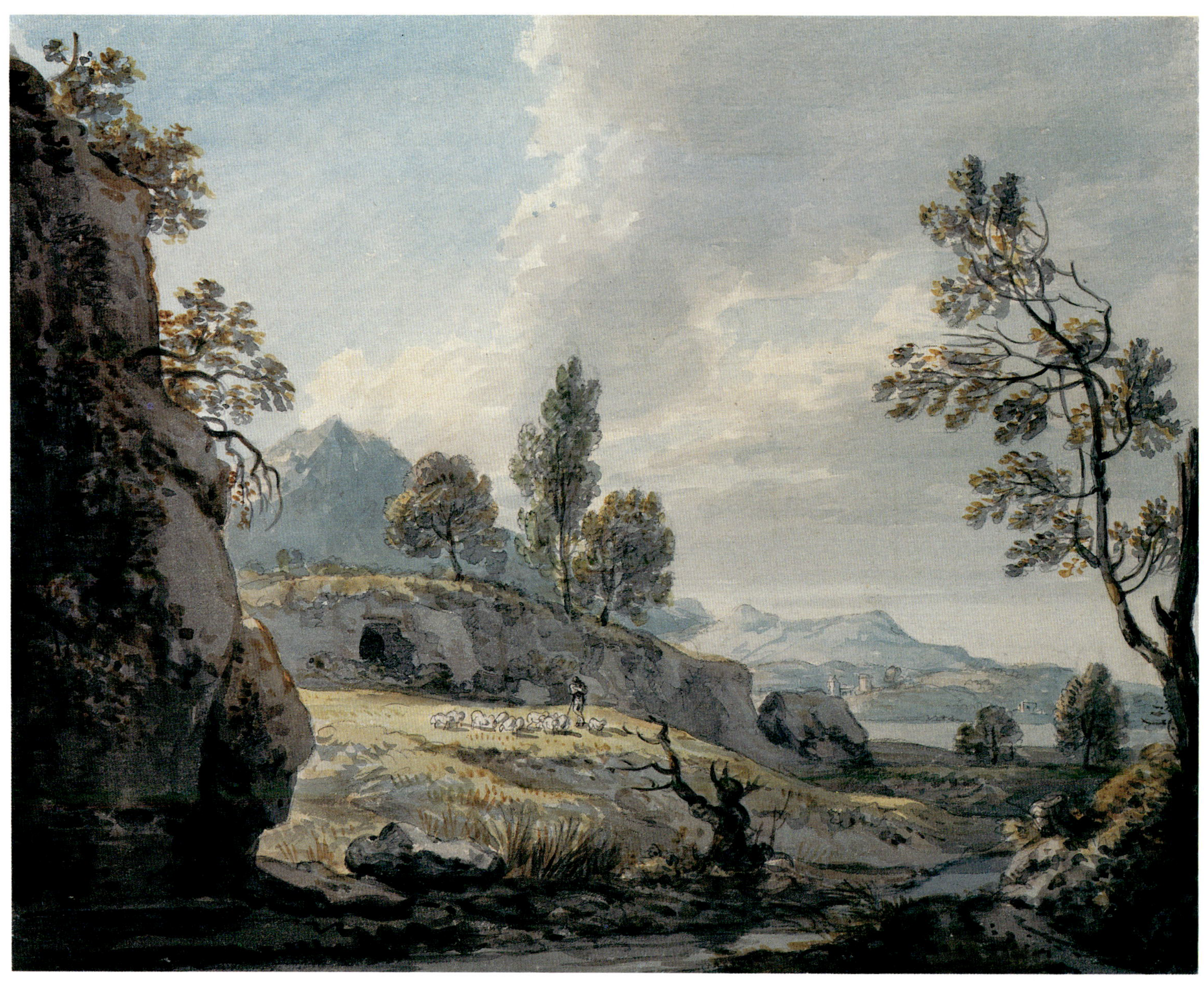

William Delamotte

Woman, Child, and Cattle by a River

(cat. no. 83)

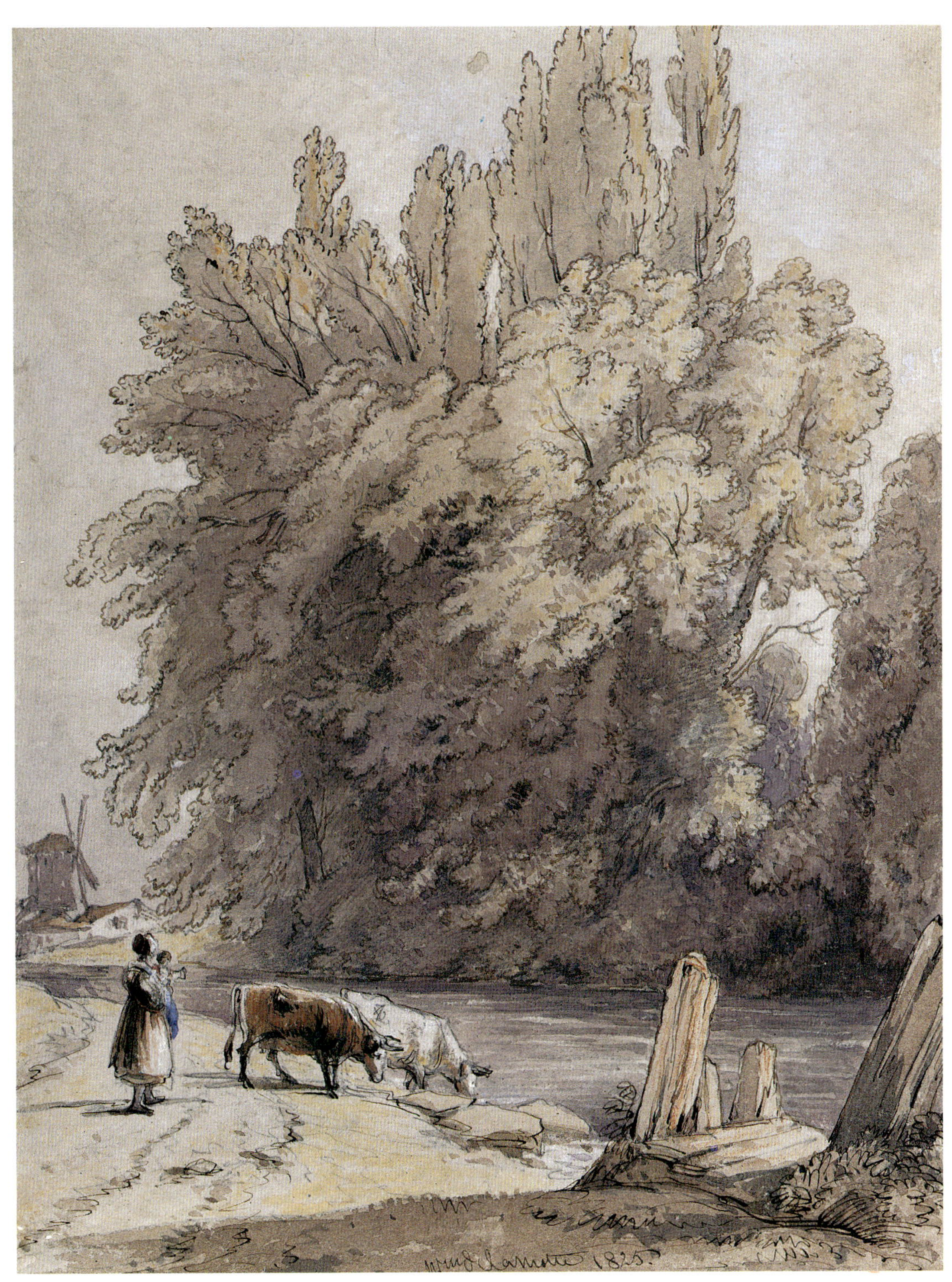

John Varley

Landscape with a Town at Sunset
(cat. no. 84)

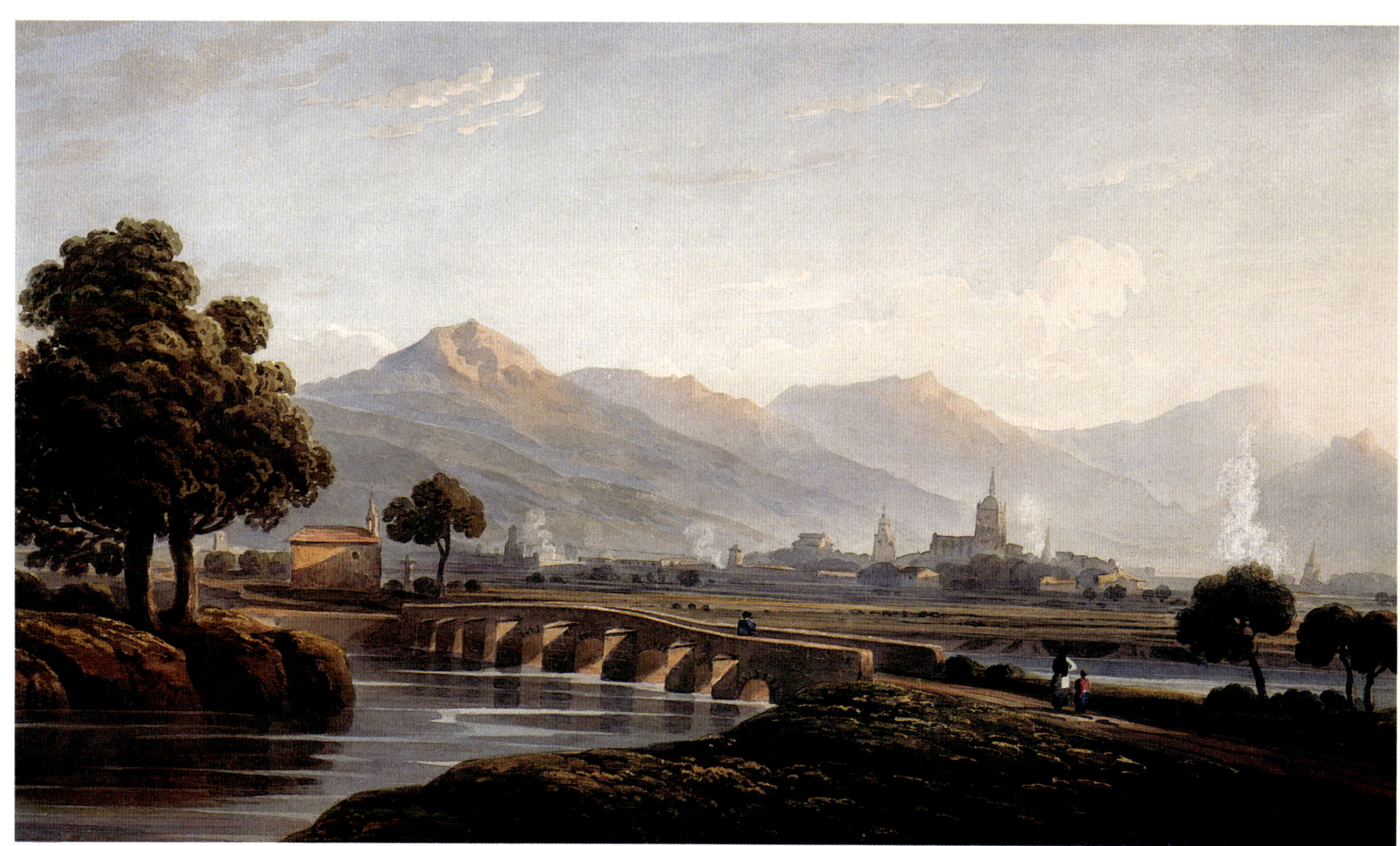

PETER DE WINT

Landscape

(cat. no. 86)

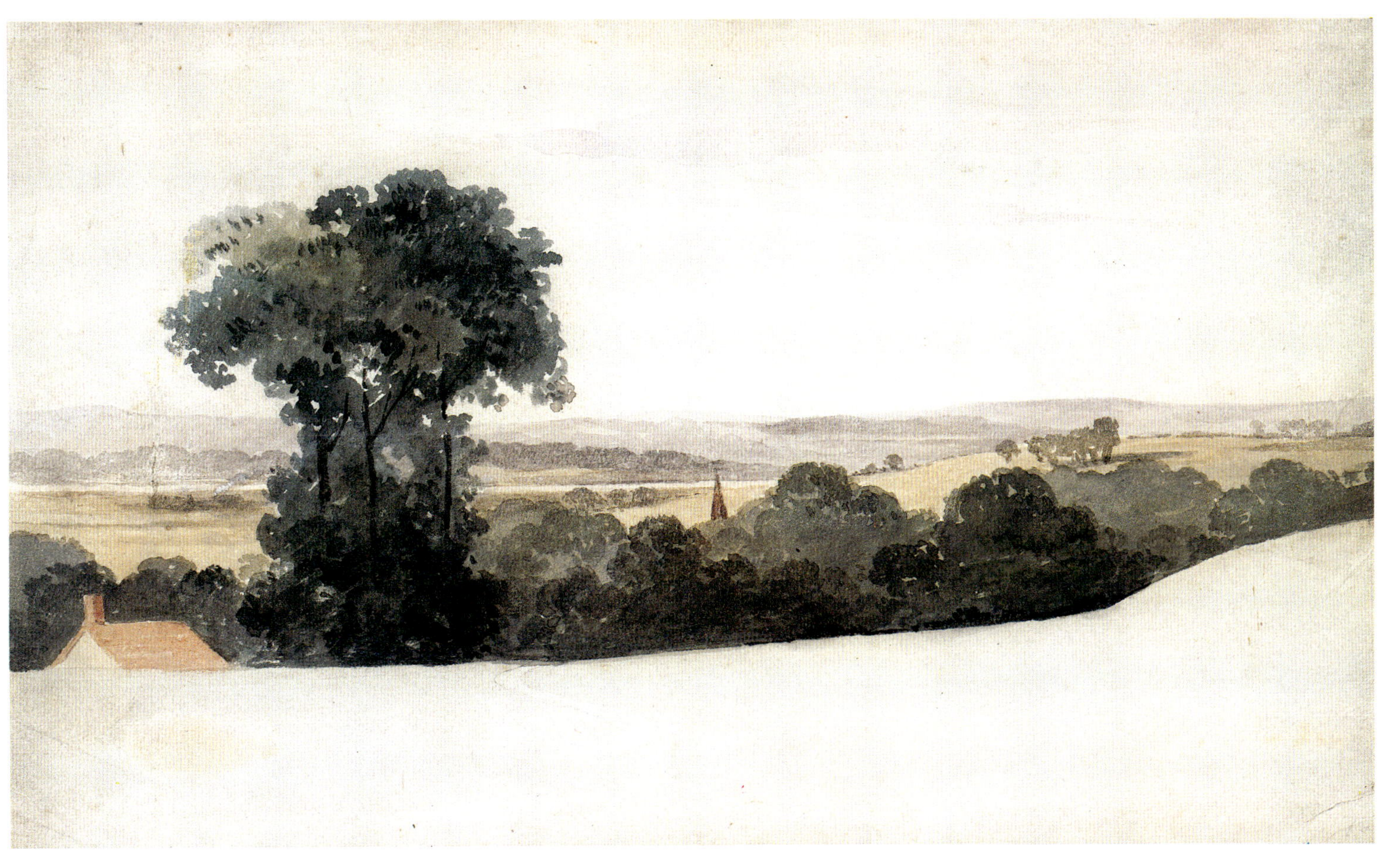

DAVID ROBERTS

Minaret of the Principal Mosque, Sioul, Upper Egypt
(cat. no. 87)

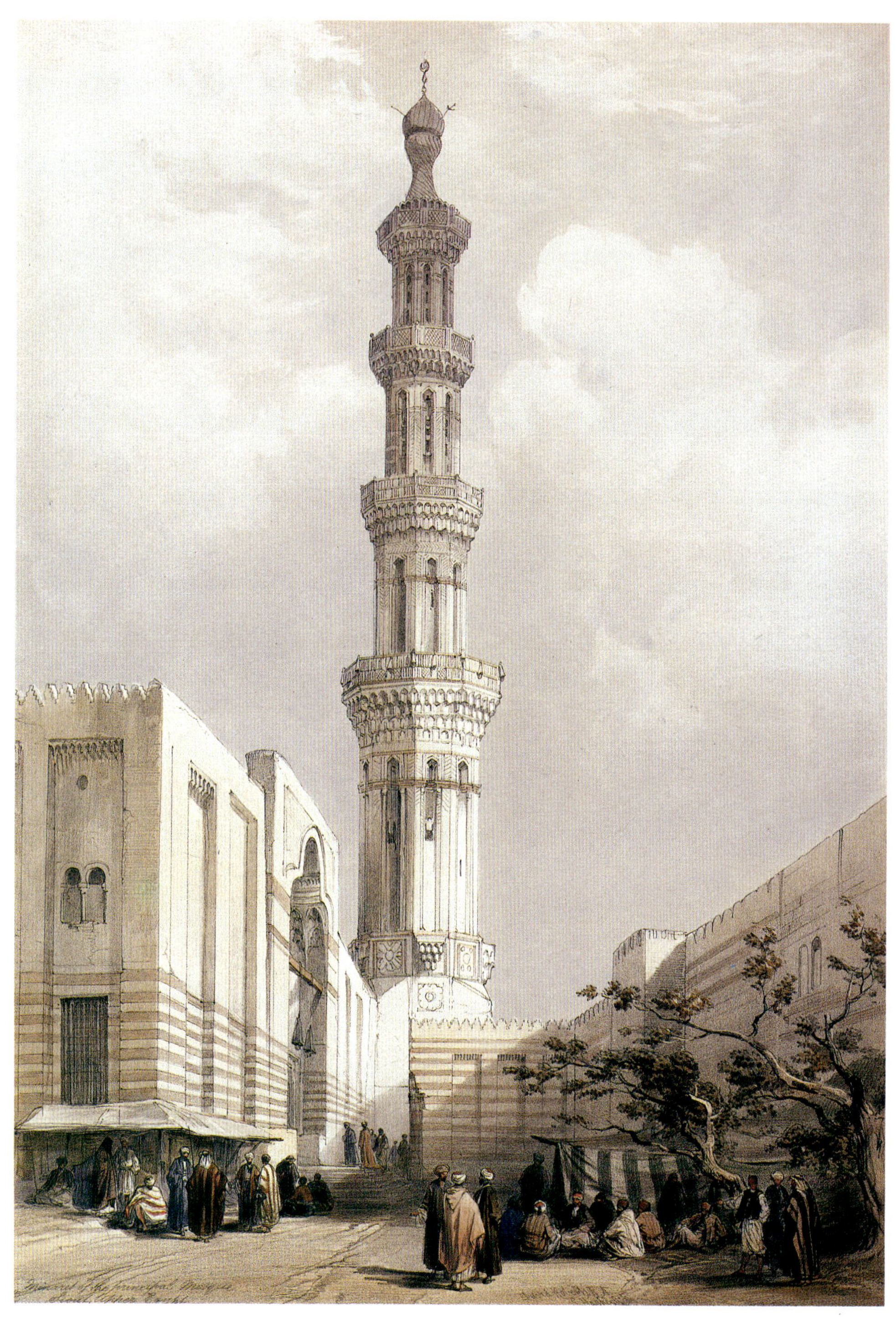

William Ward

The Seine between Mantes and Vernon
(cat. no. 96)

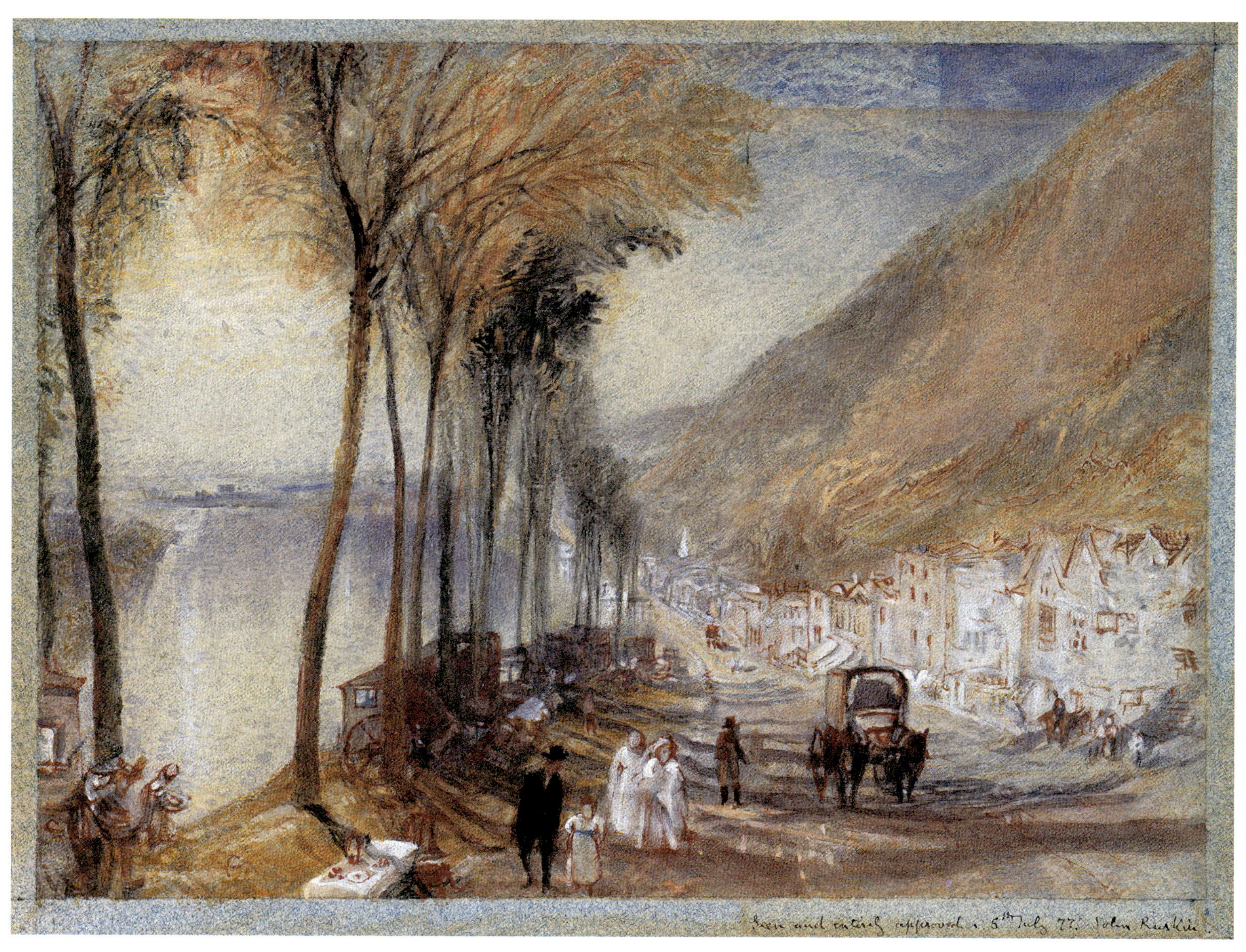

Henri-Joseph Harpignies

River Estuary
(cat. no. 124)

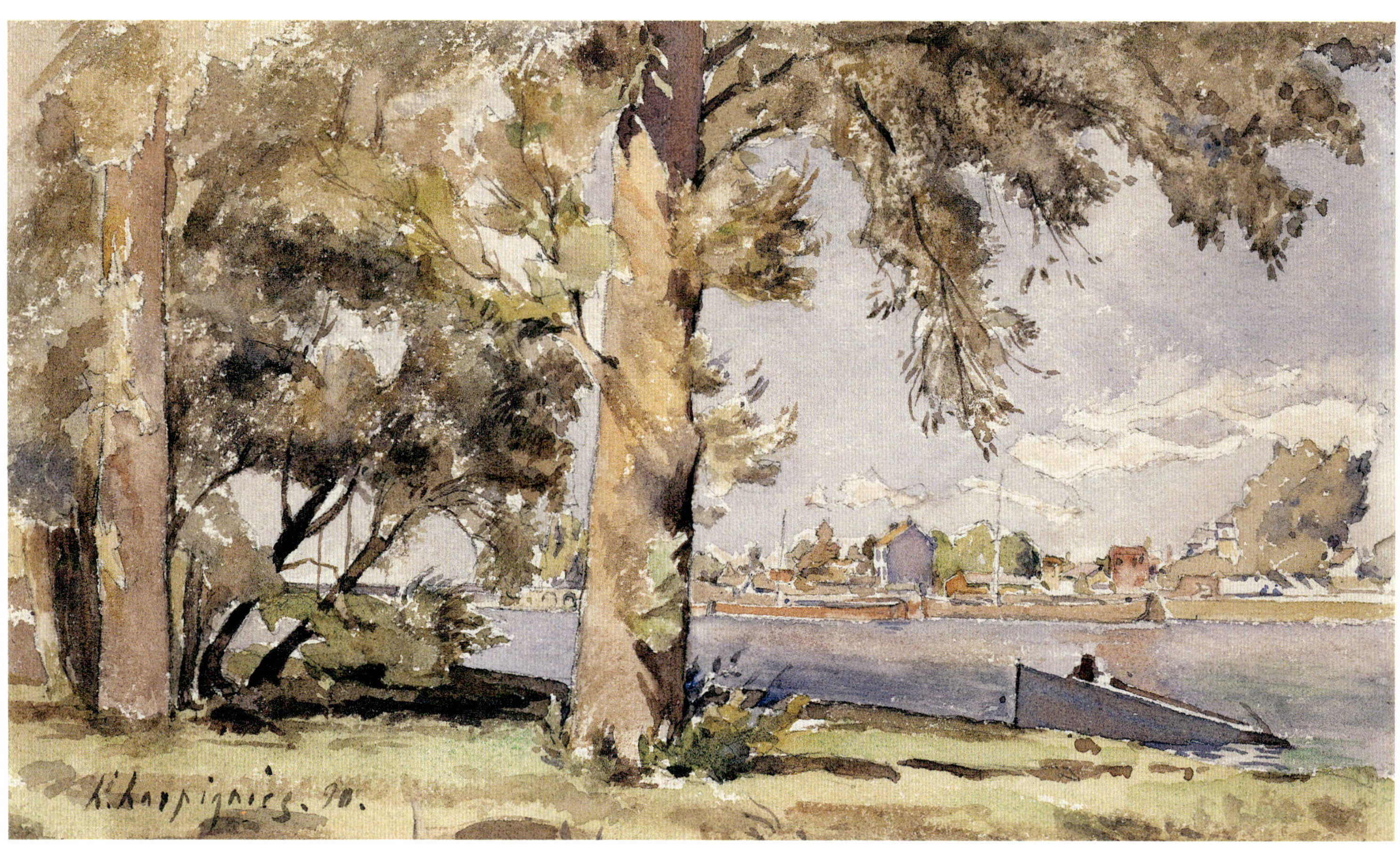

Paul Signac

Garden at Saint-Tropez
(cat. no. 133)

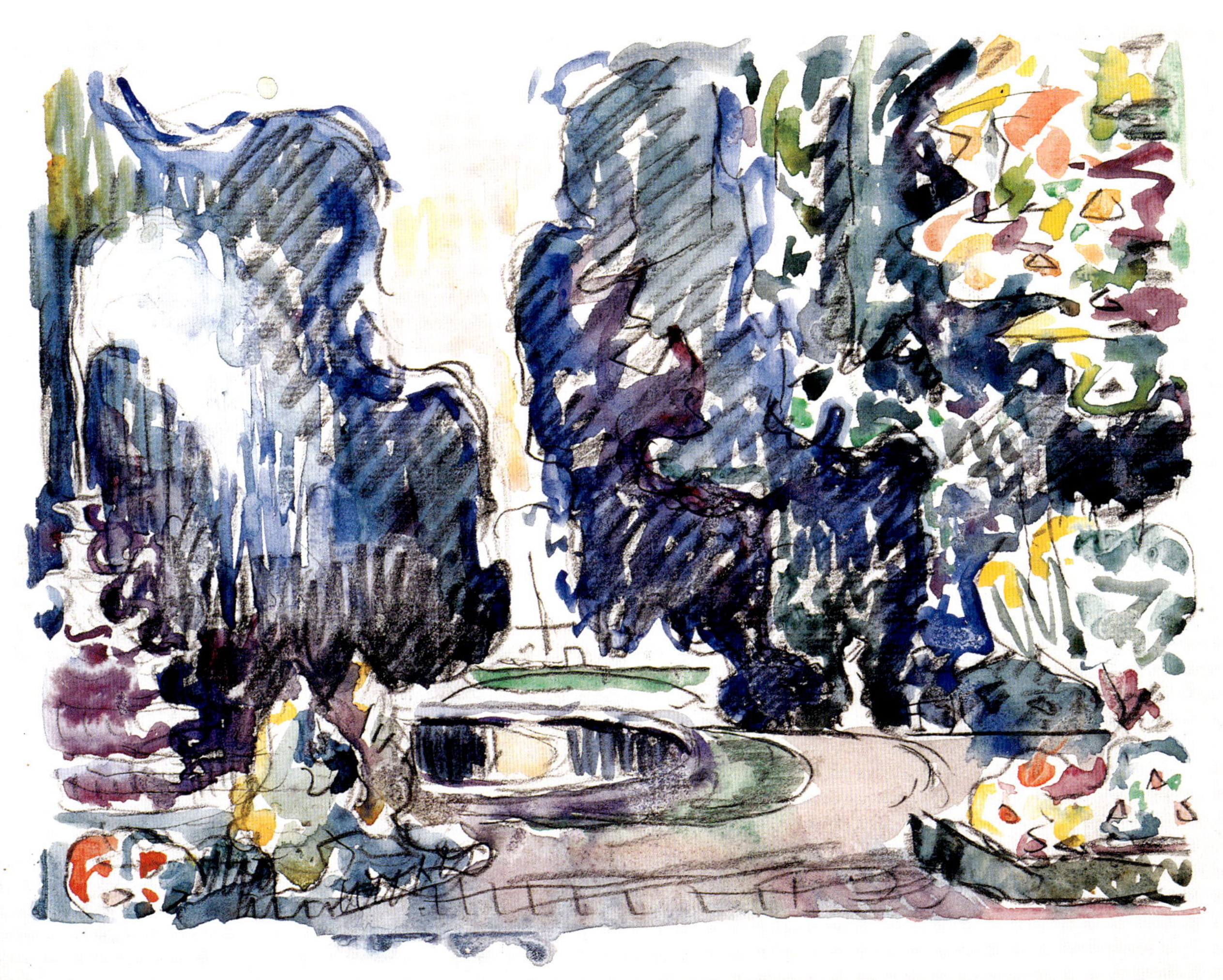

KER-XAVIER ROUSSEL

Three Tall Trees
(cat. no. 134)

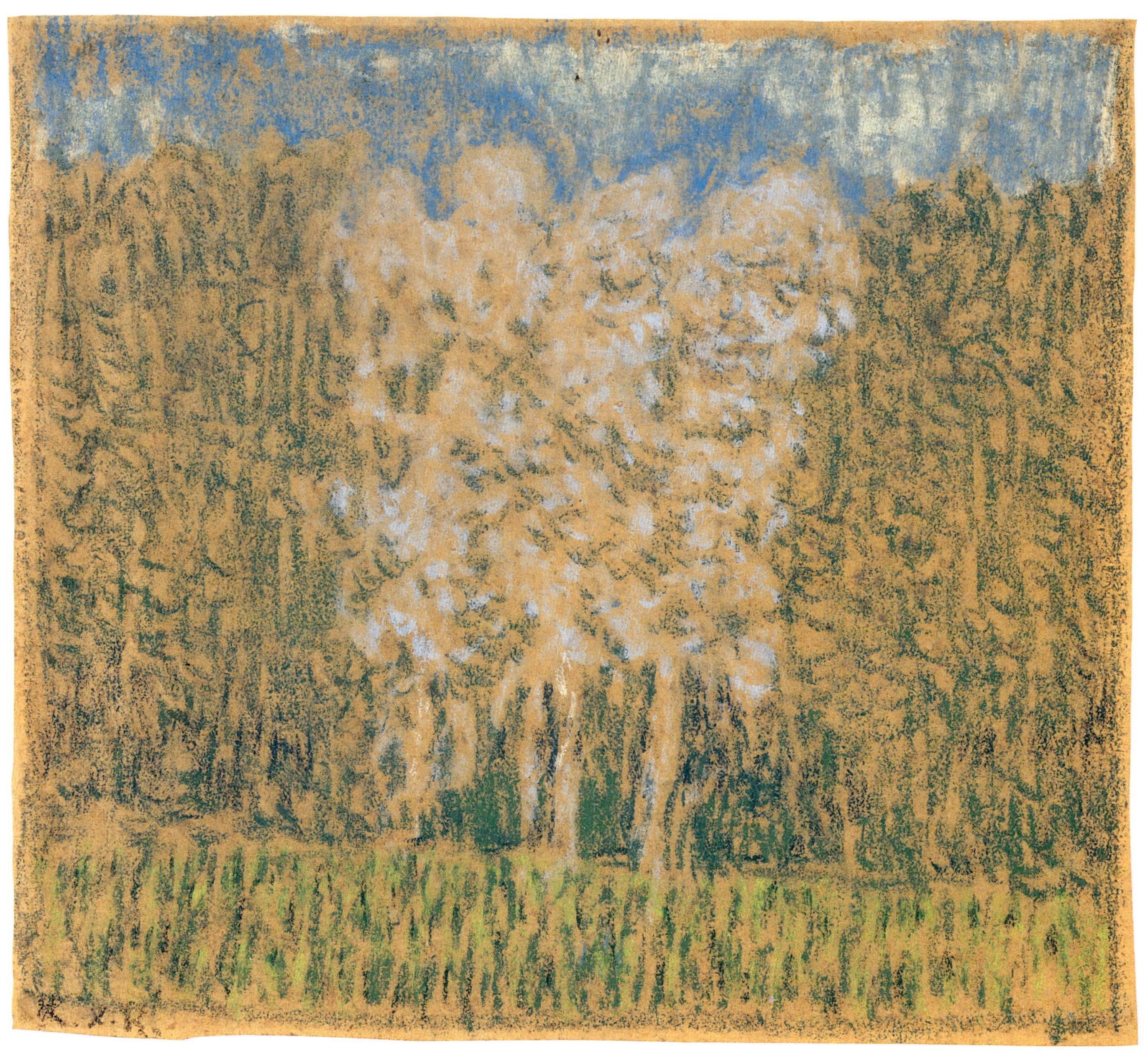

EMIL NOLDE

Harbor
(cat. no. 143)

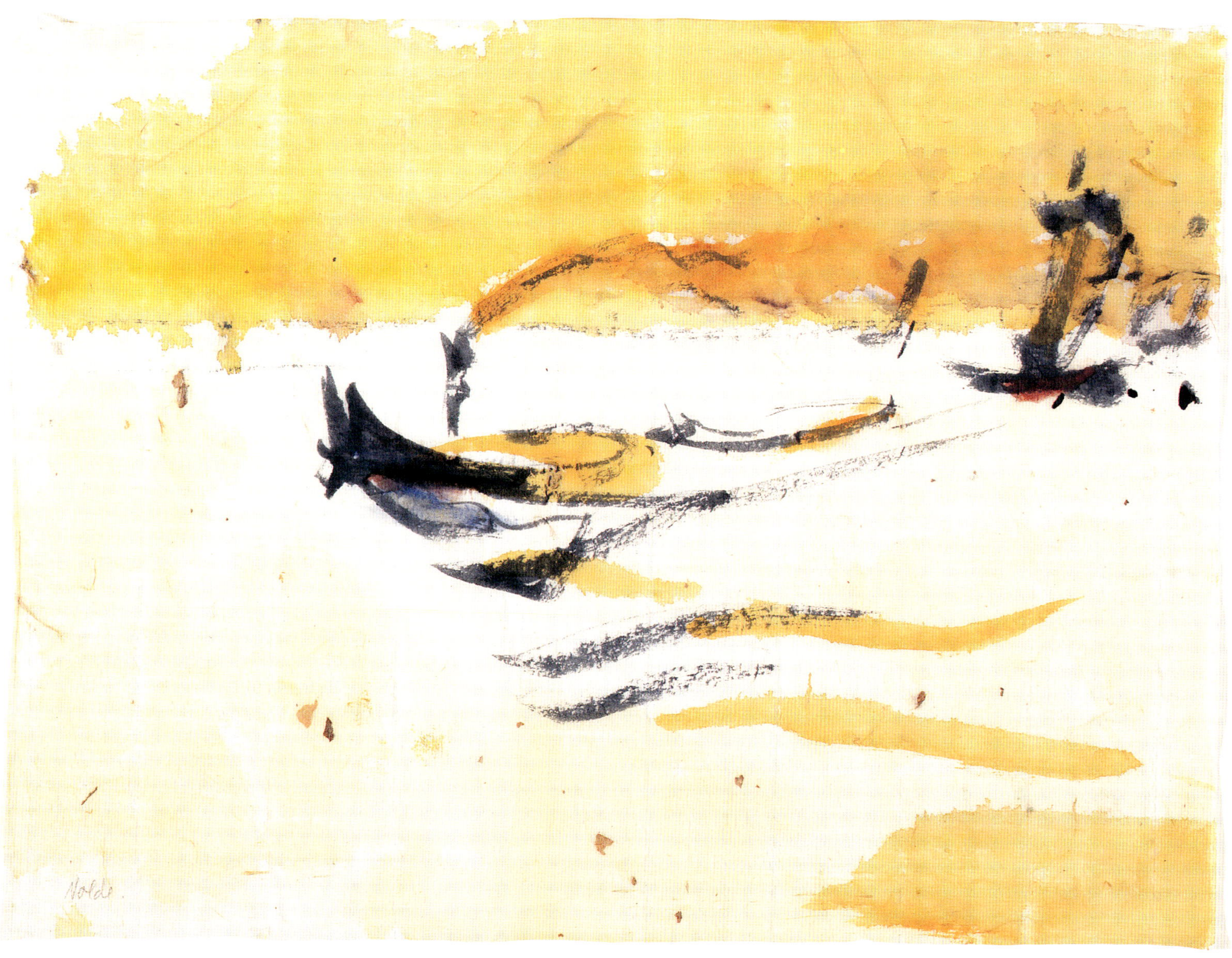

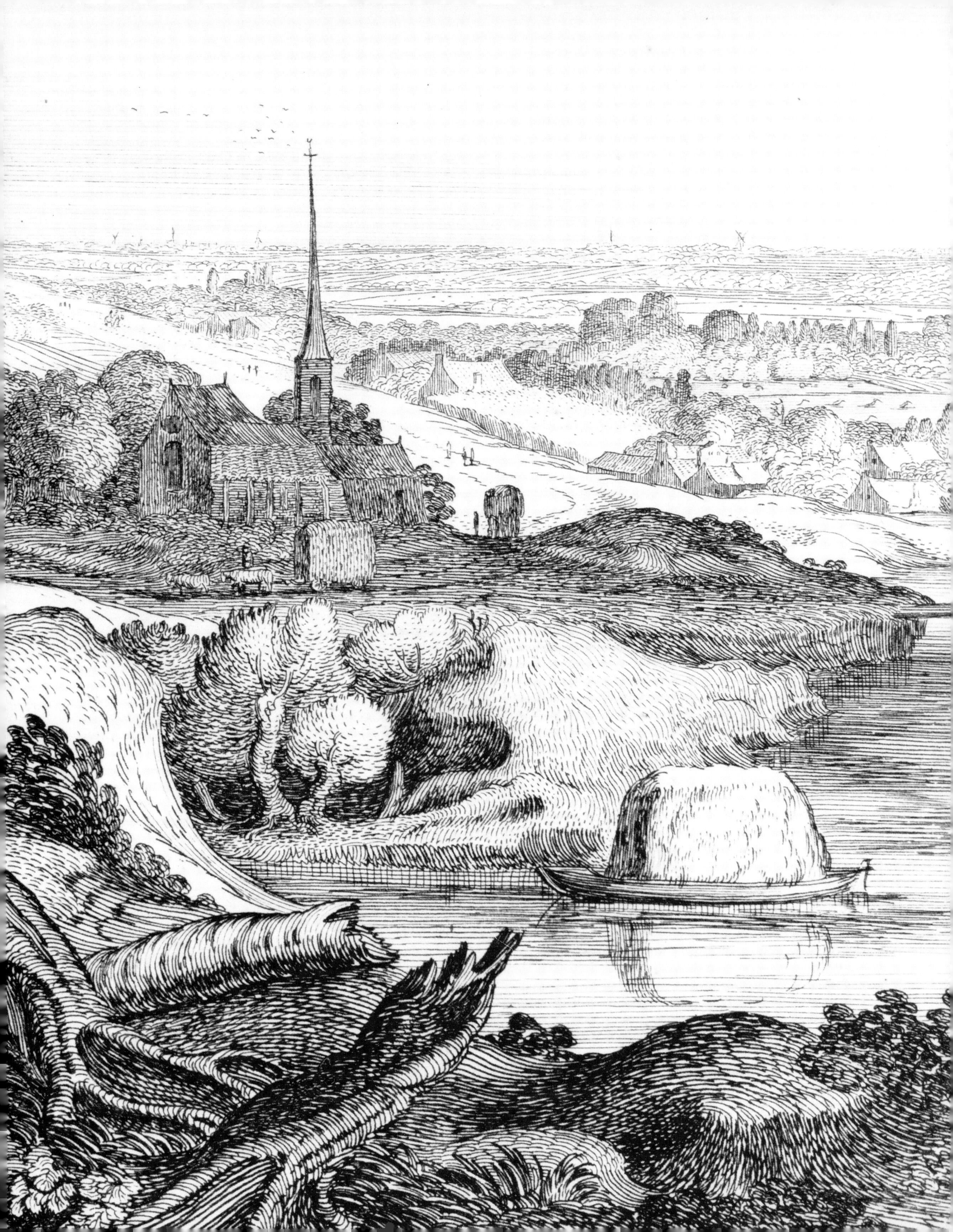

Catalogue of the Exhibition

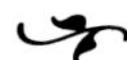

NOTE TO THE READER

EACH SECTION of the catalogue is arranged chronologically according to the artists' birth dates. Refer to the index for an alphabetical listing of artists included in the catalogue. When there is more than one work by a given artist, entries are arranged chronologically according to known or suggested dates. A biography of the artist precedes the entry or entries for that artist's work. When available, standard titles of works have been used. Unless otherwise specified, paper can be assumed to be off-white to cream in color. Measurements are given in millimeters; height precedes width. For intaglio and relief prints, measurements given are those of the plate or block; for planographic prints and drawings, measurements indicate the size of the paper. Dealer locations refer to those at the time of sale. References to books, articles, and catalogues raisonnés are generally abbreviated; full citations can be found in the bibliography.

Detail of cat. no. 42

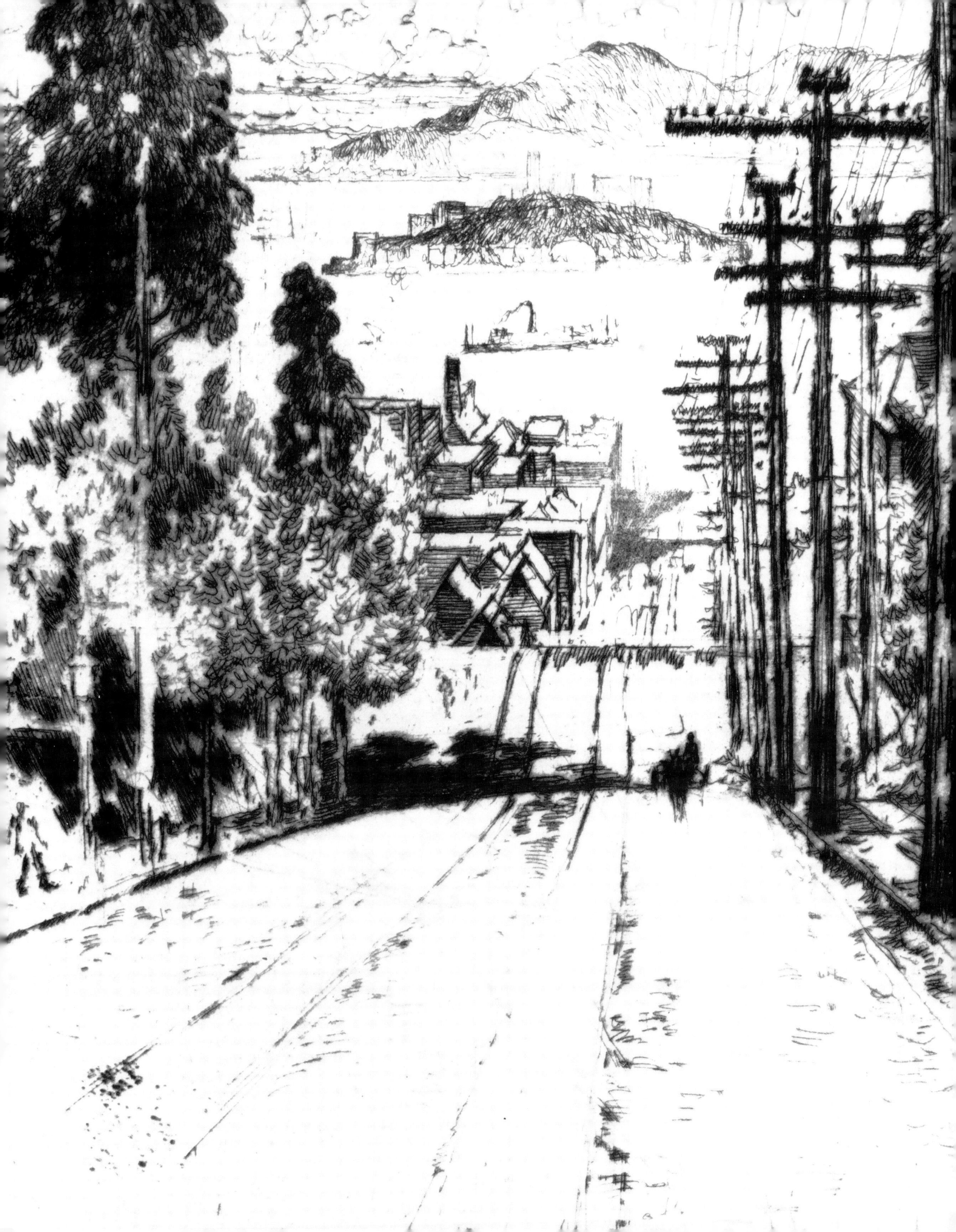

American

Detail of cat. no. 4

James McNeill Whistler

While working for the United States Coast Guard and Geodetic Survey as a surveyor and cartographer, James McNeill Whistler learned the rudiments of etching, thus beginning a lifelong preoccupation with this art form. Whistler soon decided to explore the more creative aspects of his craft and sailed for Paris in 1855, never to return to the United States. In Paris he associated with many of the leading artists of his day, including Gustave Courbet, Édouard Manet, Edgar Degas, and Henri Fantin-Latour. After traveling through northern France, Luxembourg, and the Rhineland, Whistler published Twelve Etchings from Nature in 1858.

In 1859 Whistler moved to London, where he was influenced by English artists such as Wenzel Hollar and J. M. W. Turner, and in 1871 he completed the Thames Set, which comprised sixteen etchings. In 1879 the Fine Art Society commissioned Whistler to go to Venice to complete a set of twelve etchings. A year later he returned to London with fifty plates. The First Venice Set of twelve prints was published in 1880, and six years later the Second Venice Set of twenty-six etchings was published.

During the 1880s Whistler traveled throughout Europe, and in 1887 he published a series of etchings done in Amsterdam. Aside from producing nearly 450 etchings and drypoints, he created about 180 lithographs, 550 paintings, and close to 1,500 drawings, watercolors, and pastels. By the 1890s Whistler was one of the most highly regarded artists of his day, and he had a profound influence on the generation of artists that followed him.

I

Nocturne (1878)

JAMES MCNEILL WHISTLER
(Lowell, Massachusetts 1834–1903 London)
Way 5; Levy 10 i/ii
Lithotint
172 x 264 mm
Provenance: H. S. Theobald (L. I/1376); Otto Gerstenberg (L. I/2785); R. E. Lewis, San Francisco

Whistler's first significant experiments with lithography date from 1878, when he was encouraged to work in the technique by the printer Thomas Way, who revived the art of lithography in England during the second half of the nineteenth century. Between 1878 and his departure for Venice in 1879, Whistler produced eighteen lithographs under Way's supervision. Until this time Whistler had concentrated on etching, a more portable technique that allowed the artist to sketch directly on the plate in front of his subjects, and he had shown little interest in more tonal methods of printmaking.

Beginning in the early 1870s, however, Whistler produced a series of Nocturnes depicting the Thames River, which signaled the artist's transition from more realistic modes of representation to a poetic interpretation of nature influenced by orientalist and aesthetic sentiments. In *Nocturne*, one of a group of lithotints of river subjects, the artist used veils of lithographic ink to create the moody, atmospheric effects achieved in his painted Nocturnes with translucent washes of paint, which he had been unable to produce in etching or drypoint. Drawing inspiration from Japanese prints, Whistler divided the composition of *Nocturne* into two separate zones, separated by a high horizon line. This emphasizes a two-dimensional abstract pattern and evokes the sensation of atmosphere far more than it describes the subject. The print's composition, tonal variations, and mood anticipate Whistler's views of Venice, in which the artist would return to the more portable medium of etching, using tonal printing to produce effects of mood and atmosphere.

Nocturne was one of a group of lithographs intended to be issued in a limited number of proofs. Due to a lack of interest, perhaps an indication of the low status of artistic lithography, only a few impressions of *Limehouse* and *Nocturne*, including the present print, were published in this manner.[1] In 1887 a later impression of *Nocturne* was included in the set known as Art Notes, published by Boussod, Valadan, and Company in an edition of one hundred.

1. Way (1914) records six impressions, although additional prints have since been recorded. We would like to thank Nesta Spink for her information regarding these earlier impressions.

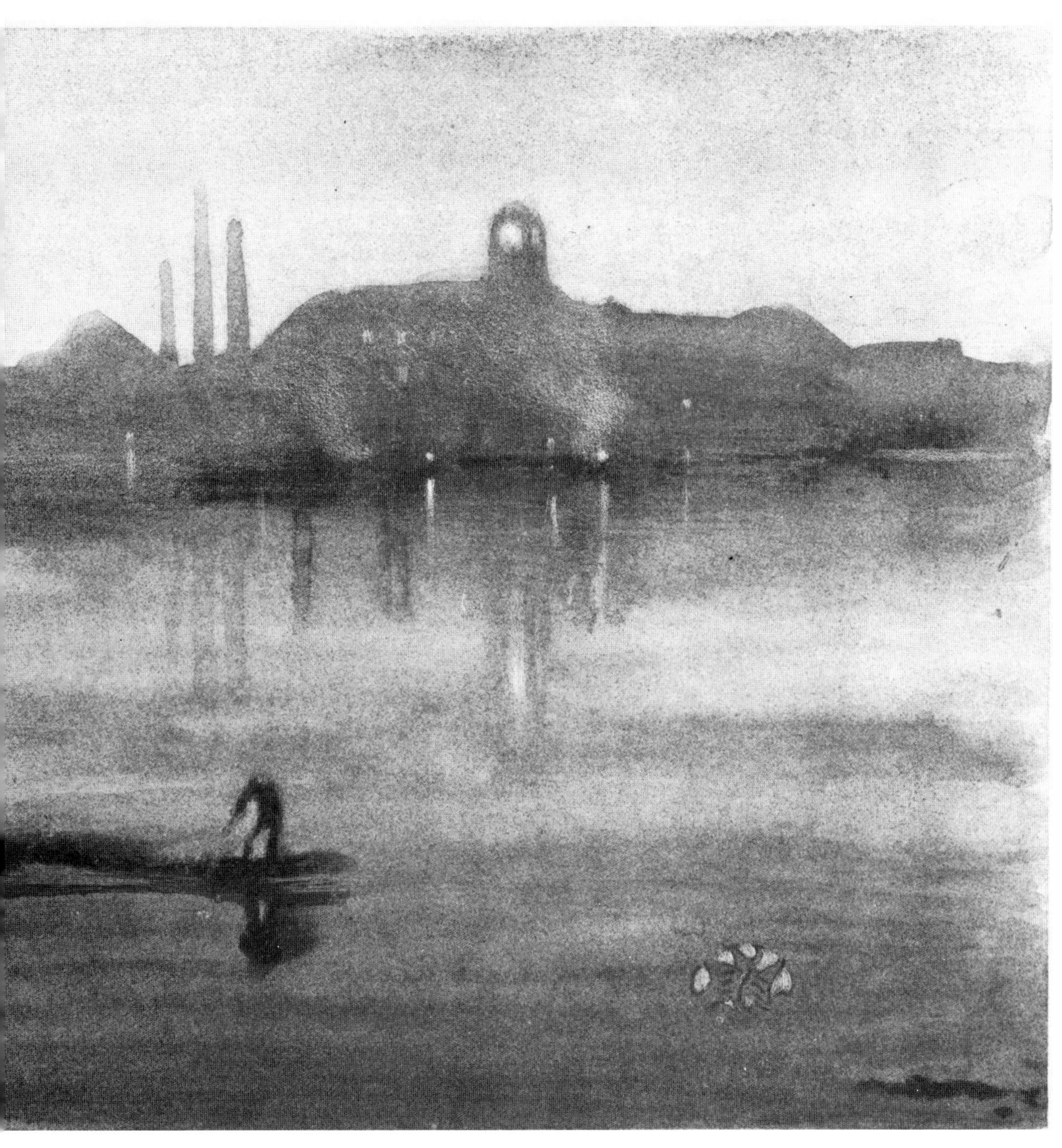

James McNeill Whistler

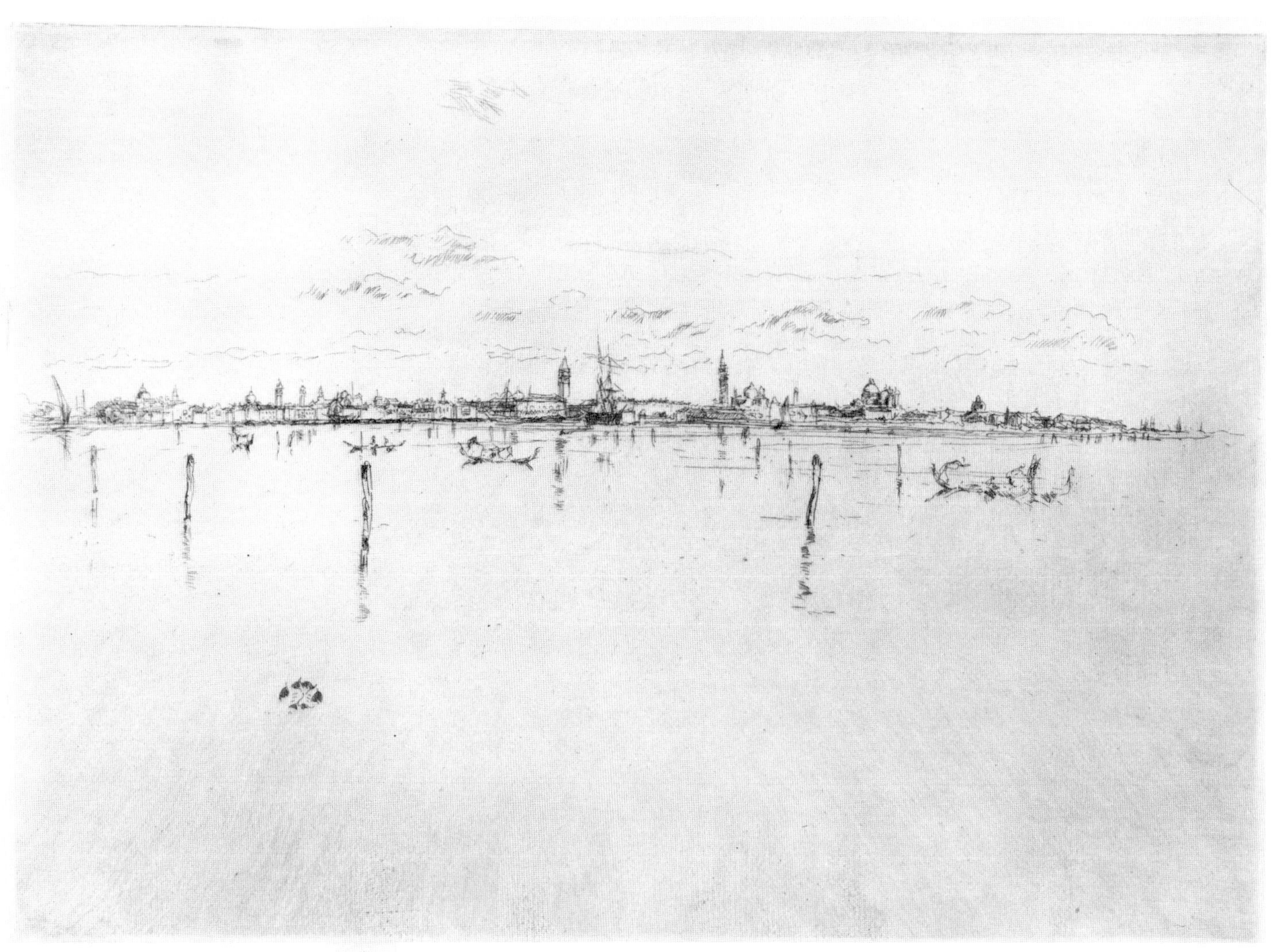

2

Little Venice (1880)

JAMES MCNEILL WHISTLER
(Lowell, Massachusetts 1834–1903 London)
From the First Venice Set (1880)
K. 183 (only state)
Etching and drypoint printed in brown ink
186 x 266 mm
Signed on tab
Provenance: Sabersky, Los Angeles

Little Venice is from the series Venice: A Series of Twelve Etchings, known as the First Venice Set, commissioned and published by the Fine Art Society, London, in 1880. Venice was a popular destination for artists, writers, and especially English tourists, thus assuring Whistler of a market for his etched views of the city. In 1879, sponsored by the Fine Art Society, Whistler traveled to Venice, where he rendered some fifty plates of this city during the following fourteen months. Setting out each day in his gondola, the artist worked from nature, drawing directly on the etching plate.

In *Little Venice* Whistler combined etching and tonal printing to produce the poetic, atmospheric effects of his 1870s Nocturne paintings and lithotints (see cat. no. 1). Whistler had not used tonal printing extensively prior to the First Venice Set, but he used it to great effect in most of the prints in this series, particularly in his sweeping vistas of the Venetian lagoon. Here he conveys the impression of a floating city, dividing the composition into two tonal areas of sky and water held together by etched lines that summarily describe the city at the horizon. In this particular impression the darkened foreground and the wiping around the horizon give the small print an expansive quality, making the city appear to recede into the distance.

JAMES MCNEILL WHISTLER

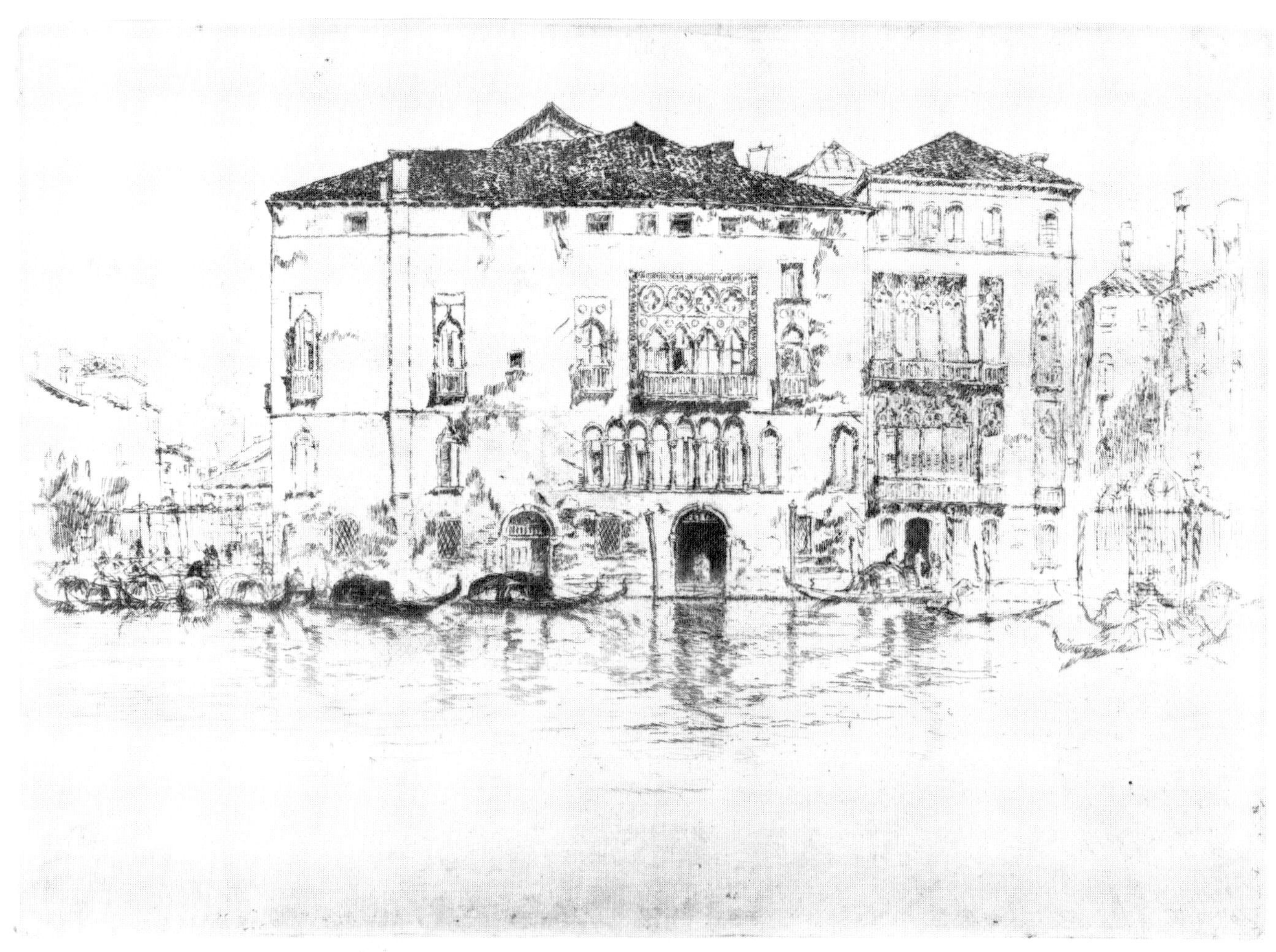

3
The Palaces (1880)

JAMES MCNEILL WHISTLER
(Lowell, Massachusetts 1834–1903 London)
From the First Venice Set (1880)
K. 187 ii/iii
Etching and drypoint
250 x 355 mm
Signed on tab
Provenance: Zeitlin and Ver Brugge, Los Angeles

The Palaces recalls some of the riverside views of the Thames Set, although here the artist does not focus on genre subjects but on the decorative effects of the ornamental palace facade. Reminiscent of Canaletto's etchings, which Whistler admired, the print displays the same interest in lively details and textural surfaces, though it is more typical of straightforward tourist views than most prints in the First Venice Set. The composition focuses on the palace itself, excluding sky, water, and surrounding buildings in accordance with Whistler's practice of working on the plate from the center outward so that one could stop at any point and have "a fine and complete picture" (Getscher and Staley 1977, p. 9).

JOSEPH PENNELL

Joseph Pennell attended classes at the Pennsylvania School of Industrial Art and in 1879 was accepted at the Pennsylvania Academy of the Fine Arts. In 1880 he was founding member of the Philadelphia Society of Etchers. In 1882 he left the Pennsylvania Academy and opened his own studio, supporting himself as an illustrator. His early work was decisively influenced by the etchings of James McNeill Whistler, which he had seen at an 1881 exhibition at the Pennsylvania Academy. In 1882 Pennell made his first journey to Europe, commissioned to execute etchings for a series of articles on Tuscan cities. He returned again in 1884, when he met Whistler in London. Their friendship did not really develop until 1893 in Paris, when Whistler invited Pennell to assist him with biting his plates. In 1917 Pennell returned permanently to New York, where he produced lithographs for the government during the war. From 1922 to 1926 he taught lithography at the Art Students' League.

As Whistler's most devoted American follower, Pennell was a leading figure of the American etching revival. A prolific printmaker, he produced more than fifteen hundred etchings and lithographs, primarily city views and landscapes.

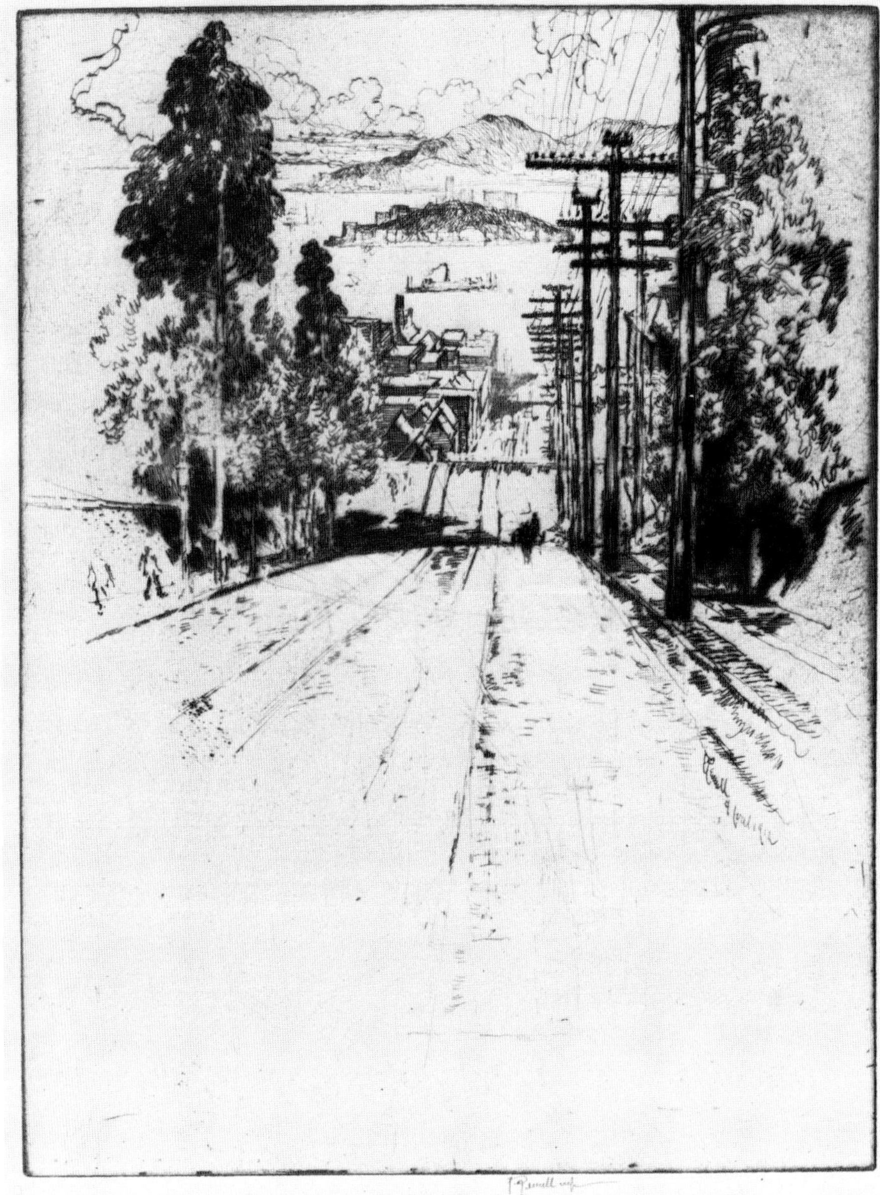

4

From R.L. Stevenson's House, San Francisco, 1912, Hyde Street with Cable Car Tracks (1912)

JOSEPH PENNELL
(Philadelphia 1857–1926 New York)
Wuerth 643
Etching
305 x 237 mm
Signed lower right
Provenance: R. E. Lewis, San Francisco

Following his rewarding trip to Central America to sketch the building of the Panama Canal in 1912, Pennell returned by way of San Francisco and the West, also stopping in Yosemite and the Grand Canyon. In San Francisco he made numerous etchings of the city, mostly views looking up or down its steep streets or vistas of skyscrapers from across the bay.

Elements of this print, such as the dramatic vertical sweep created by the steep incline of the street, the high horizon, empty foreground, and sketchy lines, reflect the influence of James McNeill Whistler, especially his strong concern for the aesthetics of composition. Typical of Pennell's more descriptive style, however, the sense of real space is never subservient to pattern or texture.

Pennell's San Francisco etchings are indicative of a new direction in American printmaking during the first quarter of the twentieth century, best exemplified by the works of John Sloan, John Marin, and the more mature works of Pennell himself. Rather than limiting his subjects to the picturesque images of old-world Europe that had become the stock in trade of American printmakers, Pennell portrayed the full range of subjects within the American industrialized urban landscape, rendering in great detail its skyscrapers, bridges, and industrial complexes.

Childe Hassam

The son of a prosperous Boston merchant, Childe Hassam began his career as a magazine and book illustrator and also studied painting at the Boston Art Club. From 1885 to 1888 he lived in Paris, studying for a short time at the Académie Julian, but he soon became more interested in the work of Claude Monet and the French impressionists. He moved to New York City in 1889 and nine years later was one of the founders of The Ten, a group of painters who broke away from the Society of American Artists. He would exhibit with the group for the better part of the next twenty years.

Already a successful painter of impressionistic, plein-air landscapes, Hassam did not seriously begin etching until 1915. During that year he made around sixty etchings, many produced during that summer in the village of Cos Cob in southern Connecticut. He continued to etch throughout the rest of his career, and his oeuvre consists of more than 350 etchings as well as forty-five lithographs produced during 1917 and 1918.

5

Cos Cob (1915)

CHILDE HASSAM
(Boston 1859–1935 East Hampton, New York)
Cortissoz 32 i/ii
Etching
173 x 124 mm
Signed with cipher and inscribed *imp* lower right
Provenance: S. V. Sterner; R. E. Lewis, San Francisco

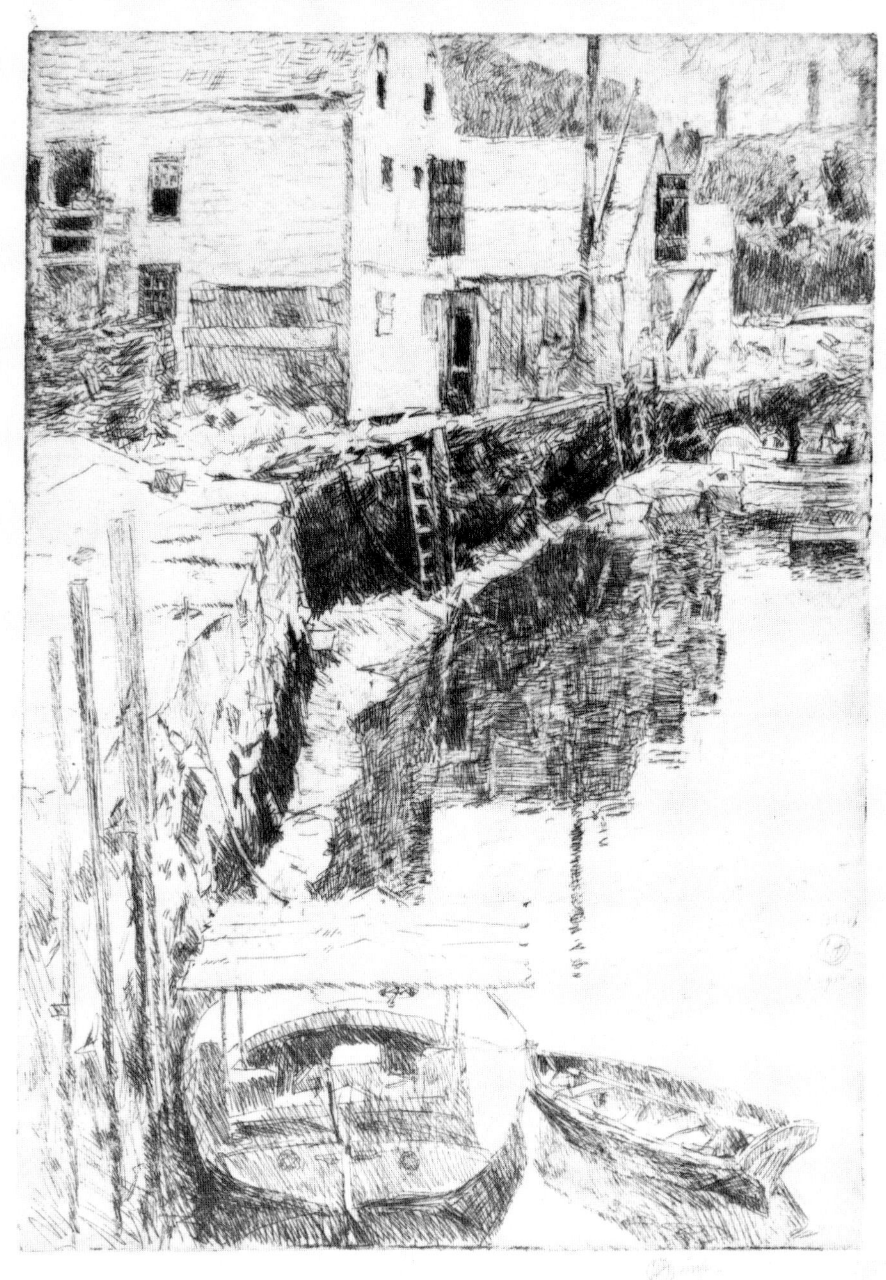

Cos Cob was one of twenty-five etchings produced by Hassam during his first experiments with etching in the summer of 1915 in Cos Cob, Connecticut, an artists' colony founded in 1890 by John Twachtman. Linked to New York by a new railroad, which made it possible for artists to work in the country while maintaining contacts with dealers and studios in the city, Cos Cob became a favorite retreat for artists around the turn of the century (Larkin 1980, p. 83). The town itself not only furnished subjects for the artists who worked there but also stimulated the development of modernism in America. Cos Cob artists were included in exhibitions of The Ten and in the Armory Show of 1913.

Hassam's first known Cos Cob works date from 1896, but he did not begin etching until much later, in 1915, when, encouraged by J. Alden Weir, he began to sketch from nature, printing the plates on printmaker Kerr Eby's etching press. *Cos Cob* is a view of Eby's studio in a waterfront warehouse, accurate in its description of an actual place and sensitive to the impressionistic play of light and shade that flickers over the surface. The low vantage point and high horizon line recall the two-dimensional approach of Japanese prints, as well as Hassam's debt to James McNeill Whistler.

John Marin

6
Quartier de la Maison Blanche (1907)

JOHN MARIN
(Rutherford, New Jersey 1870–1953 Cape Split, Maine)
Zigrosser 78
Etching
130 x 180 mm
Signed lower right
Provenance: Zeitlin and Ver Brugge, Los Angeles

After practicing architecture for a short period, John Marin entered the Pennsylvania Academy of the Fine Arts in Philadelphia, where he studied from 1899 to 1901. In 1905 he went to Paris, where he learned to etch, teaching himself the process using Maxime Lalanne's Treatise on Etching. *He traveled around Europe, working on views of Amsterdam, Laon, and Venice, and in 1907 was accepted into the Salon d'Automne. In 1909 he met Edward Steichen, who introduced him to Alfred Stieglitz, in whose 291 Gallery in New York Marin exhibited a few watercolors. The following year Stieglitz presented Marin's first solo exhibition, which included forty-three watercolors, twenty pastels, and eight etchings. With financial support from Stieglitz, Marin returned permanently to the United States in 1911 and soon became a pioneer of American abstraction, painting and etching expressionistic views of New York City. Marin participated in the Armory Show in 1913. In 1914 he spent the first of many summers on the coast of Maine, executing watercolors of the coastal landscape, which were exhibited regularly at Stieglitz's galleries.*

Marin printed most of his own plates and usually drew directly on the plate in the presence of his subject. His 180 etchings were produced primarily in Europe, and his activities as a printmaker declined after he began receiving financial support from Stieglitz. He was a prolific watercolorist throughout his life, concentrating on New York scenes and seascapes of the Maine coast.

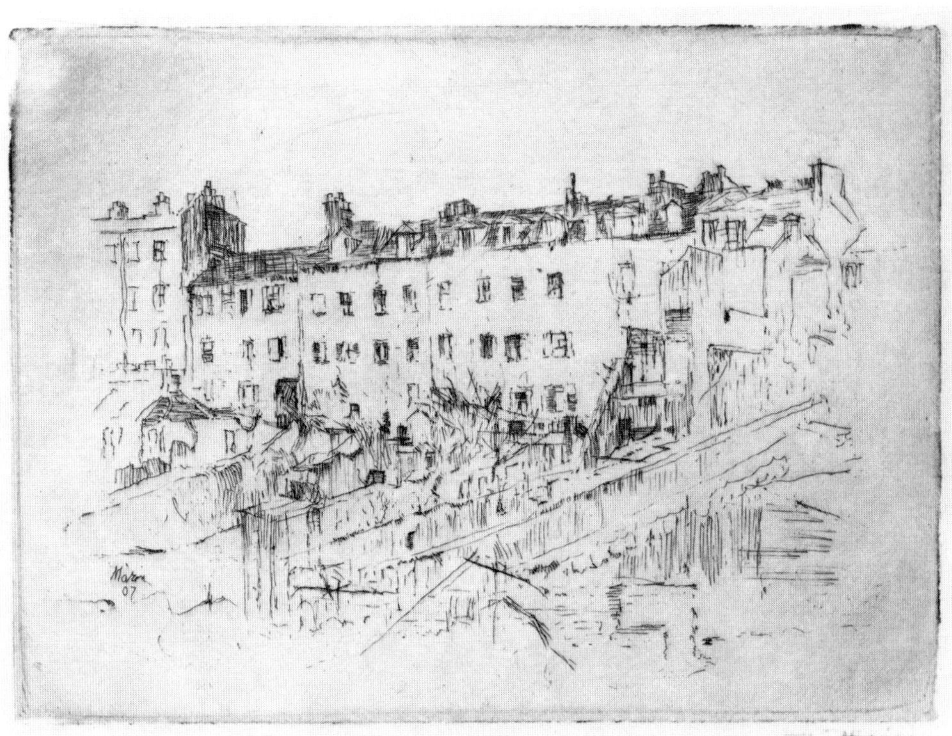

In 1905 Marin went to Europe, where he etched depictions of famous monuments as well as more generalized city scenes. As was common practice for American printmakers influenced by James McNeill Whistler and the European tradition, Marin drew directly on the plate, recording his spontaneous impression of a scene rather than meticulous descriptive details. His prints, however, range from more conventional renderings typical of those produced for the tourist market to livelier images that foretell a more radical direction in Marin's art.

One of twenty-nine etchings made in Paris in 1907, *Quartier de la Maison Blanche* lies somewhere between Marin's picturesque cathedral views and his more expressionistic etchings executed after his return to New York in 1912. In its vignette format and light tonal printing, it recalls many of Whistler's Venetian etchings, and its light, sketchy lines that suggest rather than describe the subject distinguish it from the larger, more detailed renderings desired by Marin's dealers (Watrous 1984, p. 68). Zigrosser (1969) records an edition of only twelve impressions pulled from this plate.

JOHN MARIN

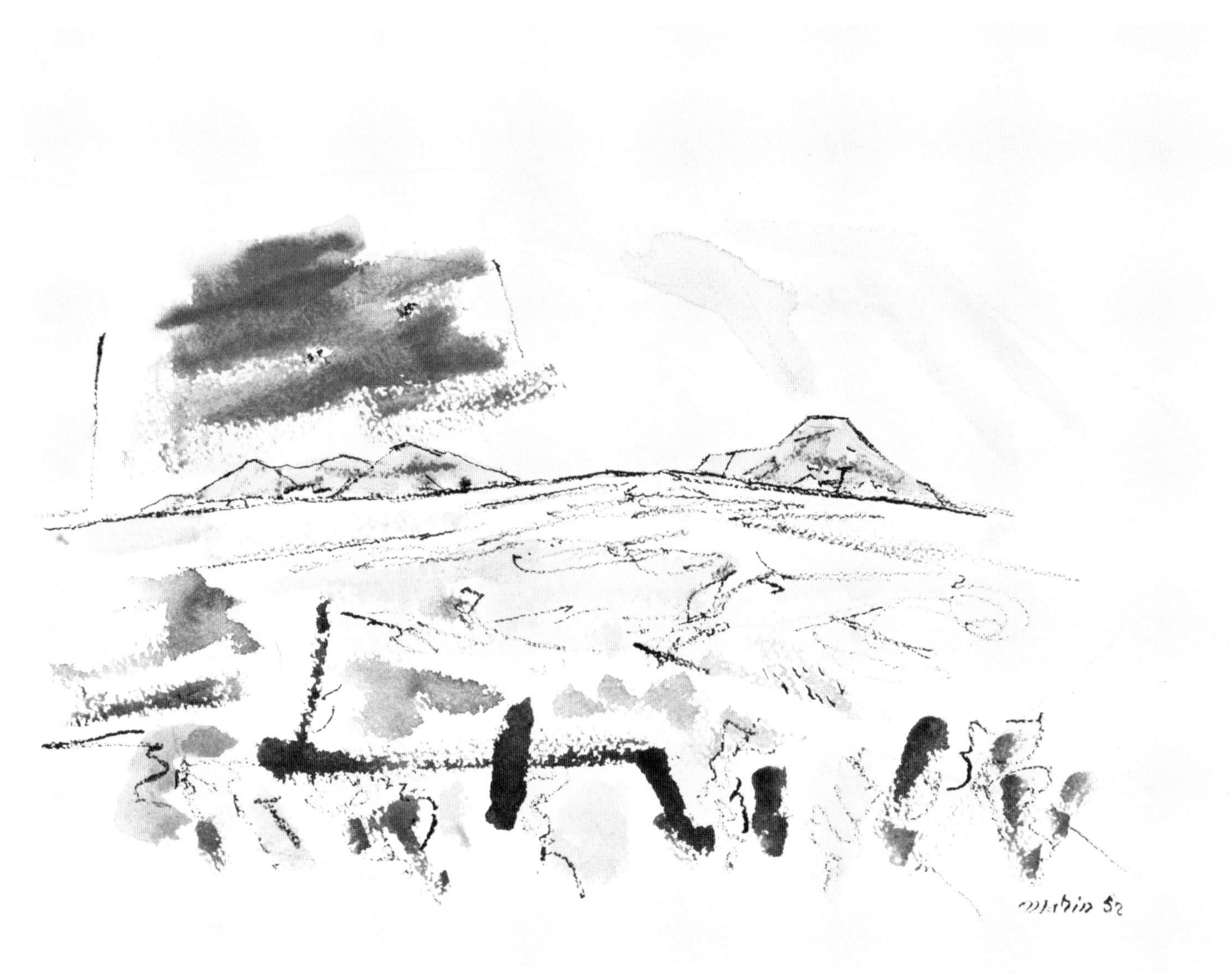

7

Autumn on the Road to Deblois, Maine, No. 2 (1952)

JOHN MARIN
(Rutherford, New Jersey 1870–1953 Cape Split, Maine)
Watercolor
362 x 483 mm
Signed and dated lower right
Provenance: Richard Loeb, New York; estate of Edith Gregor Halpert; Downtown Gallery, New York; Zeitlin and Ver Brugge, Los Angeles
Exhibition: *John Marin*, Downtown Gallery, New York, December 1952–January 1953
Bibliography: Sheldon Reich, *John Marin* (Tucson, Ariz., 1970), p. 801, no. 52.8

Beginning in 1914, and with increasing frequency during the latter part of his life, Marin spent part of almost every year in Maine, recording in watercolor, oil, and etching his impressions of its mountains and coastline. In these works he often combined abstract patterns with sensitive descriptions of natural phenomena to capture the optical vitality of the changing seasons.

Autumn was a favorite subject of Marin's. This watercolor, executed a year before his death, is related to another 1952 watercolor, *Autumn on the Road to Deblois, Maine, No. 1* (Houston, Museum of Fine Arts, Ida R. Nussbaum Bequest, inv. no. 54-3; see Reich 1970, no. 52.7). The Grunwald Center drawing is somewhat more sparsely composed, evoking the seasonal color and light with almost shorthand notations of red and gold.

This drawing was formerly in the collection of Edith Gregor Halpert, the owner of the Downtown Gallery in New York, who in 1950 gave Marin a special room to display paintings and watercolors.

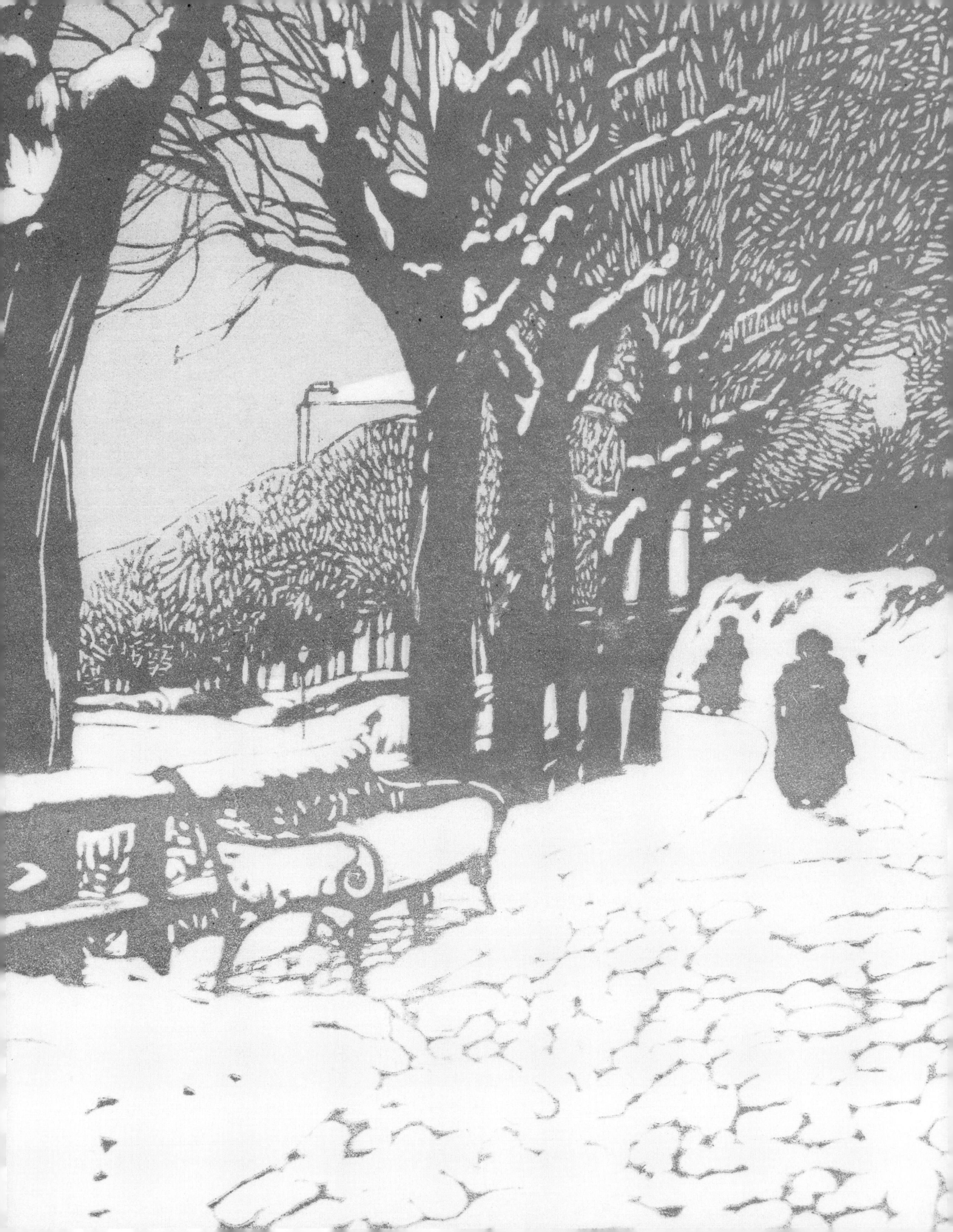

Austrian

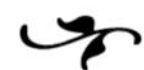

Detail of cat. no. 8

Carl Moll

Between 1880 and 1881 Carl Moll studied at the Academy in Vienna with Christian Griepenkerl. From 1881 until 1892 he was a student of the famous Viennese landscapist Emil Jakob Schindler. Moll traveled extensively during this period but remained very close to Schindler and his family until the artist's death in 1892. In 1895 he married Schindler's widow, becoming stepfather to her daughter, the future Alma Mahler-Werfel. From 1882 to 1888 he exhibited at the Künstlerhaus, becoming a member in 1892. He was among the founders of the Vienna Secession in 1897, serving as its president from 1900 to 1901 and collaborating on its journal, Ver Sacrum. *In 1908 and 1909 he participated in the organization of the Kunstschau and until 1912 was artistic director of the Galerie Miethke in Vienna. Moll traveled frequently throughout his career, and major exhibitions of his work were held in 1926, 1931, and 1936. Although his landscape style evolved from the naturalistic approach of Schindler to a more impressionistic one, he remained loyal to his former teacher, publishing a monograph on Schindler in 1930 and organizing his memoirs in 1943.*

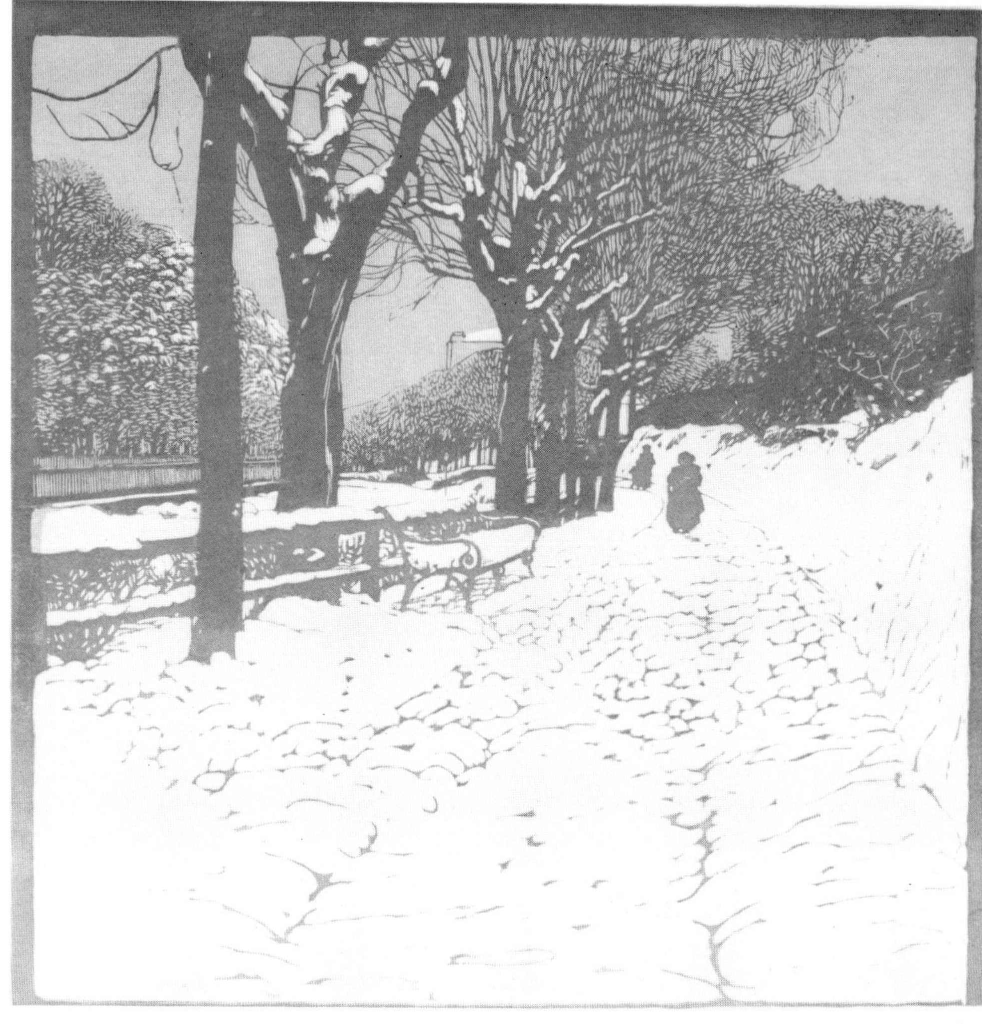

8

Winter (Hohe Warte in Vienna) (1903)

CARL MOLL
(Vienna 1861–1945 Vienna)
Color woodcut (trial proof)
425 x 430 mm
Provenance: Galerie Pabst, Vienna

This woodcut appeared in the 1903 Jahresmappe der Gesellschaft für vervielfältigende Kunst, an annual publication that featured original graphic art by Austrian and foreign artists. It depicts a winter scene in Hohe Warte, an area then on the northern fringe of Vienna. It was there in the early 1900s that Josef Hoffmann built a number of villas intended to form an artist's colony as part of a scheme devised by Secession members and their patrons. Moll lived in Hohe Warte in a double house designed by Hoffmann for him and Koloman Moser in 1900–1902.

With its square format typical of the work of Gustav Klimt and his followers, this print is similar in style and subject to Moll's paintings of the early 1900s. Like *Winter*, the paintings depict Moll's immediate surroundings: the parks and gardens of Vienna, particularly Hohe Warte, as well as intimate interior scenes of his and friends' villas. The muted chromatic range and subtle tones of the print are typical of the lighter palette evident in the artist's paintings after 1900.

Broncia Koller-Pinnell

In 1870 Broncia Koller-Pinnell moved to Vienna, where her first teachers were the sculptor J. Raab and the painter A. Delug. From 1885 to 1890 she studied at the Munich Academy with Ludwig Herterich. Her first exhibition at the Künstlerhaus in Vienna was a great success, and her first painting, Adagio, *was later acquired by Sigmund Freud. She married physicist and doctor Hugo Koller in 1896, and the couple moved to Kolling and later Nuremberg, where she learned the technique of engraving. In 1903 she returned to Vienna, where she dedicated herself to the administration of her estate at Oberwalterdorf, inherited from her father. Hugo Koller was one of the most noted patrons of the arts in Vienna, and many young artists frequented their house, including Albert Paris von Gütersloh and Egon Schiele as well as Gustav Mahler and Paul Hindemith. Among Broncia Koller's closest acquaintances were the artists of the Wiener Werkstätte and those in the circle of Gustav Klimt. She participated in the first Kunstschau in 1908 and exhibited many times with the Neue Künstlervereinigung München at the Glaspalast.*

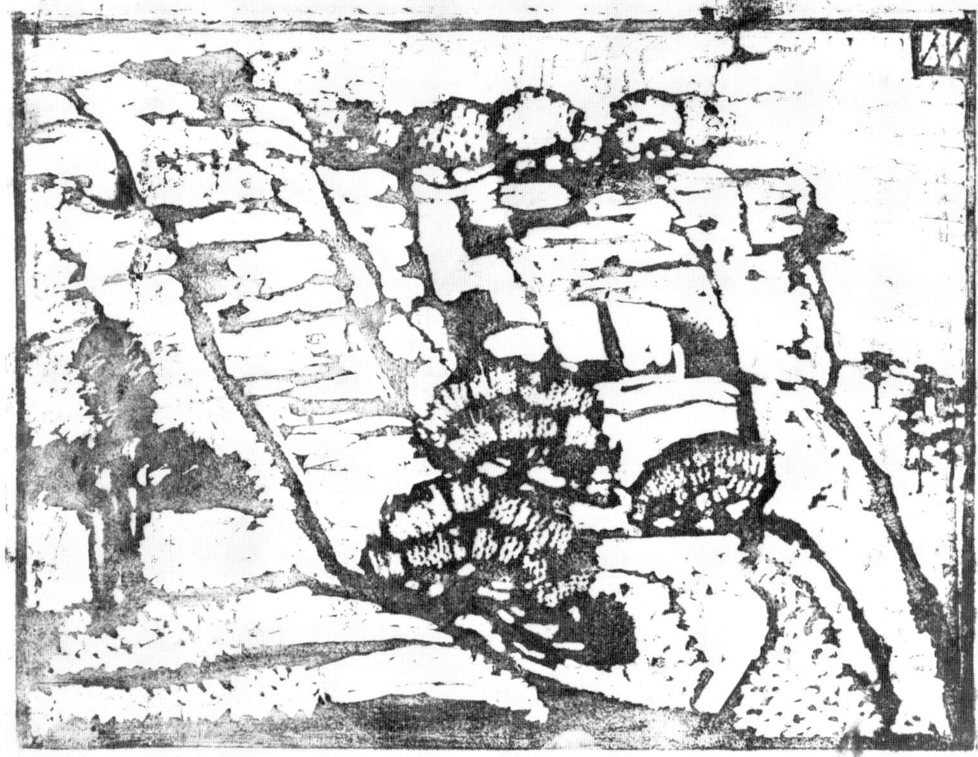

9

Rocky Landscape

BRONCIA KOLLER-PINNELL
(Sanok, Galicia 1863–1934 Vienna)
Woodcut with gouache (trial proof)
260 x 358 mm
Provenance: Galerie Pabst, Vienna

In contrast to the clean lines and tonal areas of woodcuts by other Secession artists, Koller's woodcuts exploit the rougher textural possibilities inherent in the technique. Influenced by Pierre Bonnard and Édouard Vuillard, she explored the idea of landscape as decorative pattern, combining in this print a high horizon with a pattern that defies any impression of recession or pictorial space. This woodcut was probably executed around 1905 and is similar to other landscape woodcuts of that period.[1]

1. See, for example, *Bauernhaus*, illustrated in *Kunst in Wien um 1900*, exh. cat. (Darmstadt: Hessisches Landesmuseum, 1964), no. 170

Leopold Forstner

10

Oberösterreichische Landschaft (c. 1902–3)

(Upper Austrian Landscape)

LEOPOLD FORSTNER
(Leonfelden 1878–1936 Vienna)
Watercolor and India ink
173 x 173 mm
Signed lower right; initialed upper left
Provenance: Galerie Pabst, Vienna

In 1899 Leopold Forstner went to Vienna, where he attended the Kunstgewerbeschule, studying with Karl Karger and Koloman Moser. He later attended the Munich Academy and studied with Ludwig Herterich. After traveling throughout Italy, where he studied Roman and Byzantine art, he returned to Vienna in 1906 and opened his own mosaic factory, the Wiener Mosaikwerkstätte. His first important commission was the stained-glass windows for the church in Steinhof, executed after drawings by Moser, with altar mosaics after designs by Rudolf Jettmar. He participated in the two Kunstschau exhibitions of 1908 and 1909. During this period he was influenced by the work of Gustav Klimt and Josef Hoffmann. From 1909 to 1911 he executed the mosaic frieze in the dining room of the Palais Stoclet in Brussels after Klimt's designs. Utilizing diverse media such as mosaic, metal, and ceramics, he continued to execute numerous commissions in and around Vienna until the fall of the monarchy in 1918, soon after which he left for Stockerau, where he founded a workshop for mosaics, glass, and enamel.

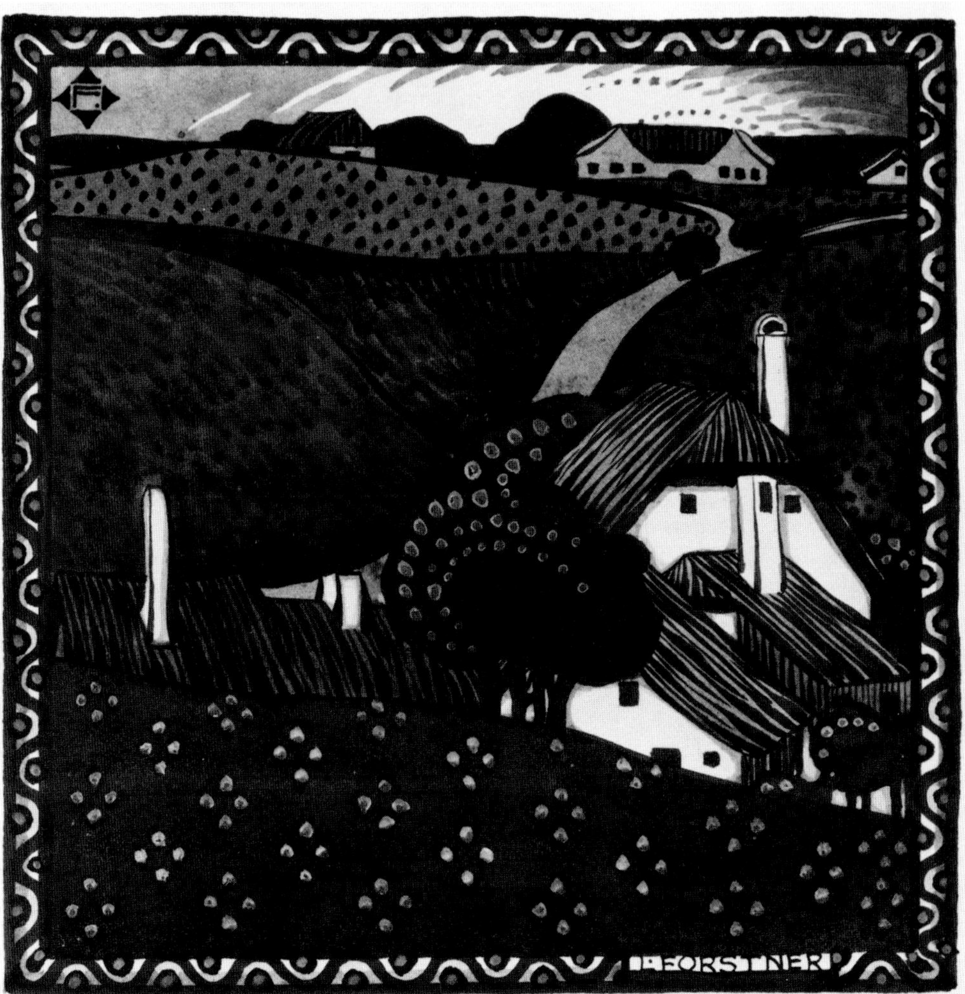

This drawing is a preliminary study for a woodcut that has been dated to 1902–3 (Mrazek 1981, p. 42). Drawn in the same direction as the print, it varies little in composition and may have served as the model from which the block was cut. Forstner uses the square format characteristic of the works of Gustav Klimt and his followers, and the high horizon line and geometric arrangement of houses, hills, and valleys recall the later landscape paintings of Klimt as well as those of Egon Schiele. The overall effect is far more decorative than expressionistic, however, characteristic of Forstner's work in the applied arts.

Franz von Zülow

11

Ziegelhaus (1912)

(Brick House)

FRANZ VON ZÜLOW
(Vienna 1888–1963 Vienna)
Koreny 373
Linocut with hand coloring
220 x 160 mm
Signed lower left; dated lower right
Provenance: Galerie Pabst, Vienna

In 1905 Franz von Zülow attended classes at the Kunstgewerbeschule in Vienna, studying with Carl Otto Czeschka. He participated in the 1908 Secession exhibitions as well as the Kunstschau and the Wiener Werkstätte exhibitions. In 1912 he traveled through Germany, France, England, and Holland. After serving in the military from 1920 to 1922, he taught at the Schleiss ceramic factory in Gmunden. He executed numerous designs in the applied arts as well as paintings.

In 1909 von Zülow began producing his Monatshefte, a book of months that appeared continuously until 1915, with each month comprising seven images plus a cover. Von Zülow initially produced the images as drawings, but in 1912 he began to print them in linocut, sometimes reproducing earlier designs. These later prints, such as *Ziegelhaus*, were produced as individual sheets bound in a wrapper. Typical of von Zülow's decorative style, the Monatshefte were executed with heavy black lines reminiscent of stained-glass windows.

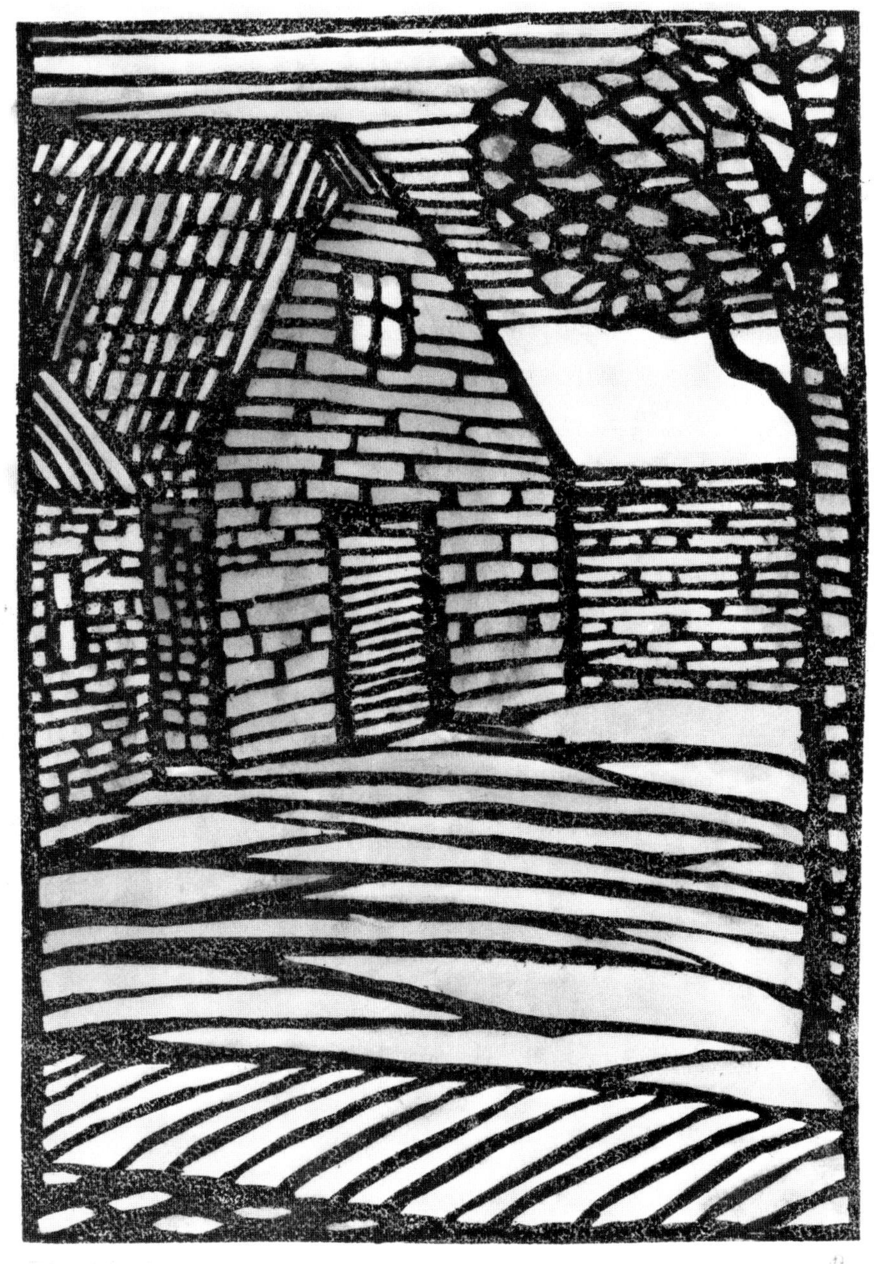

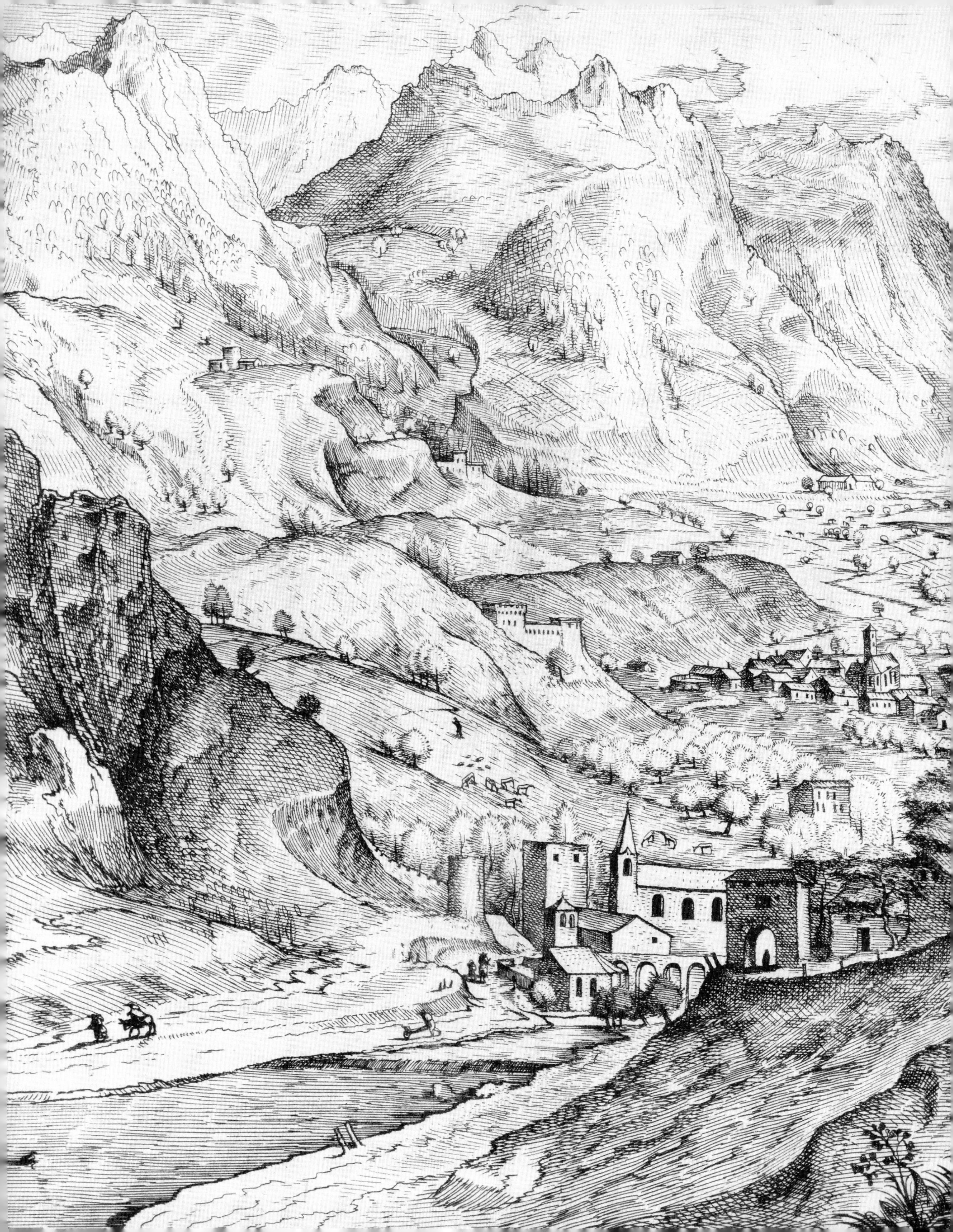

Dutch & Flemish

Detail of cat. no. 16

Master of the Small Landscapes

12

Landscape (1559)

MASTER OF THE SMALL LANDSCAPES
(Antwerp, sixteenth century)
Number 1 from the set Multifariarum casularum ruriumque lineamenata curiose ad vivum expressa (The features of various cottages and country places shown carefully and clearly from life)
Holl. 248 (as Cornelis Cort); Bast. 19 i/iv
Etching
135 x 189 mm
Provenance: William Schab, New York

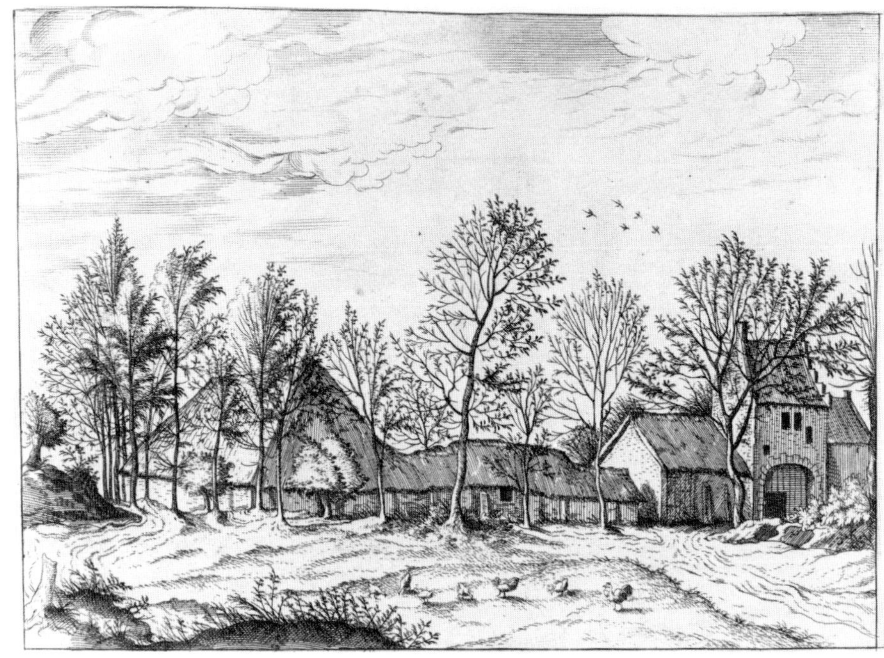

This etching is the first in a series of fourteen landscapes published by Hieronymus Cock in 1559, the majority of which represent similar small village scenes in the vicinity of Antwerp. Cock reissued the series two years later, combining it with the series Praediorum villarum et rusticarum . . . (see cat. no. 13). To this second edition at least ten more prints by the same unknown artist were added. By 1612 the series had been reissued two more times in Antwerp, and a set of copies was published in Holland by Claes Jansz. Visscher (see cat. nos. 30–38).[1]

Eleven drawings that served as designs for these prints are known, though their authorship has been the subject of much dispute. The drawings have been successively, but never entirely successfully, attributed to a number of sixteenth-century artists, including Pieter Bruegel, Cornelis Cort, Hans Bol, Cornelis van Dalem, Hieronymus Cock, and Joos van Liere. Since the exhibition of Bruegel drawings in 1975, scholars have settled on an attribution to the Master of the Small Landscapes until agreement can be reached on a known artist.[2]

Although the prints in this series did not have great impact on landscape representation at the time they were made, certain innovations, such as the abandonment of the bird's-eye view and the depiction of everyday life in the countryside around Antwerp, would prove important for developments in landscape in the first decade of the seventeenth century.

---

1. Theodor Galle published a third edition in 1601, which was ascribed to the Antwerp artist Cornelis Cort on the title page, and a fourth edition attributed to the same artist. Joan Galle published two further editions of the series. In addition Visscher copied the series, attributing the designs for the prints to Pieter Bruegel. For a full discussion of the various states and editions of this series, see Bierens de Haan 1948, nos. 248–89.
2. See Liess 1979–82 for the most recent and in-depth discussion of the attributions of the drawings. Liess reattributes most of them to Bruegel.

13

Landscape

MASTER OF THE SMALL LANDSCAPES
(Antwerp, sixteenth century)
Number 17 from the set Praediorum villarum et rusticarum casularum icones elengantissimae ad vivum in aere deformatae (Very fine images of properties, farms, and country cottages rendered in copper from life)
Bast. 50 i/iv
Etching
135 x 204 mm
Provenance: O. P. Reed, Los Angeles

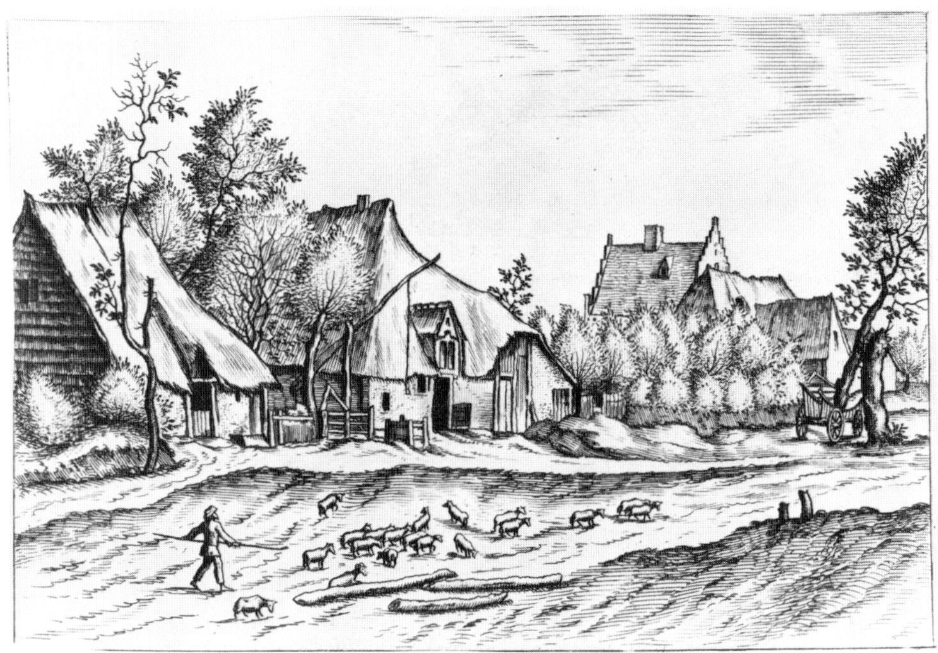

This print is from a series of twenty-eight views of the countryside surrounding Antwerp that was combined with the earlier series Multifarum casularum . . . (see cat. no. 12).

A drawing that served as a design for this print is in Chatsworth,[1] and there has been much discussion over the question of its authorship. It is, however, apparent in the drawing that another hand, whether that of Hieronymus Cock or someone else in his service, was responsible for the staffage as well as several corrections. This is also evident in the print, since the shepherd and his flock are much smaller in scale than the buildings and the cart in the background on the right.

1. Chatsworth, Duke of Devonshire inv. no. 1929.1097, T.1952,10; Haverkamp-Begemann 1975, app. 8.

HIERONYMUS COCK

Hieronymus Cock may have received his early training from his father, Jan Wellens de Cock, or his older brother Matthys. In 1548 Cock established the successful print publishing house Aux Quatres Vents, which published engravings after some of the leading Flemish artists of the sixteenth century, such as Pieter Bruegel, Frans Floris, Hans Bol, and the Master of the Small Landscapes. Although Cock was received in the Antwerp Guild of St. Luke as a painter, there are no paintings known by him. All but one of the surviving drawings by Cock are for prints. He produced sixty-two etchings after the designs of leading Netherlandish artists. Forty prints date from between 1550 and 1551, the period when his publishing business was just beginning; after that his activities as an etcher declined. He also produced fourteen prints after drawings by his elder brother Matthys, a landscape artist. Cock's greatest contribution to landscape was as a print publisher, disseminating throughout Europe the landscape styles of Flemish and Italian artists through reproductive prints.

14
Fifth View of the Colosseum (1551)

HIERONYMUS COCK
(Antwerp c. 1510/20–1570 Antwerp)
Holl. 27; Wurz. 5 i/ii; Riggs II A.6
Etching
303 x 223 mm
Provenance: David Tunick, New York

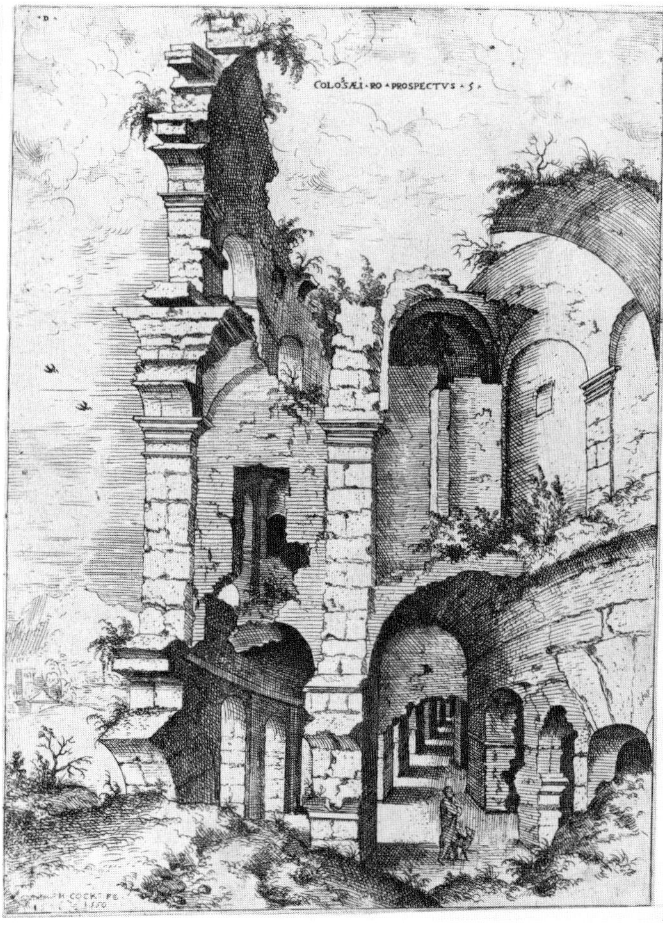

This is one of twenty-five prints in a series of views of Roman ruins, etched by Hieronymus Cock and published by him in 1551. It is one of eight views of the Colosseum in the series. While the series has been cited as proof that Cock traveled to Rome, it is not clear whether he worked from his own drawings or from those of another artist. Misleading captions on several prints in the series and the lack of identification of the ruins on others indicate that Cock employed the drawings of another artist (Riggs 1977, p. 264). Riggs has stated, however, that Cock was responsible for the additions of landscape and figures throughout the series. In this print the addition of a togaed figure and a few hillocks was less extensive than alterations Cock made to other prints in the series. He may have made the additions in order to change the strictly topographical views into more evocative landscapes (Riggs 1977, p. 264).

Despite these additions, Cock's depictions of ruins are more documentary than many of the archaeological views that appeared in the seventeenth century. Most of the ruins are identified, and the drawings were deliberately reversed when transferred onto the plate so that they would come out in the proper direction when printed.[1]

Cock's etchings of Roman ruins were important in disseminating information about these sites to northern Europe. They were also used by Italian artists as guides to ancient monuments. Copies of Cock's series by Jacques Androuet Du Cerceau and Battista Pittoni appeared almost contemporaneously with the series. Pittoni's series was in turn copied by Paolo Veronese for his frescoes in the Villa Maser (Oberhuber 1968, pp. 207–24).

1. Riggs 1977, p. 264. The drawings by Cock in Edinburgh (Riggs D2–D4) for Riggs II A. 3, 9, and 24 were traced with a stylus on the verso in order to compensate for the reversal in the printing process. They are not believed to be the original drawings from nature for this print series but were instead completely worked up by Cock after another set of drawings and then used for transfer onto the etching plate.

HIERONYMUS COCK

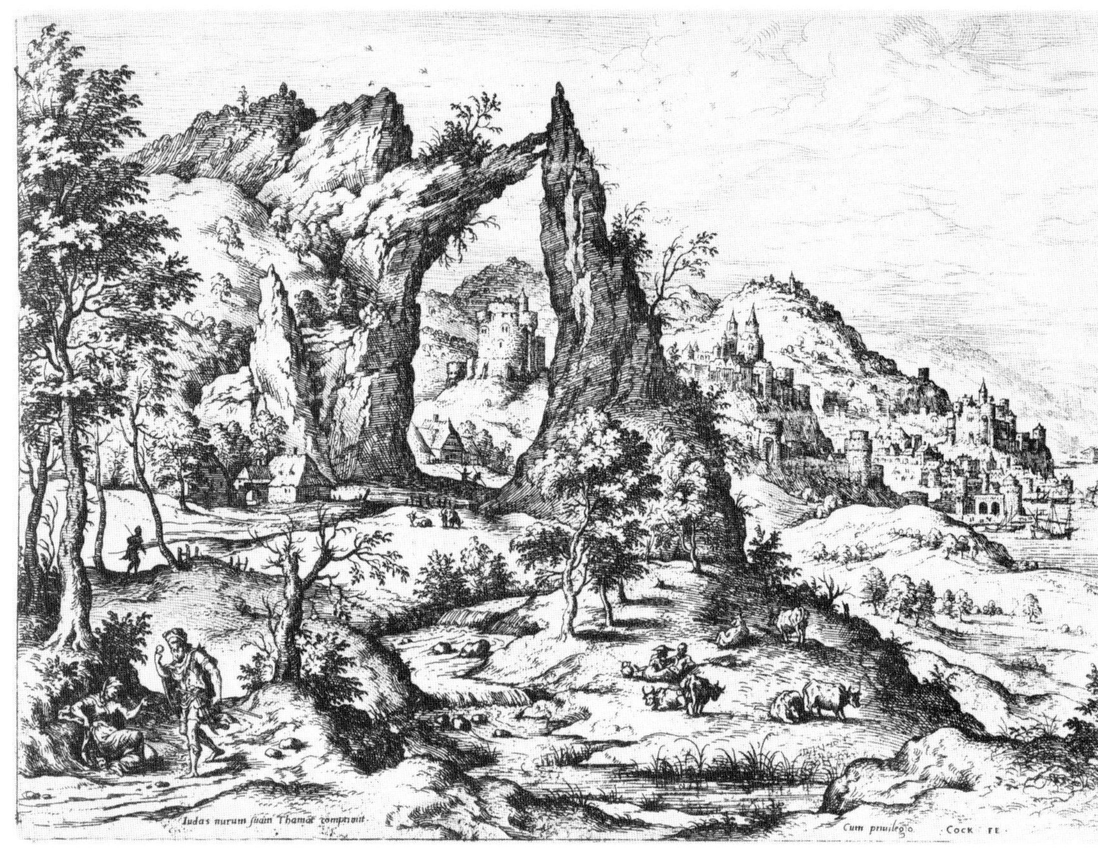

15

Judah and Tamar (1558)

HIERONYMUS COCK
(Antwerp c. 1510/20–1570 Antwerp)
After MATTHYS COCK
(c. 1509–before 1548)
Holl. 9; Riggs II A.39
Etching
225 x 306 mm
Provenance: William Schab, New York

This etching is from a series of thirteen landscapes with biblical and mythological subjects published by Hieronymus Cock in 1558. Although the designer is not specified on the print, Riggs has attributed the original design for the etching to Matthys Cock, Hieronymus's elder brother. Cock often etched prints by other artists without including their names on the printed piece (Riggs 1977, pp. 255, 273). Riggs (1977, p. 35) has also suggested that the variety in the forms of the signatures in the series indicates that, although it was published in 1558, the individual plates were etched by Cock over a long period of time.

This fantastic, expansive landscape, combining sea and mountains with craggy rocks that frame the landscape behind them, follows the landscape tradition popularized by Joachim Patinir (c. 1485–1524). The story of Judah and Tamar occupies a minor position in the landscape and would be difficult to identify were it not for the legend provided. Not a mere backdrop for the biblical narrative, the landscape is the most prominent element in the print. Cock's emphasis on the variety of landscapes is apparent in the title-page text, which describes the topographical subject first and mentions the presence of biblical and mythological illustrations only in the secondary Dutch title.[1]

---

1. Riggs 1977, pp. 184–85. The full title-page text reads: "VARIAE VARARVM REGIONVM TYPOGRAPHICAE ADVMBRATIONES / IN PVBLICVM PICTORVM VSVM A / HIERONIMO COCK DELINEATAE / IN AES INCISAE ET AEDITAE / veelderleye ordinantien van lantschappen, met fyne historien / daer in gheordineert, wt den ouden ende niewen testamente, / ende sommighe lustighe Poeteryen, seer bequaem voer Schil- / ders, ende andere liefhebbers der consten: Nu eerst niew in de / Printe ghebracht, ende ghemaect by Ieronymus Cock Schilder. / Men salse vinden Thantwerpen inde vier winden. / Met gratie ende priuilegie. / IMPRIME EN ANVERS / aupres la bourse neuue au quatre vens, en la mayson / de Hironymus Cocq Paintre / 1558."

Pieter Bruegel the Elder

Pieter Bruegel's early life is not documented. Van Mander states that he was a pupil of Pieter Coecke van Aelst (1502–1550), but this is not certain. Bruegel joined the Guild of St. Luke in Antwerp in 1551 or 1552 and shortly thereafter departed on a journey to Italy that lasted until 1554. On this trip he produced numerous drawings depicting monumental Alpine views and the Italian countryside, which had a significant influence on later landscape. Upon his return to Antwerp in 1555 Bruegel was active as a painter and designer of prints, working for the print publisher Hieronymus Cock. During their long association Bruegel produced nearly forty designs, including landscapes, religious themes, and secular subjects. In 1563 he moved to Brussels, where he remained for the rest of his life.

In addition to the ninety-six prints by and after Bruegel, his oeuvre consists of approximately forty paintings and fifty securely attributed drawings. Bruegel ranks among the greatest Renaissance landscape artists, and his landscape paintings, drawings, and engravings influenced artists well into the seventeenth century.

16

Insidiosus Auceps (c. 1555–56)

(The Cunning Bird Catcher)

After PIETER BRUEGEL the Elder
(Breda c. 1525/30–1569 Brussels)
Holl. 10; Bast. 10; Lebeer 5
(as etched by Hieronymus Cock); Riggs 28, 5 (as etched by Jan or Lucas van Deutecum)
Etching and engraving
320 x 421 mm
Provenance: William Schab, New York

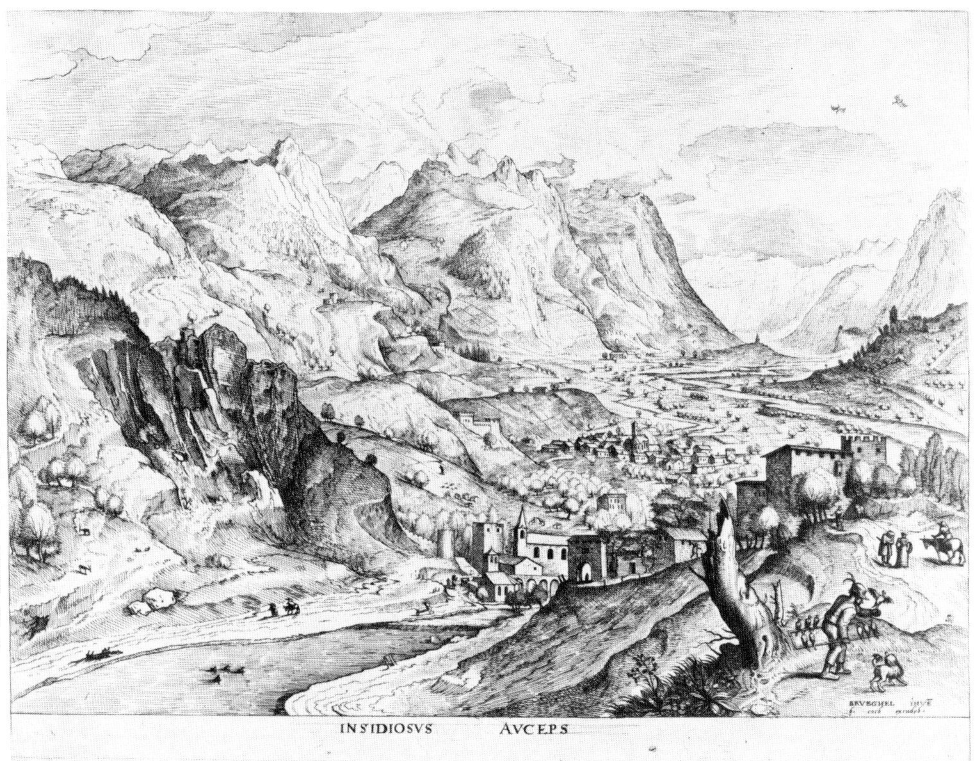

This print is one of a series of thirteen landscapes after Pieter Bruegel published by Hieronymus Cock. The series, dated about 1555–56, was one of the earliest collaborations between Bruegel and Cock and was executed soon after the artist's return to Antwerp from Italy. There are varying opinions as to the identity of the engraver. Though Cock signed the print only as publisher, Lebeer has stated that he also engraved it after Bruegel's design. Bastelaer has suggested furthermore that Cock was responsible for the addition of the figures. Riggs, however, attributed the engraving of the design to Jan or Lucas van Deutecum.[1]

Each print in the series depicts a sweeping "universal landscape" with a narrative scene in the foreground. In this case the scene depicts a bird catcher returning from the hunt with a load of birds. In fifteenth- and sixteenth-century German prints, the motif of the bird catcher with his trap, which appears in two other works by Bruegel,[2] symbolizes the Devil, who sets a trap to snare human souls. The title of the print implies that the subject has this meaning here as well.[3] The allegorical meaning of the print is, however, secondary to Bruegel's interest in illustrating sweeping vistas with views of high mountains and the sea.

Bruegel's mountain views were often based on sketches that he made on a journey through the Alps to Italy. Lebeer identified the site depicted in the print as the valley of Yvorne. Although certain mountains or valleys in this series have been identified, it should be remembered that Bruegel did not intend the final designs for his prints to represent specific sites, but rather invented mountainscapes based on his memories. Romdahl has noted that part of a drawing in Dresden was incorporated into the present landscape,[4] and Tolnay and Popham have remarked that rocks in a drawing in Chatsworth and one formerly in the Seilern collection were included in the engraved landscape.[5]

1. Brussels 1980, p. 104; Riggs 1977, p. 318. Riggs cites variations in the freedom of drawing among the plates as reflecting the different styles of the two Deutecum brothers.
2. *Triumph of Death* (Madrid, Museo del Prado) and *Winter Landscape with Skaters and Bird Trap* (Brussels, Musées Royaux des Beaux-Arts).
3. For a discussion of the bird trap motif in Bruegel's work, see Bauer 1984.
4. Dresden, Kupferstichkabinett (Tolnay 18, Münz 7); Romdahl 1905.
5. Chatsworth, Duke of Devonshire (Tolnay 19, Münz 16), formerly collection of Count Seilern, London (Tolnay 20, Münz 15); see Popham 1949.

PIETER BRUEGEL THE ELDER

17

Man of War, Sailing Right, with the Fall of Icarus

FRANS HUYS
(1522–1562)
After PIETER BRUEGEL the Elder
(Breda c. 1525/30–1569 Brussels)
Bast. 101 i/ii; Lebeer 44 i/ii
Engraving
222 x 287 mm
Provenance: Metropolitan Museum of Art, New York; Zeitlin and Ver Brugge, Los Angeles

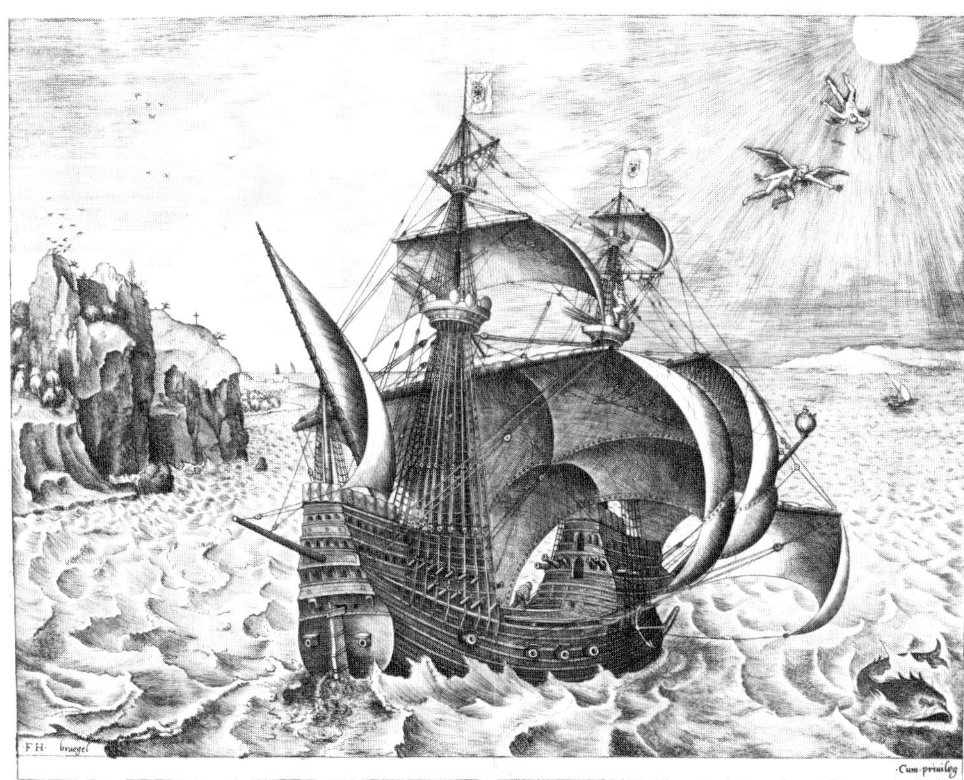

This print belongs to a series of ten or eleven engravings of ships after Pieter Bruegel.[1] The series, dated about 1561–62,[2] contains only three prints with secondary mythological scenes. Lebeer (1969, p. 116) has questioned whether these figures were in Bruegel's original designs or whether they were added by another artist. Two paintings by Bruegel include the Fall of Icarus, and another seascape engraved after Bruegel includes a similar falling Icarus.[3] The choice of a story from Ovid reflects the popularity of the stories from the *Metamorphoses* (see cat. nos. 19–22), which had been published in numerous illustrated editions by the end of the sixteenth century.

The engraving of ships has antecedents in fifteenth-century Florentine and Venetian prints, such as the set of ship engravings dated about 1480–1500 by an anonymous Venetian master (Hind 1938–48, vol. 1, nos. A.I.63–65, E.III.8–12) or the prints by the Netherlandish Master WA with an anchor, active in the 1470s and 1480s.[4] Marine painting became an important genre in the northern Netherlands in the seventeenth century in the works of artists such as Jan Porcellis (1584/87–1632) and Hendrick Vroom (c. 1566–1640), whose seascapes influenced the compositions of early Haarlem landscapes.

1. There has been much discussion over the unusual number of plates in this series, eleven. While some authors have proposed additions to the series, Lebeer believes that Bast. 108 should be eliminated from the series since it depicts sixteen ships. See Lebeer 1969, p. 113, for a discussion of the problem.
2. The problems in dating the series are discussed in ibid., p. 112.
3. Bruegel's two paintings of the Fall of Icarus are in Brussels, one in the Musées Royaux des Beaux-Arts (inv. no. 4030) and the other in the Museum Van Buuren. The attribution of the latter painting to Bruegel has been questioned by some scholars. According to Lebeer, the print, *Landscape with a River and the Fall of Icarus* (Bast. 2, Lebeer 82), is after a work by Bruegel that was never intended as a model for a print.
4. Lehrs 1908–34, vol. 7, pp. 8–9, 62–69, nos. 34–41.

Hans Bol

In Mechlin Hans Bol was trained in the local specialty of painting in watercolor on canvas. He traveled in Germany, lived in Heidelberg for two years, and then returned to Mechlin. He moved to Antwerp after the Spanish occupation of Mechlin in 1572 and joined the guild there in 1574. To escape political and religious turbulence, Bol moved in 1584 to the northern Netherlands, where he lived in Bergen op Zoom, Dordrecht, and Delft, finally settling in Amsterdam in 1591. His pupils were Frans Boels, Jacques Savery, and Joris Hoefnagel.

Although few paintings by Bol survive, several hundred drawings and approximately 350 prints after his designs are known. Bol himself etched about 27 prints, most of them landscapes influenced by the work of Pieter Bruegel. With these he contributed to the development of landscape representation in Holland, serving as a link in the transmission of Bruegel's innovative landscape style to the northern Netherlands.

18

Saint John the Baptist Preaching in the Desert

HANS BOL
(Mechlin 1534–1593 Amsterdam)
Holl. 9; Wurz. 9; Dut. IV, p. 65
Etching
Diameter: 181 mm
Provenance: Lucien Goldschmidt, New York

Overwhelmed by the mountainous landscape, an almost imperceptible Saint John the Baptist in the center middle ground preaches to the multitude, who turn their backs to the viewer as they gather around him beneath a large cliff that rises toward the right. This print appears to be part of a series that also includes *The Reconciliation between Esau and Jacob* (Holl. 8), which is similar in composition and of the same size. The subject matter of this print, one of the few etched by Bol himself, may have been inspired by Pieter Bruegel's painting *Saint John Preaching* (Budapest, Szépmüvészeti Múzeum). Bruegel's painting, copied numerous times, depicts a mass of people gathered around the saint, their backs to the viewer.

It has been suggested that Bruegel's painting was inspired by actual clandestine sermons delivered by Protestant preachers in the Flemish countryside (Gluck 1963, p. 64). Perhaps Bol, one of many artists who fled to the northern Netherlands to escape religious persecution in Flanders, was also referring to these sermons in his depiction of Saint John preaching.

Bruegel's views of the Alps also influenced Bol's landscapes, as evidenced by the steep mountain landscape receding into the distance in this print. Bol, who did not travel to Italy, would have become familiar with the mountainous terrain of the Alps from Bruegel's prints (see cat. no. 16).

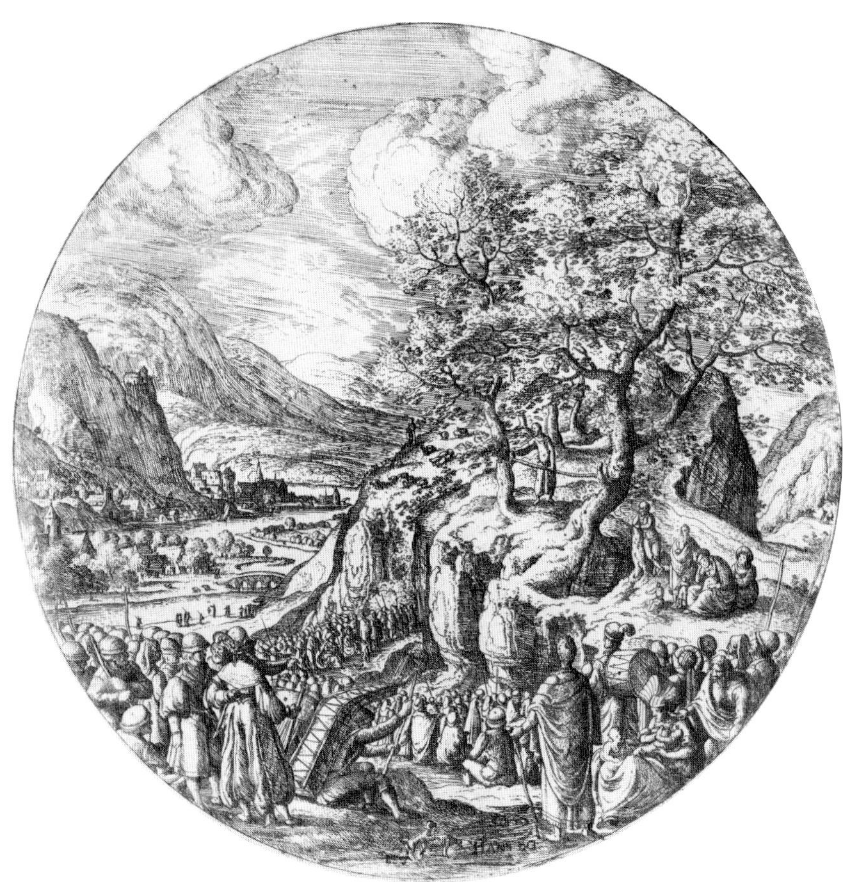

JOHANNES SADELER I

Johannes Sadeler's earliest engravings date from 1570. In 1572 he was admitted into the Brussels Guild of St. Luke. After that he traveled to Germany and worked in Cologne, Munich, and Frankfurt. Sadeler later went to Rome and around 1593 settled in Venice, where he probably died in 1600. Among his pupils was Gillis Sadeler in 1585.

Sadeler was mainly a reproductive engraver, transferring to copper the designs of artists such as Marten de Vos, Hans Bol, and Dirck Barendsz. Sadeler engraved about 622 prints.

19

Pan Following the Nymph Syrinx

JOHANNES SADELER I
(Brussels 1550–c. 1600 Venice?)
After GILLIS MOSTAERT
(Hulst near Antwerp 1534–1598 Antwerp)
Holl. 481
Engraving
138 x 197 mm
Provenance: William Schab, New York

20

Latona Changing the Lycians into Frogs

JOHANNES SADELER I
(Brussels 1550–c. 1600 Venice?)
After GILLIS MOSTAERT
(Hulst near Antwerp 1534–1598 Antwerp)
Holl. 482
Engraving
138 x 200 mm
Provenance: William Schab, New York

21

Venus and Adonis

JOHANNES SADELER I
(Brussels 1550–c. 1600 Venice?)
After GILLIS MOSTAERT
(Hulst near Antwerp 1534–1598 Antwerp)
Holl. 483
Engraving
138 x 200 mm
Provenance: William Schab, New York

22

Orpheus among the Animals

JOHANNES SADELER I
(Brussels 1550–c. 1600 Venice?)
After GILLIS MOSTAERT
(Hulst near Antwerp 1534–1598 Antwerp)
Holl. 485
Engraving
138 x 197 mm
Provenance: William Schab, New York

The narratives illustrated in these engraved landscapes from a set of six mythological scenes were taken from Ovid's *Metamorphoses*: Pan tries to capture the nymph Syrinx as she turns into reeds (1:689–713); Latona changes the Lycians, who prevented her from drinking from their lake (or in this case river), into frogs (6:317–81); Venus holds the dying Adonis, who was gored by a wild boar (10:708–39); and Orpheus charms the wild animals with the music of his lyre (10:86–105). The series of six prints was engraved by Johannes Sadeler I. The Grunwald Center impressions are possibly proofs before inscriptions; the images are the same in all other respects and are not described by Hollstein.

A drawing by Gillis Mostaert in an *album amicorum* in Wolfenbüttel was recently recognized as the model for the engraving of Venus and Adonis.[1] The drawing, in reverse of the engraved image, is the only one that can be connected with this series; it is believed, however, that the entire series is after drawings by Mostaert.

1. In the *album amicorum* of Philipp Hainhofer, Wolfenbüttel, Herzog-August Bibliothek, Cod. Guelf. 210 Extrav., p. 207; see also Zwollo 1985.

JOHANNES SADELER I

19

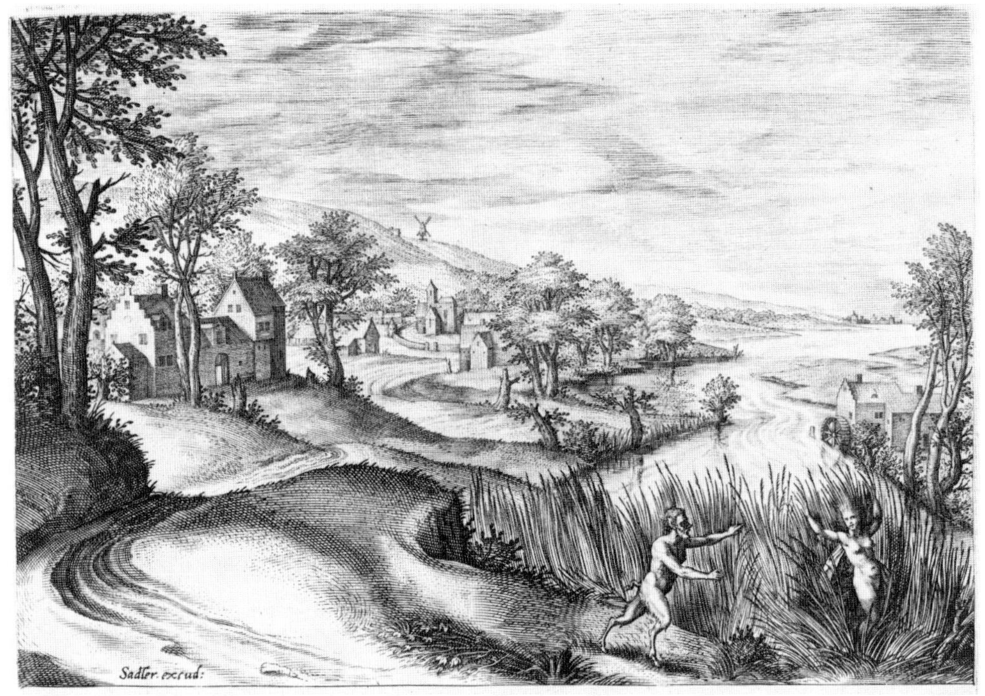

20

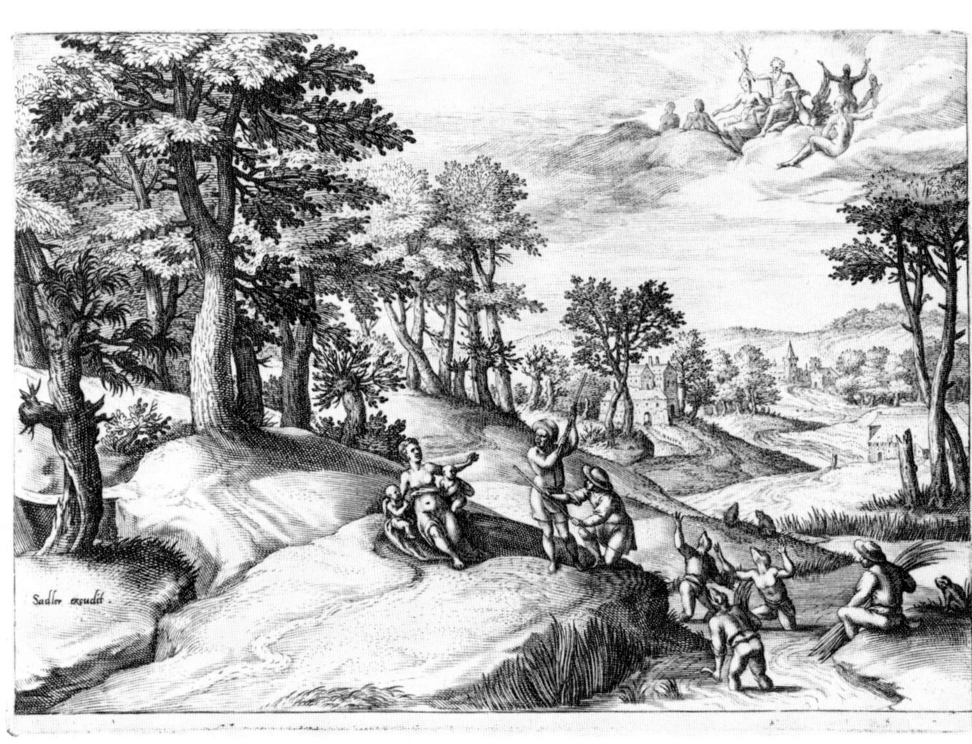

Johannes Sadeler I

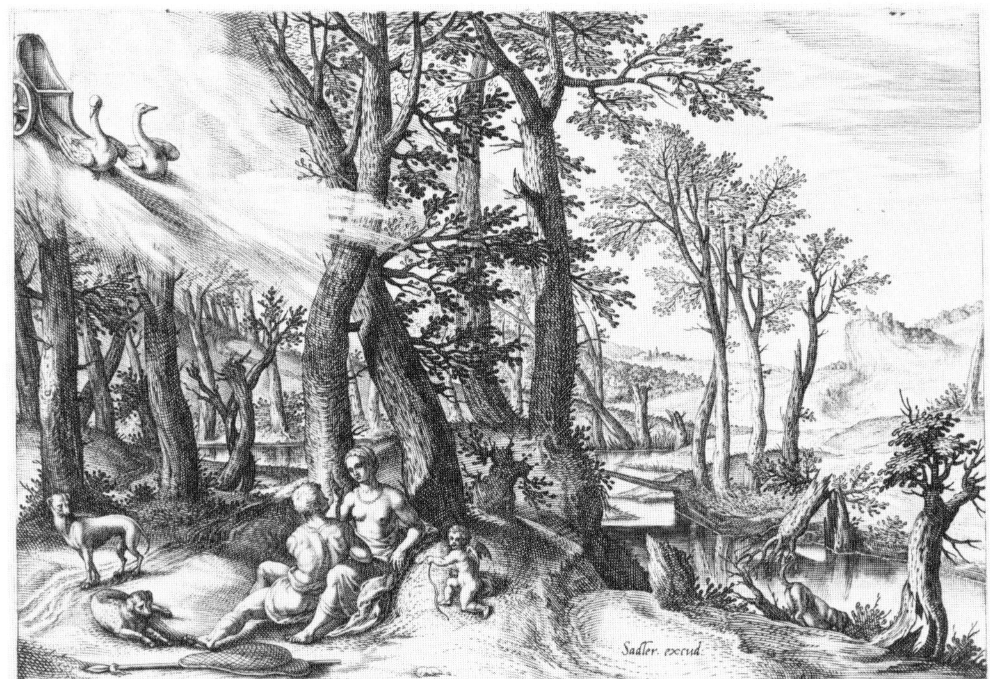

21

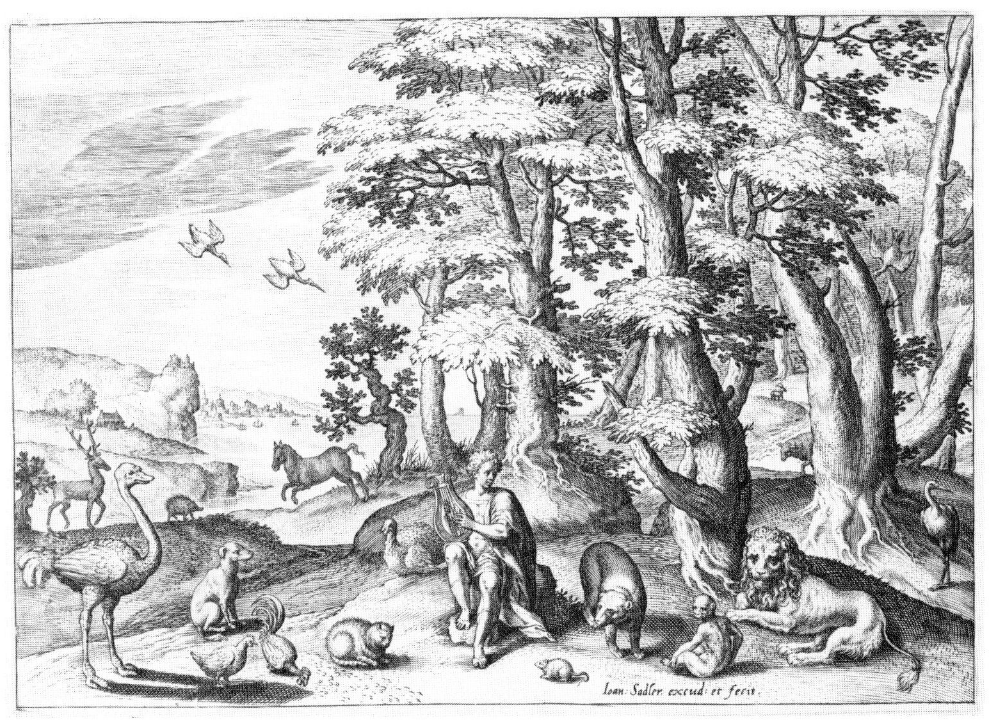

22

Paul Bril

Paul Bril received his early training with the painter Damian Ortelmans. According to van Mander, he left Antwerp when he was twenty, staying first in Lyons and then joining his older brother Matthias in Rome, where he remained until his death. In Rome Bril's landscape style was strongly influenced by the Venetian landscape painter Girolamo Muziano, who had settled in Rome around 1548. Before Matthias's death in 1583 the two brothers collaborated on landscape decorations in Rome. After his brother's death Bril continued to paint numerous fresco cycles for papal and other patrons. Probably around 1590 he began to make small easel paintings as well as designs for prints. Though Bril's mannerist landscapes, with their elaborate rocks and mountains, remained idealized, around 1600 his work began to display the influence of the more naturalistic landscape paintings of the Carracci and Adam Elsheimer. Bril was a pivotal figure for generations of artists who journeyed to Rome. Many of his compositions were engraved and circulated widely in northern Europe.

23

River Landscape with a Shepherd on a Hill to the Right (1590)

PAUL BRIL
(Antwerp 1554–1626 Rome)
Holl. 2 i/iv
Etching
203 x 276 mm
Provenance: Catherine Bullard, Washington, D.C.

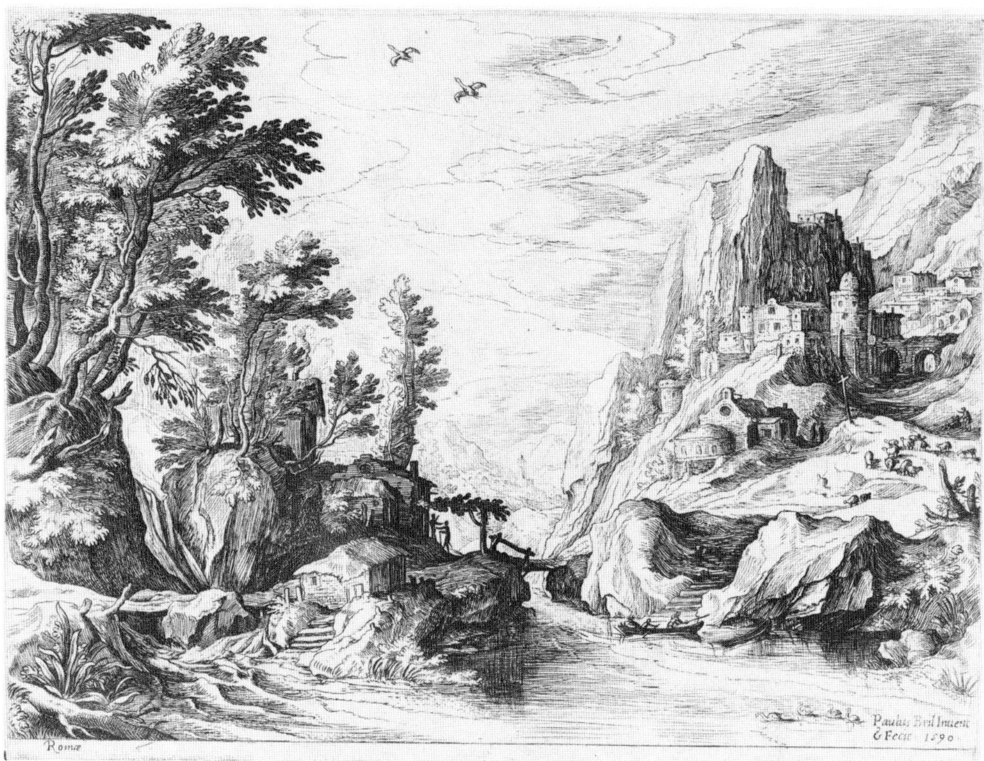

This etching of an imaginary rocky landscape, part of a set of views of the coast of Campania, is one of the few prints actually signed by Paul Bril. The use of the wood on the left as a repoussoir element and the strong diagonal emphasis of the composition are characteristic of Bril's mannerist style of the 1590s, when he was influenced by the work of Girolamo Muziano (Rotterdam 1988, p. 86, no. 48). A close inspection of the etching reveals light traces of Bril's original sketch on the plate. This is particularly evident in the depiction of the first sheep on the right, which bends its head down to graze. Just above the head is a lightly etched pentimento of a raised head, which was changed in the final working of the plate. A drawing of Bril's composition exists in Frankfurt (Städelsches Kunstinstitut inv. no. 3773, as by Matthias Bril).

Hendrik Goltzius

Hendrik Goltius studied first with his father, Jan Goltz, a painter, and around 1575 he apprenticed with Dirck Volckertsz. Coornhert, an engraver and controversial humanist writer. Goltzius's first prints were published by Phillips Galle, the successor to Hieronymus Cock in Antwerp. In 1582 Goltzius began publishing his own prints in Haarlem, having moved there in 1576 following the pacification of Ghent. Soon after Karel van Mander, Goltzius's friend and biographer, introduced him to the work of Bartholomeus Spranger, and in 1585 Goltzius published his first works either after Spranger or in Spranger's international mannerist style. In 1590 he traveled to Italy, returning in 1591 to Haarlem, where he remained until his death. Around 1600 he turned to painting and was seldom active as a printmaker after that date.

Goltzius enjoyed an international reputation thanks to the large number of prints that he produced and published. Many of his designs were engraved by pupils such as Jacob Matham, Jacques de Gheyn II, and Jan Saenredam. His printed oeuvre comprises approximately 350 engravings, about twenty woodcuts, twelve etchings, and three drypoints. The majority of his prints were of figure subjects in which landscape was relegated to a minor role. His primary importance for the history of landscape lies in a small group of drawings dated to the early years of the seventeenth century, which are among the earliest depictions of the countryside around Haarlem.

24
Landscape with Farmhouse (c.1595–1600)

HENDRIK GOLTZIUS
(Mühlbracht 1558–1617 Haarlem)
B. 244; Holl. 380 ii/ii;
Strauss 411; Hirschmann 380
Chiaroscuro woodcut from 1 line block and 2 tone blocks
113 x 145 mm
Provenance: William Schab, New York

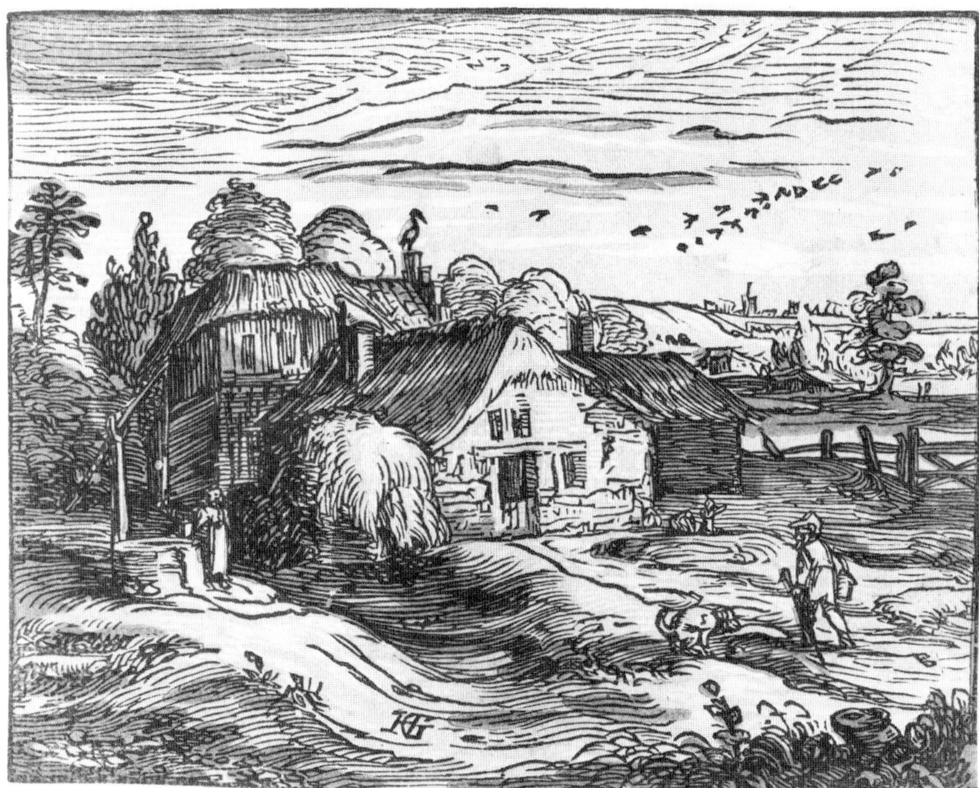

Landscape with Farmhouse is part of a series of four chiaroscuro woodcuts depicting various landscapes. The date of this series, like those of all Goltzius's woodcuts, is disputed. Scholars generally place them sometime between 1595 and 1600 and agree that they were made following his return from Italy, since the influence of Venetian woodcuts is so readily apparent in the style and technique of these prints.[1]

While other woodcuts in this series depict Arcadian or Italianate landscapes, this image is the most "Dutch" in composition and anticipates future developments in the genre. Though the fluid, curvilinear strokes are reminiscent of prints and drawings by the sixteenth-century Venetian artist Domenico Campagnola, the rusticity of the scene and the naturalism of individual motifs such as the excreting dog are typically Dutch.[2] The stork, for instance, appears often in Dutch prints and was considered a sign of good luck in seventeenth-century Holland (Lawrence 1983, p. 167, no. 45; Zumthor 1962, p. 151).

While Goltzius's woodcuts were not as influential as his drawings for the development of landscape, they are still indicative of the predilection, particularly among Haarlem artists, for more realistic views of contemporary local landscapes rather than the fantastic Flemish vistas that had been in vogue up to this time.

Strauss has suggested that Goltzius, who began his career as an engraver, may not have cut these woodcuts himself, but that the artist's stepson, Jacob Matham, may have been responsible for cutting the blocks.[3] The early impressions in this series were printed with only the line block on blue paper; only later were impressions printed with a chiaroscuro block, as in the present example.[4]

1. Hirschmann (1921, pp. 137–38) dates the series between 1598 and 1600, as does Reznicek (1961, pp. 110, 173, 180). Strauss (1977, p. 720) notes that *Landscape with Waterfall* (B. 242) is related to a drawing by Goltzius dated 1595.
2. See, for example, Rembrandt's print *The Good Samaritan* (B. 90).
3. Strauss (1977, p. 718) has distinguished the word *Matham* within areas of shading in each of the prints in this series. We have not been able to detect this word in the present impression, however.
4. Strauss (ibid.) has suggested that the tone blocks were not originally intended to be part of the prints and were added later, possibly by a member of Goltzius's workshop.

ABRAHAM BLOEMAERT

Abraham Bloemaert studied first with his father, a sculptor, architect, and engineer, and then with numerous teachers in Utrecht. At age fifteen or sixteen he went to Paris, where he studied with the Flemish artist Hieronymus Francken. In 1591 he moved with his father to Amsterdam and returned the next year to Utrecht, where he would remain for the rest of his long artistic career. Bloemaert was not only a successful artist in his own right but was a notable teacher as well; his pupils included Hendrik Terbrugghen, Gerard Honthorst, Jan Baptist Weenix, Cornelis van Poelenburgh, Andries Both, and probably Bartholomeus Breenbergh.

Although more than six hundred engravings, etchings, and woodcuts were executed after his designs, Bloemaert appears to have etched only one print himself, Juno *(Holl. 4). He was a prolific draftsman and painter, and his picturesque landscapes with farmhouses played an important role in the development of landscape prints in the early seventeenth century.*

25

Study of an Old Tree with a Shepherd

ABRAHAM BLOEMAERT
(Gorinchem 1564–1651 Utrecht)
Black chalk, brown pen and wash
180 x 243 mm
Provenance: Earl of Spencer (L. I/1530); Ernst Jurgen Otto (L. II/1873b); Dr. Kurt Otto (L. II/611c); C. G. Boerner, Leipzig, 7 November 1929, lot 16; Dr. A. Welcker, Amsterdam (L. II/2793c); Zeitlin and Ver Brugge, Los Angeles

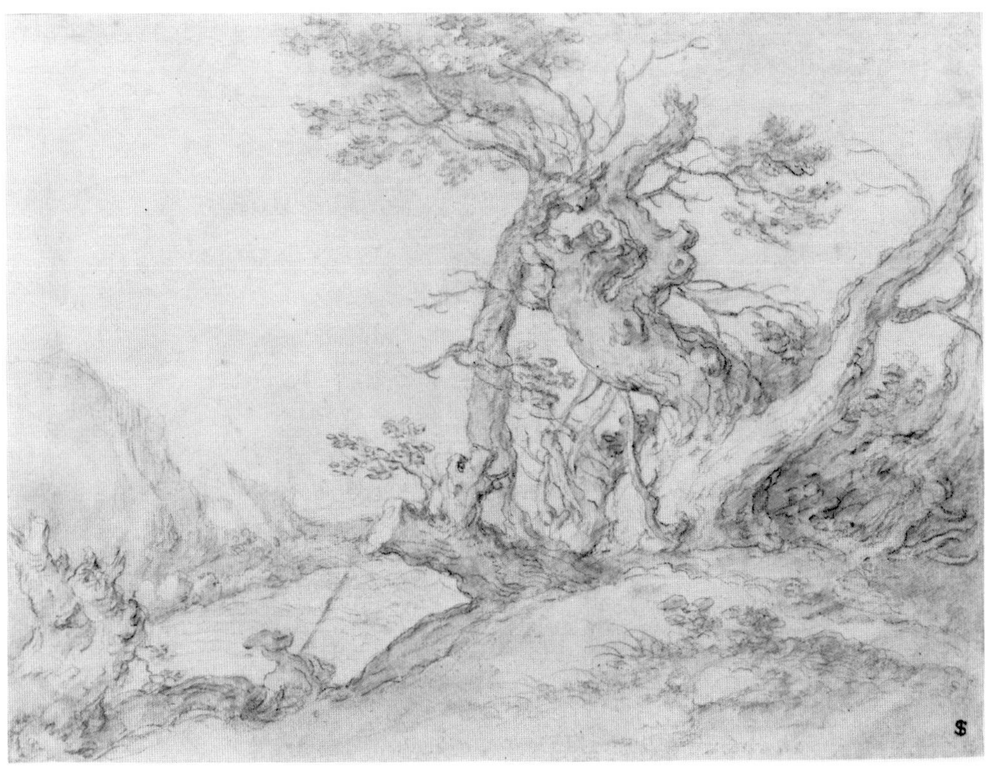

This drawing depicting a landscape with gnarled trees on a softly sloping hillside was created by Bloemaert quite late in his career.[1] It is similar in subject and technique to a group of late landscape drawings by the artist that includes examples in Edinburgh (*Landscape with Sleeping Wanderer and a Peasant with Sheep,* National Gallery of Scotland inv. no. D. 1320) and Munich (*Landscape,* Staatliche Graphische Sammlung inv. no. 42440).

Bloemaert's late drawings are characterized by a painterly style achieved with undulating lines that describe form rather than contour and a subtle use of washes. While this drawing is typical of his late style, the motifs of the gnarled tree and the unassuming shepherd viewed from behind were used by Bloemaert throughout his career, for example, in the drawing *Landscape with Rising Sun* (Amsterdam, Rijksprentenkabinet inv. no. A3740), dated around 1600–1610. The gnarled tree was in fact a popular subject at the beginning of the seventeenth century. It can be found not only in Bloemaert's works but also in those of contemporary artists such as Roelandt Savery, and these works no doubt influenced later artists such as Jacob van Ruisdael.

1. We would like to thank Jaap Bolten for sharing his information on this drawing.

Abraham Bloemaert

26–29

Title Page and Three Landscapes (1614)

BOETIUS ADAM BOLSWERT
(Bolsward 1580–1633 Antwerp)
After ABRAHAM BLOEMAERT
(Gorinchem 1564–1651 Utrecht)
Numbers 1, 2, 8, and 19 from a set of landscapes with farmhouses
Holl. 338 i/ii, 339 i/ii, 345 i/ii, 356 i/ii (under Bolswert); Wurz. 26
Etchings
Each approximately 155 x 243 mm
Provenance: Zeitlin and Ver Brugge, Los Angeles

These four prints belong to a series of twenty plates dated 1614, etched after Abraham Bloemaert's designs by Boetius Adam Bolswert. The series consists mainly of landscapes with farmhouses, a few seascapes, and one landscape dominated by vines in the foreground.[1]

The farmhouses that are prominent in many of the prints in this series are typical of Bloemaert's drawings and paintings. Although he depicts native Dutch farmyards and countryside, Bloemaert's conception of landscape was still quite mannerist in 1614, as evidenced by the stylized twisted trees and almost deserted, worn farmhouses placed in carefully contrived compositions. The one or two figures that occupy the foreground are typically mannerist in form, with small heads, small feet, and elegantly twisted bodies.

In its variety of landscapes this series is in some ways similar to Hendrik Goltzius's series of chiaroscuro woodcuts of farmhouses, seascapes, and wood scenes (see cat. no. 24). Bloemaert, however, applied mannerist principles to the naturalistic depiction of the Dutch landscape of the type practiced by Goltzius and Claes Jansz. Visscher (see cat. nos. 30–38) in the first decades of the seventeenth century. Although Bloemaert's mannerism was not influential for later landscapists, his motifs, such as the crumbling farmhouses, influenced artists such as Pieter Molijn (1595–1661) (Freedberg 1980, p. 39) and, in the following century, François Boucher (1703–1770).

---

1. Drawings exist in Vienna (Graphische Sammlung Albertina) for nos. 3 and 17 of the series.

ABRAHAM BLOEMAERT

26

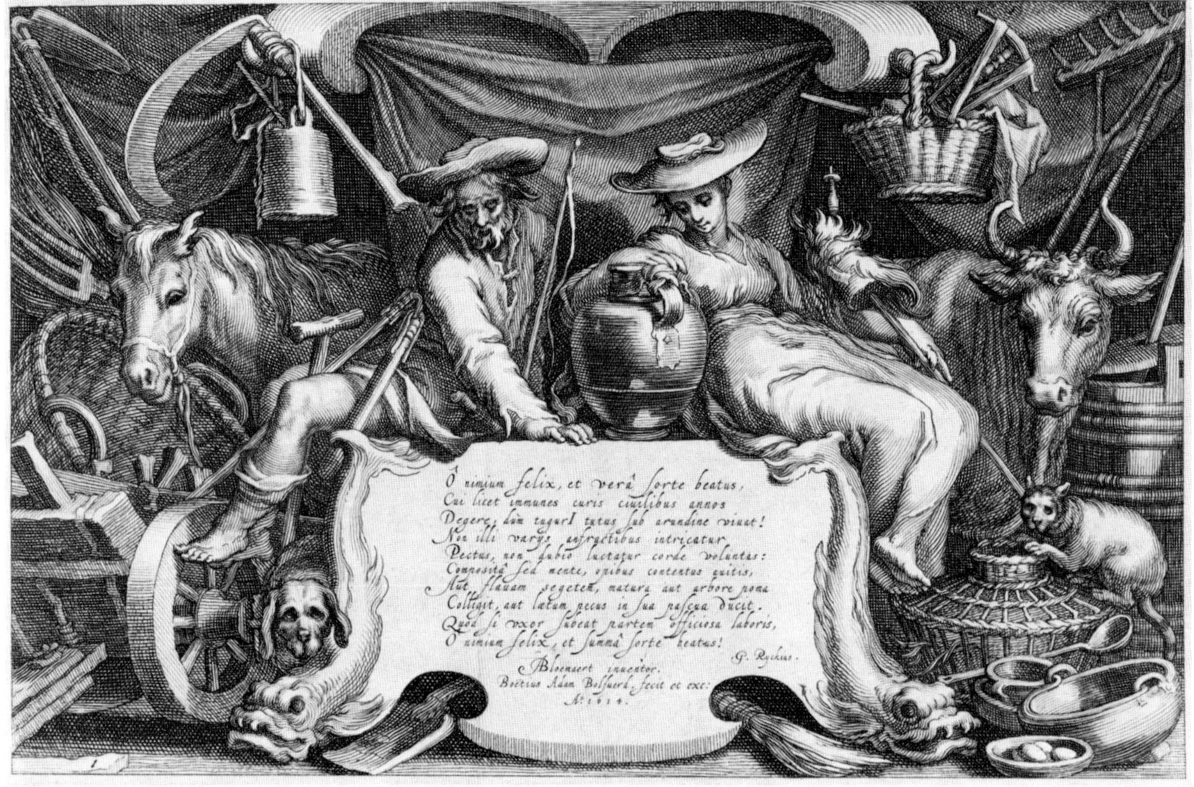

27

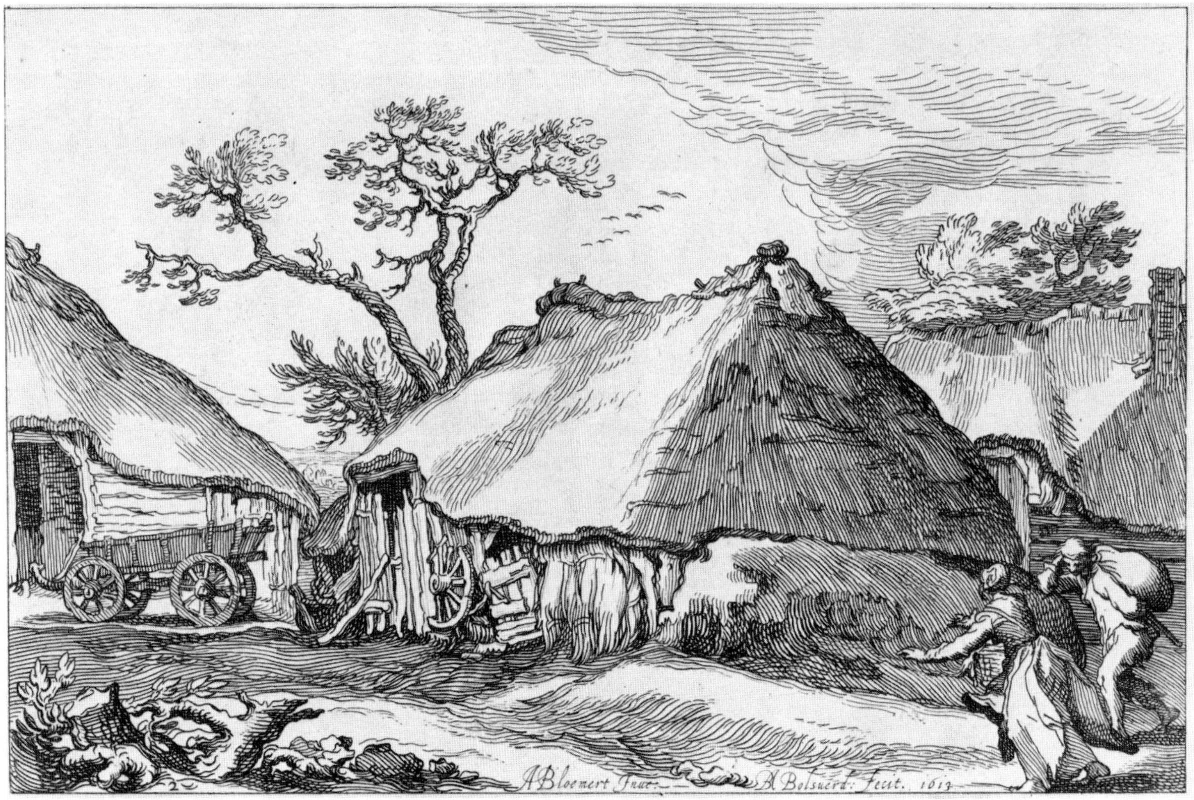

Abraham Bloemaert

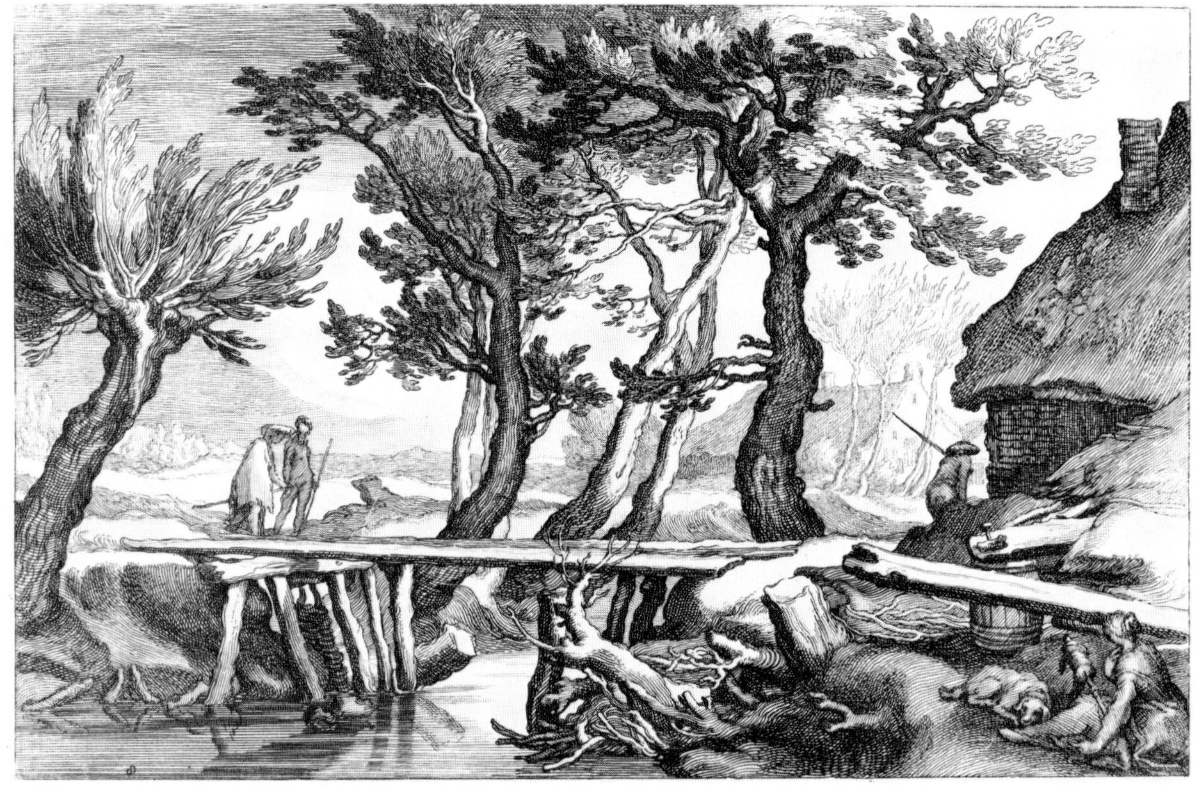

28

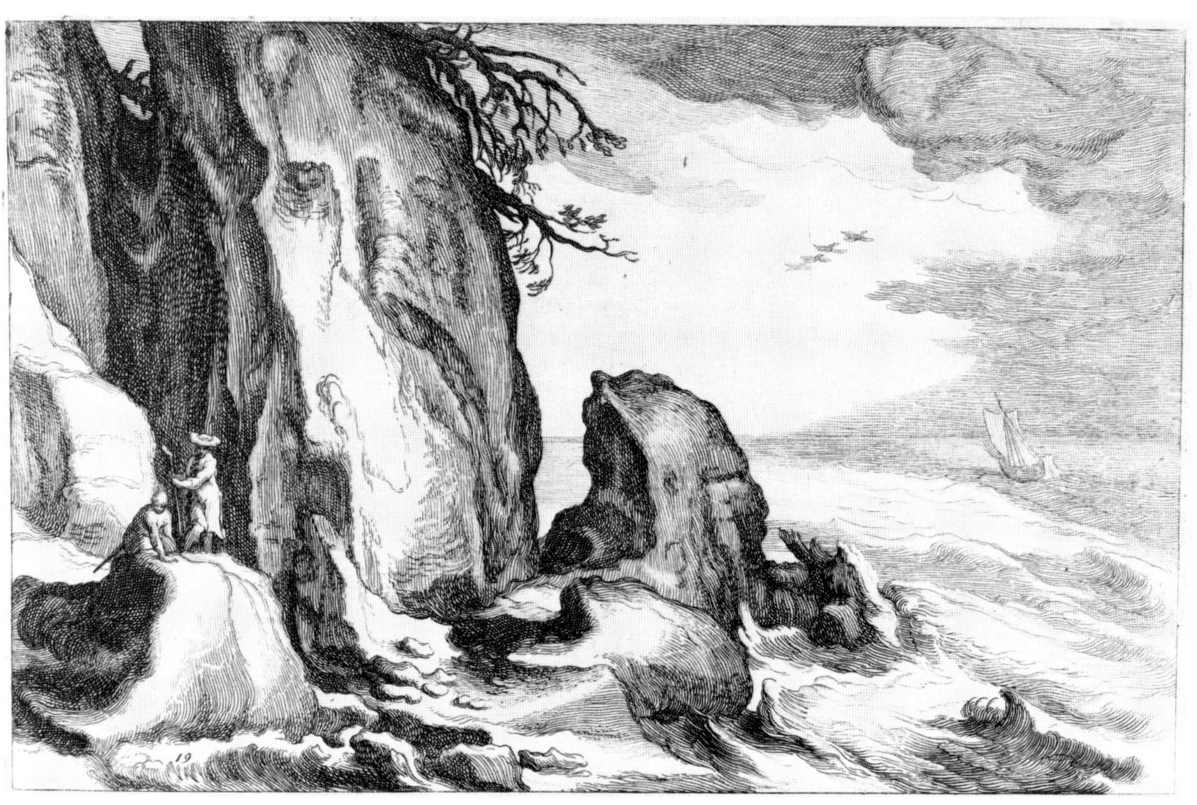

29

Claes Jansz. Visscher

Although Claes Jansz. Visscher was one of the most important publishers of prints during the first half of the seventeenth century, little is known about his artistic training. In his biography of Jacques de Gheyn II, Constantijn Huygens states that de Gheyn taught Visscher to etch.

Visscher etched more than two hundred plates from his own designs and after the designs of others. He also published or republished prints by contemporary artists, notably Esaias and Jan van de Velde and Willem Buytewech, and reworked and republished numerous older plates. His series of pen sketches of the countryside around Haarlem and Amsterdam made between 1606 and 1608 was influential for the history of landscape, as was Pleasant Places around Haarlem, a series of eleven prints published in 1611–12.

30–38

Title Page and Eight Landscapes

CLAES JANSZ. VISSCHER
(Amsterdam 1587–1652 Amsterdam)
After THE MASTER OF THE SMALL LANDSCAPES
(Antwerp, sixteenth century)
From the series Regiunculae et Villae aliquot ducatus Brabantiae (Some country farms and cottages of the duchy of Brabant)
Etchings
Each approximately 103 x 157 mm
Provenance: William Schab, New York

The earlier series depicting the environs of Antwerp (see cat. no. 12), attributed to the Master of the Small Landscapes and published by Hieronymus Cock, served as a model for this series of twenty-five etchings published about half a century later. In copying the series of etchings by the earlier artist, which depict small houses with triangular roofs nestled among trees along dirt roads, as well as several castles around Antwerp, Visscher made the prints smaller in size, dressed the figures in contemporary costume, and etched the entire series with a lighter touch. He also included two prints that did not belong to the original series: number 25, after Abraham Bloemaert, and number 20, after an unknown artist.

The republication of the series by Visscher, with his attribution of the original designs to Pieter Bruegel, is related to the "Bruegel renaissance" that occurred during the first decades of the seventeenth century (see Gerszi 1976 and 1982). Visscher's copies were far more influential for subsequent Netherlandish landscape art than the original series, indicating a rise in the popularity of local topographical views during the half century since Cock's original publication. Their naturalistic depictions of a variety of subjects, including villages, farms, rivers, and harbors, served as models for artists during the ensuing decades.

Visscher's own compositions were influenced by the earlier prints even before he published his own copies of them. In the previous year he had published a series of etchings after his own sketches of the outskirts of Haarlem, which, with their naturalistic approach and low horizons, were quite close in style to the village views by the Master of the Small Landscapes.

Claes Jansz. Visscher

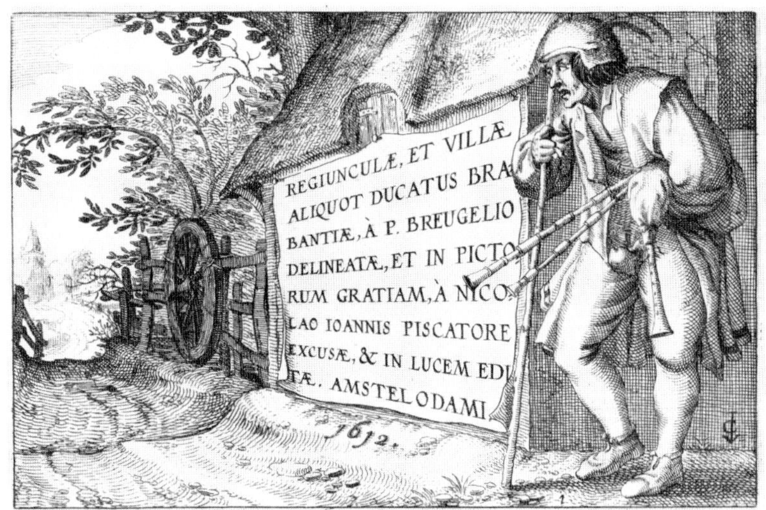

30

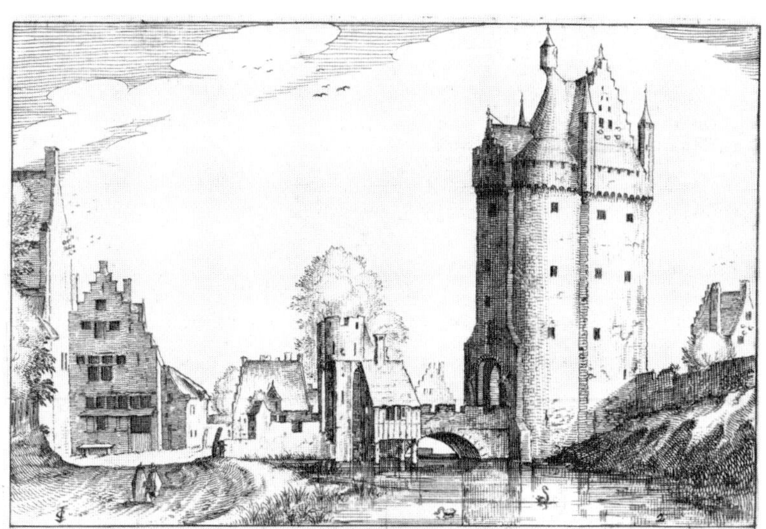

31

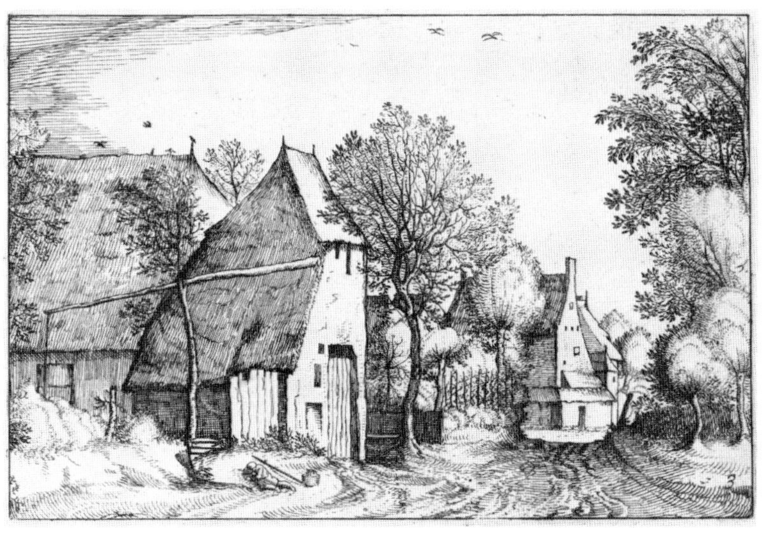

32

Claes Jansz. Visscher

33

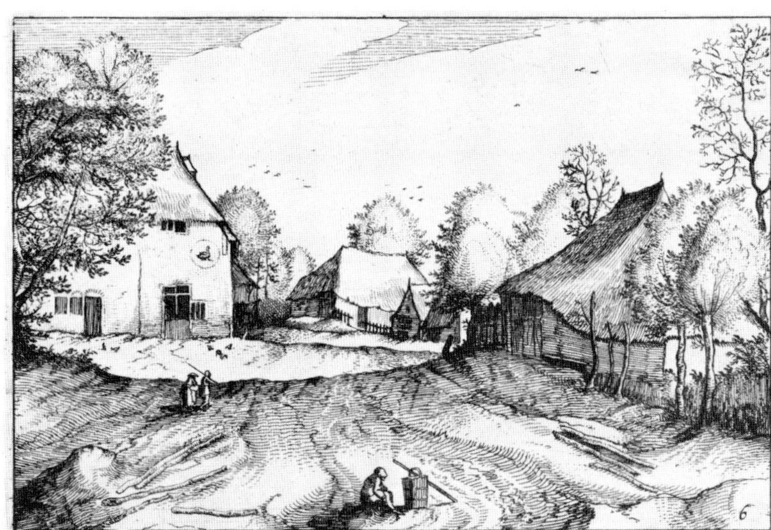

34

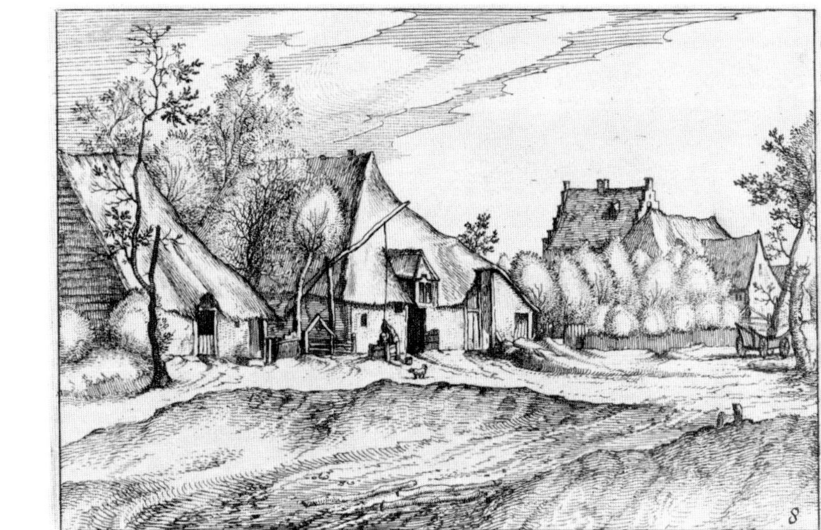

35

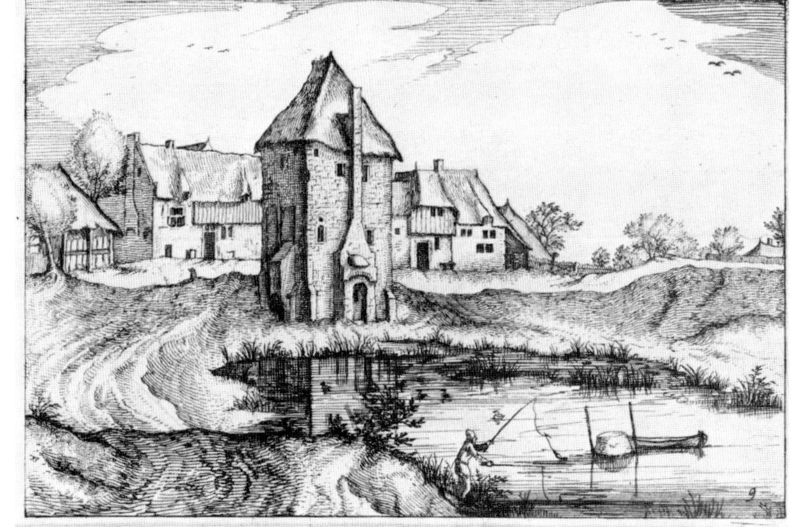

Claes Jansz. Visscher

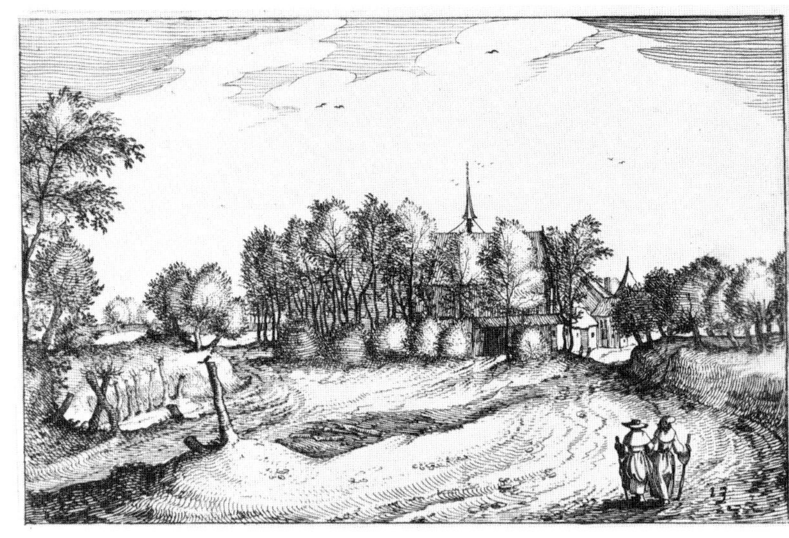

36

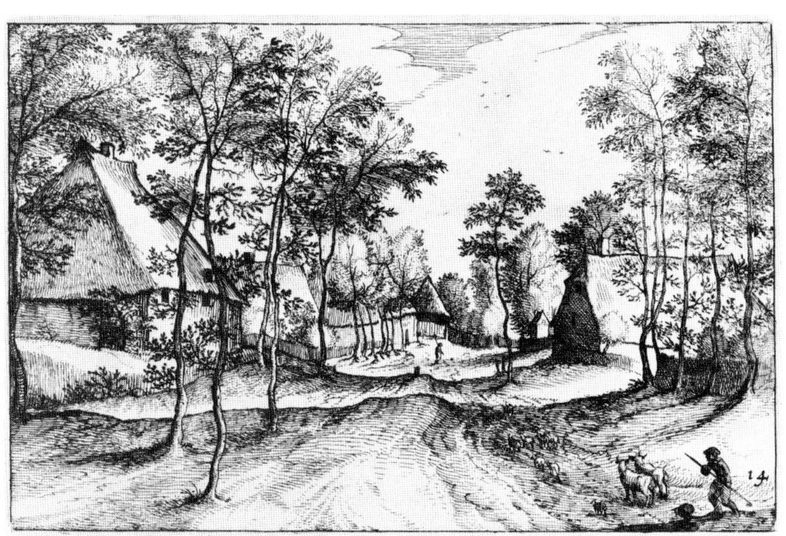

37

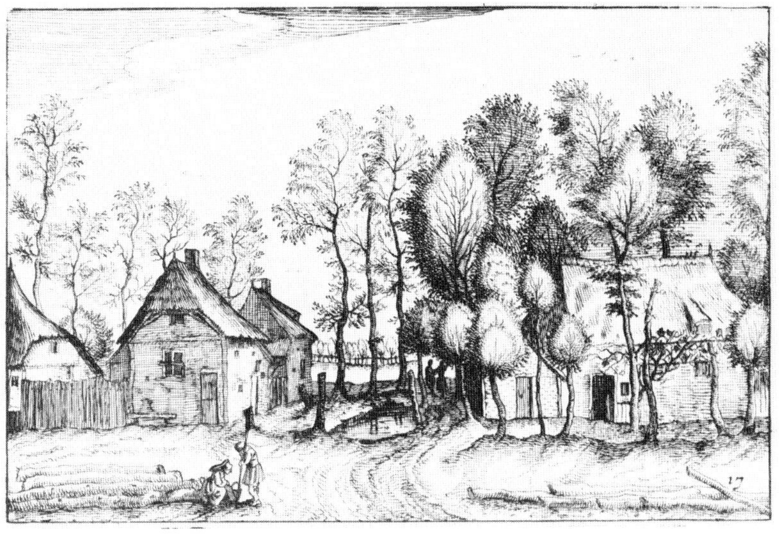

38

Jan van de Velde II

Son of the calligrapher Jan van de Velde I and cousin of Esaias van de Velde, Jan van de Velde II was apprenticed in 1613 in Haarlem to Jacob Matham, the stepson of Hendrik Goltzius. There he joined the Guild of St. Luke, and his first print series from his own designs was published in 1615 and 1616. He may have gone to Italy in 1617 but returned to Haarlem the following year and devoted himself to printing designs by other artists, including Willem Buytewech and Pieter Molijn. In 1636 he moved to Enkhuizen, where he remained until his death in 1641.

Van de Velde's substantial body of work comprises approximately 490 prints dating between 1615 and 1633. Of these nearly 200 are landscapes, many from his own designs.

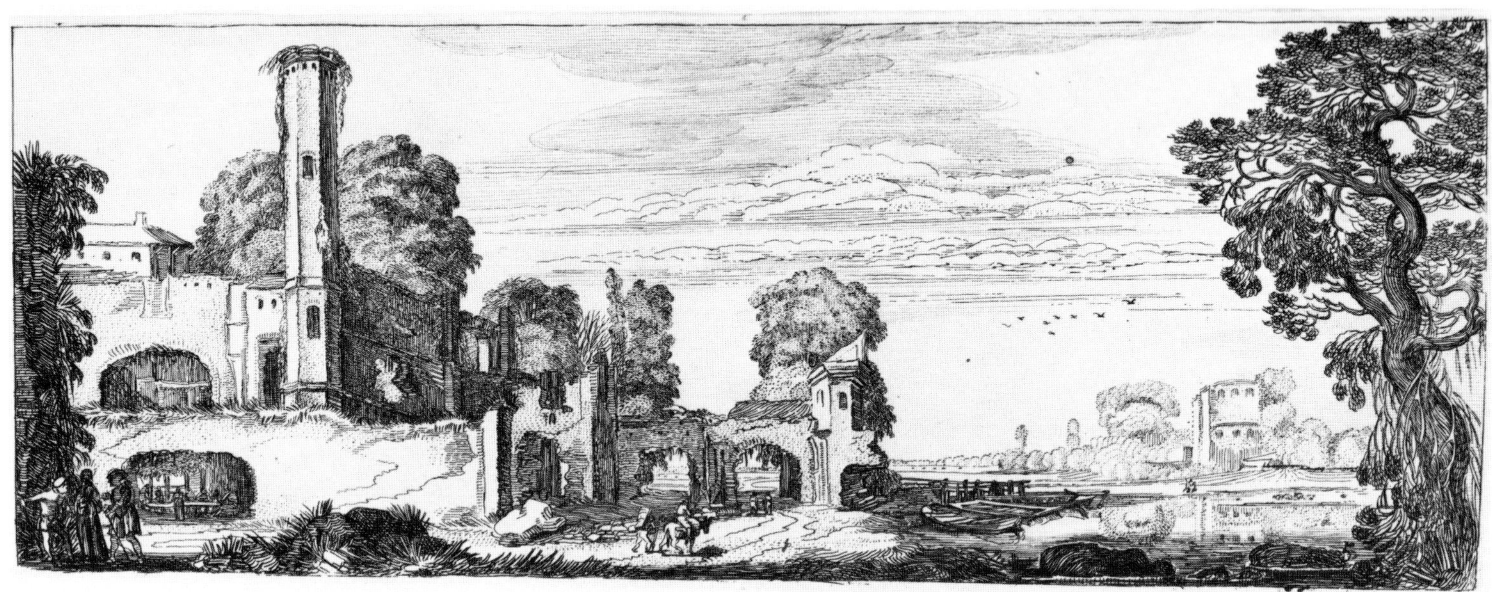

39

Landscape with Ruin of a Castle (1615)

JAN VAN DE VELDE II
(Rotterdam 1593–1641 Enkhuisen)
From the series Amoenissimae aliquot regiunculae et antiquorum monumentorum ruinae (Some of the most pleasant landscapes and ruins of ancient monuments)
Franken 221
Etching
111 x 310 mm
Provenance: R. E. Lewis, San Francisco

This print is from van de Velde's earliest dated series, one of two series of panoramic landscapes that he etched from his own designs. The ruins depicted in this series have not been identified, but they are evidence of the general antiquarian and archaeological interests of the time, which are also reflected in prints by Bartholomeus Breenbergh (see cat. nos. 46–47) and Johannes Ruisscher (see cat. no. 66). The representation of local ruins may also have had a special significance for van de Velde and his contemporaries. Ruins of Dutch medieval monuments, similar in structure to the ruins in this print, were represented by numerous Dutch artists, proud of their distinctive history. At the same time, however, the depiction of crumbling ruins also demonstrated the temporality of man's creations (Ackley 1981, p. 72).

Jan van de Velde II

40

January (1618)

(Ianuarius)

JAN VAN DE VELDE II
(Rotterdam 1593–1641 Enkhuisen)
Franken 150
Etching
271 x 365 mm
Provenance: Colnaghi, London

41

February (1618)

(Februarius)

JAN VAN DE VELDE II
(Rotterdam 1593–1641 Enkhuisen)
Franken 151
Etching
275 x 365 mm
Provenance: Colnaghi, London

42

July (1618)

(Julius)

JAN VAN DE VELDE II
(Rotterdam 1593–1641 Enkhuisen)
Franken 156
Etching
275 x 365 mm
Provenance: Colnaghi, London

43

September (1618)

(September)

JAN VAN DE VELDE II
(Rotterdam 1593–1641 Enkhuisen)
Franken 158
Etching
272 x 365 mm
Provenance: Colnaghi, London

These four prints belong to a series of the twelve months engraved by Jan van de Velde II. In each plate van de Velde skillfully illustrates the subtle atmospheric changes of the seasons as they affect the land and the people: the blustery winds of February tossing a ship and forcing man and tree alike to bend and the late afternoon sun of July compelling figures to take refuge in the shade. The corresponding sign of the zodiac appears at the top of each plate, and verses relating to the month appear in the lower margin.

The series is dedicated by Claes Jansz. Visscher (see cat. nos. 30–38) to Pieter van Veen, the brother of Rubens's teacher Otto van Veen, who was an influential lawyer in The Hague.

Stylistically the series recalls the prints of Willem Buytewech, particularly in the delineation of the bare-branched trees and the depiction of elegantly dressed figures in *January*. After 1618, the date of this series, van de Velde stopped making prints after his own designs.

Van de Velde often produced prints in somewhat old-fashioned series types such as series of the months, the seasons, and the elements (Freedberg 1980, p. 33). Similar series were produced by sixteenth-century Flemish artists such as Pieter Bruegel and Hans Bol but are part of a tradition that goes back even farther, to medieval depictions of the Labors of the Months. Though van de Velde worked in this traditional form, he experimented by depicting the local Dutch landscape and a variety of atmospheric changes.

Jan van de Velde II

40

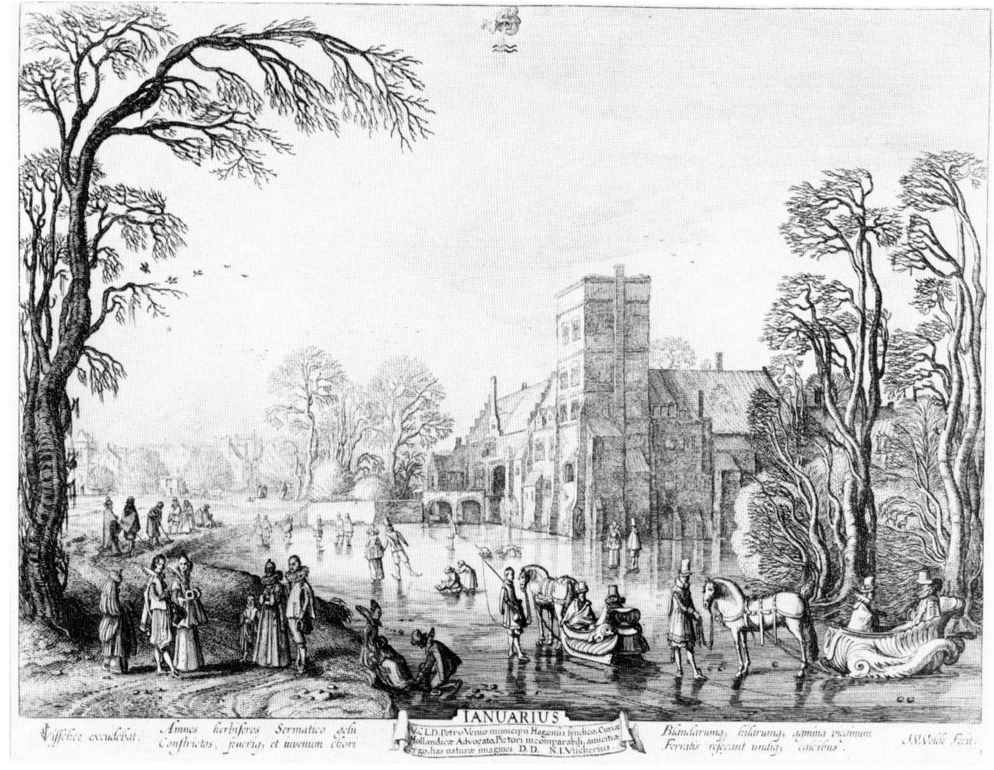

41

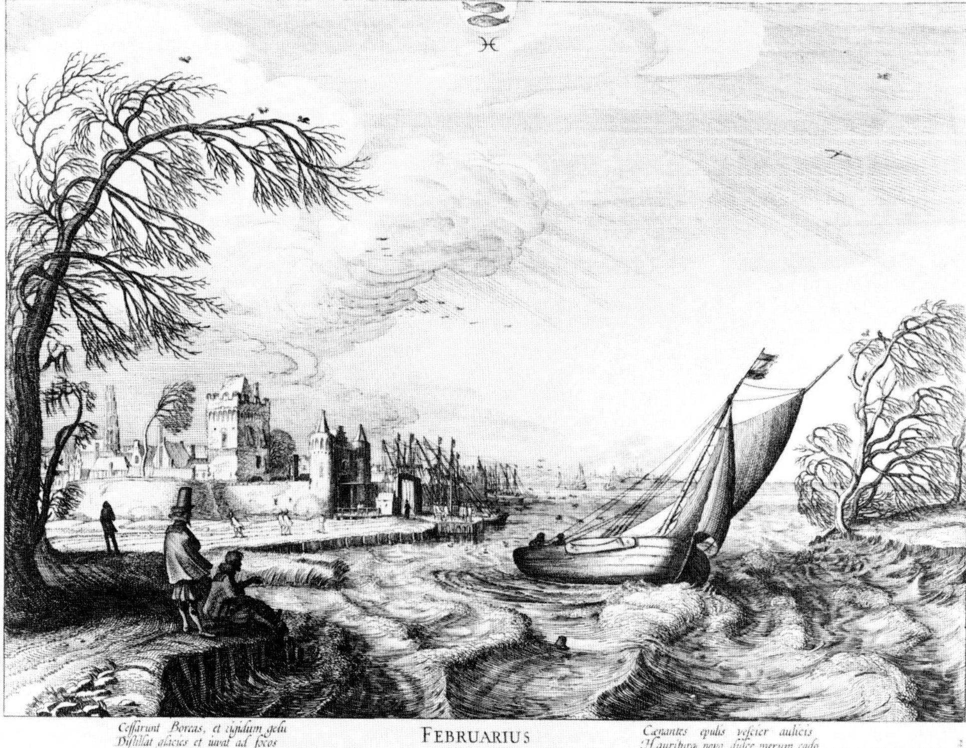

Jan van de Velde II

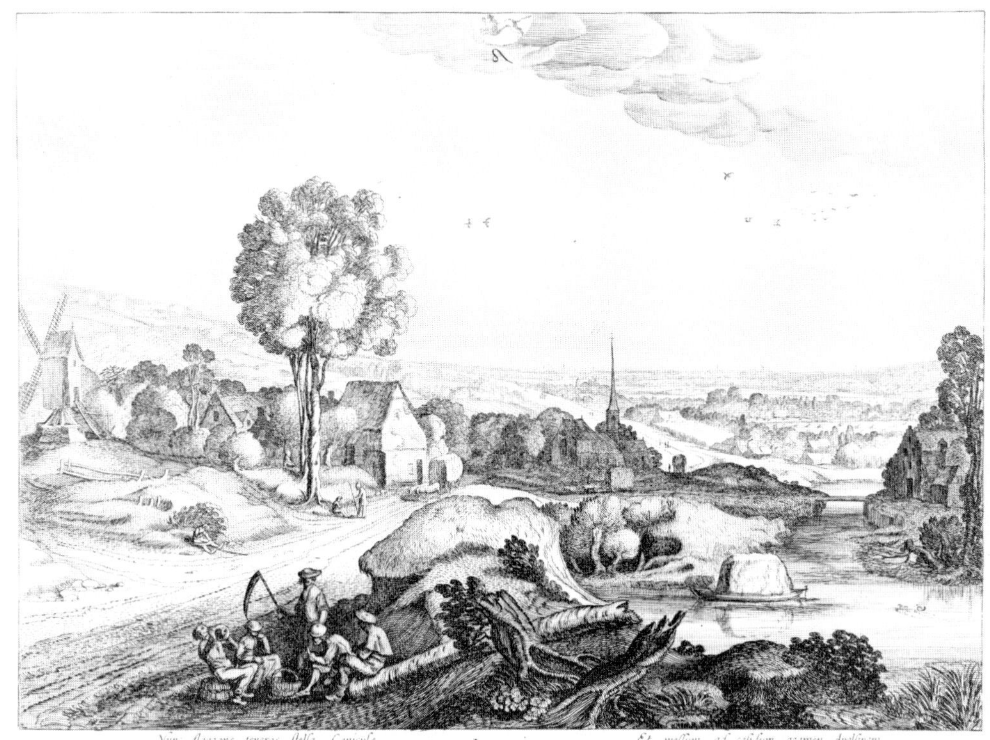

42

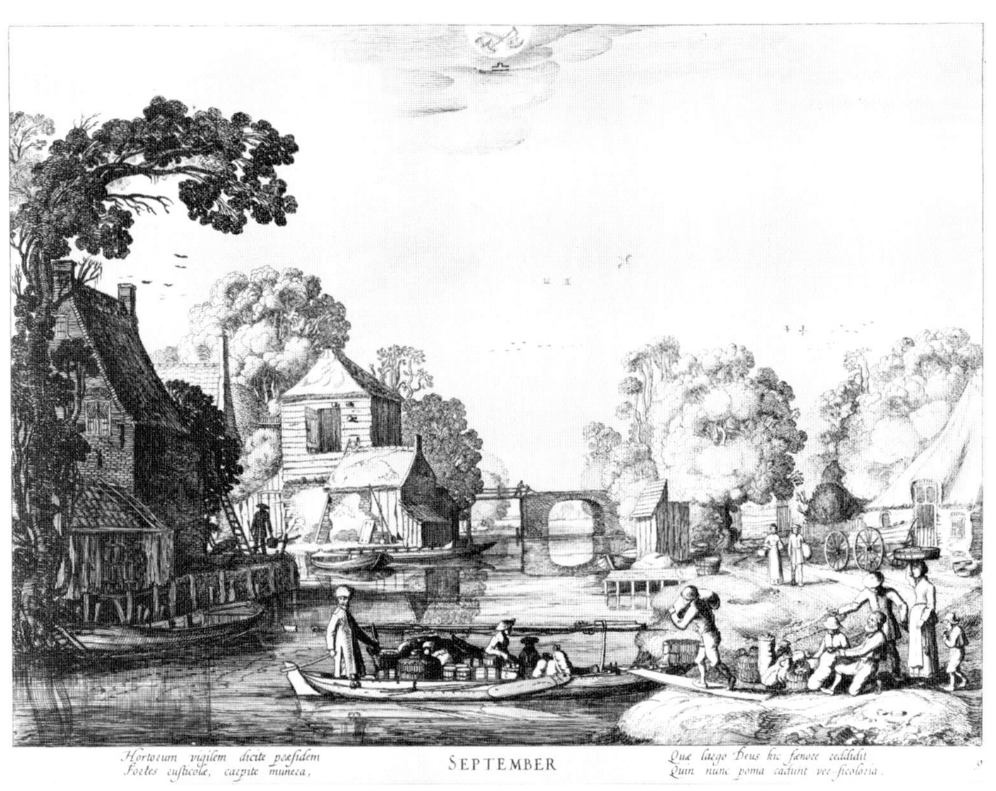

43

JAN VAN GOYEN

Jan van Goyen was born in Leiden in 1596. According to Orlers, from 1606 on he had a number of teachers. In Leiden he studied with Coenraet van Schilperoort, Isaac Nicolai van Swanenburgh, Jan Arentsz. de Man, and the glass painter Hendrick Clock; then he studied with Willem Gerritsz. in Hoorn for two years. His most important teacher was Esaias van de Velde, with whom he studied in Haarlem in 1617. In 1618 van Goyen returned to Leiden, and in 1634 he acquired citizenship in The Hague. Despite his prolific output and popularity as an artist, he died poor in 1656. This may have been due in part to precarious financial speculations. For example, he suffered heavy losses in the "tulipmania" of 1636–37.

Van Goyen was one of the most important and prolific Dutch landscape artists of the seventeenth century, and his oeuvre comprises about fifteen hundred landscape prints and two thousand drawings, the majority of them signed and dated. There are also about five sketchbooks that testify to his travels to Antwerp, Brussels, and the Rhineland. Van Goyen's early colorful village scenes show the influence of van de Velde, while his early marine paintings bear the imprint of Jan Porcellis. By 1630 van Goyen had come under the influence of Pieter Molijn and developed the monochrome landscape palette for which he is well known.

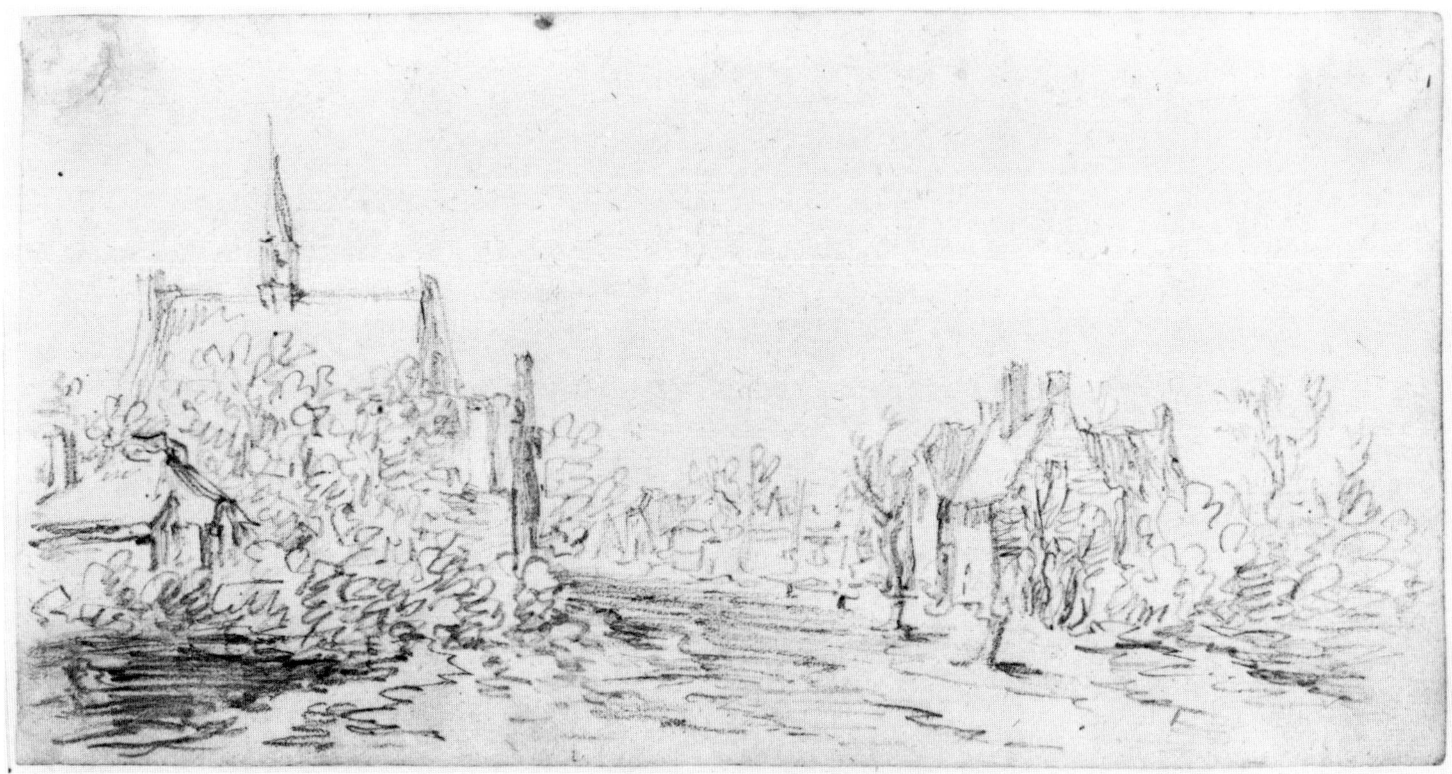

44
View of Leiderdorp (c. 1627–29)

JAN VAN GOYEN
(Leiden 1596–1656 The Hague)
Beck 844a, no. 38
Black chalk
114 x 225 mm
Provenance: General George C. Morgan and Sophia Pollard; Colnaghi, London

In contrast to van Goyen's more finished *River Landscape* (cat. no. 45), this depiction of a village road is a quick sketch of a particular site made by the artist early in his career. The drawing is a leaf from a sketchbook reconstructed by Beck and dated by him to 1627–29. The sketchbook contains two views of the town of Leiderdorp in addition to the present example. While the other views in the book are unidentified, they were probably also sketched in the countryside around Leiden, where van Goyen was living at the time.

The drawing is quite freely sketched in comparison with some of the other leaves in the book, such as number 24, which depicts three figures standing on a frozen river, stylistically more akin to those of van Goyen's teacher, Esaias van de Velde. The period around 1627 was transitional for van Goyen. He departed from the narrative style of his teacher, and his drawing style became freer, with figures assuming a minor role (Beck 1972, p. 53). This drawing, however, does not yet exhibit the emphasis on empty space that is evident in van Goyen's later sketchbook drawings, for example, that of 1650–51 (Beck 847).

45

River Landscape (1652)

JAN VAN GOYEN
(Leiden 1596–1656 The Hague)
Beck 324
Black chalk and gray wash
122 x 196 mm
Inscribed *VG 1652* lower left

Provenance: D. Vis Blokhuyzen, Rotterdam, 23 October 1871, possibly lot 233; Herman de Kat; Neville D. Goldsmid, Paris, 25 April 1876, lot 69; O. Gerstenberg (L. II/2785); Klipstein and Kornfeld, Bern, 19 May 1963, lot 123; R. M. Light and Co., Boston
Bibliography: *Die Weltkunst*, 1 May 1963, p. 19

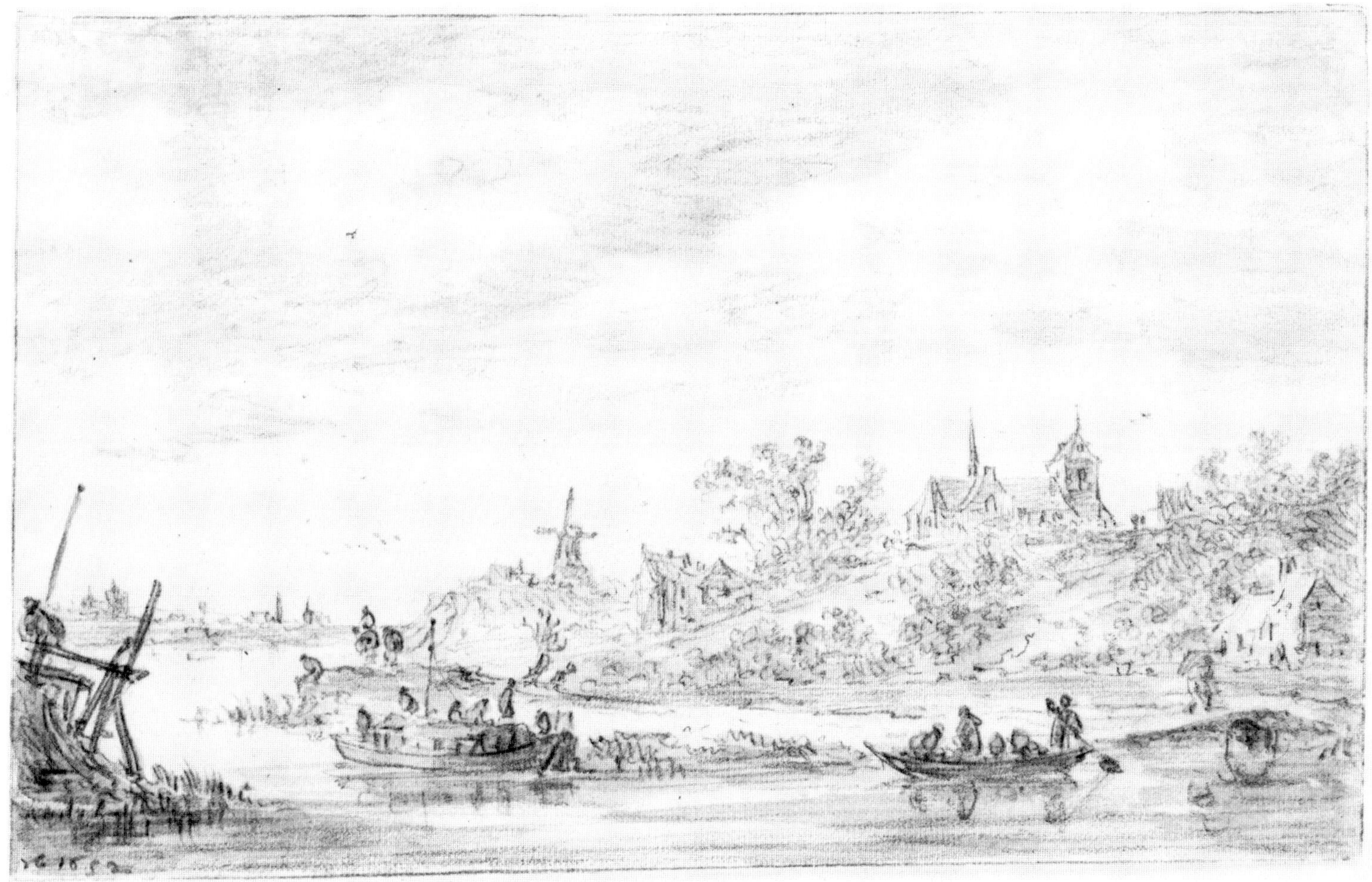

Despite its sketchiness, the artist would have considered this drawing a finished work rather than a sketch for another work of art. In comparison with van Goyen's sketchbook drawings (see cat. no. 44), this drawing, with touches of gray wash, is more carefully composed. The quick black chalk lines are typical of the artist's style during his most prolific period as a draftsman, between 1651 and 1653. Although van Goyen made few paintings during this period, Beck (1972, p. 51) has suggested that the great number of drawings he produced then prepared him for the high point of his career in painting during the years 1655 and 1656.

Bartholomeus Breenbergh

Bartholomeus Breenbergh lived in Rome from 1619 to 1629. There in 1623 he was one of the founders of Bentvueghels, the confraternity of Netherlandish artists. Part of the first generation of Netherlandish artists in Rome, Breenbergh was influenced in the early part of his career by the landscapes of Adam Elsheimer and Paul Bril. His paintings of Italian ruins with historical subjects are closely related to those of Cornelis van Poelenburgh. By 1633 Breenbergh was in Amsterdam, where he remained until his death. After 1644 he turned away from landscape, concentrating on history subjects. Breenbergh made about thirty etchings, most of which date from 1639 to 1640.

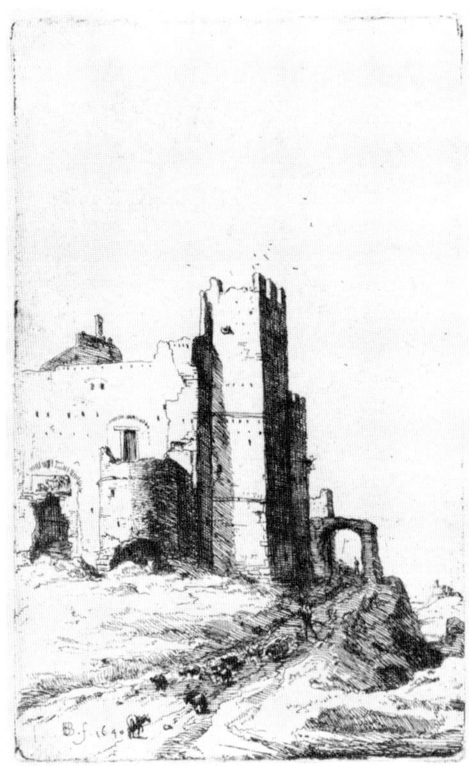

46

The Tower of Leoni near Frascati (1640)

BARTHOLOMEUS BREENBERGH
(Deventer c. 1598–1657 Amsterdam)
From the series Various Ruined Buildings within and without Rome (Verscheyden vervallen gebouwe soo binnen als buyten Romen)
B. 9; Holl. 9
Etching
101 x 64 mm
Provenance: R. E. Lewis, San Francisco

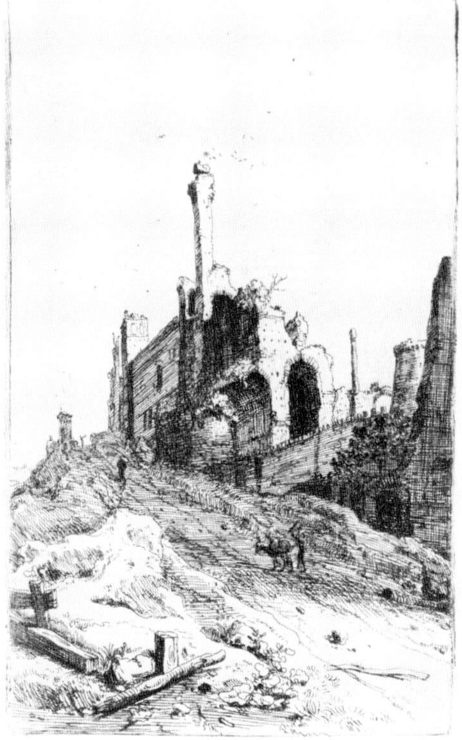

47

Ruins of a Palace at Tivoli (1640)

BARTHOLOMEUS BREENBERGH
(Deventer c. 1598–1657 Amsterdam)
From the series Various Ruined Buildings within and without Rome (Verscheyden vervallen gebouwe soo binnen als buyten Romen)
B. 16; Holl. 16
Etching
101 x 64 mm
Provenance: P. Davidsohn (L. I/654); F. Rumpf (L. I/2161); Artaria and Co. (L. I/90); H. E. Ten Cate (L. II/533b); R. E. Lewis, San Francisco

These two etchings belong to a series of seventeen small and delicate vertical views of ruins published in 1640.[1] While a number of the ruins depicted in the series can be identified, such as the Tower of Leoni near Frascati, the ruins at Tivoli pictured here are unidentified, though they also appear in a print and a painting by Jan Both.[2] In general the images in this series are probably more idealized than topographical.

Drawings exist for a number of the plates in this series. The design for the Tower of Leoni is a wash drawing[3] in which the composition has been sketched out in terms of the patterns of light and shadow. A drawing for the palace at Tivoli was sketched in pen.[4] Both drawings have been dated by Roethlisberger to Breenbergh's stay in Rome. If this is the case, he probably made the etchings several years after the drawings, as the majority of Breenbergh's prints date from 1639 to 1640.

Breenbergh is well known for his evocative depictions of ruins, which he included in paintings, drawings, and prints until 1644, when he began to concentrate on history subjects. This series is part of the tradition of illustrating Roman ruins begun by Hieronymus Cock in 1551 (see cat. no. 14). The Italianate painters contemporary with Breenbergh, such as Paul Bril and Cornelis van Poelenburgh, combined the traditional Flemish landscape with the depiction of ruins. In contrast to Cock's earlier, more archaeological depictions of ruins, they emphasized the intense southern light rather than the details of crumbling stone monuments.

1. The title page reads: "Verscheyden / vervallen gebouwe / Soo binnen als buyten / ROMEN. / Geteykent en Ghets / Door / Bartholomeus Breenbergh / Schilder. / Gedaen in't Jaer 1640."
2. For the print *Landscape with Ruins and Two Cows at the Waterside* (Holl. 16) and for the painting *Buildings on the Edge of a Lake*, see Burke 1976, nos. 8, 28.
3. Paris, Musée du Louvre inv. no. 22 539a; brown wash. See Roethlisberger 1969, no. 27.
4. Berlin, Kupferstichkabinett inv. no. 12462; pen and ink. See ibid., no. 59.

48

Landscape with a Stone Bridge

ANONYMOUS
(Dutch, seventeenth century)
B. 34 (as by H. van Saftleven); Holl. 5 (as by J. van Capelle); Dut. 5 (as by J. van Goyen); Wurz. 5 (as by J. van Goyen); Bierens de Haan 5 iv/v (as by J. van Capelle)
Etching
131 x 173 mm
Provenance: Zeitlin and Ver Brugge, Los Angeles

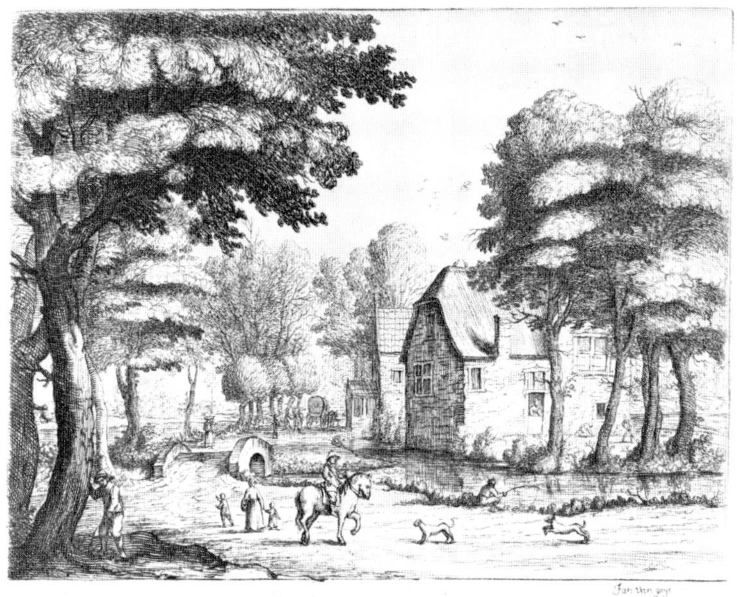

This print, along with five others from the same series, has been attributed to a variety of artists but has in the end been left without an author. Because of the signature that appears on this print in the fourth state, the series was once attributed to Jan van Goyen. This print is stylistically similar to works of van Goyen's early period, which resemble those of Esaias van de Velde.[1] Beck, however, along with a number of scholars before him, has disputed this attribution (1972, p. 55). Bierens de Haan was the first to attribute the print to the marine painter Jan van Capelle. Hollstein, following his lead, attributed a total of eleven prints to Capelle in an attempt to retrace the eleven copper plates that are mentioned in the artist's inventory. Russell has refuted this attribution, however, claiming only one of the prints cited by Hollstein for Capelle. There is no indication that the copper plates that appear in Capelle's inventory were by the artist.[2]

Typically Dutch naturalistic genre details populate the scene, including a man in the foreground on the left urinating under a tree. The town view follows the tradition of city views with genre scenes established by Haarlem artists of the second decade of the seventeenth century such as van de Velde and Willem Buytewech.

1. Although the etching is similar in composition to those of early Haarlem artists such as van de Velde, the execution of the puffy foliage differs considerably from their work.
2. Russell 1975, p. 35. Russell concurs with Stechow in accepting *The Bank of a Wide River with Fishing Boats* (Holl. 1), of which there is only one known impression, in London, as the only known print by Capelle.

49

View of Antwerp

ANONYMOUS
(Flemish, seventeenth century)
Graphite and lightly colored washes
190 x 304 mm
Inscribed *Antwerp* upper right
Provenance: Walter Schatzki, New York

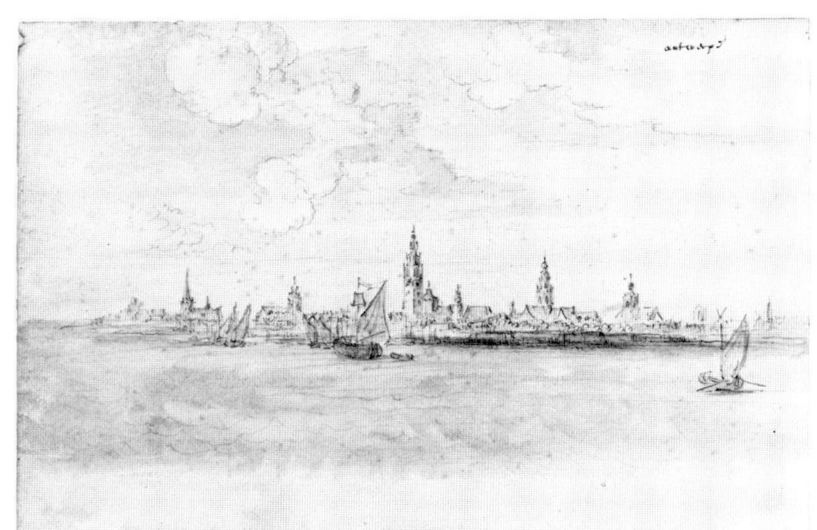

The steeple of the Onze Lieve Vrouwe church, which rises in the center of the drawing, clearly identifies it as a depiction of the Antwerp skyline as viewed from the west across the Scheldt River.

Although the sketchy quality of the drawing suggests an attribution to a seventeenth-century artist, the style is not distinctive enough to be associated with any specific artist. It is clear that the artist was more interested in giving a shorthand description of the city than in faithfully rendering the skyline, since Antwerp, even in the sixteenth century, had more churches and towers than are visible here.

Rembrandt Harmensz. van Rijn

Rembrandt Harmensz. van Rijn was taught painting by Jacob van Swanenburgh in Leiden. In 1624 he studied in Amsterdam with Pieter Lastman, whose style had a greater impact on the young artist. In Leiden as an independent artist from about 1624 to 1631, Rembrandt worked in close association with his friend and fellow artist Jan Lievens. Sometime between 1631 and 1632 he moved to Amsterdam and for several years was one of the most successful portraitists in that city, maintaining a large number of apprentices in his studio. At the end of the 1630s his production declined, although he received several important commissions. In 1656 he was declared insolvent, and his possessions, including a large art collection, were sold at auction in 1658. Rembrandt died impoverished in Amsterdam in 1669. His financial misfortunes did not reflect his international artistic reputation, however; his work was held in high esteem throughout his life.

Rembrandt's oeuvre includes about three hundred etchings, some twenty-seven of which are landscapes dating from 1640 to 1657, the period in which he painted the majority of his landscape pictures as well. His landscape etchings were inspired by the countryside surrounding Amsterdam but were almost never etched from nature. Rembrandt's work as a printmaker compares with that of no other artist except Hercules Segers in the variety of techniques and papers used, and certainly no other Dutch artist of the period made such a large number of radical revisions to his plates.

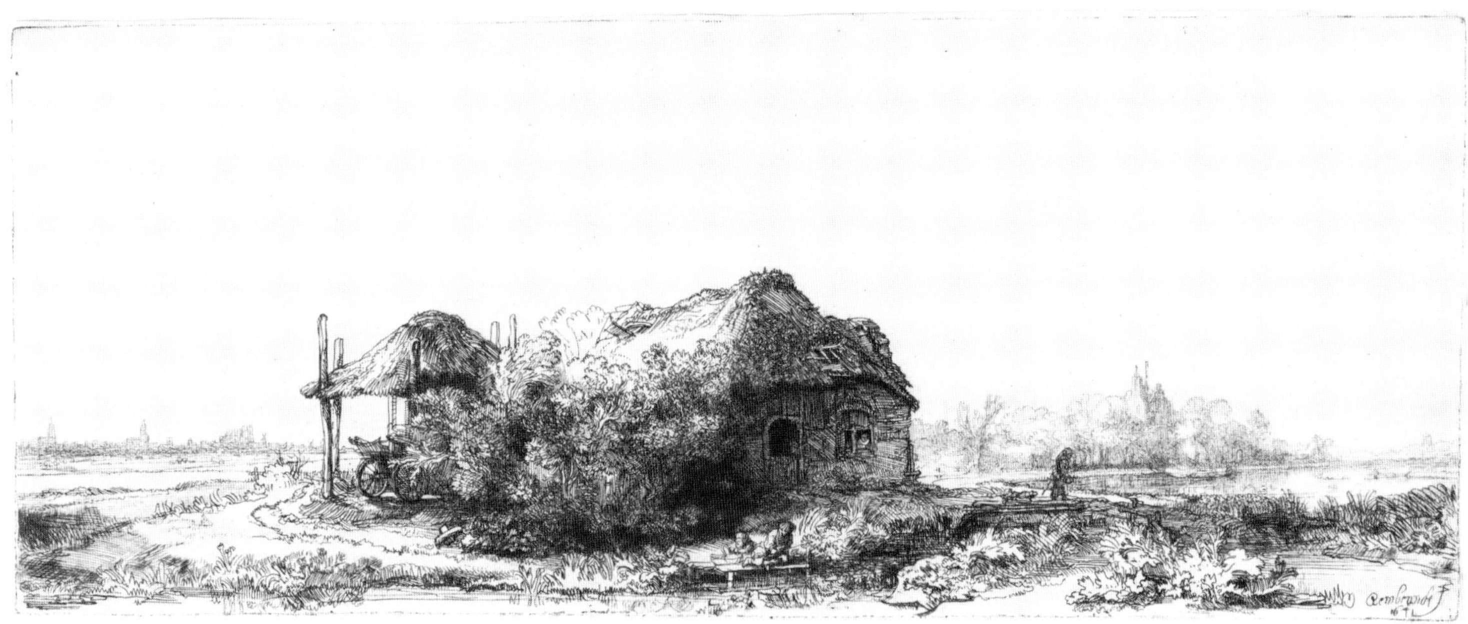

50

Cottage and Hay Barn (1641)

REMBRANDT HARMENSZ. VAN RIJN
(Leiden 1606–1669 Amsterdam)
B. 225; Hind 177; Münz 147; Biörklund and Barnard 41-A
Etching and drypoint
128 x 323 mm
Provenance: Kupferstichkabinett der Staatlichen Museen, Berlin (L. I/1606); Thiermann (L. I/2434); O. P. Reed, Los Angeles

The house on the right amidst the trees has been identified as Kostverloren, a house along the Amstel that was a readily recognizable landmark for Rembrandt's contemporaries and was often depicted in paintings, drawings, and prints by seventeenth-century Dutch artists.[1] Kostverloren, whose name (which means "lost money") was recorded as early as 1563, was built around 1500 on swampy land on the riverbank, which resulted in the expenditure of large sums of money on its preservation by its various owners (Groesbeek 1966, pp. 125–26, pls. 46–48).

While Rembrandt depicted an actual site, its placement in relation to the city of Amsterdam, seen at left, is entirely imaginary. Indeed, probably only two of the artist's landscape prints were actually drawn from nature.[2] Rembrandt intentionally juxtaposed the bustling city in the background with the deteriorating house, a symbol of decay. The image could be interpreted moralistically, as illustrating the decay of the farmhouse in the center, whose inhabitants fish rather than tend to their property, as in a drawing of a neglected farmhouse by Jacques de Gheyn (van Regteren Altena 1983, no. 950, pl. 24). In any case, Rembrandt certainly meant the farmhouse in the center to act as a mediating image between the neglected Kostverloren and the busy, crowded city.

---

1. Six 1909, p. 96; Lugt 1915, p. 109ff., pls. 65–69. Kostverloren has been identified in the following drawings by Rembrandt: Benesch 1265, 1266, 1268, 1269, 1270, 1220 recto, 1220 verso. For the depiction of Kostverloren by Dutch artists of the period, see Seymour Slive, "Kostverloren: The Vicissitudes of a Seventeenth-Century Dutch Landscape Motif" (Paper delivered at the annual meeting of the College Art Association, Boston, 1987).
2. White 1969, p. 191; these were two drypoints: the first state of *The Clump of Trees with a Vista* (B. 222) and *Landscape with a Road beside a Canal* (B. 221).

51

Canal with Large Boat and Bridge (1650)

REMBRANDT HARMENSZ. VAN RIJN
(Amsterdam 1606–1669 Amsterdam)
B. 236 ii/ii; Hind 239 ii/ii; Münz 162 ii/ii;
Biörklund and Barnard 50-B ii/ii
Etching and drypoint
83 x 108 mm
Provenance: S. Bermann (L. II/236); William Schab, New York

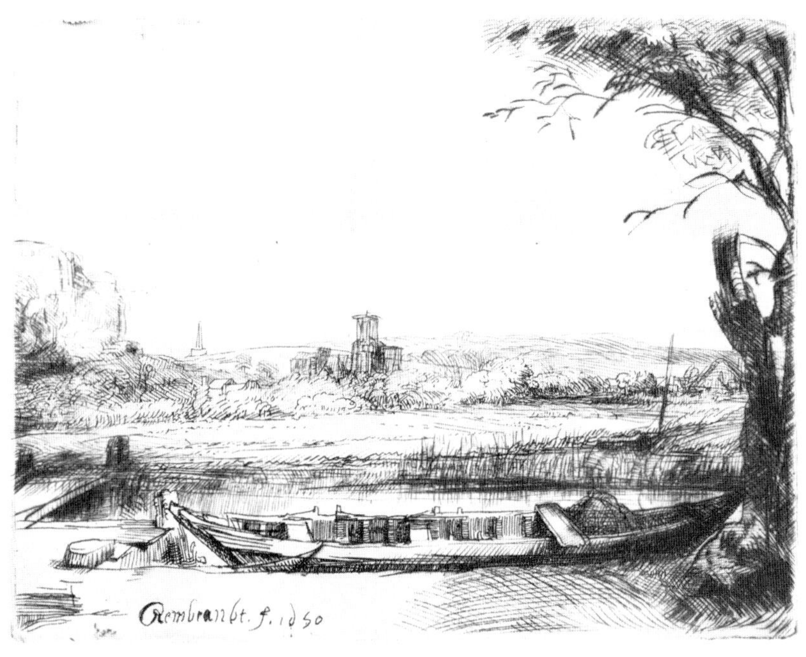

In the second state of Rembrandt's etching, as exemplified by this impression, shading was added to the trees below the square tower, and the outline of the hill was changed to include three vertical lines that cut the horizon.

The view depicted, although naturalistic in the foreground, appears somewhat more fantastic in the background because of the inclusion of rolling hills that are foreign to the surroundings of Amsterdam. The composition, rather than having been sketched from nature, is probably derived entirely from Rembrandt's imagination. While Rembrandt sketched landscapes in the outskirts of Amsterdam, his prints seldom faithfully depict the landscape but include realistic details within imaginary settings. As White (1969, p. 192) states, Rembrandt's landscape etchings moved "in the direction of an idealistic landscape expressed through natural means."

REMBRANDT HARMENSZ. VAN RIJN

52

Landscape with Three Gabled Cottages beside a Road (1650)

REMBRANDT HARMENSZ. VAN RIJN
(Leiden 1606–1669 Amsterdam)
B. 217 iii/iii; Hind 246 iii/iii; Münz 163 iii/iii; Biörklund and Barnard 50-D iii/iii
Etching and drypoint
162 x 203 mm
Provenance: A. J. Hachette; O. P. Reed, Los Angeles

This print, dated 1650, is similar in composition not only to *Landscape with an Obelisk* (cat. no. 53), which has been dated to the same year, but also to prints by Rembrandt's predecessors, such as the Master of the Small Landscapes (see cat. nos. 12–13) and Jan van de Velde II (see cat. nos. 39–43). While Rembrandt adopts the traditional diagonal composition, his interpretation of it is entirely original, combining etching with drypoint and using richly descriptive strokes.

The print is related to two drawings by Rembrandt. A drawing in Stockholm is much earlier than the etching of three cottages and quite different in style.[1] A drawing in Berlin, however, is dated around 1653 and represents a cottage and a tree by a road, which resemble the first cottage and the tree in the foreground of this etching.[2] Although Rembrandt often sketched in the countryside surrounding Amsterdam, he never used his drawings from nature as direct models for prints. He sometimes used drawings as starting points for prints, however, and that may have been what occurred in this instance (White 1969, p. 192).

1. *Three Cottages,* Stockholm, Nationalmuseum (Benesch 1973, no. 795, fig. 946).
2. *Cottage and Tree by a Road,* Berlin, Kupferstichkabinett (ibid., no. 1306, fig. 1536).

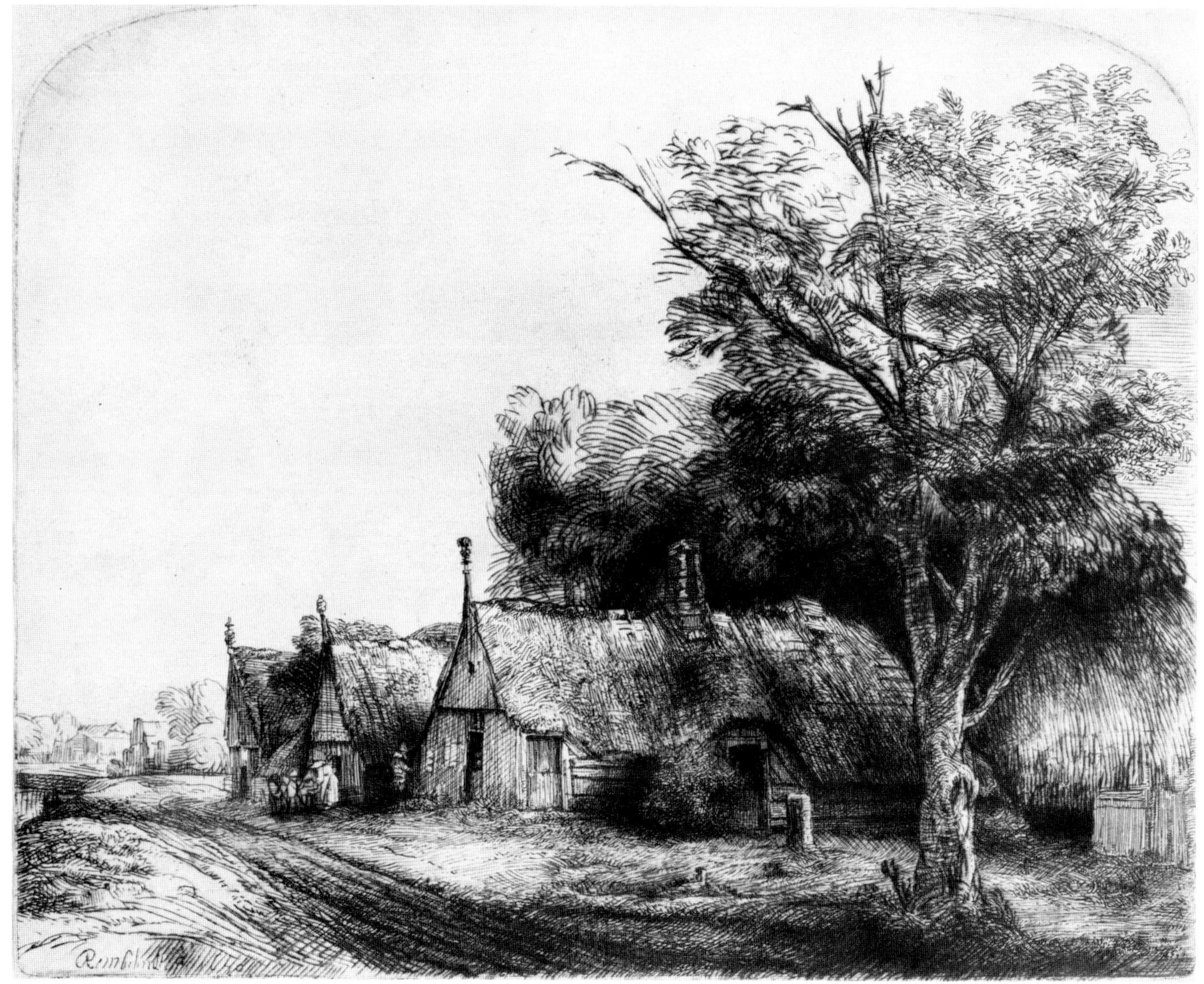

53

Landscape with an Obelisk (c. 1650)

REMBRANDT HARMENSZ. VAN RIJN
(Leiden 1606–1669 Amsterdam)
B. 227 ii/ii; Hind 243 ii/ii; Münz 157 ii/ii; Biörklund and Barnard 50-3 ii/ii
Etching and drypoint
85 x 162 mm
Provenance: Zeitlin and Ver Brugge, Los Angeles

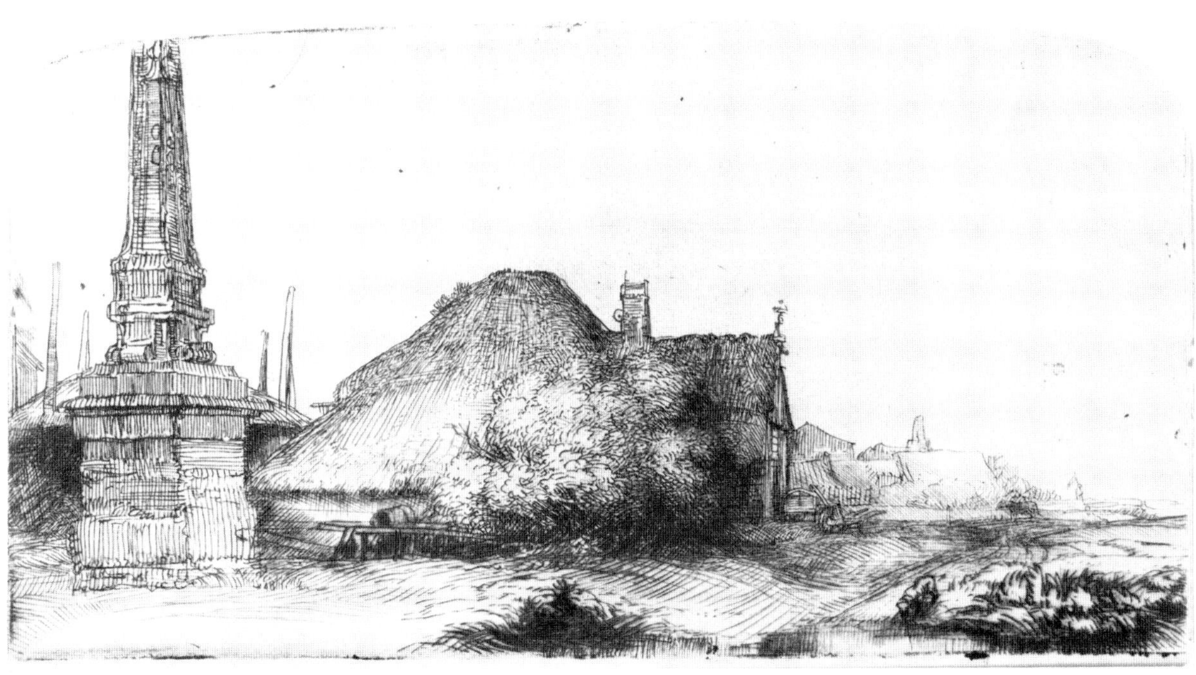

This impression is from the second state of Rembrandt's small but monumental image, and the changes to the plate in this state resulted in a more unified and visually satisfying treatment of the image. Although he added shading to the once-blank houses in the background on the right in order to moderate the abrupt shift into the distance, he also scraped away some of the foreground burr from the cottage roof.[1] While the rich, velvety burr was often used to great advantage by Rembrandt, its abundance in the foreground of the first state was overwhelming.

The obelisk that anchors the composition had a particular association for the seventeenth-century Dutchman. Obelisks such as this marked the boundaries of a city's jurisdiction, delineating the division between town and countryside. The obelisk in this print was identified by Lugt (1915, p. 153) as one near Spieringerhorn on the road between Amsterdam and Haarlem. Obelisks also appear in a number of Rembrandt's paintings and drawings as well as in works by other seventeenth-century artists, such as Govaert Flinck's *Landscape with an Obelisk* in the Isabella Stewart Gardner Museum, Boston (Bredius 1969, no. 443).

1. White (1969, p. 209) was among the first to observe that Rembrandt actually scraped away some of the burr but left it intact in other areas of the print.

Jan Lievens

The son of a Flemish embroiderer, Jan Lievens was apprenticed in 1615, at the age of eight, to an artist in Leiden, Joris van Schooten. From about 1619 to 1621 he studied with Pieter Lastman in Amsterdam, before returning to Leiden, where from about 1624 to 1631 he worked in close association with Rembrandt. From 1632 to 1635 Lievens was in England painting portraits for the court of Charles I. In 1635 he registered with the Guild of St. Luke in Antwerp, where one of his close artistic associates was Adriaen Brouwer, but by 1644 he had moved back to Amsterdam, where he received a number of official commissions, including paintings for the new Town Hall in Amsterdam and the Huis ten Bosch near The Hague.

Lievens's paintings and prints comprise mainly history subjects and portraits, although he made numerous landscape drawings. His printed oeuvre comprises sixty to sixty-five etchings and eight to ten woodcuts. Lievens's early style was quite close to Rembrandt's, especially during their collaboration in Leiden in the 1620s. In England he was influenced by Anthony van Dyck, while in Antwerp he developed a landscape style close to that of Brouwer.

54

A Farmhouse and a Man by a Fence

JAN LIEVENS
(Leiden 1607–1674 Amsterdam)
Reed pen and brown ink with blue wash
194 x 313 mm
Provenance: William Schab, New York
Bibliography: Schneider and Ekkart 1973, no. Z. 390; Bernt 1958, vol. 2, no. 365 (as in Albertina, Vienna); Meder 1922, vol. 1, no. 42., pl. 22; Nebahay, Vienna, sale cat., 1928, lot 66 (ill.); R. W. P. de Vries, Amsterdam, sale cat., 9 December 1930, lot 283 (size as 195 x 315 mm); Sotheby's, London, sale cat., 9 April 1981, lot 35 (ill.)

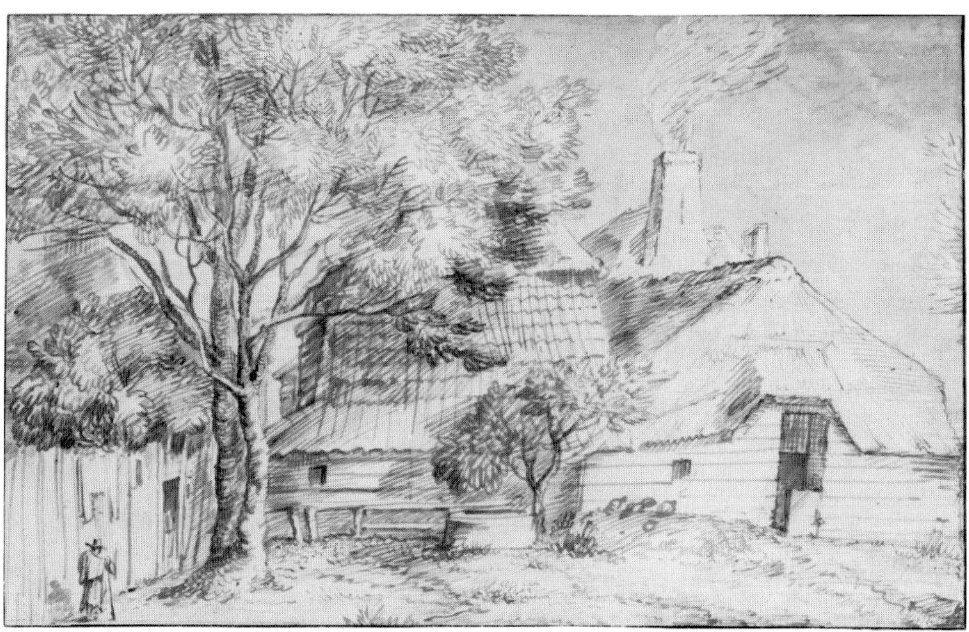

A large number of Lievens's drawings depict wooded landscapes with farm buildings or small villages. Although they are not dated, they are usually placed between the years 1654 and 1660 (Schneider and Ekkart 1973, pp. 73–74). Sumowski (1980), among others, has noted that Lievens relied on sketches of trees and landscapes made in nature for some of his more finished drawings. The balanced composition and the small figure with a walking stick at the left suggest that this drawing may have been made in the studio, although no related preparatory sketches are known. The blue wash may have been added by a later hand.

Anthonie Waterloo

Little is known of Anthonie Waterloo's artistic training, and he may have been self-taught. He first settled near Utrecht but is recorded as living in Amsterdam in 1640. After that time he lived alternately in Leeuwarden and Amsterdam, finally settling in Utrecht, where he remained until his death. Waterloo also traveled extensively in Germany, the southern Netherlands, and possibly Italy.

Though paintings by Waterloo are rare, a large number of drawings and about 126 etchings survive, all undated. He was primarily a landscape artist, and his work reflects a familiarity with the styles of a variety of artists, such as Jan van Goyen, Jacob van Ruisdael, Anthony van Dyck, and in particular Simon de Vlieger.

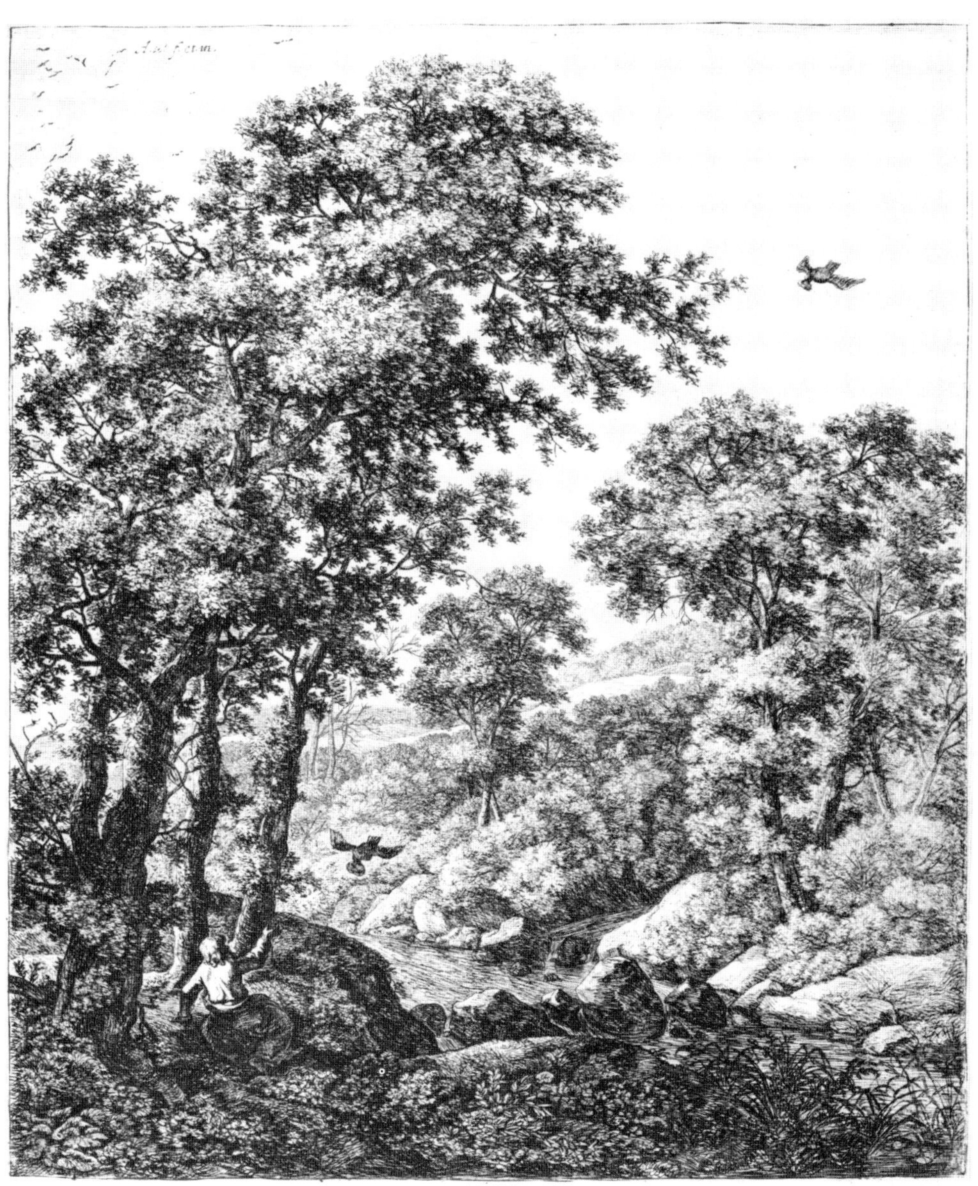

55

Elias in the Desert

ANTHONIE WATERLOO
(Lille c. 1610–1690 Utrecht)
B. 136; Dut. 136
Etching
294 x 250 mm
Provenance: Zeitlin and Ver Brugge, Los Angeles

This print is one of a series of six landscapes with biblical scenes. In conception it parallels several series published by Herman van Swanevelt (c. 1600–1655) in the 1650s consisting of forest landscapes with secondary biblical and mythological scenes in the foreground. In this particular print Elijah is seated on the left, reaching out to two ravens who bring him bread and meat. According to the Old Testament (1 Kings 17:1–6), Elijah, during a drought, went to dwell by the brook Cherith, where he was fed by ravens. Waterloo's forest landscape, however, depicts lush trees and shrubs on the shore of the rushing stream.

The pictorial tradition of relegating a biblical subject to a secondary position in order to emphasize the landscape can be seen in prints by Johannes Sadeler (see cat. nos. 19–22) but goes back to the landscapes of Joachim Patinir (c. 1485–1524). Waterloo's treatment of the flickering light passing through the dense foliage is closer to the landscapes of his contemporaries Jacob van Ruisdael (see cat. nos. 67–68) and Meindert Hobbema (1638–1709).

Jan Both

According to Sandrart, Jan Both trained first with his father, a glass painter, and then, like his older brother Andries, with Abraham Bloemaert. In 1638, 1639, and 1641 Both was recorded as living in Rome but soon returned to Utrecht, where he remained until his death.

Both was part of the second generation of Netherlandish artists in Rome, which also included Jan Asselijn and later Nicolaes Berchem, who painted views of the Roman Campagna. In Rome Both was in contact with Herman van Swanevelt and Claude Lorrain, and their idyllic Italian landscapes influenced his style. The majority of Both's sun-drenched landscape paintings, however, as well as his fifteen etchings, were created after his return from Rome, typical of numerous Dutch artists who responded to the northern demand for Italianate subjects.

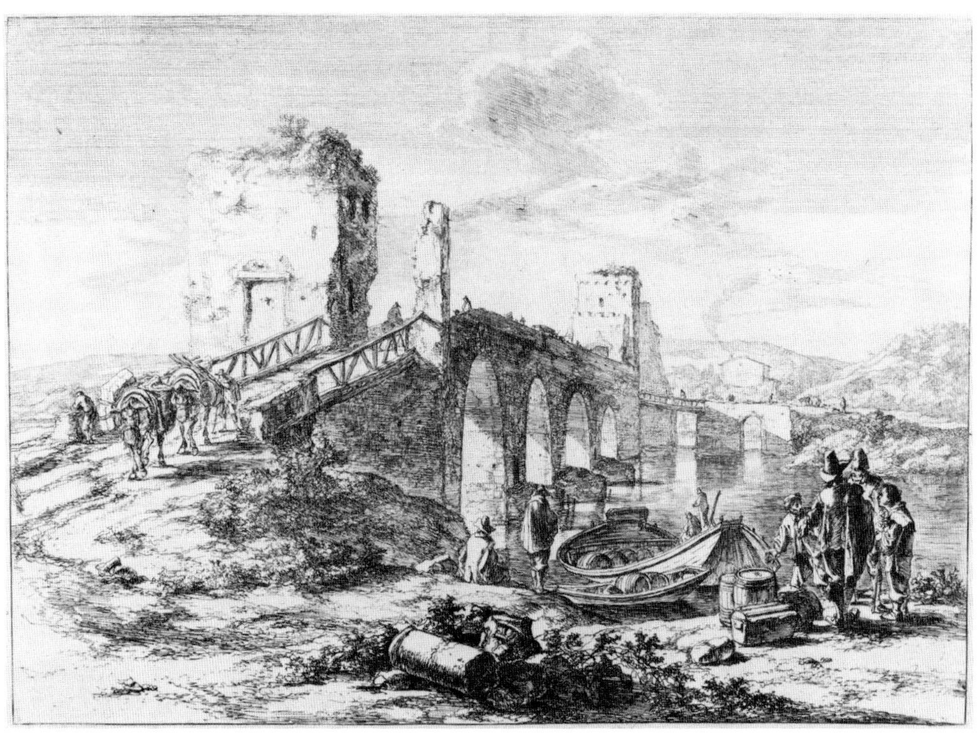

56

Ponte Molle

JAN BOTH
(Utrecht c. 1615/18–1652 Utrecht)
B. 5; Holl. 5 ii or iii/vi; Wurz. 5 ii/vi;
Dut. 5; Burke 5 ii/vi
Etching
197 x 275 mm
Provenance: R. E. Lewis, San Francisco

Ponte Molle belongs to a series of four to six prints by Jan Both depicting the environs of Rome.[1] The second state, exhibited here, is the most complete treatment of this image by Both himself. The first state of this print exists in a unique impression in London, a trial proof with corrections by the artist in pen and brown ink, indicating lines to be added to the foreground, parts of the bridge, and small areas of the background. These changes were carried out in this second state. The third state, in which the sky was completed, was engraved by another hand (Burke 1976, p. 298).

While most of Both's prints are directly related to his paintings, there is no painting known that can be linked to this print. A drawing in reverse, an early study for the image, is in Hamburg.[2] The drawing differs from the etching in that the foreground is still unresolved and the perspective of the bridge is incorrect.

In his prints Both was able to translate the golden southern light, characteristic of the works of Italianate painters, into large areas of white that give the illusion of light reflecting off stone monuments. Bartholomeus Breenbergh achieved a similar effect in his prints of Roman ruins (see cat. nos. 46–47). The Ponte Molle was frequently depicted by northern artists of Both's generation who worked in Rome, such as Jan Asselijn (before 1610–1652) and Claude Lorrain.

1. While Hollstein catalogues the series of six plates, Ackley and Burke maintain that numbers 9 and 10 are after Both rather than by his hand. See Ackley 1981, p. 176, and Burke 1976, p. 287.
2. Hamburg, Kunsthalle inv. no. 21740; black chalk with touches of wash, possibly added later.

ROELAND ROGHMAN

Little is known about the life and artistic training of Roeland Roghman. He was the son of the engraver Hendrick Lambertsz. Roghman and Maria Savery. A landscape painter and topographical draftsman as well as a printmaker, he may have been taught first by his uncle, Roelandt Savery. In 1646 and 1647 he made at least 241 drawings of castles and manors in the Dutch countryside. He was apparently active in Amsterdam in the 1660s and is presumed from his one series of Alpine landscapes to have made a trip to Italy. Roghman's paintings depict fantastic mountain landscapes related to those of Rembrandt and Hercules Segers. His drawings are either invented mountain views or topographical subjects, and his forty etchings are topographical views of the Dutch countryside.

57
Rocky Landscape with Fir (no. 4)

ROELAND ROGHMAN
(Amsterdam c. 1620–1692 Amsterdam)
Holl. 28
Etching
130 x 166 mm
Provenance: Zeitlin and Ver Brugge, Los Angeles

58
Rocky Landscape with Cross (no. 5)

ROELAND ROGHMAN
(Amsterdam c. 1620–1692 Amsterdam)
Holl. 29
Etching
131 x 162 mm
Provenance: Zeitlin and Ver Brugge, Los Angeles

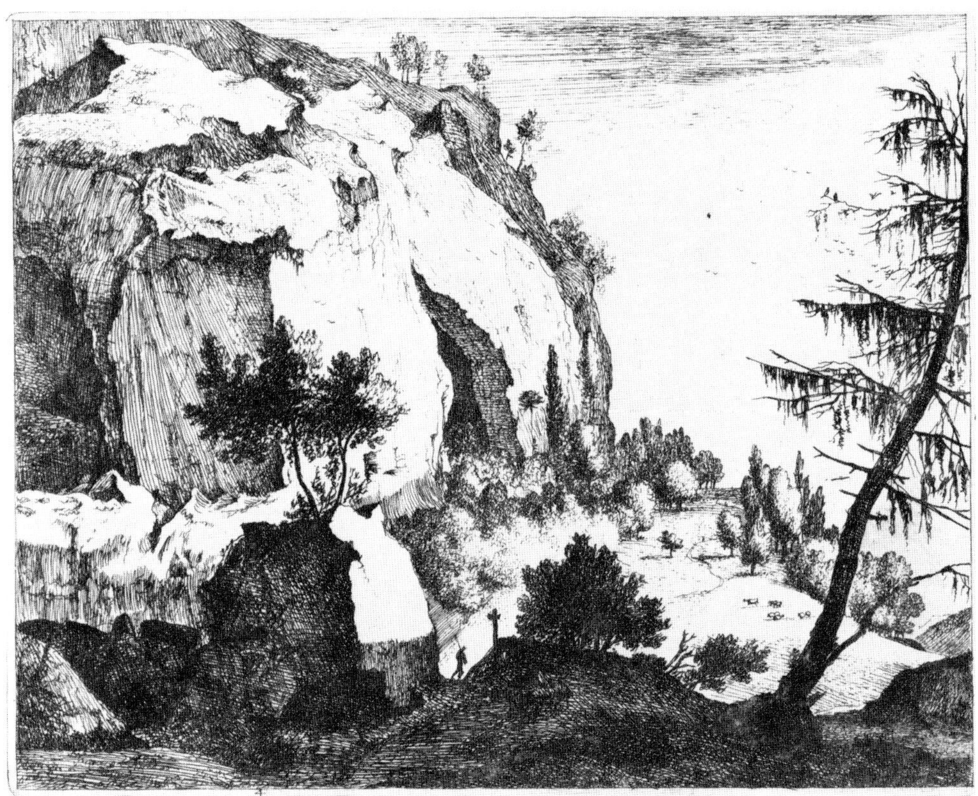

57

59
The Bridge (no. 7)

ROELAND ROGHMAN
(Amsterdam c. 1620–1692 Amsterdam)
Holl. 31
Etching
125 x 161 mm
Provenance: Zeitlin and Ver Brugge, Los Angeles

These three etchings belong to a series of eight prints depicting the mountainous region of Tirol. Roghman's style in this series is quite different from that of his other etchings. He illuminates his scenes with a striking bright sunlight that strongly delineates the boundaries between light and shadow and silhouettes repoussoir forms against lighter background areas. Though figures populate Roghman's Alpine views, they are subordinate to the landscape, always appearing in shadow.

While this series stands out among Roghman's prints, which consist mainly of illustrations of his native Dutch countryside, it is close to his landscape paintings, which comprise mostly foreign mountain scenes. In contrast to prints by Pieter Bruegel (see cat. no. 16) or Jan Both (see cat. no. 56), the locations or monuments in Roghman's prints cannot be identified, as they are creations of the artist's imagination inspired by a trip to Italy generally thought to have taken place around 1640.

Roeland Roghman

58

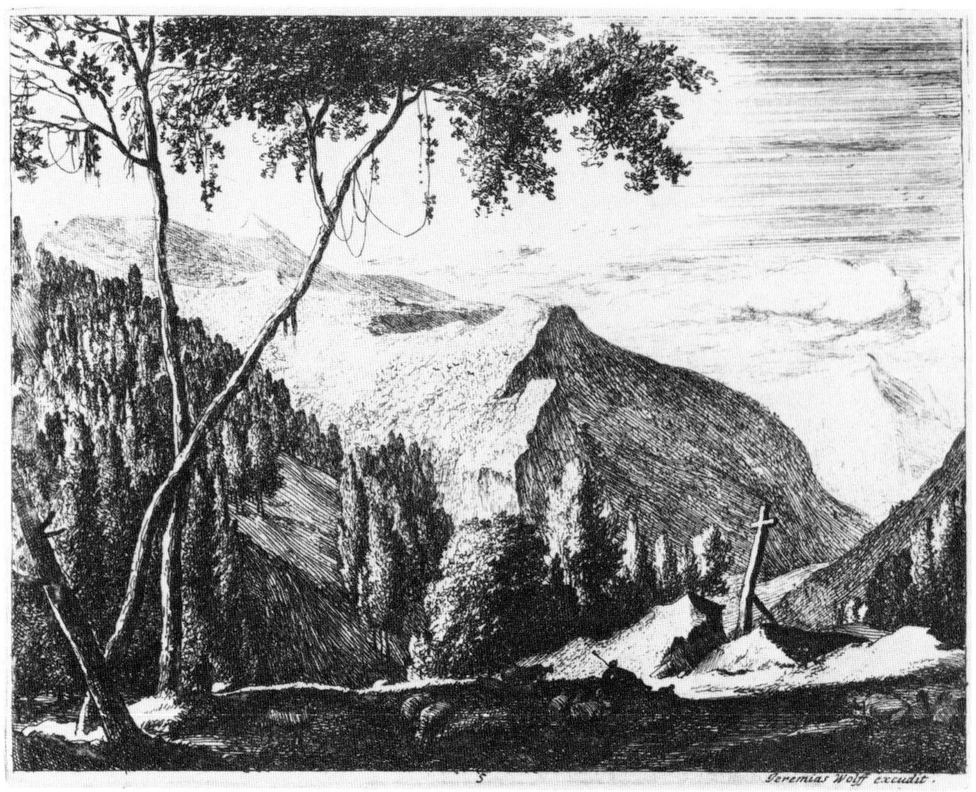

59

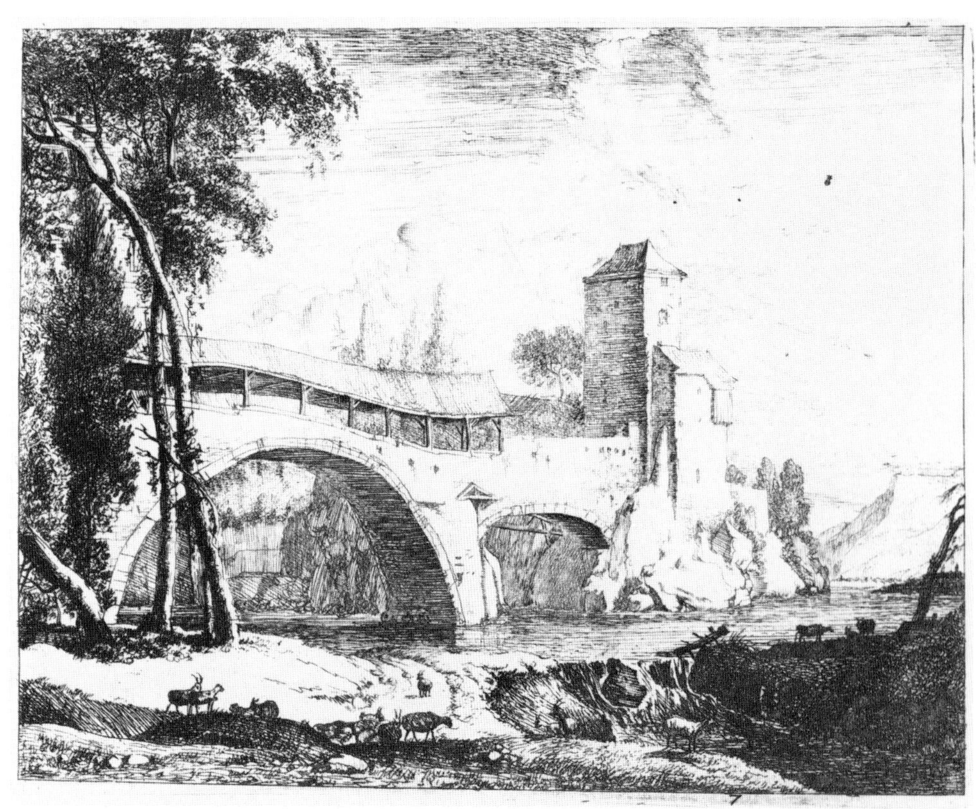

Allart van Everdingen

According to Houbraken, Allart van Everdingen studied with Roelandt Savery and then with Pieter Molijn in Haarlem. Between 1640 and 1644 he made a trip to Sweden and Norway, which is documented by drawings made during the trip. The landscapes he subsequently painted included Scandinavian motifs such as rock formations, log cabins, and firs, which he introduced into the vocabulary of Dutch landscape art. In 1645 Everdingen was back in Haarlem, where he lived until 1655. In 1657 he became a citizen of Amsterdam, remaining there until his death. In addition to painting, Everdingen appears to have supported himself as an art dealer.

Everdingen produced a large graphic oeuvre, the bulk of which is composed of a series of fifty-seven illustrations for Reynard the Fox. *He also made a series of four etchings depicting the mineral springs of Spa, which he probably visited around 1660.*

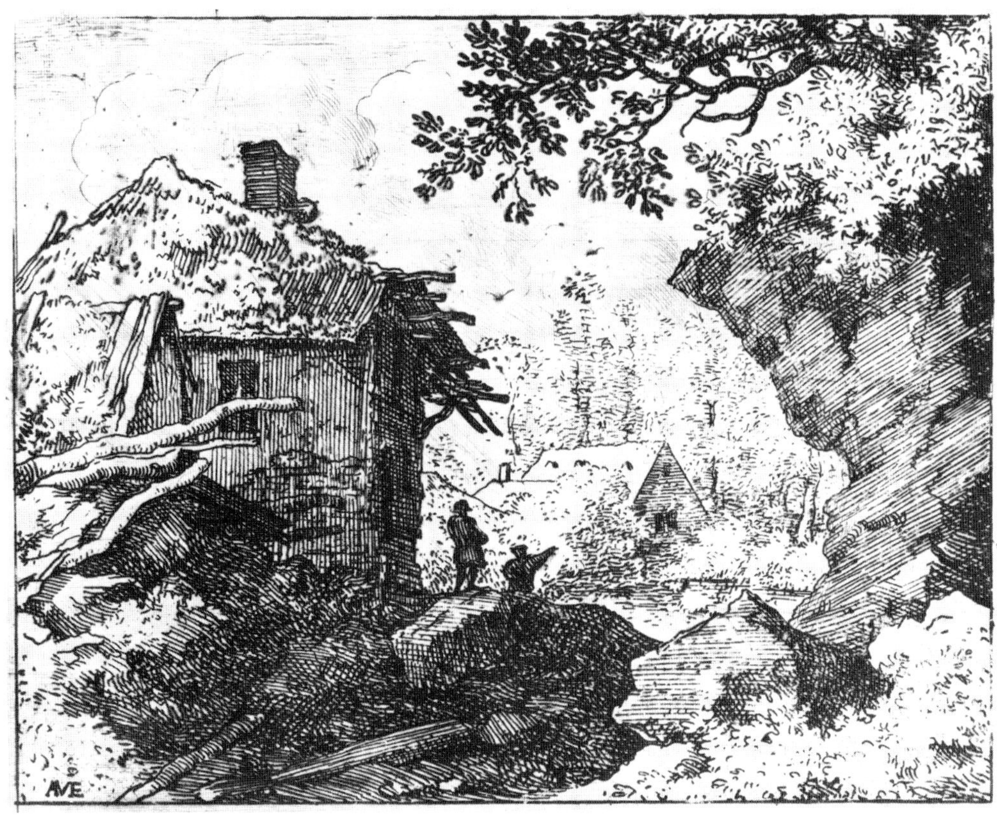

60

The Hut Seen from Behind

ALLART VAN EVERDINGEN
(Alkmaar 1621–1675 Amsterdam)
B. 30; Holl. 30 iii/iii; Dut. 30; Drugulin 29
Etching
105 x 134 mm
Provenance: H. S. Theobald (L. I/1375); Kennedy Galleries, New York

Based on a drawing in reverse now in Berlin, this print reveals some significant changes in the depiction of the landscape elements.[1] Everdingen changed the staffage from figures working with large wooden barrels to two figures conversing. He also turned the house from a wooden cottage into a straw hut of the type more typically found in Dutch prints by Abraham Bloemaert or Jacques de Gheyn. In addition Everdingen added a background landscape with an A-frame house emerging from the foliage that quite closely resembles the village views of the Master of the Small Landscapes (see cat. nos. 12–13) and related landscapes by Claes Jansz. Visscher (see cat. nos. 30–38). In this print Everdingen makes the Scandinavian motifs that so often appear in his work conform more closely to the Dutch landscape tradition.

1. Berlin, Kupferstichkabinett inv. no. 2351; *Landscape with Cottage*, black chalk and brown wash.

ALLART VAN EVERDINGEN

61

The Two Boats on the River

ALLART VAN EVERDINGEN
(Alkmaar 1621–1675 Amsterdam)
B. 58; Holl. 58 ii/iv;
Dut. 58; Drugulin 58
Etching
83 x 149 mm
Provenance: Bree (L. I/2630); R. E. Lewis, San Francisco

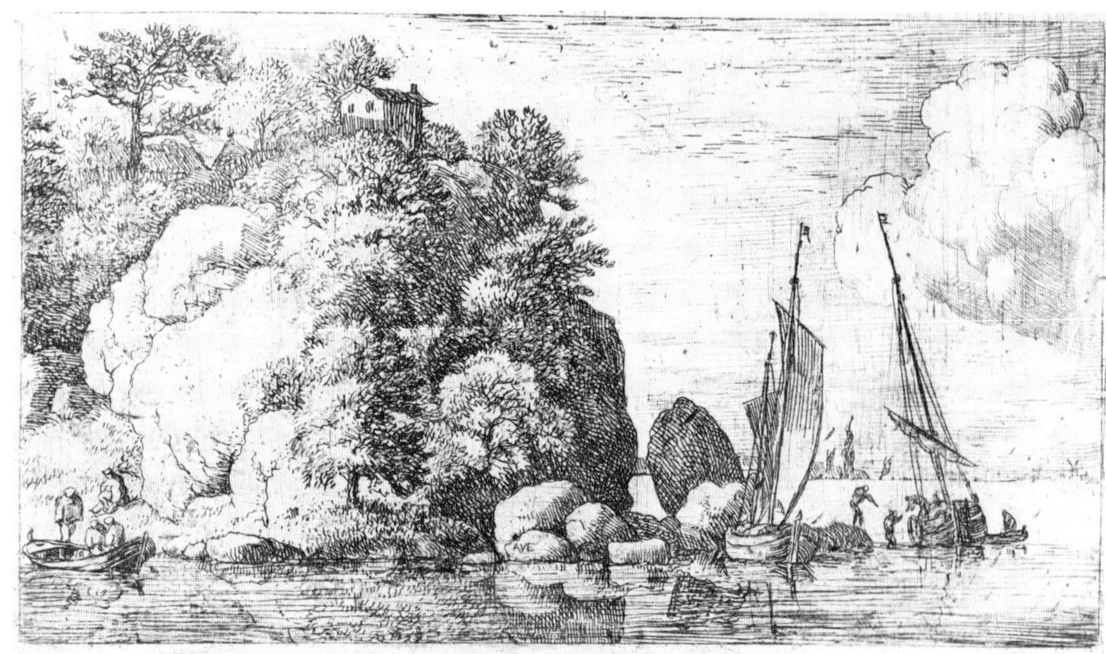

Everdingen, best known for his Scandinavian mountain landscapes, also made a number of seascapes. This type of calm sea is typical of his graphic works, while stormy seas dominate his painted seascapes. In creating his tranquil seascapes, Everdingen looked to river scenes by Salomon van Ruysdael and Jan van Goyen of the 1650s, in which the composition, similarly divided among land, river, and clouded sky, features boats reflected in calm waters. Everdingen still includes Scandinavian motifs such as the rocky cliff with the little hut perched above it.

Jacob van der Ulft

Jacob van der Ulft was baptized in Gorinchem on March 26, 1621. Like his father, Abraham Albertsz. van der Ulft, he became a glassmaker. It is not known whether he studied painting and drawing under an artist or received his training from his father. In 1643 he married Helena Willemsdr. de Wijn, and they had six children. Between 1660 and 1679 he was mayor of Gorinchem. It is now believed that van der Ulft, whose oeuvre consists mainly of Italianate paintings and drawings, did not go to Italy but derived his motifs and style from prints and drawings by other artists, particularly his contemporary Jan de Bisschop. He died in Noordwijk in 1689.

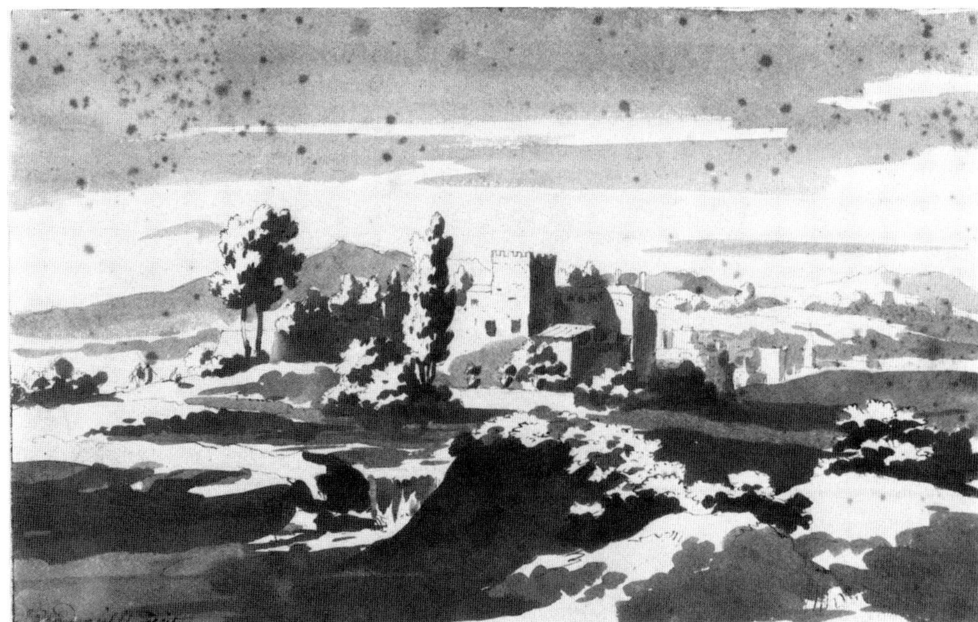

62

Castle outside the Porta del Popolo

JACOB VAN DER ULFT
(Gorinchem 1621–1689 Noordwijk)
Pen and brown ink with sepia wash
131 x 212 mm
Signed lower left
Provenance: Zeitlin and Ver Brugge, Los Angeles

The use of broad washes in this drawing combined with thin pen lines that define the details of the landscape is typical of van der Ulft's drawing style. His use of pen and washes, closely related to the style of his contemporary Jan de Bisschop, evokes the bright Italian sunlight characteristic of the works of many Dutch landscapists in the mid-seventeenth century.

A drawing of the same subject exists in van der Ulft's sketchbook in Paris (Institut Néerlandais inv. no. 6481; inscribed *gezigten naar het leven / in Italien / door / van der Ulft / 58 stuks*). The sketchbook drawing, however, entitled *Buyten Porte del Poplo,* is done only in washes. In addition the distribution of light and dark washes in the two drawings differs, as do small details such as the two figures in the left background, both standing in the sketchbook drawing. A number of the sketchbook drawings were made after drawings of Italian sites by dc Bisschop (Florence 1966, p. 72, no. 49). This, coupled with inaccuracies in the titling of a number of views of Rome, suggests that van der Ulft probably never visited Italy (Tissink and de Wit 1987, pp. 36–39). Whether the Grunwald Center drawing was meant as a preparatory drawing for the sketchbook or made after it is not clear.

A drawing by Giovanni Francesco Grimaldi depicts the same central section as the present drawing.[1] Although the two drawings are not exactly alike, they are close enough to suggest that they might be related. Much closer to the van der Ulft drawing is one attributed to Gaspar van Wittel in the collection of Hans van Leeuwen, Utrecht.[2] The drawings are quite close in composition, particularly in the shading and the placement of the shrubs.

---

1. Didier Bossart, *Dessins de la collection Thomas Ashby à la Bibliothèque Vaticane* (Vatican City: Bibliotheca Apostolica Vaticana, 1975), no. 146, pl. LVII.
2. Centraal Museum, *Nederlandse Tekeningen uit drie Eeuwen*, exh. cat. (Utrecht: Centraal Museum, 1978), no. 117.

Karel Dujardin

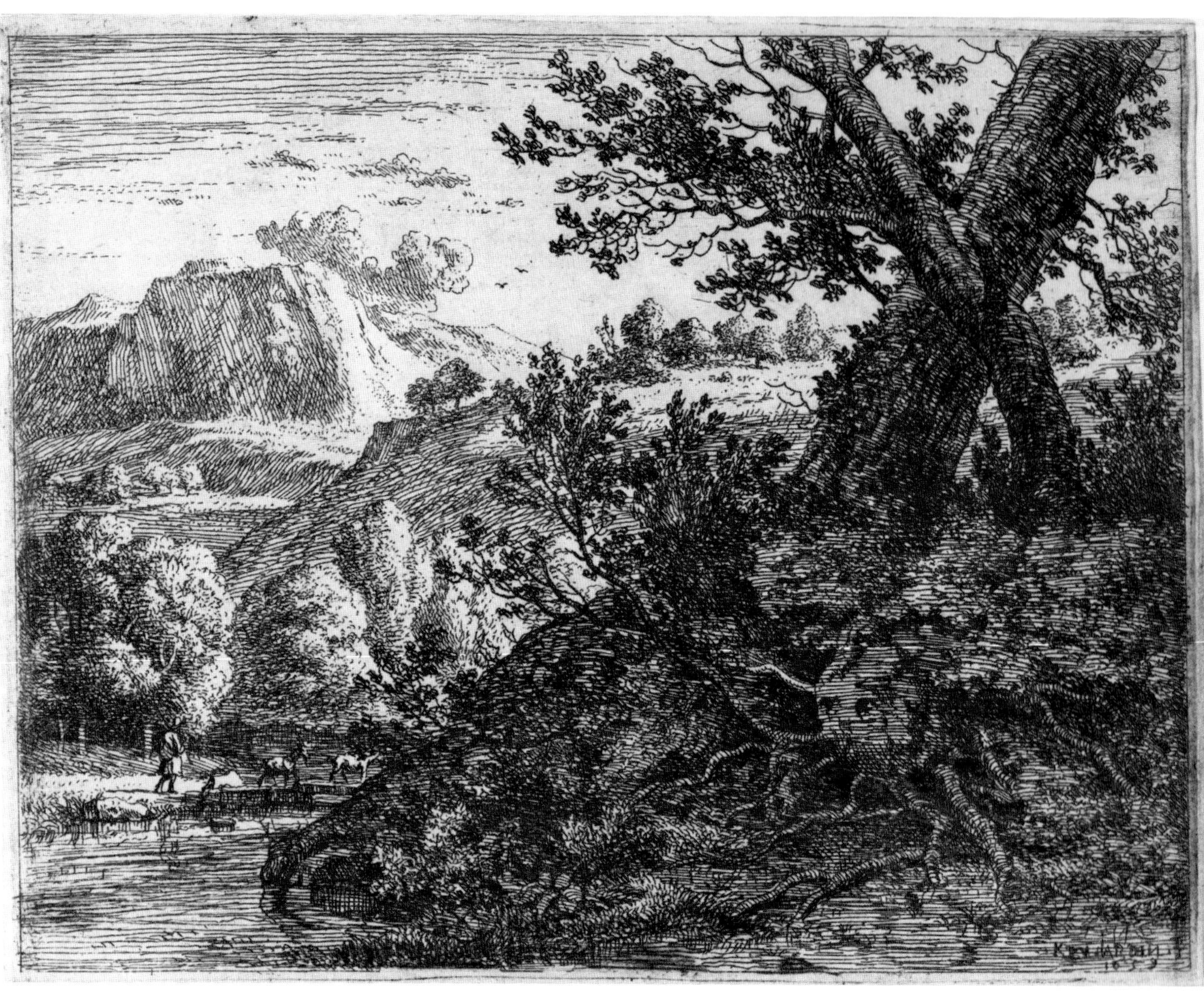

Karel Dujardin probably studied with Nicolaes Berchem, and it is presumed that he traveled to Italy between 1640 and 1652. In 1650 he traveled to Paris as a merchant and then to Lyons, where he married. His early Italianate work betrays the influence of Berchem and Jan Asselijn, while around 1655 he incorporated the influence of Paulus Potter's animal scenes into his work. In 1656 he was in The Hague as a founding member of the painters' association Pictura. In 1659 Dujardin was in Amsterdam. In 1675 he was in Rome on a trip that had taken him through Tangier, and in 1678, after a productive period in Rome, he moved to Venice, where he died later that year.

Dujardin is well known for his Italian landscapes, genre scenes, portraits, and religious subjects. His fifty-two prints, dating from 1652 to 1660, are primarily Italian landscapes and animal subjects.

63

The Trees with Roots Laid Bare (1659)

KAREL DUJARDIN
(Amsterdam c. 1622–1678 Venice)
Holl. 17 i/ii
Etching
136 x 176 mm
Provenance: Duke of Portland; R. E. Lewis, San Francisco

This print and Dujardin's *The Packer and the Two Asses* (cat. no. 64) are separated by one year in date and were published, in the second state, as part of the same series.

While the background of this print, with its brightly lit mountains and the shepherd tending his herd across the river, is typical of the Dutch Italianate style, the massive uprooted trees in the foreground are more akin to the depictions of untamed nature in Jacob van Ruisdael's prints of the 1650s (see cat. nos. 67–68). Dujardin, who created these prints in Amsterdam in 1659, was no doubt influenced by the work of Ruisdael, who became a citizen of Amsterdam that same year. Dujardin may have been attempting in this print to cater to two trends in landscape that were popular in Amsterdam at the time.

Karel Dujardin

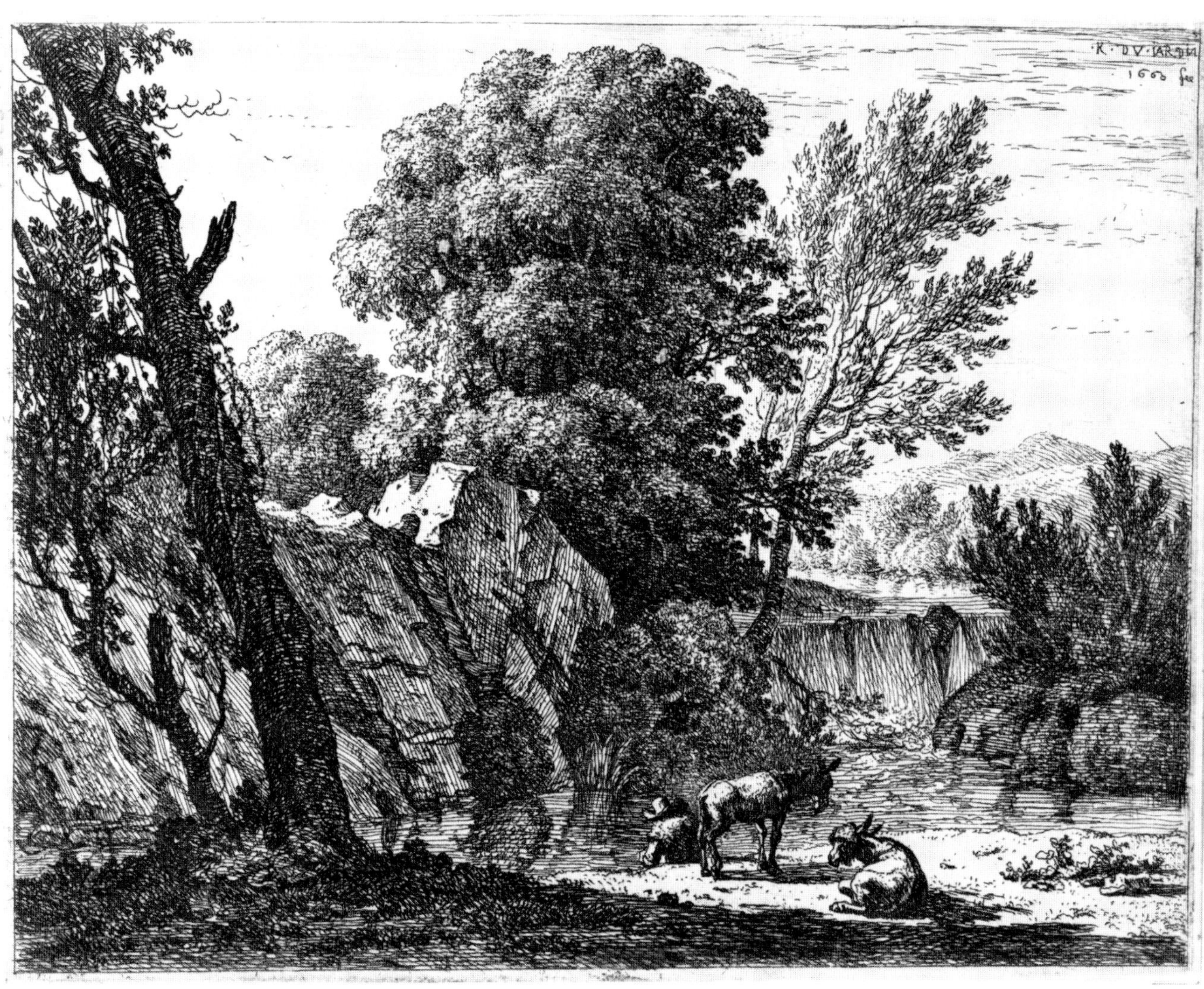

64

The Packer and the Two Asses (1660)

KAREL DUJARDIN
(Amsterdam c. 1622–1678 Venice)
Holl. 19 i/ii
Etching
136 x 176 mm
Provenance: Duke of Portland; R. E. Lewis, San Francisco

In this etching Dujardin was able to render the luminous quality of the Italian landscape that he captured in his paintings. Dujardin derived this luminosity not only from the southern landscape, which he may have visited around 1650, but also from the works of artists such as Jan Both (see cat. no. 56), who had been to Italy before him, and his teacher Nicolaes Berchem (1620–1683), who may not have gone to Italy but who incorporated this type of luminosity into his work.

The large tree that looms in the foreground differs from the thin birches that normally appear in the paintings of Italianates. The trees in this print and in *The Trees with Roots Laid Bare* (cat. no. 63) are similar to the massive, untamed trees found in the prints of Jacob van Ruisdael (see cat. nos. 67–68).

HERMAN NAIWINCX

Very little is known about the life of Herman Naiwincx. He was active mainly in Amsterdam, where he is mentioned as a merchant in 1648 and 1650, and may have traveled to Italy, as mountain landscapes are prominent in his work.

Naiwincx's rare paintings show an influence of the Italianate artists Jan Both and Jan Asselijn. He made eighteen etchings and a number of drawings, which have often been misattributed. His drawings are quite close in style to those of Jacob van Ruisdael and Herman Saftleven.

65

The Large Rock to the Left of a Riverbank

HERMAN NAIWINCX
(Schoonhoven c. 1624–after 1651 Hamburg?)
B. 2; Holl. 2 i/iii
Etching
112 x 125 mm
Provenance: R. E. Lewis, San Francisco

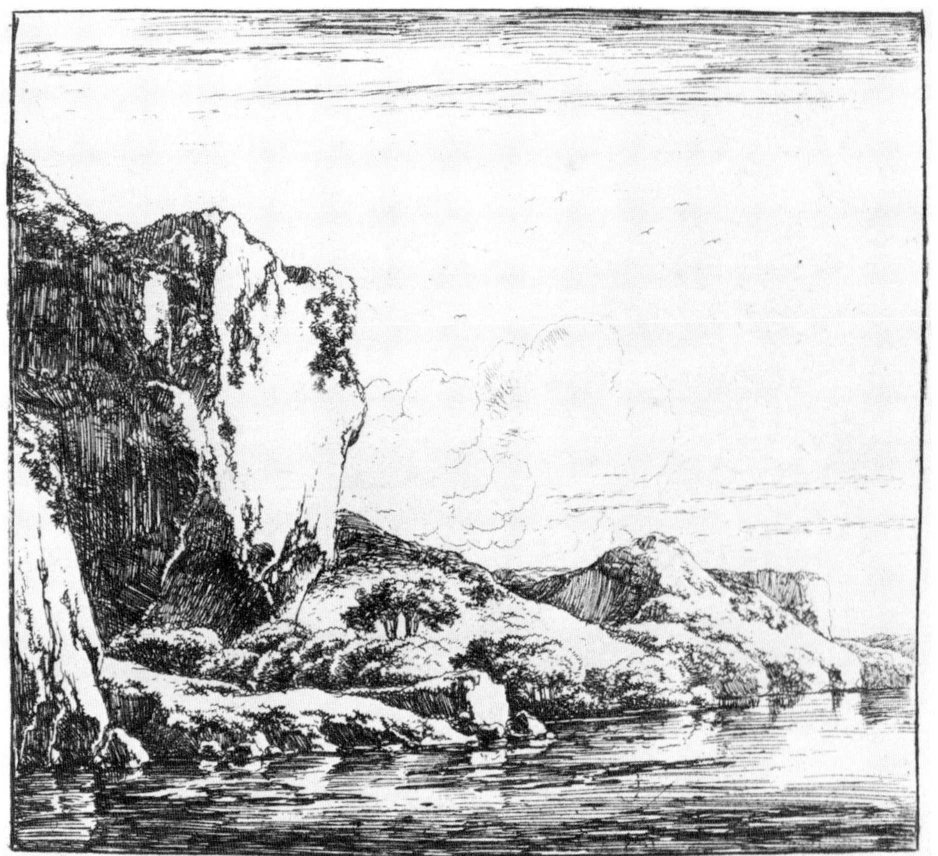

This print is the second plate from a series of eight landscapes. Naiwincx's representations of wooded cliffs on the shores of a large body of water were influenced by the works of Herman Saftleven, who was the first to adopt this theme. Such views are also found in drawings by Naiwincx, such as one in the Lugt collection (see Brussels 1968–69, no. 108). Naiwincx's bright lighting of the cliffs is probably derived from the works of Jan Both (see cat. no. 56), who also influenced Naiwincx (Brussels 1968–69, p. 108).

This type of rocky landscape is not typical of the Dutch countryside but suggests some foreign land, as does the landscape in Allart van Everdingen's *The Two Boats on the River* (cat. no. 61). It is not known, however, whether Naiwincx traveled or, like many other Dutch artists, picked up foreign motifs from the works of others.

Johannes Ruisscher

Following a period of activity in Dordrecht and in the area of Cleves, Johannes Ruisscher worked as a landscape painter at the Brandenburg court in Berlin until 1661. From 1662 to 1675 he was court painter for Elector Johann Georg of Saxony. The date and place of his death are unknown.

Ruisscher was known in Holland as "the young Hercules" because of the influence of Hercules Segers's technical innovations evident in his twenty-nine landscape etchings. Ruisscher's drawings of around 1648 betray the influence of Rembrandt and his circle, however, while his later prints made in Germany are less experimental and consist mainly of topographical views. A number of Ruisscher's plates were acquired by Anthonie Waterloo, who reworked and republished them under his own name.

66

The Ruin

JOHANNES RUISSCHER
(Franeker c. 1625–after 1675)
B. 2 (under Waterloo); Holl. 4 ii/iii; Tr. 4 ii/iii
Etching, reworked by Anthonie Waterloo
86 x 102 mm
Provenance: Wald-Blondell; W. Roscoe; C. G. Boerner, Düsseldorf

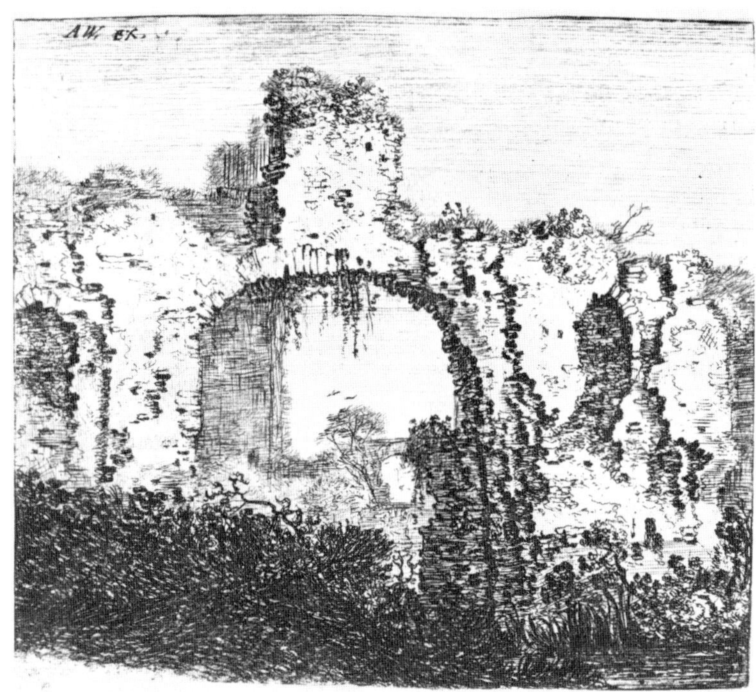

The only known impression of the first state of this print is in London. This second state was reworked and published by Anthonie Waterloo.

This print was thought by Fraenger (1922, pp. 26–27) to have been an early work by Hercules Segers (1589/90–1633/38). Indeed Ruisscher's treatment of the decaying ruins is quite similar to Segers's handling of ruins in his etchings of Brederode Castle and the Tomb of the Horatii and Curiatii (Haverkamp-Begemann 1975, nos. 39, 40, 45). The ruins in this instance have not been identified; Trautscholdt (1973, p. 119), however, has suggested a relation to Roman ruins.

In contrast to Hieronymus Cock's more archaeological representation of the Colosseum (see cat. no. 14), Ruisscher's depiction of ruins is instead a *vanitas* symbol, pointing to the temporality of man's creations.

Jacob van Ruisdael

The son of a frame maker and art dealer, Jacob van Ruisdael probably studied with his father and with his uncle the painter Salomon van Ruysdael, although his early work shows none of their influence. His earliest known works date from the 1640s, and he became a member of the Haarlem guild in 1648. In 1650 Ruisdael visited Bentheim, probably in the company of Nicolaes Berchem, and around 1656 he settled in Amsterdam, where he lived until his death in 1682. His only documented pupil was Meindert Hobbema.

Ruisdael's early work of 1648–49 shows the influence of Cornelis Vroom, but following his trip to Germany in 1650, his landscapes become more monumental and his trees more massive. Ruisdael's numerous paintings include examples of every type of landscape, including marines, city views, and winter scenes. His paintings of waterfalls of the 1650s show the influence of Scandinavian motifs found in the work of Allart van Everdingen. Considering his prolific output as a painter, his graphic oeuvre is relatively small, including twelve etchings, all landscapes, and 110 drawings.

67

The Little Bridge (c. 1651–55)

JACOB VAN RUISDAEL
(Haarlem c. 1628/29–1682 Amsterdam)
B. 1; Holl. 1 ii/iii; Dut. 1; Wurz. 1; Keyes 8
196 x 277 mm
Etching
Provenance: Oswald Stein; P. Davidsohn (L. I/654); W. Esdaile (L. I/2617) F. Lehmann (L. I/1024); O. P. Reed, Los Angeles

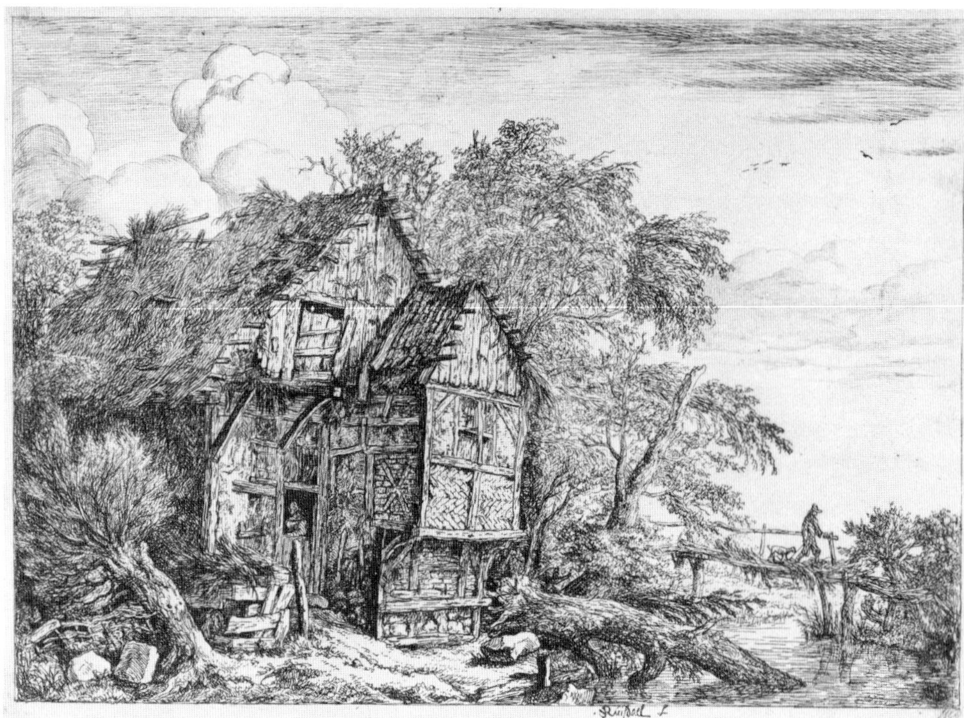

This print and *The Thatched Cottage at the Top of the Hill* (cat. no. 68) are part of a group of four prints related in size, style, and technique, usually considered a set but not numbered as such.[1] Although they are dated relatively early in Ruisdael's career, about 1651–55, they appear to be the last of his thirteen essays in the technique of printmaking, done over a span of about ten years at the beginning of his career.

The reasons for Ruisdael's having ceased to make prints by the time he reached the age of twenty-seven are not clear. It has been suggested that in his etching he could not attain the spatial recession and variations of light that he was capable of achieving in his paintings and that perhaps he did not want to attempt the more complex technique of multiple bitings of the etching plate used by earlier printmakers to suggest deep space (Slive 1982, pp. 232–34).

The cottage depicted in this image is of gable and tie-beam construction, typical of the houses that Ruisdael saw on his travels in the early 1650s in the area of Bentheim.[2] This trip to the region near the border between the United Provinces and Germany was to have a lasting influence on the artist, who thereafter incorporated distinctly German motifs such as this cottage or the Castle of Bentheim into his work. A drawing by Ruisdael in the Teylers Museum, Haarlem (inv. no. Q*51), depicts similar cottages.

This second state of the etching, the one most frequently found, is characterized not only by drypoint additions to the trees but also by the addition of clouds to the sky by another hand. It is not known if these changes, like the print itself, were made by a professional etcher following a drawing or instructions by Ruisdael. The clouds that appear in the first state of *Landscape with Travelers* (B. 2), the only clouds in this group of etchings that were present in Ruisdael's original design, are quite different, appearing as flat striations rather than the puffy clouds found in this state.[3]

---

1. Keyes (1977) divides Ruisdael's etchings into three categories: the five Haarlem-period works, which are signed and dated (nos. 1–5); these four prints (nos. 6–10); and four supposedly very early works (nos. 11–14).
2. Schepers 1976, cited by Slive 1982, p. 253.
3. Weigel (1843) wrote that the plate for this print as well as those for *The Thatched Cottage at the Top of the Hill* and *The Great Beech* (B. 2) had been in the possession of Pierre-François Basan (1723–1793) and were then in England. Wurzbach (1910) mentioned only this plate as being in existence but did not mention its location.

Jacob van Ruisdael

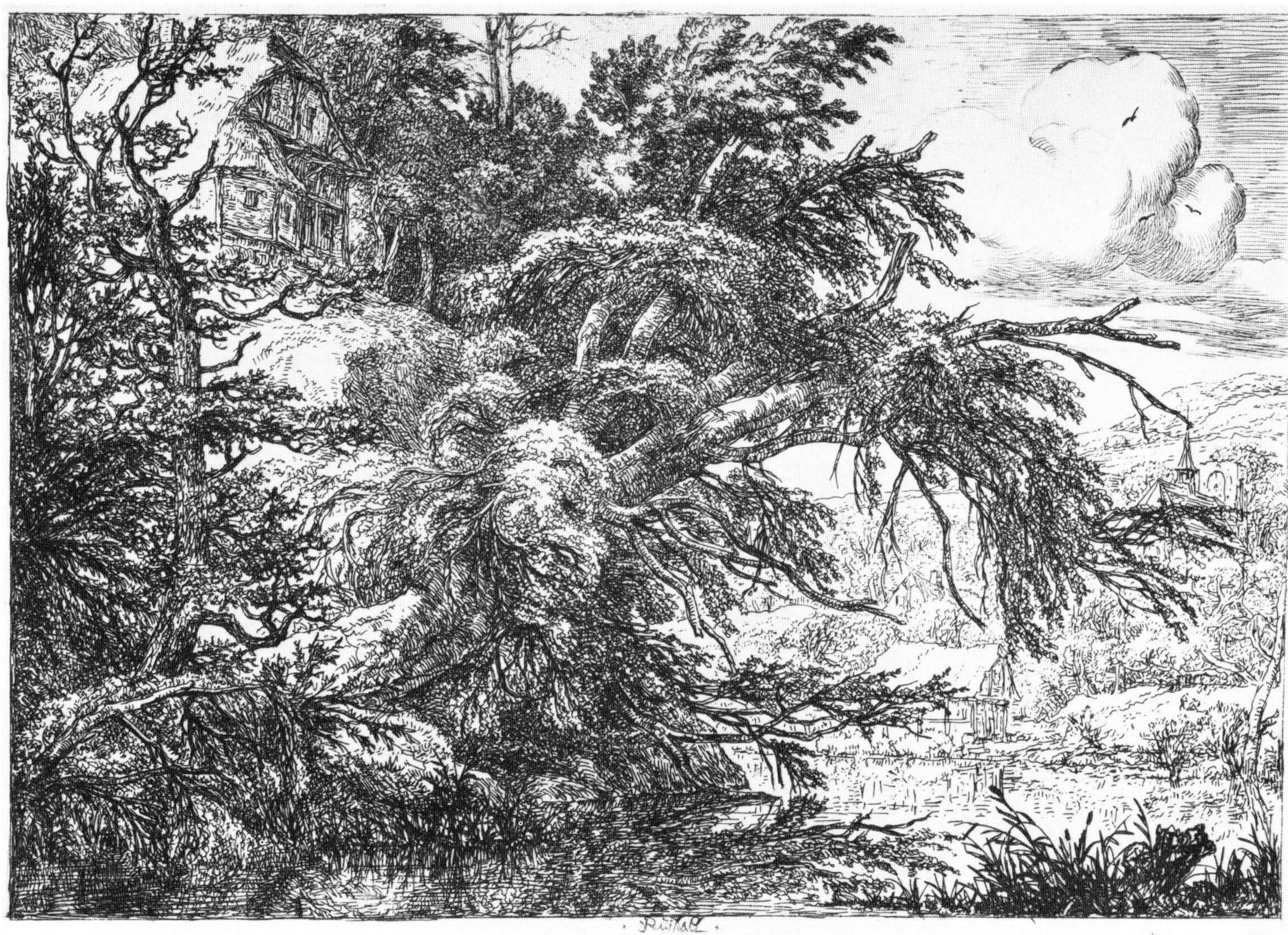

68

The Thatched Cottage at the Top of the Hill (c. 1651–55)

JACOB VAN RUISDAEL
(Haarlem c. 1628/29–1682 Amsterdam)
B. 3; Holl. 3 ii/ii; Dut. 3; Wurz. 3; Keyes 7
Etching
186 x 273 mm
Provenance: William Schab, New York

This etching and *The Little Bridge* (cat. no. 67) are part of the same series. The motif of the cottage encompassed by the encroaching, untamed forest, with a large beech balancing precariously on the edge of the hill, is typical of van Ruisdael's early prints.

The clouds in the upper right were added in the second state by another hand. They may have been added in order to make the print more closely approximate Ruisdael's work of the 1660s, in which clouds such as these were more prominent (Keyes 1977, p. 12). Clearly the execution of the clouds is much cruder than that of the rest of the etching. This, however, is the most frequently found state of the print.[1]

1. Weigel (1843, no. 3) stated that Pierre-François Basan (1723–1793) had been in possession of the plate for this print but that at the time Weigel was writing the plate was in England.

Adriaen Verboom

69
The Hamlet

ADRIAEN VERBOOM
(Rotterdam 1628–c. 1670 Amsterdam?)
B. 1; Wurz. 1 ii/ii; Dut. 1 ii/ii
Etching
130 x 175 mm
Provenance: R. E. Lewis, San Francisco

70
The Pond

ADRIAEN VERBOOM
(Rotterdam 1628–c. 1670 Amsterdam?)
B. 2; Wurz. 2 ii/ii, Dut. 2 ii/ii
Etching
130 x 173 mm
Provenance: R. E. Lewis, San Francisco

Very little is known about the life of Adriaen Verboom. Brother of the landscape painter Willem Verboom, he worked first in Haarlem and then in Amsterdam, where he died around 1670. A landscape painter, etcher, and draftsman, he developed a style, especially in his paintings, that was strongly influenced by the work of Jacob van Ruisdael. His drawings from around 1640–50 are sometimes mistaken for those of Cornelis Vroom and Claes van Beresteyn. Only six etchings, all landscapes, have been attributed to Verboom.

Because of their similar dimensions and compositions, *The Hamlet* and *The Pond* are generally considered to have been composed as a pair. The delicate etching of the trees and clouds recalls Verboom's drawings. His style is similar to that of Cornelis Vroom (1590/91–1661) but is probably derived from the early works of Vroom's student Jacob van Ruisdael (see cat. nos. 67–68) (Brussels 1968–69, p. 161).

While very different in character, *The Pond* was clearly derived from an earlier source, namely Esaias van de Velde's print *Wooded Landscape with Travelers* (Burchard 1917, no. 5). Verboom, like van de Velde, placed a large, twisted tree on the right, silhouetted against the sky, and a smaller clump of trees in the left background. In addition the small tree in the center of Verboom's composition is a reduced version of a similarly placed tree in van de Velde's print. Verboom's treatment of the landscape is, however, less stylized than that of his predecessor.

Ackley (1981, p. 263) has dated the two prints around 1663, comparing their style with that of Verboom's drawings from that period. These second states were reworked in engraving, probably by a publisher.

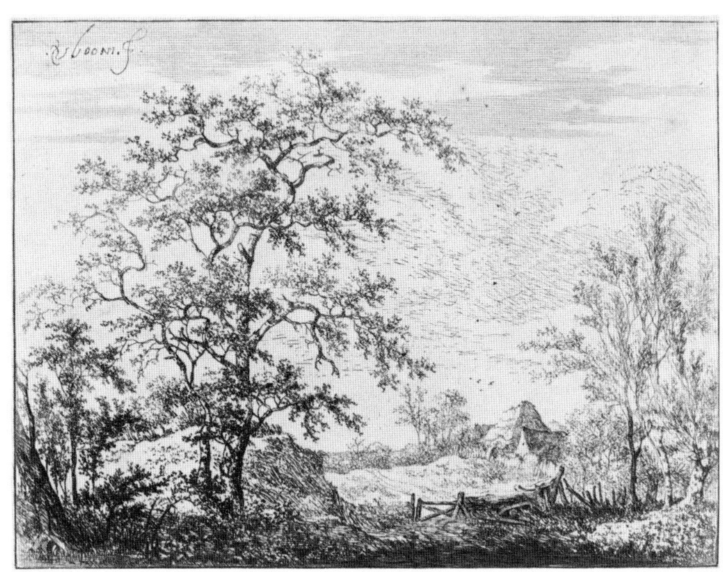

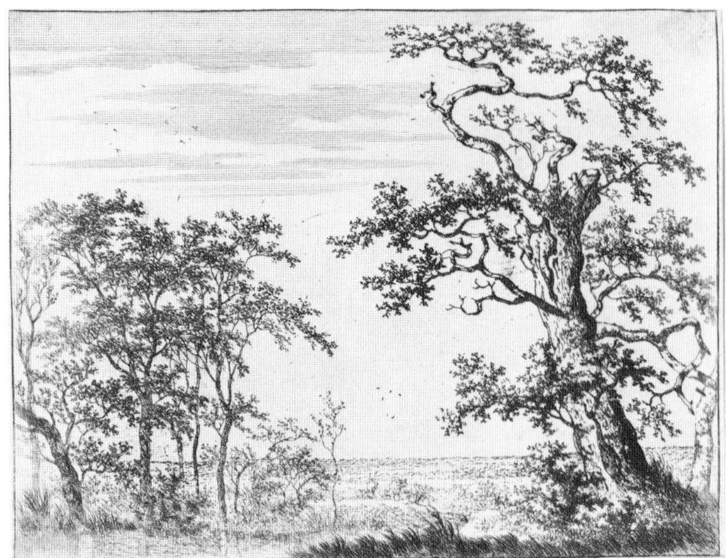

Josua de Grave

71

The Town of Grave (1674)

JOSUA DE GRAVE
(Amsterdam 1643–1712 The Hague)
Pen and brown ink with gray wash
102 x 156 mm
Inscribed *J de Grave fecit* lower right; dated and titled on mount
Provenance: Zeitlin and Ver Brugge, Los Angeles
Bibliography: van Hasselt 1967, no. 123a

Josua de Grave entered the Guild of St. Luke in Haarlem as an apprentice in 1659. Around 1667 he traveled to France, returning to Holland in 1668. He was married in Maastricht in 1670 and the following year moved to The Hague, where he lived until his death in 1712.

De Grave worked very closely with two other artists, Valentin Klotz and Barnardus Klotz. The three traveled together throughout the Netherlands, sketching cities and towns and often drawing the same sites and copying one another's drawings. Between 1674 and 1676 they traveled with the Dutch army, sketching the towns they passed through and the activities of the troops at rest. De Grave, known mainly for his topographical drawings of cities, also drew and painted imaginary landscapes and gardens.

The date assigned to this drawing assumes added significance as the town of Grave was liberated by William III in October 1674 after having been besieged for two years by the French under the Marquis de Chavigny (Breitbarth-van der Stok 1969, p. 104). While de Grave depicts the town in a traditional cityscape, the presence of the Dutch army is duly indicated by the boat in the center filled with several small figures and two cannons as well as two additional cannons standing on the shore. De Grave usually drew the everyday activities of the army rather than its battles.

De Grave made another drawing of this subject (Amsterdam, Rijksmuseum inv. no. A4549), which is dated by the artist on the image November 15, 1674, just as the Grunwald Center drawing is dated by another hand on the mount.[1] While the two drawings are almost identical, the Amsterdam version displays slightly looser handling of details such as the boats on the left and the small church on the right.[2] It is possible that this drawing was made by de Grave after the one in Amsterdam, but the purpose of the drawings that he made on his travels with the army or of copies of these drawings is still unclear.

1. Both drawings are accepted by van Hasselt as by de Grave (van Hasselt 1965, no. 12e, and van Hasselt 1967, no. 123a).

2. The Grunwald Center version extends slightly further on the right and upper edges; it is possible, however, that the Amsterdam drawing was cut down.

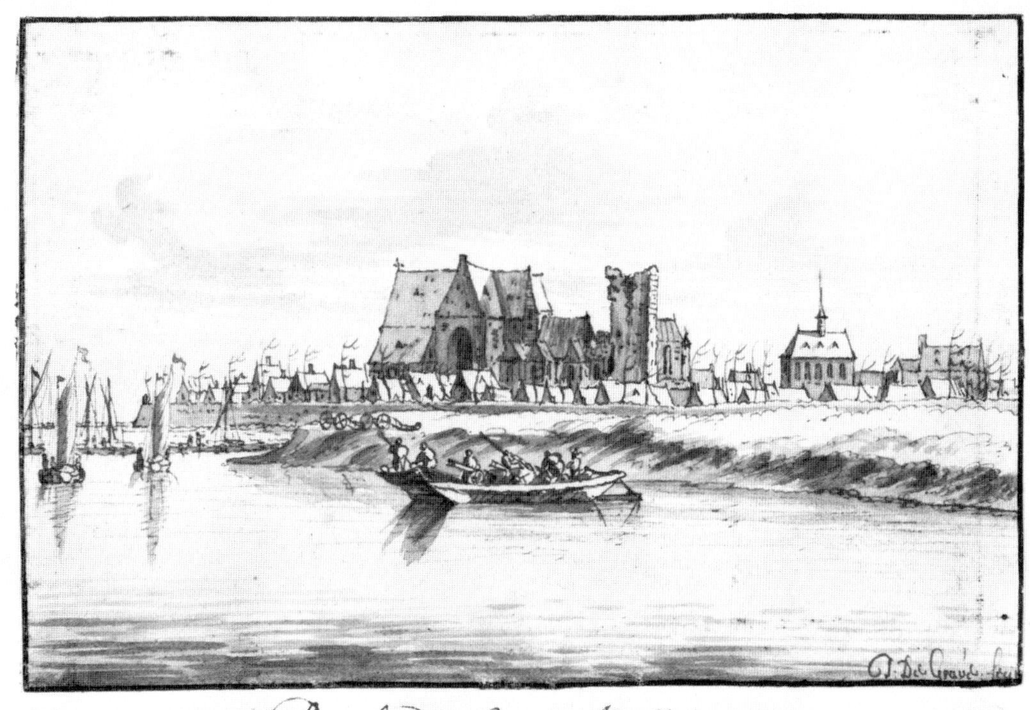

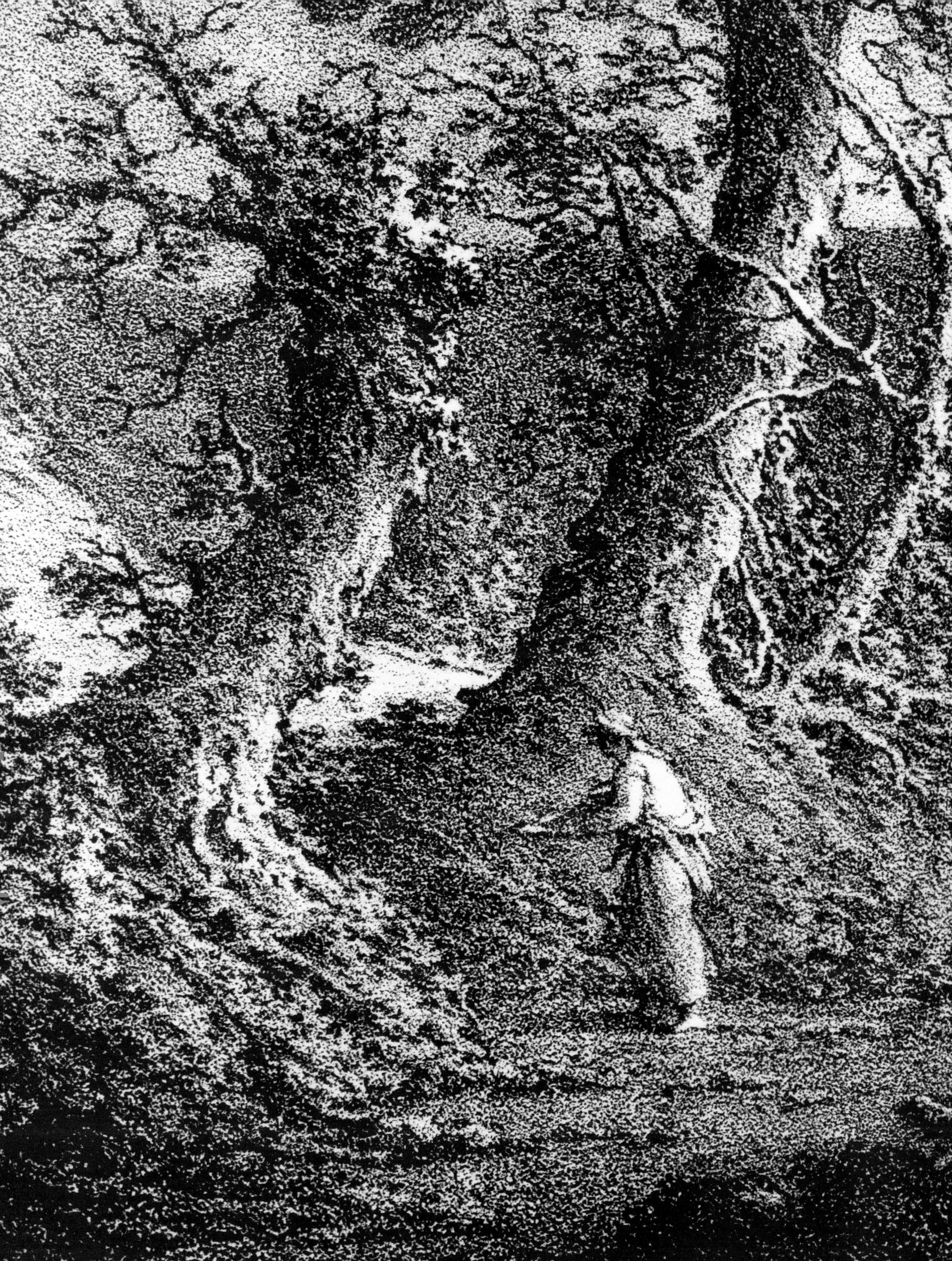

English & Scottish

Detail of cat. no. 75

Wenzel Hollar

Trained as a topographical draftsman and etcher in Frankfurt, Wenzel Hollar traveled and lived in present-day Germany and the Netherlands until he joined Thomas Howard, the first earl of Arundel, on his journey to the Bohemian imperial court in Prague in 1636. Hollar accompanied the earl to England later that year and took up residence there, except for several years of exile (1644–52) in Antwerp during the English Civil War. He continued to earn his living as a topographical landscape artist and etcher of other artists' designs, first in the employ of the earl of Arundel and later in the service of the duke of York. In 1639 or 1640 Hollar also served as drawing master to the young Prince of Wales, the future Charles II.

Although he was a prolific artist who painted history pictures and portraits as well as making numerous figure, animal, and botanical studies, Hollar's primary contribution to the history of British art was as one of the most significant and influential topographical artists of the seventeenth century. His exact yet sensitive drawings and prints displayed a real understanding of both pictorial principles and the topographic features unique to each site he recorded. In this respect he set the standard for all British landscape artists who followed him.

In 1668 he was commissioned by Charles II to accompany the expedition of Lord Henry Howard to record the town and fortifications of Tangier. This turned out to be his last major commission, as he was never again able to secure such patronage and spent his final years producing plates for booksellers, dying in poverty in London in 1677.

72
Cathedral at Strasbourg

WENZEL HOLLAR
(Prague 1607–1677 London)
Parthey 892
Etching
209 x 177 mm
Provenance: T. J. Thompson (L. I/2442); F. Schindler (L. I/2351); Kennedy Galleries, New York

The Strasbourg Cathedral is an important example of the Rayonnant style of Gothic architecture, which takes its name from the French word *rayonner,* meaning to radiate or shine, and is characterized by extensive use of elaborate window tracery. Whitney Stoddard has defined the style as a distinct phase of late Gothic dominant in France and extending northward to Strasbourg from the 1230s through the fourteenth century, reaching its purest form in Sainte-Chapelle, Paris (Stoddard 1972, pp. 279–310).

Like Sainte-Chapelle, the Strasbourg Cathedral emphasizes a vertical sweep of elegantly articulated windows that reduce the mass of the walls to a nearly weblike support for the colored glass. This attracted Hollar's attention and challenged his mastery of the delicate working of the etching needle. In this print of the cathedral, we see just how capable he was of rendering the most minute detail: the tracery in the rose window of the facade, for example, the details of which are visible despite the severe angle from which it is drawn, and the sculptural ornamentation of the single tower, which diminishes in scale without losing its legibility.

Similarly, Hollar is capable of concentrating on the life around the cathedral, however diminished by the high vantage point from which the activity is seen. A crowd of people have gathered on market day and mingle around the carts and booths set up for the exchange of goods. However crowded it is, the scene is not congested; one can make out clearly just what each person is doing and even, in some cases, what a person is carrying or holding.

This print is among Hollar's most monumental depictions of notable ecclesiastical architecture and was executed during his brief tenure on the Continent between 1644 and 1652 (see entry for cat. no. 73). It demonstrates Hollar's ability to bring his accurate and precise descriptive talents to bear on the life of the city as it is acted out on the grounds of its great cathedral.

WENZEL HOLLAR

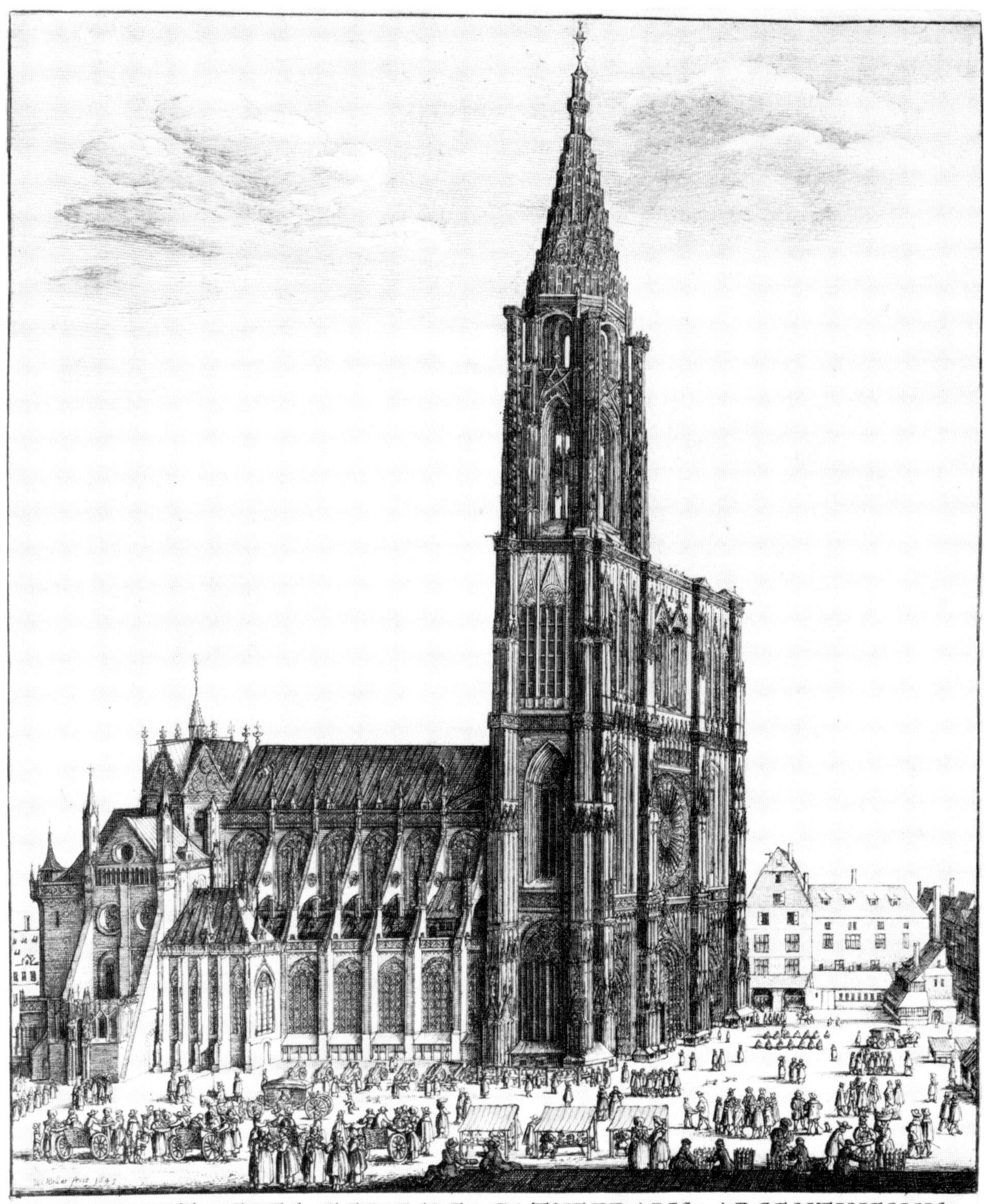

TVRRIS ET ÆDES ECCLESIÆ CATHEDRALIS ARGENTINENSIS.

à Wenceslao Hollar Bohemo, primo ad vivum delineata, et aquæ forti æri insculpta. A.° 1630. denuoq facta Antuerpiæ, A.° 1645.

WENZEL HOLLAR

73
Landscape (1645)

WENZEL HOLLAR
(Prague 1607–1677 London)
From the series Six Views of Albury
Parthey 938
Etching
81 x 157 mm
Provenance: Zeitlin and Ver Brugge, Los Angeles

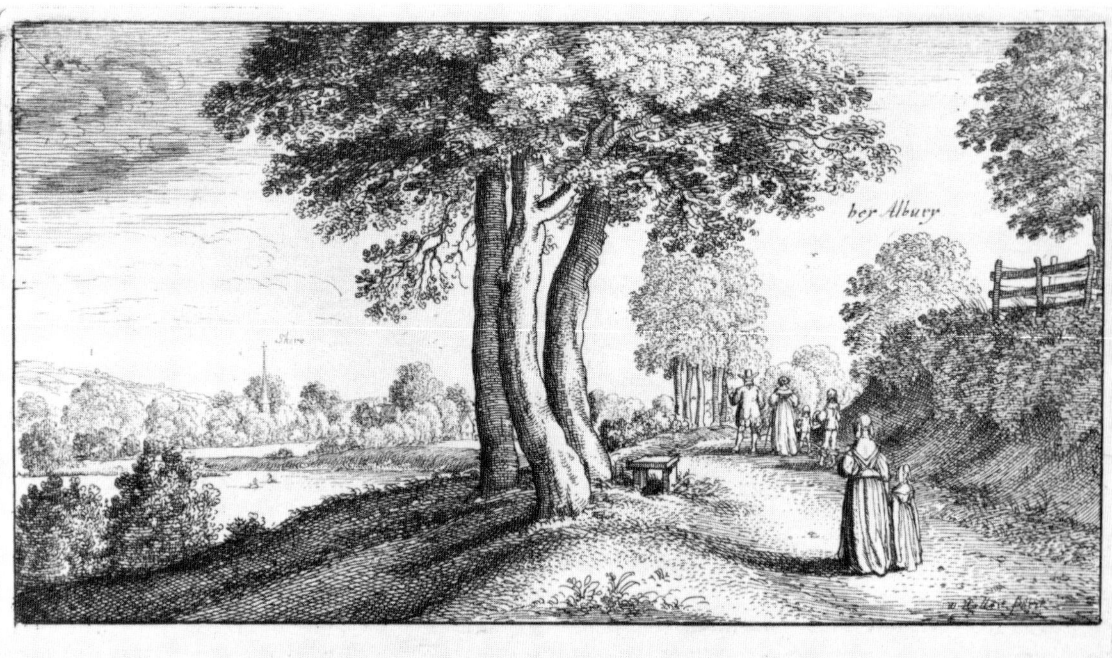

This print is from a series of six etchings of the countryside around Albury, the country seat of the earl of Arundel. Its subject is Albury Park, near Guildford in Surrey, purchased by the earl in 1638, whose gardens were redesigned in the 1650s and 1660s by Lord Henry Howard.

Hollar's work had come to the attention of Lord Arundel when the famous collector was ambassador to the court of Ferdinand II of Vienna in 1636. Perhaps with the intention of engaging the artist to illustrate his travels on the Continent, Lord Arundel purchased Hollar's suite of twenty-three etchings entitled Amoenissimae Effigies. These comprised views of Prague, Strasbourg, Nuremberg, Augsburg, and other German cities, and were published in 1635 (Parthey 1853, nos. 695–718). Hollar then joined Lord Arundel and in 1636 published for him a view of Würzburg (Parthey 1853, no. 735). In the same year Hollar accompanied Lord Arundel to England and in the following year etched his first plates there. With constant commissions from his patron as well as printsellers, Hollar's years in England brought him his greatest success. Unfortunately Lord Arundel was forced to flee England in 1642, during the Civil War, and Hollar himself was arrested in 1644, only to escape and join his patron in Antwerp. There, despite the earl's death in 1646, Hollar produced an enormous amount of work, etching more than 350 plates over the next six years, including the suite to which this print belongs.

In this print a family walks along a path at the edge of the river Tillingbourne with the Shere Church of Albury barely visible in the distance. Hollar's sure sense of topographical draftsmanship is well served by his control of the etching technique. A wide range of etched marks, from parallel lines in the sky to delicate webs of lines in the trees to densely cross-hatched lines describing shadows across the foreground, render the landscape around Albury with verisimilitude. Indeed the precision of Hollar's technique and the formality of his composition give Albury a calm, peaceful, well-managed air, benefiting, no doubt, from the earl's generous patronage. One would not sense that Lord Arundel had been driven from England only four years earlier and never again saw his country seat. Thus this is in a sense a memorial image, a representation of the peaceful and bountiful life that the earl was forced to leave behind.

Paul Sandby

Paul Sandby began his career in 1747 as a draftsman with the Board of Ordnance in London. He left the board in 1757 and spent considerable time at Windsor with his brother Thomas, drawing views of the castle and surrounding grounds and forest. Settling in London in 1760, he pursued a career as an independent artist specializing in landscapes and views of London, which he produced in etching, watercolor, and after 1774, aquatint. In 1768 Sandby was appointed chief drawing master at the Royal Military Academy in Woolwich, a position he occupied until his retirement in 1796. In 1768 Sandby and several other artists founded the Royal Academy, where he frequently exhibited watercolors of Windsor Castle and other country house portraits, thus contributing to the acceptance of the medium as one worthy of exhibition and patronage.

Sandby achieved preeminence for his pioneering achievements in the media of aquatint and watercolor. Although not the inventor of the aquatint process, he was the first to call it aquatinta, *and his very early and skillful use of it in England produced several series of prints between 1775 and 1789, most notably a three-part set comprising thirty-six views of Wales. By the time of his retirement, public interest in Sandby's work had declined; his advances had been superceded within his own lifetime by those of younger, more innovative artists. Yet more than any other artist of his generation, Sandby developed the art of watercolor as a major form of pictorial expression upon which younger artists could build.*

74

Hilly Landscape

PAUL SANDBY
(Nottingham 1730/31–1809 Paddington)
Watercolor and graphite
212 x 273 mm
Provenance: Zeitlin and Ver Brugge, Los Angeles

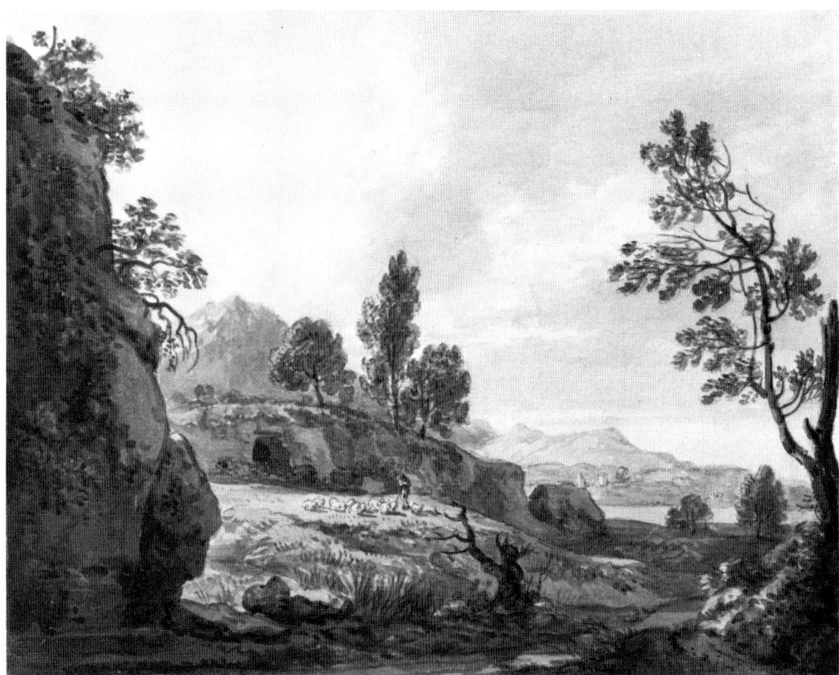

This small, idealized watercolor is one of a large group of landscape drawings executed by Sandby or his students as a practical exercise in technique and composition. The watercolor is undated, as is the case with many of Sandby's capriccios. Bruce Robertson has suggested that it was drawn at least a decade into the artist's career but prior to the last ten years of his life, noting that the relative delicacy and variety of brush strokes in the foliage point to the mature artist, while the relative tightness in the execution and lack of exaggeration in tree forms suggest it was drawn before Sandby's landscape compositions slipped into stylized formulas.[1]

Generally drawn or painted without reference to a specific location, Sandby's idealized landscapes, including this one, often depict a mountainous or hilly Italian countryside that recalls the work of such artists as Gaspar Dughet, Marco Ricci, or, less frequently, the dramatic landscapes of Salvator Rosa. *Hilly Landscape*, however, also includes particularized foreground elements more reminiscent of motifs found in Sandby's watercolors, aquatints, or etchings of actual English or, more specifically, Welsh vistas.[2] This drawing nevertheless provides a more intimate close-up view of the landscape as well as a gentler, more freely rendered composition than those depicted in his formal, topographical portraits of country estates, ancient castles, or coastal towns.

Although seemingly informal in the depiction of forms and objects, this watercolor contains several conventions common in Sandby's landscapes, particularly in his later years: the use of the tall yet scraggly tree on the right and the steep hill on the left as framing devices and the inclusion of a small flock of sheep with a shepherd toward the center. This drawing is a characteristic example of Sandby's innovative use of watercolor, which helped transform the medium from one of tinted drawings to one in which color and tone provided form and definition in addition to achieving atmospheric effects.

Executed primarily for aristocratic patrons, Sandby's landscapes, both imaginary and topographical, present an almost nostalgic, idealized view of man's relationship to nature. Any reference to the enclosure of common lands is presented naturally as a pleasingly geometric and regulated aspect of a country estate. Typical of Sandby's capriccios, this drawing depicts an untamed yet gentle landscape that provides sustenance and pleasure for animals and human beings alike, as suggested by the combination of the rural (sheep and shepherd) with the peaceful urban presences (the buildings of a small town across the lake in the distant middle ground) in this watercolor. As such, *Hilly Landscape* and drawings like it contributed to the development of the rustic and picturesque traditions of English landscape painting.

1. Correspondence with author, 31 January 1989.
2. Yale Center for British Art, *The Art of Paul Sandby*, selection and catalogue entries by Bruce Robertson (New Haven, Conn.: Yale Center for British Art, 1985), nos. 97–101.

RICHARD COOPER II

75

Landscape with an Oak Tree (c. 1805–6)

RICHARD COOPER II
(Edinburgh 1740–1814 London)
Man 40
Lithograph
237 x 310 mm
Provenance: Victoria Dailey, Los Angeles

Richard Cooper II was a draftsman, etcher, and engraver of portraits and topographical views, as well as a lithographer of landscapes after his own designs. He trained in Edinburgh under his father, painter and engraver Richard Cooper I, and later studied engraving with Jacques-Philippe Le Bas in Paris. Already settled in London by 1761, he traveled to Italy during the 1770s, sketching views, which led to the publication of a series of aquatints entitled Rome and Its Environs in 1778–79. During the following decade he was drawing master at Eton, after which he executed an important series of twelve landscapes in soft-ground etching, which were published in 1799–1800. One of the first artists to experiment with lithography, Cooper was among those whose pen lithographs were included in the two editions of Specimens of Polyautography, published in 1803 and 1806, the most important publication of early lithographs in England.

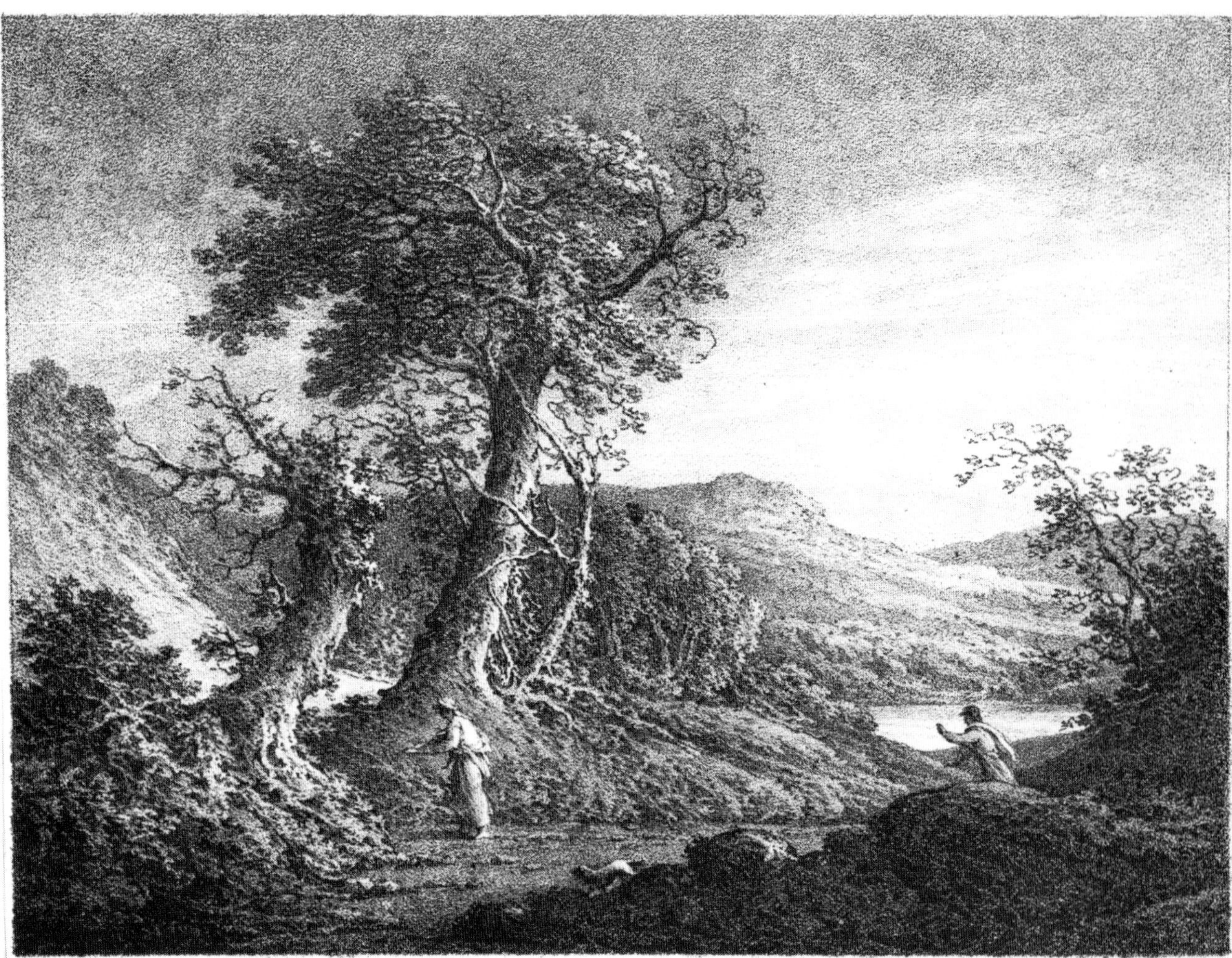

In this dramatic scene a man pursues a woman within a forest lit by the silvery light of a setting sun. The craggy shapes of the wind-ripped trees heighten the drama, animating the darkening sky and echoing the fury of the pursuing man. It is an evocative subject, alluding perhaps to a typical scene from a Highland legend of Scottish bandits.

The print's drama is also conveyed by the character of its lithographic crayon marks. Drawn in the manner of soft-ground etching, which Thomas Gainsborough had used so effectively in the 1780s in imitation of his own chalk drawings and which Cooper had himself explored in a set of twelve landscapes published in 1799–1800, the image is composed entirely of tonal gradations from black to very light gray. But the waxy lithographic crayon has a viscid effect that textures the image and enriches the dark tones. In this respect it is quite unlike the crayon lithographs of the Swiss artist Conrad Gessner, which appeared regularly in 1801 and 1802 and were included in Specimens of Polyautography.

John Robert Cozens

John Robert Cozens learned to draw from his father, Alexander, the well-known landscape artist and teacher. Unlike the elder Cozens, however, who created imaginary vistas, John Robert based his drawings and watercolors on actual locations encountered during his extended travels through the Swiss Alps and Italy in 1776–79 and 1782–83. The many commissioned paintings thus derived from his travel sketchbooks earned John Robert a reputation as one of England's most original and accomplished landscape watercolorists.

Cozens created his own poetic and melancholic style by combining topographical precision with compositional conventions derived from the landscape paintings of Claude Lorrain, such as repoussoir motifs and atmospheric recession. Employing a limited palette of soft grays and blues and touches of green, Cozens's watercolors of the Swiss Alps and the Alban Hills and lakes near Rome (some painted in as many as eight or nine versions for his many patrons) helped usher in the romantic era in painting and gave early pictorial form to the aesthetic category of the sublime. Cozens's romantic interpretation of the Italian countryside was very influential for the younger Thomas Girtin and J. M. W. Turner, both of whom copied many of his sketches at the informal academy established by Dr. Thomas Monro.

By 1794 Cozens was suffering from an incurable mental illness and spent the last years of his life in the care of Dr. Monro, supported through the aid of former patrons and a grant from the Royal Academy, which many years earlier (1776) had denied his application for associate membership.

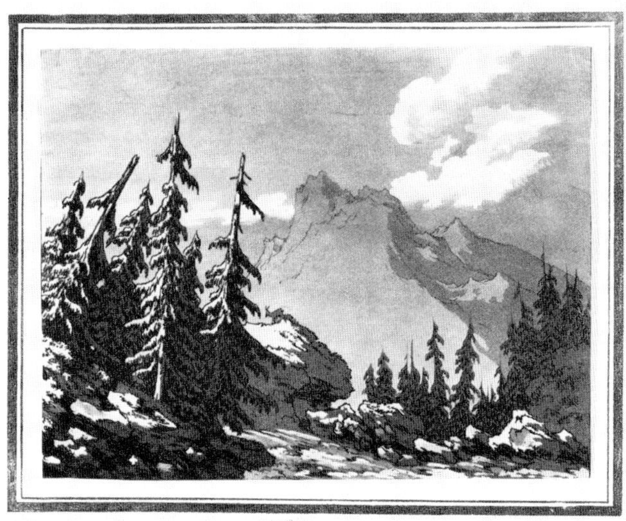

Fir (1789)

JOHN ROBERT COZENS
(London 1752–1797 Smithfield)
From the series Delineations of the General Character, Ramifications and Foliage of Forest Trees (1789)
Soft-ground etching with aquatint
237 x 315 mm
Titled lower center
Provenance: R. E. Lewis, San Francisco

When John Robert Cozens produced his suite of fourteen plates of forest trees entitled Delineations of the General Character, Ramifications and Foliage of Forest Trees, he was following in part the example of his father, Alexander Cozens. In 1771 the elder Cozens had published an engraved set entitled The Shape, Skeleton and Foliage of Thirty-two Species of Trees. According to Andrew Wilton, an album of the original drawings of Alexander's trees contains a manuscript title page dated 1789 with the same title as John Robert's published edition (Wilton 1980, pp. 27–28). Beyond their subject matter and title, however, there is no further resemblance between these two series.

The image in the Grunwald Center is unsigned and aquatinted and is therefore not one of the proof series, which, according to Wilton, were colored by hand and bore etched signatures (Wilton 1980, p. 28). Sets of the published series located in the print room of the British Museum, London, and at the Huntington Library, San Marino, California, although aquatinted, carry formal engraved signatures, however, and are inscribed *Published Feby 1st, 1789.*[1] It is highly probable that the Grunwald Center etching was produced prior to publication, at which time the signature and inscriptions would have been added to each plate.

It is not clear to what purpose John Robert executed this collection of forest trees in landscape settings ranging from "upland slopes of wild grandeur" to "broad meadows" and "Mediterranean coasts" (Wilton 1980, p. 28). Alexander's set (in which trees were drawn singly or in pairs, isolated from their natural environments) was devised specifically as a heuristic device for his students and other artists wishing to depict various trees accurately, yet not necessarily with scientific precision. Although John Robert's soft-ground etchings are not executed in the same diagrammatic manner, he did teach drawing after his return to England in 1783, and this set may have been prepared as an instructional guide in landscape technique and composition. In *Fir,* for example, the viewer is presented with a "Swiss" scene of a massive, barren, and craggy mountain at some distance from the rocky, snowy hillside in the foreground covered by clumps of tall fir trees. A lone mountain goat is visible on a substantial outcropping in the middle distance. The trees in the left foreground and those in the right middle ground serve to frame both the mountain goat and the grand mountain in the background and are pictorial devices often found in Cozens's more ambitious and finished watercolors. The technique of soft-ground etching lends itself well to the suggestion of a variety of textures, tonal subtleties, and contrasts between deep shade and bright sunlight seen in this image.

Although on a significantly smaller, more intimate scale, these etched landscapes fit well within Cozens's oeuvre of dramatic, melancholic watercolor renderings of the Roman Campagna and the Swiss Alps, encompassing the aesthetics of both the sublime and the beautiful.

1. A. P. Oppé, "Fresh Light on Alexander Cozens," *Print Collector's Quarterly* 8 (1921): 90. The set in the rare book collection of the Huntington Library is bound without a title page.

Gainsborough Dupont

The eldest surviving son of Thomas Gainsborough's sister Sarah, Gainsborough Dupont was formally apprenticed to his uncle in January 1772. He received additional training at the Royal Academy Schools beginning in 1775, after which he continued to serve as his uncle's studio assistant until the latter's death in 1788. Dupont survived his uncle by only nine years and during that brief time earned his living as both a portraitist and a landscape artist, patronized by members of the royal family.

His sixteen years of study and work with Gainsborough indelibly marked Dupont's own artistic technique, style, and choice of subject matter. Although known primarily for his portraits, he also executed numerous landscape paintings, drawings, and watercolors, several of which are copies of Gainsborough's compositions. The landscapes most similar to those of Thomas Gainsborough are in black and white chalk on blue paper and in pen and ink with gray wash.

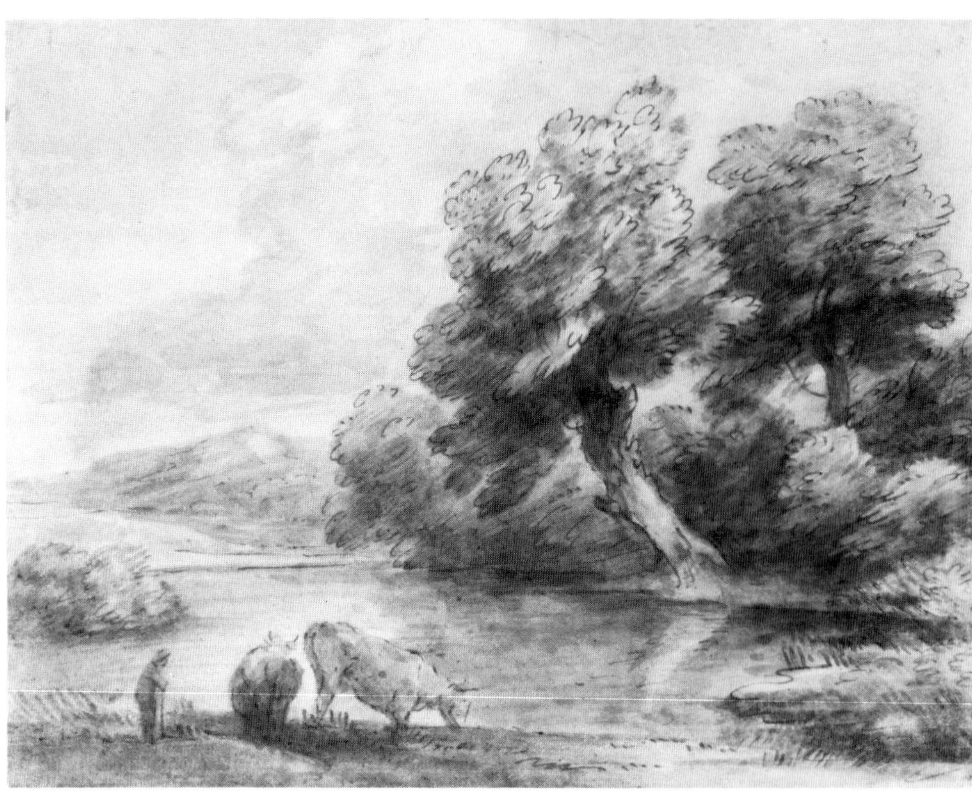

77

Cattle Watering at a Pond (c. 1780)

Attributed to GAINSBOROUGH DUPONT
(1754–1797 London)
Black chalk, ink, and gray wash
261 x 343 mm
Provenance: George Donaldson; H. Schniewind; Zeitlin and Ver Brugge, Los Angeles

Cattle Watering at a Pond is one of a group of drawings now thought to be by Gainsborough Dupont that are so similar in content, materials, and execution to those of Thomas Gainsborough that they had been attributed to the elder artist. John Hayes cites several elements of technique and style that led to his attribution to Dupont: staccato contours, shapeless clouds, a too-small figure, the lack of an organic relationship between the main tree and the ground, and an unbalanced composition (Hayes 1965, p. 253). Hayes compares it with a securely attributed Gainsborough drawing dated to the late 1770s in the collection of the earl of Spencer. Although the drawings are strikingly similar in composition, the differences noted by Hayes are apparent.

The composition of *Cattle Watering at a Pond* exemplifies the differences between the drawings of Dupont and those executed by his uncle late in his career. Generally speaking, Gainsborough structured his more intimate landscapes as enclosed spaces with few avenues of access. Such points of entrance and exit as do exist are often blocked by trees, cattle, or some other impediment (Bermingham 1986, pp. 40–41). In contrast Dupont opens up the composition, providing access by moving the cattle to the near side of the water and placing the trees more to one side of the pond, thus "exposing" an expansive background of rolling hills.

In subject the Dupont drawing is reminiscent of an entire class of rustic scenes composed by Gainsborough throughout his lengthy career, which were identified by contemporary critics and theorists of the picturesque (including Uvedale Price, who had known Gainsborough) as the embodiment of certain quintessentially English pictorial and philosophical values (Bermingham 1986, pp. 59–60).

Ann Bermingham (1986, pp. 40–41) asserts that Gainsborough's later rustic landscapes, drawn in the 1760s and 1770s, when he was living in Bath and London, were more a rejection of the city itself than of the eighteenth-century practices of enclosure that he had found so disturbing and disruptive in his youth. These scenes are idyllic rural retreats free of topographical landmarks or other urban features, often set deep within an all-enveloping forest, enclosing animals and people within its leafy branches, providing an "unmediated organic relationship between man and nature" (Bermingham 1986, p. 41). In such an idyllic environment the issues of labor and capital, enclosure, and the agrarian and industrial revolutions become irrelevant. According to Hayes (1965, p. 253), it is these later, almost schematic landscapes that Dupont emulated in *Cattle Watering at a Pond* and other drawings, without, however, capturing the more personal, introspective element found in Gainsborough's compositions.

THOMAS ROWLANDSON

Thomas Rowlandson is most often considered in terms of his contribution to the tradition of British caricature. His landscape art is seldom examined, yet he produced a large body of drawings depicting rural, town, and harbor scenes that display great sensitivity to the particularities of these settings.

Rowlandson's rapid drawing style depended primarily on broken pen outlines. He used color washes sparingly, ignoring the innovations introduced by his contemporaries Thomas Girtin and J. M. W. Turner in watercolor and by Edward Dayes in topographical landscape, each of whom contributed to the trend toward a more atmospheric treatment, with modeling accomplished through color rather than line.

Despite his concern for the depiction of landscape, figures remained the principal subject of Rowlandson's art. Indeed the fine art publisher Rudolph Ackermann often paired Rowlandson with architectural draftsmen such as Augustus Pugin to produce plates for topographical publications such as The Microcosm of London *(1808–11). It should be noted that Rowlandson's delight in caricature led him to satirize theorists and artists associated with the picturesque style of landscape in his drawings for William Combe's* Tours of Dr. Syntax in Search of the Picturesque, *first published in 1812.*

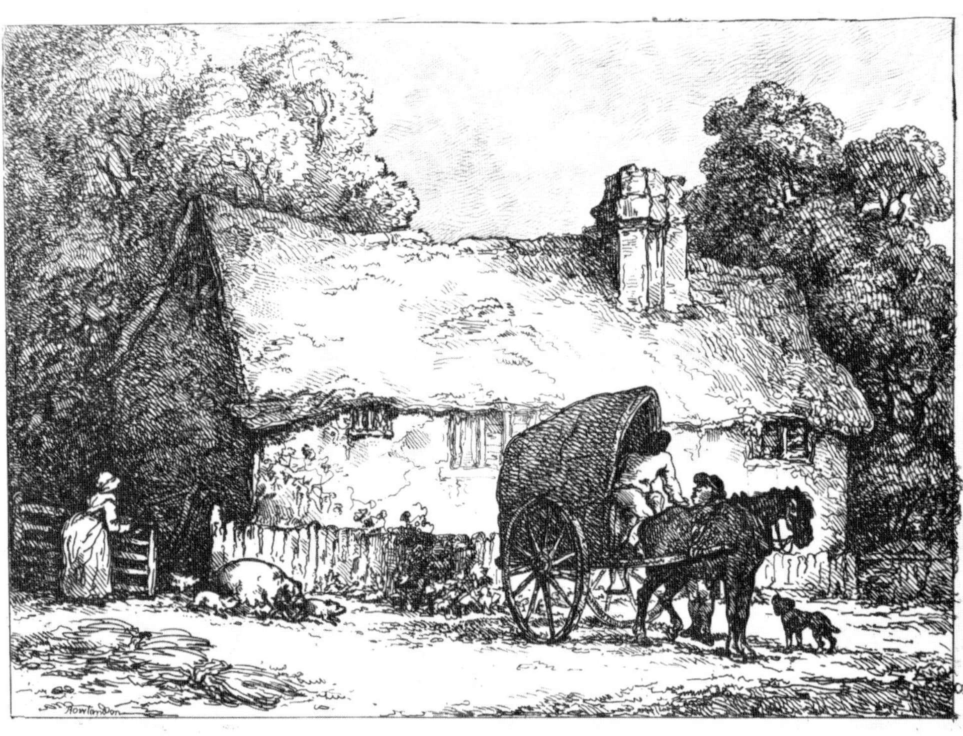

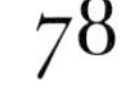

78

Cart before a Thatched Cottage (c. 1787)

THOMAS ROWLANDSON
(London 1756–1827 London)
Soft-ground etching
170 x 240 mm
Provenance: R. E. Lewis, San Francisco

This soft-ground etching by Thomas Rowlandson is datable to approximately the late 1780s, based on comparisons with securely dated landscapes. Soft-ground etching was the technique preferred by the artist when he was producing his series Imitations of Modern Drawings (1788), in which he actually copied specific drawings as well as the individual styles of Thomas Gainsborough, Sawrey Gilpin, John Mortimer, and other artists whose works influenced his own development.[1] *Cart before a Thatched Cottage* is not a copy or imitation, although features characteristic of the works of both Gainsborough and George Morland are apparent here, for example, the sense of enclosed space and the horse and cart found in many of Gainsborough's drawings and the easy, almost cozy quality of country life depicted by Morland. It is an original composition featuring figures, trees, and a building rendered in Rowlandson's familiar style, reminiscent of his drawings with rapid broken pen outlines.

The etching also contains a characteristic comic element, the just-released family of pigs scurrying from behind the open gate to the left of the cottage. The scene lacks Rowlandson's biting sarcasm, however, as is usually the case with his landscapes. They are more often gentle in nature, except when he is satirizing certain tendencies of the genre, as he did in *Tours of Dr. Syntax in Search of the Picturesque.* Despite his apparent contempt for the picturesque, Rowlandson's landscapes fall squarely within the rustic tradition that is variously considered an artistic precursor of the picturesque or one aspect of that larger tradition.

1. Ronald Paulson, *Rowlandson: A New Interpretation* (New York: Oxford University Press, 1972), pp. 15, 17. Paulson refers to this publication variously as Imitations of Modern Masters or as Imitations of Modern Drawings. A catalogue from the William Weston Gallery, London, *An Exhibition of Printmaking in England, 1770–1950*, vol. 1 (1985), cites it as Imitations of Modern Drawings.

DR. THOMAS MONRO

Dr. Thomas Monro's primary career was as a physician specializing in insanity. From 1792 until his death he served as principal physician at Bethlehem Hospital in London. His passion was for art rather than medicine, however, particularly watercolors, drawings, and prints, which he avidly collected and made available in his informal academy for study and copying by promising young artists such as Thomas Girtin and J. M. W. Turner. In the years following, a younger generation of artists, including John Sell Cotman, Peter De Wint, and John and Cornelius Varley, spent their evenings at one of Monro's residences, sharing a hot meal, after which they would copy the drawings and watercolors of Canaletto, Claude Lorrain, John Robert Cozens, Thomas Gainsborough, Thomas Hearne, Paul Sandby, and Richard Wilson, to name the most important artists whose work Monro collected.

In addition to being a patron of the arts, Monro spent considerable time sketching, particularly outdoors. He had been a drawing pupil of J. Laporte but found his real inspiration in the sketches of Gainsborough, whose techniques and style in the execution of landscapes he enthusiastically emulated.

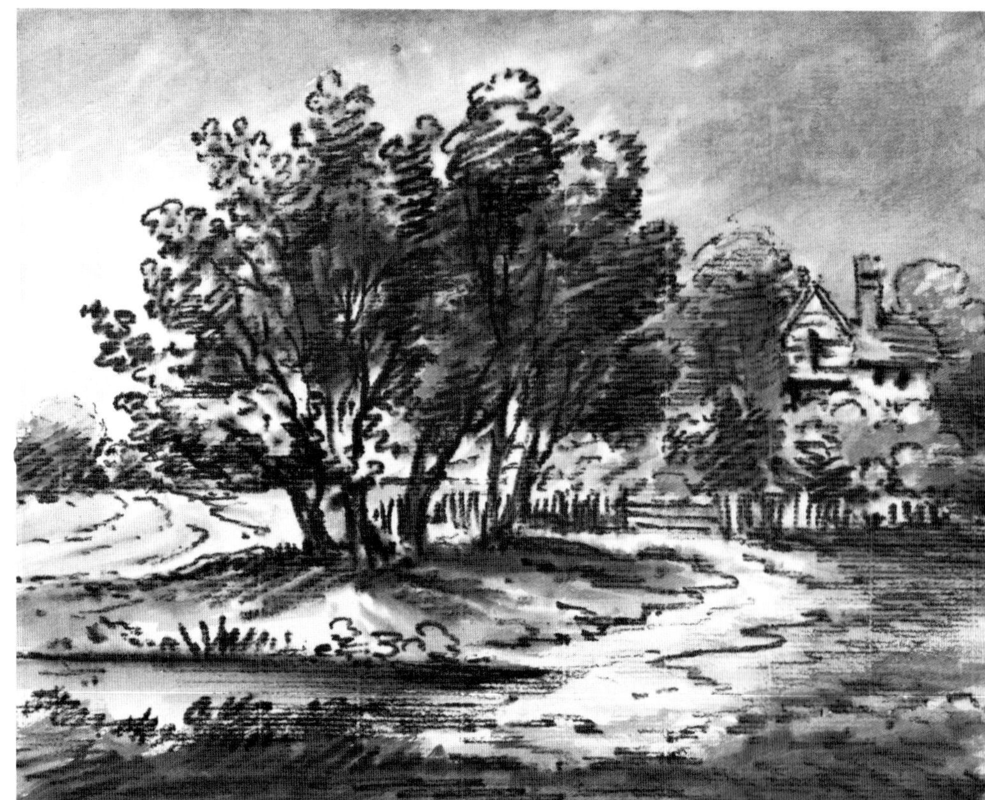

79
Trees and Cottage

DR. THOMAS MONRO
(London 1759–1833 Bushey)
Charcoal with gray wash
183 x 234 mm
Provenance: Zeitlin and Ver Brugge, Los Angeles

Monro's drawing of a cottage near a pond with trees is very much in keeping with other landscapes sketched by him in the style of Thomas Gainsborough. As was common practice for amateurs and professional artists alike during the era of rustic and picturesque landscape painting in England, Monro probably began this sketch outdoors, perhaps near his country home in Bushey. He was frequently accompanied on these sojourns by one or more of the young artists who participated in his informal academy, whom he encouraged to sketch from nature. His usual practice involved using either Payne's gray or India ink washes on gray, blue, or white paper while outside, which he then took home to be outlined and retouched in charcoal, crayon, or dry sticks of India ink dipped in water.[1] It is highly probable that the Grunwald Center drawing was executed in this manner.

1. Martin Hardie, *The Victorian Period*, vol. 3 of *Water-Colour Painting in Britain* (London: B. T. Batsford, 1968), p. 277.

John Crome

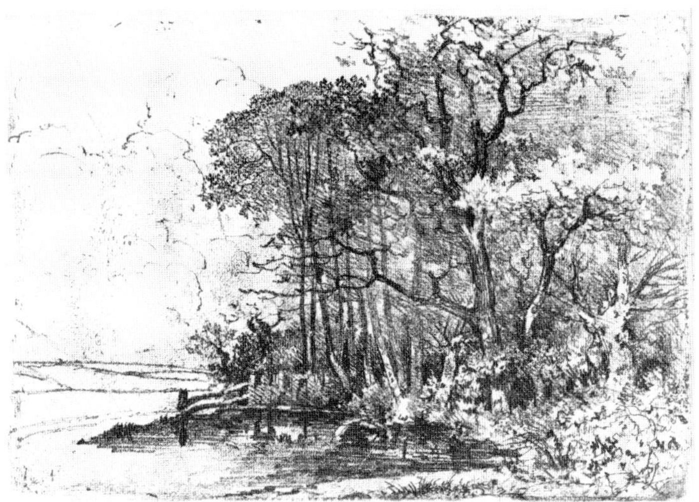

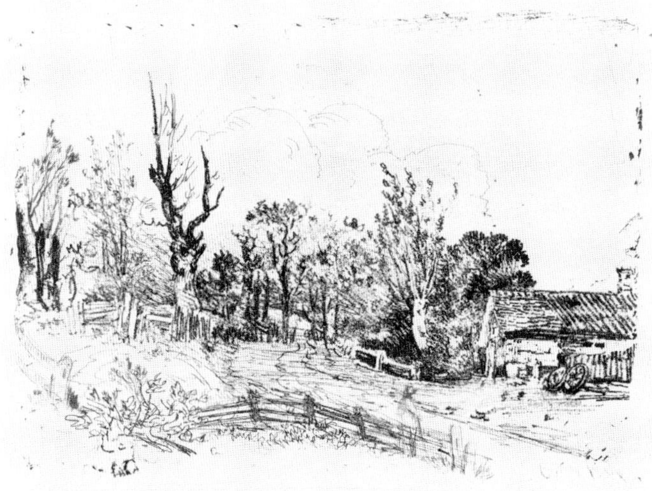

Founder in 1803 of the Norwich Society, and its president from 1808, John Crome was responsible for establishing and nurturing one of the most recognizable regional schools of art outside London. Beginning his career as an apprentice to a house, sign, and carriage painter, he remained in Norwich throughout his life, documenting the Norfolk landscape in oil, watercolor, and etching.

Crome's early artistic influences were Meindert Hobbema and Richard Wilson, whose landscapes he copied at the home of Thomas Harvey, a local collector as well as an amateur painter and etcher. During these years Crome also met William Beechey, who acknowledged the young artist's talents and encouraged his ambitions. He became a drawing master to the children of many wealthy local families, particularly those of John Gurney, a prominent Norfolk Quaker banker with whose family he often traveled and summered.

Crome devoted his life to painting the countryside around his home, depicting country lanes, cottages, and open lands in a direct and unaffected yet almost picturesque manner. Along with Thomas Gainsborough, he was one of the first English artists to exploit etching for its own artistic possibilities rather than simply as a means of reproducing already existing designs.

80

Hoveton St. Peter (1809, published 1834)

JOHN CROME
(Norwich 1768–1821 Norwich)
From *Norfolk Picturesque Scenery* (1834)
Theobald 30
Soft-ground etching
162 x 233 mm
Provenance: R. E. Lewis, San Francisco

81

Colney (1809, published 1834)

JOHN CROME
(Norwich 1768–1821 Norwich)
From *Norfolk Picturesque Scenery* (1834)
Theobald 32
Soft-ground etching and drypoint
162 x 226 mm
Provenance: R. E. Lewis, San Francisco

These two etchings were printed on one page of *Norfolk Picturesque Scenery*, published posthumously in 1834. Colney is signed and dated 1809 in the plate, with the *9* reversed, in the lower right-hand corner. It is the earliest date for an etching by Crome. Of the thirty-three etchings completed by Crome, eleven are done with the soft-ground process, a technique at which he excelled, and during his lifetime he actually printed a few of them for himself and friends. According to Henry Studdy Theobald (1906, p. 95), there are no differences of state in the soft-ground etchings.

As with most of Crome's work, whether painting, drawing, or etching, the scenery depicted is located close to his Norwich home. Each of these two etchings is representative of a particular aspect of his landscape art. *Colney*, on the one hand, portrays a country road meandering past a cottage at the edge of a small wooded area; across the road is a rough-hewn curving fence, against which a laborer leans. In *Hoveton St. Peter*, on the other hand, one sees only forest, water, sky, and fields, without people or buildings, accessible and inviting, but virtually untouched. Only the remains of broken fencing are visible on the far side of the pond. Nature, with or without human presence, is portrayed as a comfortable, nurturing environment.

Crome was a master of the representation of trees, and the technique of soft-ground etching permitted a full range of textures and tones suitable for the rendering of wooded areas. Of the soft-ground etchings in *Norfolk Picturesque Scenery, Hoveton St. Peter* is the most finished composition, presenting a variety of trees and shrubs, full-leafed or dying, while *Colney* is more typical in its incompleteness; the trees are defined by a few rapidly executed lines, the fence on the left is lightly sketched, and the figure in the right foreground is ghostly in its transparency. Although relatively unfinished, the trees and shrubs are drawn with convincing substantiality.

John Crome

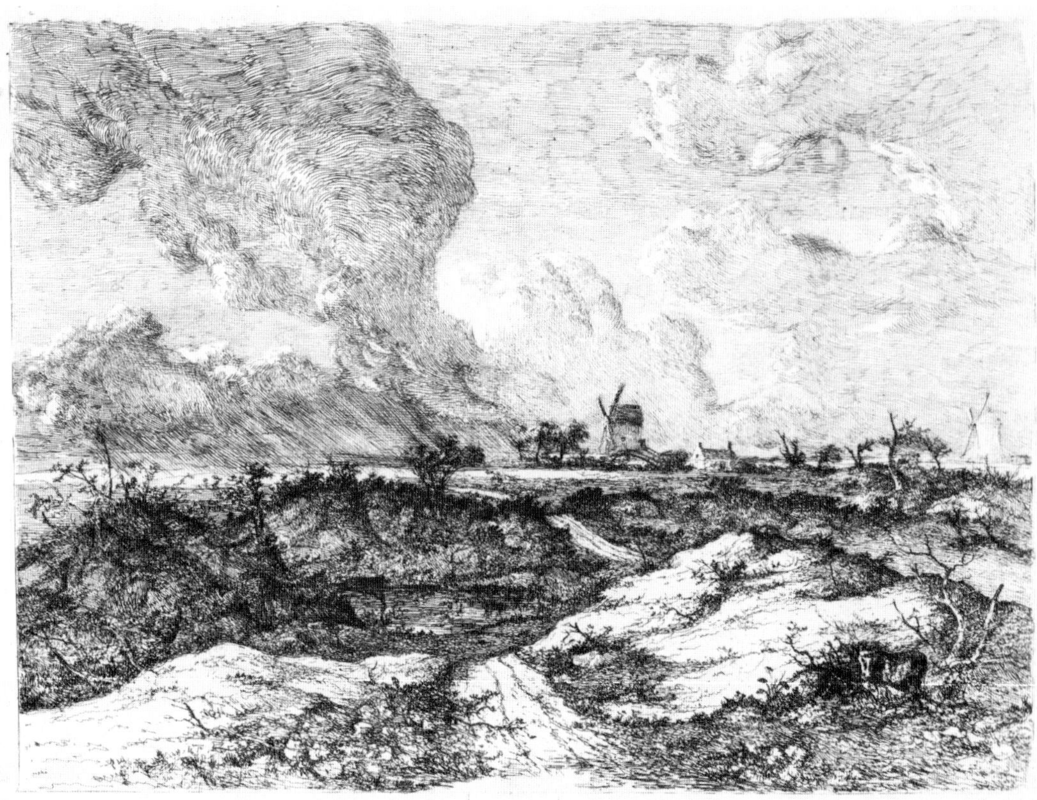

82

Mousehold Heath

(c. 1810–13, published 1834)

JOHN CROME
(Norwich 1768–1821 Norwich)
From *Norfolk Picturesque Scenery* (1834)
Theobald 3 ii/iv
Etching
206 x 300 mm
Provenance: R. E. Lewis, San Francisco

The Norwich school, so closely identified with John Crome's career, became a center of the etching revival in the early decades of the nineteenth century. Although Crome issued a prospectus in 1812 for a proposed issue of etchings, thirty-three of which were completed between 1809 and 1813, he declined to proceed with the project. Thirty-one were published by Crome's widow as *Norfolk Picturesque Scenery* in 1834.

Mousehold Heath, the tenth plate in the posthumous volume, is the most dramatic of Crome's etchings. His other etchings depict more intimate landscapes, woodland paths, and humble farmyards (see cat. nos. 80, 81). Only in his drawings and paintings do we find other panoramas with low-lying horizons, and these present more tranquil vistas. Unfortunately the stormy, windswept sky, perhaps the most prominent feature of this etching, was materially altered in subsequent states, diminishing the power of the natural forces depicted by Crome.[1]

Mousehold Heath was a favorite location for Crome and is the subject of more than one painting.[2] In the paintings, however, there is evidence of man-made creation, such as farm buildings or windmills. Derek and Timothy Clifford have suggested that Crome, particularly in his etchings, treated everything—trees, water, sky as well as buildings—as part of the landscape, that is, as part of nature.[3] Here not only has man been brought into harmony with nature (albeit a tempestuous nature), typical of landscapes within the rustic tradition, but the objects of man's technical ingenuity and creation have also become part of nature.

Yet there is perhaps an unintended irony within *Mousehold Heath*, namely, the juxtaposition of untamed, uncultivated land with the two windmills in the background, instruments invented by man to harness nature and make it complicit in its own taming and domestication (also represented by the donkey in the right foreground). This landscape depicts a part of the English countryside that in 1812 had not yet been either completely enclosed or transformed into a picturesque garden on a country estate. It is rough and bumpy, covered by straggling, thorny bushes and dusty earth, homely, not pretty, a composition inspired by the land itself, rather than an idealized notion of the land. It is perhaps that aspect of Crome's etching that prevents *Mousehold Heath* from becoming merely a wishful, nostalgic vision.

1. The first alteration resulted in the removal of the sky; the second, in the addition of a ruled sky crudely executed with diamond point by W. C. Edwards of Bungay. In addition, a portion of the shading in the water was burnished out, destroying the balance of light and shadow (Theobald 1906, p. 72; White 1977, p. 59).
2. See Derek and Timothy Clifford, *John Crome* (Greenwich, Conn.: New York Graphic Society, 1968), pls. 93, 111.
3. Ibid., p. 67.

William Delamotte

William Delamotte was one of the first artists in England to practice open-air oil sketching. He and other young artists studying with John Varley (William Havell, William Henry Hunt, John Linnell, and William Mulready) gathered to sketch along the banks of the Thames between 1805 and 1807. He may also have produced one of the first landscapes in oil completed on location in 1805, nearly ten years before any that are known to have been painted by John Constable.

As one of the early practitioners of lithography, Delamotte contributed a landscape to the first and second editions of Specimens of Polyautography, published in 1803 and 1806. From 1810, however, his artistic production decreased drastically, perhaps owing to his 1803 appointment as drawing master at the Royal Military Academy in Great Marlow, a post he held for thirty-five years.

83

Woman, Child, and Cattle by a River (1825)

WILLIAM DELAMOTTE
(Weymouth 1775–1863 Oxford)
Ink, black chalk, and watercolor
290 x 222 mm
Signed and dated lower center
Provenance: Zeitlin and Ver Brugge, Los Angeles

Quite similar in feel and sentiment to certain drawings by John Varley, with whom Delamotte studied,[1] this drawing depicts by rather simple means a young woman and child along the banks of a river in the cool light of a late afternoon. The figures, cows, and principal landscape elements were quickly drawn with soft black chalk. Watercolor washes were then added to give body and character to these forms, while ink was added to strengthen their edges and define details in the woman's dress, the cow's neck and head, and the grass in the lower right. The cool light is the effect of the gray paper, which reads as a color buffed by light yellow, tan, and chalky blue washes in the sky and foliage and along the path in the foreground. The bright touches of blue and red in the figures' dress and of brown and white in the cows' coats provide momentary focus for the image and draw our attention from the overall effect of the monochromatic softness of the landscape to the diminutive but charming woman and child out for a walk along a country lane. It is in the softness of the image and its suggestion of a kind of gentle somnolence that one sees Varley's influence.

1. See the drawings by Varley in the Yale Center for British Art, New Haven, reproduced in White 1977 (no. 177) and Wilcox 1985 (no. 37).

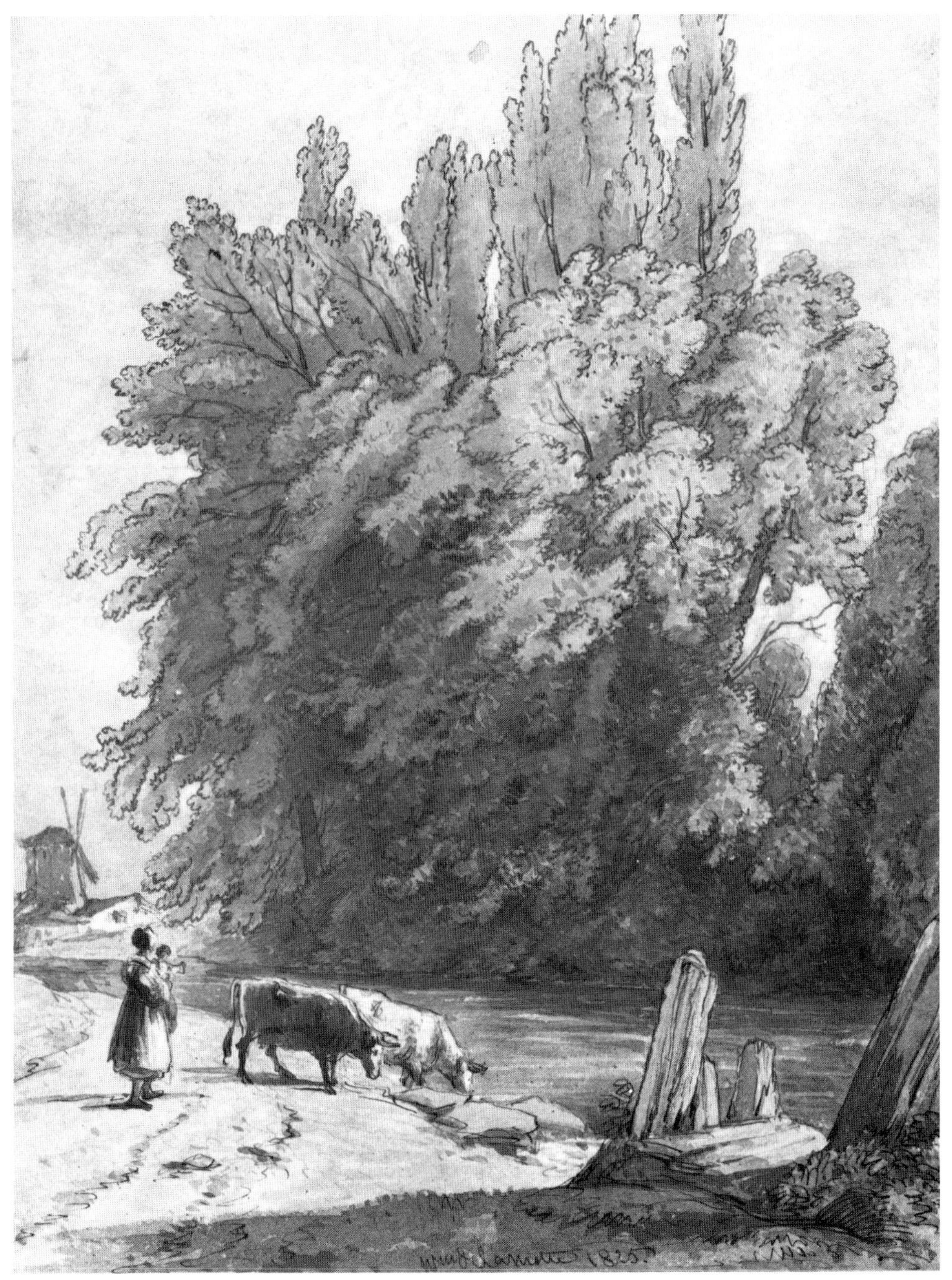

JOHN VARLEY

One of the more important landscape watercolorists of his generation, John Varley was perhaps most influential as a teacher and writer of treatises on art. Although his artistic training began in 1793 in J. C. Barrow's drawing school, Varley's real education occurred after 1800 at Dr. Thomas Monro's informal academy, where he was introduced to the landscape watercolors of John Robert Cozens and, more importantly, Thomas Girtin. The latter's direct, simplified approach was fundamental to the developing style of the young Varley, as well as to the formulation of his didactic methodology. The theories of picture making he expounded in his art manuals published between 1815 and 1826 were structured and conventional, however, providing pupils and other readers with strict guidelines for composing picturesque landscapes.

Through his connection with Monro, Varley met future patrons and began to take on students, both amateur and professional. He encouraged them to develop their individual styles, study nature, sketch out-of-doors, and maintain a direct, spontaneous quality about their work. Among those who took lessons from Varley were David Cox, Peter De Wint, and John Linnell.

Varley exhibited at the Royal Academy between 1798 and 1804, after which he showed his works often and almost exclusively for the next forty years at the Old Water-Colour Society, of which he was a founding member. He was also briefly a member of the Sketching Club (1802–4).

Until about 1806 Varley's drawings exemplified the simplicity and subdued color scheme typical of Girtin's work while exhibiting Varley's own mastery of line and color. Although later pieces retained those qualities of fine draftsmanship and characteristically simplified areas of wash, his compositions were increasingly dependent on generalized forms and the conventionally picturesque rather than on direct observation of nature. This later reliance on compositional formulas resulted from Varley's devotion to teaching, which after 1820 increasingly took precedence over his own artistic work.

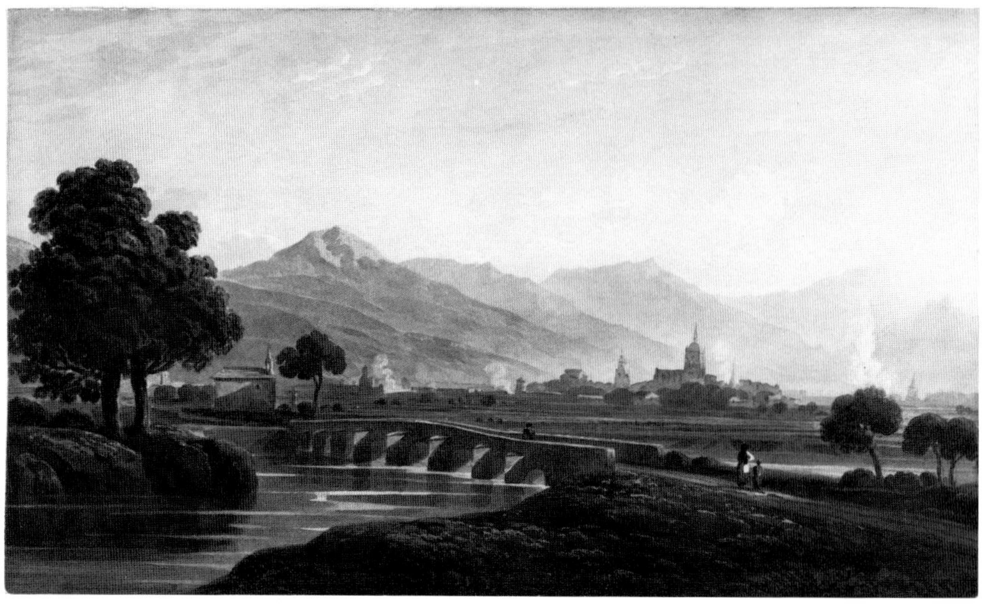

84

Landscape with a Town at Sunset

JOHN VARLEY
(London 1778–1842 London)
Watercolor
264 x 453 mm
Provenance: Zeitlin and Ver Brugge, Los Angeles

This watercolor, quite large in size and rigidly structured in composition, has a highly finished quality, indicating that it was probably painted specifically for exhibition, perhaps at the Old Water-Colour Society. It exemplifies principles of composition and tonality that Varley developed in his early years as an artist and followed throughout his career, such as leaving foreground areas in shadow in order to contrast with alternating bursts of light and varying darker tones receding into the distance (Kauffmann 1984, p. 22). The steep angle of the afternoon sunlight further accentuates the difference between the darkening foreground and middle ground and the hazy brightness of the mountains in the far distance on the right side of the composition, creating crisply delineated shadows on the bridge and small chapel.

Although it is undated and the locale is unidentified, this watercolor appears, through comparisons with other signed and dated works, to depict a northern Welsh town and was probably painted between 1806 and 1810 (see Kauffmann 1984, nos. 2, 20, 32). While Varley's landscapes were always created within the framework of the picturesque as defined by William Gilpin, after 1805 he departed from the naturalistic style of Thomas Girtin, characterized by broad washes of color. From 1806 to 1810 his watercolors became closer to the formal compositions of Claude Lorrain and Richard Wilson, while from about 1810 onward, Varley turned increasingly to a broader panoramic model encompassing longer, narrower vistas (see Kauffmann 1984, pp. 20–21, 47). Varley's broad areas of wash are virtually absent in this watercolor, and although the setting is a Welsh town and its surrounding countryside, the composition is reminiscent of other classicizing works done around 1808 in the style of Nicolas Poussin's seventeenth-century pastoral landscapes (see Kauffmann 1984, p. 46, fig. 19). Varley's two or three sketching expeditions through northern Wales between the years 1798 or 1799 and 1802 provided sufficient inspiration and subject matter for works of the following forty years and may have inspired this watercolor.

David Cox

David Cox began his artistic studies with John Varley in 1807, after traveling through Wales with Charles Barber to develop his drawing skills and watercolor technique in the representation of landscape. He was further influenced by the art of Thomas Girtin, whose straightforward depictions of the English landscape avoided the more popular romantic or idealized interpretations. Cox's own watercolors, worked from sketches made on the spot, are notable for their uncluttered compositions and their forceful, unprettified directness. The contemporary critic A. L. Baldry wrote of Cox's work, "No straining after elegant formality, no precise insistence on particular rules of composition, no substitution of convention for direct inspiration." His primary subject matter—nature, light, and atmosphere—occupied Cox throughout his life, leading to a style that was almost impressionistic in nature.

As Cox matured into a successful artist, his professional commitments and affiliations grew. Between 1805 and 1844 he often exhibited watercolors at the Royal Academy. In 1809 he became a member of Associated Artists in Water-Colours and served as its president from 1810 (when its name was changed to Associated Painters in Water-Colours) until its demise two years later. He was also an associate member of the Old Water-Colour Society. In 1815 Cox was appointed drawing master at the Military College at Farnham, leaving shortly thereafter for Hereford, where he taught and published treatises on art.

Cox traveled to the Continent three times between 1826 and 1832 to sketch and study the work of Dutch, Belgian, and French artists. By 1827, once again living in London, he developed his late technique of using pure watercolor, the medium in which he worked almost exclusively. In 1841, when he was fifty-eight, Cox returned to the Birmingham area to live and work, making yearly drawing excursions to the Welsh hills.

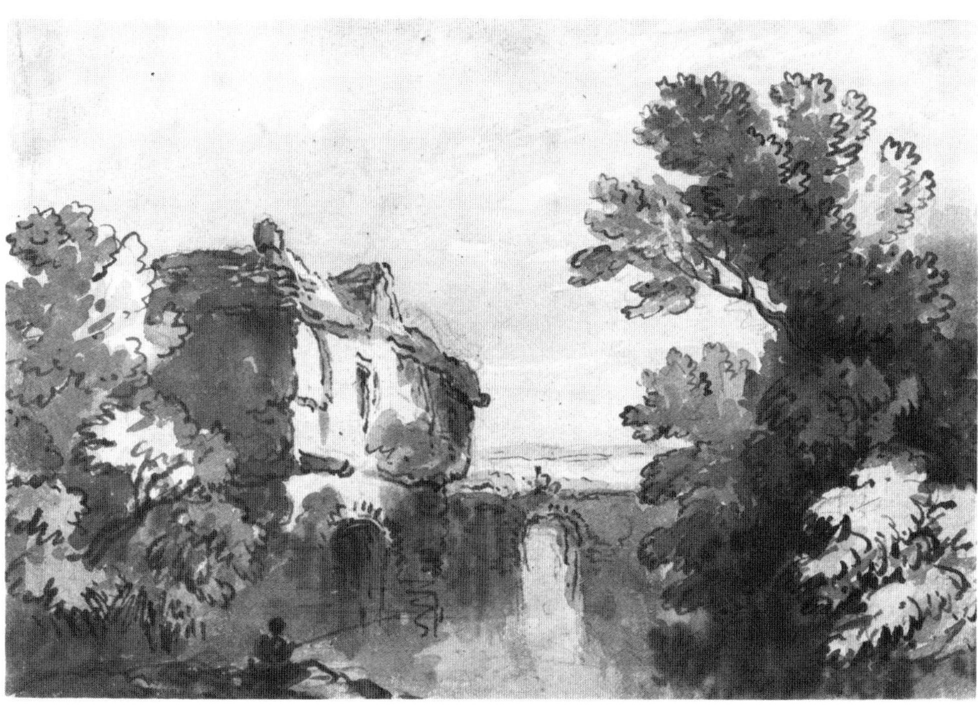

85

Landscape with a House by a Stream (c. 1804–7)

DAVID COX
(Deritend 1783–1859 Harborne)
Sepia ink and washes over graphite
182 x 270 mm
Provenance: Lucien Goldschmidt, New York

Cox is best known for his early watercolors executed under the influence of his teacher John Varley, characterized by broad rich washes in pigment, or for his later, more distinctive impressionistic landscapes, in which he developed a technique for "animating the surface of his work with repeated small strokes of the brush."[1] The sepia wash drawing in the Grunwald Center most probably dates from a much earlier period, perhaps between 1804 and 1807, after he arrived in London and prior to his studies with Varley. It was during this period that he produced many small studies in sepia or India ink for sale to drawing masters through a London art dealer, one of several jobs undertaken to support himself.[2] As he developed his craft, Cox devoted himself almost exclusively to watercolor, moving away from monochrome washes.

The assignment of an early date is further supported by comparing Cox's technique in the Grunwald Center drawing with that of works executed from 1814 through the 1820s and 1830s.[3] Although it has a schematic, sketchy quality often found in Cox's later work, the drawing is most notable for its rapid, almost nervous outlining of the house and foliage, a characteristic that disappeared after Cox began painting with Varley.[4] His later landscapes—whether they illustrate fall harvests, the banks of the Thames, or ancient British castles—provide panoramic vistas open to a far horizon line, generally unframed by techniques of repoussoir or other compositional conventions.

Considered along with John Crome, Peter De Wint, and Varley, among others, to be part of the rustic landscape tradition, Cox portrays a bucolic, unproblematic relationship between man and nature in this early drawing. Landscapes painted by the mature artist are more complex, however, and those from his later visits to Wales, for example, present images more within the tradition of the sublime and J. M. W. Turner.[5]

1. Lindsay Stainton, *British Landscape Watercolours, 1600–1860* (Cambridge: Cambridge University Press, 1985), p. 62, no. 136.
2. Martin Hardie, *The Romantic Period*, vol. 2 of *Water-Colour Painting in Britain* (London: B. T. Batsford, 1967), p. 192.
3. See, for example, Stainton, *British Landscape Watercolours*, nos. 136–39, pls. 95–99.
4. Hardie refers to Cox's use of outline while on his 1805 sketching tour of Wales (*The Romantic Period*, p. 192).
5. See Stainton, *British Landscape Watercolours*, no. 139, pl. 98.

PETER DE WINT

Peter De Wint began his career in 1802 as an apprentice to the portrait artist and engraver John Raphael Smith. His subsequent affiliation with the circle of John Varley and Dr. Thomas Monro influenced his decision to turn to watercolor, the medium for which he is best known, although he continued to paint in oil throughout his life.

In 1809 De Wint began attending the Royal Academy School. By 1810 he had been made an associate of the Old Water-Colour Society, becoming a full member the following year. Exhibiting approximately 326 watercolors and paintings between his first Royal Academy showing and his death in 1849, De Wint was a prolific landscape artist who mastered the large-scale exhibition piece as well as the rapid sketch, both of which were avidly collected by his patrons. He was considered one of the best drawing teachers in England by many, including John Ruskin, and his students included a variety of amateur as well as professional artists.

De Wint's landscapes avoided the picturesque and sublime in favor of a simple and unprettified depiction of the British countryside. Although he toured every summer, traveling once each to Normandy and Wales, De Wint preferred to remain in England. His landscapes, often painted outdoors, were executed with broad strokes in rich gold and earth tones, reminiscent of the style of Thomas Girtin, whose work profoundly influenced De Wint.

86

Landscape

PETER DE WINT
(Hanley, Staffordshire 1784–1849 London)
Watercolor over graphite
260 x 439 mm
Provenance: Zeitlin and Ver Brugge, Los Angeles

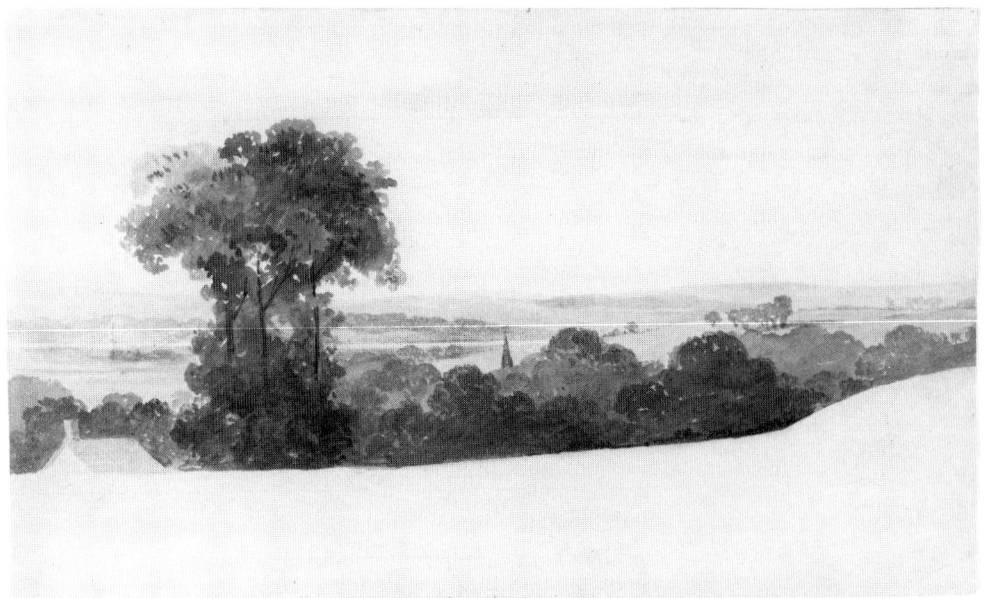

This unfinished watercolor showing deep, broad expanses of gently rolling British countryside, complete with rivers and almost hidden villages with only a cottage roof and church spire visible above the densely wooded middle ground, is characteristic of a type of landscape painted by De Wint. The elevated viewpoint provides a vista that is panoramic yet that drops sharply below the unfinished foreground hill, with a barely visible path indicating access to the woods and village at the bottom. The influence of seventeenth-century Dutch landscape paintings and more particularly the watercolors of Thomas Girtin is evident in this work.

The most prominent feature in the landscape is a cluster of three towering trees that is placed to the left of center, not at the edge of the composition, where it would serve as a traditional framing or repoussoir device. De Wint was perhaps best known for his unconventional, naturalistic approach to drawing directly from nature, using broad washes of color laid down in single strokes, often leaving first layers untouched by further brushwork.[1]

De Wint was a prolific artist, and many of his rapid watercolor sketches, such as this one, are unfinished. They were often drawn in pencil and partly completed outdoors on damp paper with brushes drenched in pure color. The subject matter and its treatment (broad washes of color; a high viewpoint, reminiscent of Girtin's landscapes; and the massing of trees to form clusters, reminiscent of Alexander Cozens) are characteristic of much of De Wint's oeuvre. Because he rarely signed his work, it is difficult if not impossible to date most of his watercolors and drawings.

De Wint is usually considered part of the British rustic landscape tradition, along with David Cox, John Crome, and John Varley, among others (Bermingham 1986, p. 197, n. 5). It has frequently been noted that during De Wint's lifetime England was transformed from a rural agricultural country to an industrialized urban nation. Though this affected the work of John Constable, Thomas Gainsborough, and Thomas Wright of Derby, many landscape artists, including De Wint, chose not to portray directly any of the dislocations that resulted from rural enclosure or urban industrialization.[2] Many of De Wint's patrons were wealthy landowners, and there is no evidence of his interest in or concern about such matters.[3] It was De Wint's innovations in style and technique within the medium and genre of watercolor landscape that attracted patrons as well as contemporary writers such as John Ruskin and the "peasant poet" John Clare, who both praised his treatment of the English countryside as innovative, fresh, and unaffected.[4]

---

1. Hammond Smith, *Peter De Wint, 1784–1849* (London: F. Lewis, 1982), p. 49.
2. John Barrell, *The Dark Side of the Landscape* (Cambridge: Cambridge University Press, 1980); Bermingham 1986. Both these books discuss at length issues of eighteenth- and nineteenth-century landscape painting and the industrialization of agriculture and manufacturing in England; see also Smith, *Peter De Wint*, p. 2.
3. Smith, *Peter De Wint*, app. B, pp. 114–28. In the biography of De Wint written by his wife, there is no indication of his interest in this phenomenon.
4. Ibid., p. 2.

David Roberts

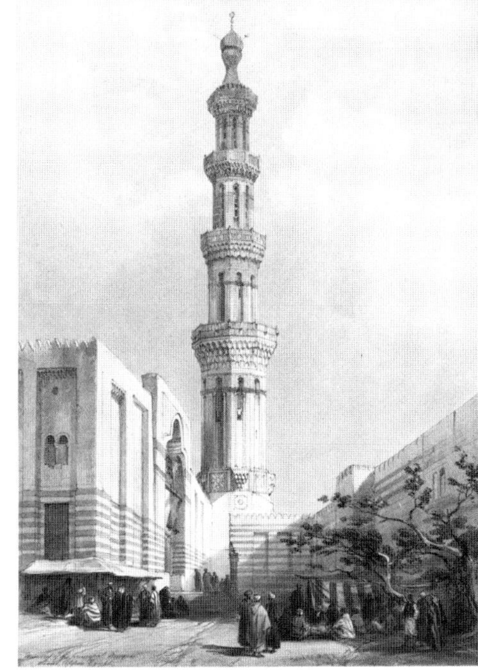

David Roberts first earned his reputation as a successful theatrical artist in London at the Drury Lane Theatre and was commissioned in 1827 to paint the scenery for the first production of Mozart's The Abduction from the Seraglio *at Covent Garden. During these early years Roberts trained himself to paint and draw on a smaller, less dramatic scale, eventually turning to landscape and topographical illustration. Although he was one of several artists who became known in the 1820s and 1830s for depicting foreign settings, Roberts specialized in particularly exotic scenery and subject matter.*

In the 1830s he traveled through Spain and to Tangier, and in 1837 he produced his first illustrated travel book, Picturesque Sketches in Spain in 1832 and 1833. *His most famous publication, however, the result of an extensive Middle Eastern sojourn in 1838, was entitled Views in the Holy Land, Syria, Idumea, Arabia, Egypt, and Nubia. Consisting of 248 tinted lithographs by Louis Haghe after watercolors by Roberts, it appeared in several parts between 1842 and 1849. Both publications proved extremely popular, presenting straightforward images of the architecture and costumes of sacred places read about, but generally not yet illustrated, in Europe.*

Roberts exhibited his oil paintings and watercolors consistently throughout his career at both the British Institution (between 1825 and 1859) and the Royal Academy, to which he was elected an associate in 1838 and a Royal Academician in 1841. Eighteen years earlier he had been elected vice president of the Society of British Artists at its founding, and he was made an honorary Royal Scottish Academician in 1829. His contribution to British art was acknowledged in 1851, when he was appointed one of the commissioners for the Great Exhibition of that year.

87

Minaret of the Principal Mosque, Sioul, Upper Egypt

LOUIS HAGHE
(Tournai 1806–1885 Stockwell)
After DAVID ROBERTS
(Edinburgh 1796–1864 London)
From the series Views in the Holy Land, Syria, Idumea, Arabia, Egypt, and Nubia (1842–49)
Lithograph with hand coloring
338 x 237 mm
Provenance: Zeitlin and Ver Brugge, Los Angeles

The exotic, Near Eastern equivalent of Richard Parkes Bonington's *Tour du Gros Horloge, Evreux* (cat. no. 89), this print emphasizes the vertical rise of the minaret as it dominates the architecture of the Egyptian cityscape. From its decorative balcony, the muezzin would give the daily call to prayer, drawing the berobed figures below into the large mosque to the left.

The color tinting of this lithograph is quite comparable to Roberts's original watercolors. Typically he would draw outlines in graphite and lay on a series of washes that would allow the original drawing to show through. These were usually monochrome, leaving color to be added later to the robes of the figures. This technique was similar to the lithographic technique of Louis Haghe, to whom Roberts entrusted the printing of his Holy Land drawings (Twyman 1970, pp. 206–8, 221–23).

Haghe was among the most prolific reproductive lithographers of the 1830s and 1840s, specializing in the tinted style. Born in Belgium, he came to England in 1823, when he was only seventeen. Three years later he formed a partnership with the lithographic printer William Day and from around 1830 lent his name to Day's company, thereafter known as Day & Haghe, Haghe being the artist who drew on the stones and Day being the printer.

Haghe's most important work was his translation of Roberts's drawings of the Holy Land. The numerous tones in the sky—various blues, browns, grays, and whites—are a trademark of Haghe's work, as is the way they blend so carefully into one another without losing their distinct qualities. This was achieved by a variety of techniques, including rubbing, scraping, and etching away the foundation marks and then brushing the inks over the colored base and printing as many as two stones and three colors. Roberts was fully appreciative of Haghe's work and wrote of him, "He has rendered the views in a style clear, simple, and unlaboured, with a masterly vigour and boldness which none but a painter like him could have transferred to stone" (Twyman 1970, p. 223).

Joseph Stannard

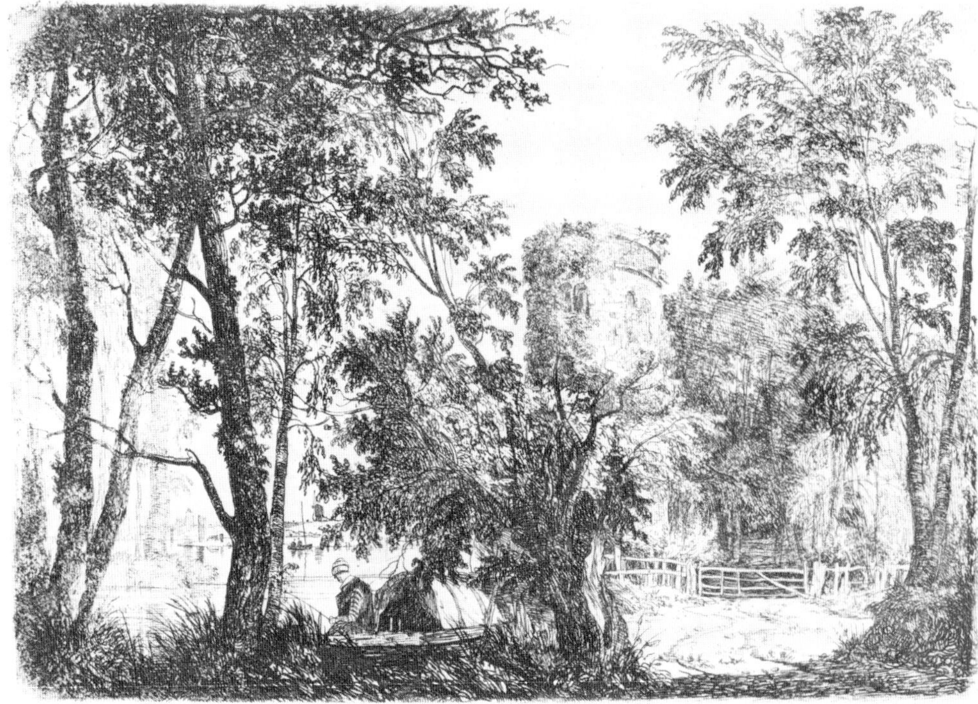

At the age of twelve Joseph Stannard was sent to study drawing with Robert Ladbrooke, one of the founding members of the Norwich Society, and remained with him for seven years. In 1811, at age fourteen, he exhibited at Wrench's Court in Norwich, ultimately showing more than forty-five paintings in oil in the Norwich Society's annual exhibitions before his death in 1830. Although he also exhibited a number of paintings at the British Institution from 1824 to 1828 and at the Society of British Artists in 1824 and 1825, he is most closely associated with his hometown and its regional school of landscape.

More preoccupied with the figure than other members of the Norwich school, Stannard never specialized in a particular genre, executing portraits, still lifes, marine and pastoral landscapes. Stannard's 1821 trip to Holland, where he painted copies of the Dutch masters in the Rijksmuseum, influenced his later choice of landscape as a subject for his paintings and etchings. Though he was a gifted printmaker, he produced only twelve etchings.

88

Old Whittlingham Church (1824)

JOSEPH STANNARD
(Norwich 1797–1830 Norwich)
Etching
105 x 150 mm
Provenance: William Weston Gallery, London

Scratchy in texture and alluding to Dutch precedents, this etching betrays the influence of John Crome, with whom Stannard exhibited in the Norwich Society as early as 1811.

A man is fishing from a boat pulled along the bank of a river's backwater, deep within the shadows of trees and reedy grasses. A rutted path leads past him to a wooden fence, on the other side of which is a tower of Old Whittlingham Church. Beyond and to the left of the church is the open river, smooth and glassy, on which sails a single-masted boat. Cows graze at the far edge of the river, while the hill behind rises to a picturesque windmill.

The charm of the scene is not only in its subject, however, but also in its texture; the way the scratchy lines simulate the coarse bark of the trees to the left and the light-dappled, delicate foliage of the trees to the right and in the middle ground. Stannard used a very fine etching needle and worked it in quick, swirling, criss-crossed patterns to suggest the density of landscape textures and to distinguish among them. He structured his composition very simply by biting the foreground elements longer, contrasting their darkened, shadowy forms with the light-bathed trees, tower, and river in the middle ground and background. The bright white of the soft wove paper only emphasizes the contrast between foreground and background, thus contributing to the suggestion of deep recession in this small but accomplished etching.

RICHARD PARKES BONINGTON

Richard Parkes Bonington began his brief creative life in earnest when his family emigrated to Calais in 1817 and he studied with the watercolorist Louis Francia, who had in turn studied with Thomas Girtin and John Sell Cotman in England. Having developed a passion for landscape, Bonington entered the École des Beaux-Arts in Paris, working in the studio of Baron Gros for two years (1820–22). Bonington is often considered in connection with those younger French artists who rebelled against the neoclassicism of the earlier generation.

Bonington's enthusiasm for watercolor as an independent medium was combined with a fascination with the Near East and a profound curiosity about the history and architecture of medieval France. Bonington contributed to the multivolume Voyages pittoresques et romantiques dans l'ancienne France, sponsored by the state and published by Baron Isidore Taylor between 1820 and 1878, one of the first publications to illustrate French medieval architecture. He took a leave from the École in 1821 for an extended architectural and landscape sketching tour of Normandy, which led to the illustrated travel book Restes et Fragmens *(sic)* d'architecture du moyen âge *in 1824.*

Bonington was also captivated by the French seacoast, rendering appealing yet undramatic paintings and watercolors of several locales, emphasizing his study of light and atmosphere. He was known as a colorist who often took license with perspective, and his early work is characterized by low tones, almost monochromatic in their effect, the result of Girtin's influence by way of Francia.

Bonington first exhibited his work in France. Along with fellow British artists John Constable, Copley Fielding, and Charles Thomson, he was awarded a gold medal at the famous 1824 Paris Salon, at which eighteen British artists displayed fifty-two paintings and watercolors. Bonington's paintings and watercolors were exhibited at the British Institution from 1826 to 1829 and at the Royal Academy in 1827 and 1828. On his third trip to England, in 1828, Bonington succumbed to consumption at the age of twenty-six.

89

Tour du Gros Horloge, Evreux (1824)

GODEFREY ENGLEMANN
(active c. 1820–1830)
After RICHARD PARKES BONINGTON
(Nottingham 1802–1828 London)
From *Normandie*, vol. 2 of Voyages pittoresques et romantiques dans l'ancienne France (1825), pl. 226
Curtis 19 ii/ii
Lithograph printed in colors
332 x 200 mm
Provenance: R. E. Lewis, San Francisco

The first volume of Voyages pittoresques et romantiques dans l'ancienne France appeared in 1820; nineteen volumes would appear over the next fifty-eight years (see Twyman 1970, pp. 226–53). Initiated by Baron Isidore Taylor and the poet Charles Nodier, the series of lithographic albums was meant not only to document architectural monuments and scenery throughout France but also to evoke their exotic and nostalgic charms for an urban public in Paris. As Nodier wrote in the preface to this first volume, the series meant to suggest "a certain melancholy disposition of thought, a certain involuntary predilection for the poetic customs and the arts of our ancestors, the sentiment of I know not what mysterious correspondence of decay and misfortune between these old structures and the generation which has just passed" (Grad and Riggs 1982, p. 17).

The first volume was dedicated to the province of Normandy, an area rich in medieval architecture and prehistoric monuments, and appeared in two parts in 1820 and 1825. Bonington's first contribution to Voyages pittoresques appeared in the second part of the first volume, with five lithographs depicting the great clock tower at Rouen, the church of Saint-Gervais at Gisors, a tower at Vernon, the clock tower at Evreux, and the church of Saint-Taurin at Evreux. The first print, *Rue du Gros-Horloge, Rouen*, described in detail the bustle of a provincial street, with figures in contemporary dress going about their daily business in the shadow of richly

RICHARD PARKES BONINGTON

89

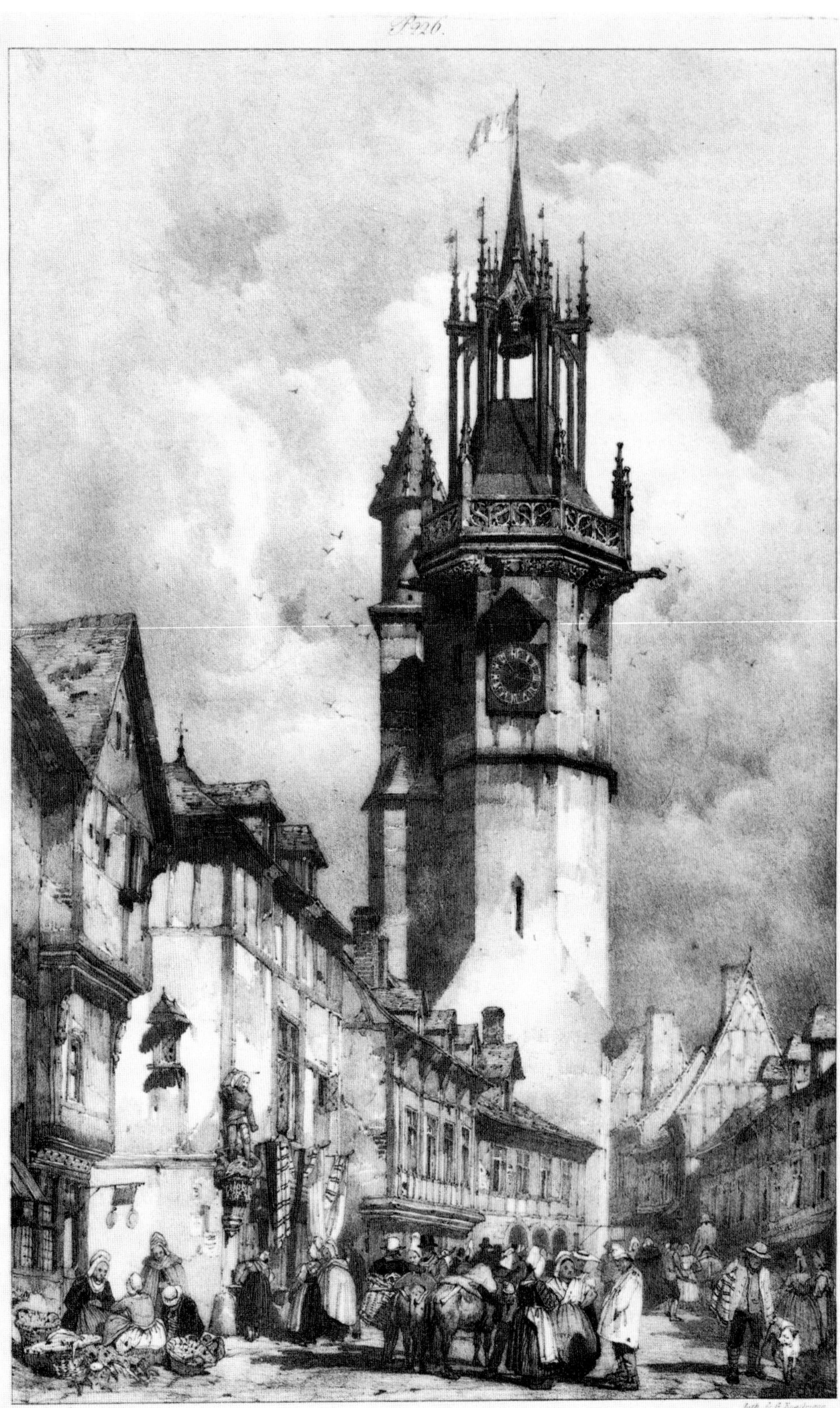

ornamented, diverse, and charming houses. The great clock tower, squat in proportion and straddling the street above an arch through which figures pass, is far in the distance, the end point of the diagonally receding street. *Tour du Gros Horloge, Evreux,* by contrast, emphasizes the vertical thrust of the medieval clock tower as it rises forcefully above the town, dominating the timbered houses that line the street below. It is an image of the clock tower as defender of the town, a remnant, perhaps, of a castle that once stood on that site and that may have once formed the town itself. Indeed, as the caption below the print states, the tower was built in 1417, when Evreux was under the domination of the English. It thus bears witness to foreign occupation and tells of a violent past that continues to inform the character of the peaceful townspeople of provincial Normandy, who carry on in its presence.

Bonington's sure sense of the lithographic technique is evident here, in the play of silvery marks in the small details of the house facades as well as in the more dramatic tonal passages in the clouds. His use of a low vantage point is equally effective, exaggerating the scale of the tower, which dwarfs the diminutive figures. It is a monumental work in Bonington's oeuvre and, according to Michael Twyman (1970, p. 247), the model by which one assesses the other lithographs of Voyages pittoresques. As many of the leading artists of the formative years of lithography contributed to the series, this is no mean achievement. The series included around three thousand lithographs and stands as a major monument in the history not only of lithography but also of romanticism.

THOMAS SHOTTER BOYS

At the age of fourteen Thomas Shotter Boys was apprenticed to the engraver George Cooke, who, with his brother W. B. Cooke, is best known for having commissioned drawings from J. M. W. Turner, which they had engraved and published in 1811 as Views of the Southern Coast of England. Boys completed his apprenticeship in 1823 but continued his association with George Cooke, providing numerous drawings of flowers, which Cooke had engraved for inclusion in Conrad Loddiges's Botanical Cabinet, a series of twenty volumes published between 1818 and 1833.

Boys went to Paris as early as 1823. There he met Richard Parkes Bonington, under whose influence he began working in watercolor and lithography. Between 1833 and 1837 Boys contributed lithographs to the famous topographical series Voyages pittoresques, specifically to the volumes on Languedoc and Picardy. These were simple chalk lithographs with lithotint and scraping for highlights. Boys did not publish colored lithographs until his own Picturesque Architecture in Paris, Ghent, Antwerp, and Rouen in 1839. The subtle beauty of these prints closely approximates the delicate color washes of his watercolors, and the publication was an instant success. Indeed the similarity was so great and the effect so stunning and new that Boys felt it necessary to explain in a descriptive "notice" included in the publication that the color was not added by hand but printed: "Every touch is the work of the artist," he concluded, "and every impression the product of the press."

Following the success of Picturesque Architecture, Boys published Original Views of London as It Is, an album of twenty-seven drawn and tinted lithographs colored by hand that brought him fame in London equal to that he had achieved in Paris. This was, however, his last major lithographic work. As his fortunes declined throughout the 1840s and 1850s, Boys was reduced to contributing occasional illustrations to various publications, including John Ruskin's Examples of the Architecture of Venice *(1851) and* The Stones of Venice *(1851–53). He died impoverished in 1874.*

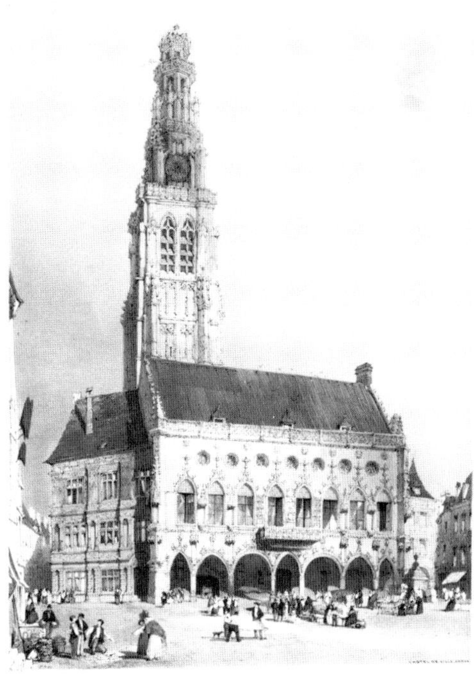

90

L'Hôtel de Ville, Arras (1839)

THOMAS SHOTTER BOYS
(Petonville 1803–1874 London)
From Picturesque Architecture in Paris, Ghent, Antwerp, and Rouen (1839)
Groschwitz 24L
Lithograph printed in colors
380 x 273 mm
Provenance: R. E. Lewis, San Francisco

While French topographical publications, particularly Voyages pittoresques (see entry for cat. no. 89), were concerned with the architectural monuments and scenery of provincial France, the depiction of romantic Paris was left to the Englishman Thomas Shotter Boys in his Picturesque Architecture in Paris, Ghent, Antwerp, and Rouen, published in London in 1839. Comprising twenty-nine lithographs, the work is not only one of the finest topographical albums ever produced but is also a landmark in the development of color printmaking (Twyman 1970, p. 211). Its delicate printing and subtle use of chromolithography testify to the artist's close collaboration with the album's printer, Charles Hullmandel, to whom the album is dedicated in acknowledgment of the printer's many innovations in the technique of lithographic printing.

Typical of Boys's compositions, and similar to those of Richard Parkes Bonington in Voyages pittoresques, the viewpoint taken in *L'Hôtel de Ville, Arras* is from below, exaggerating the scale of the architecture and opening the image up to a dramatic skyward sweep. The chalk drawing is crisp and precise, articulating the numerous details of the ornamented facade of the Gothic town hall. The entire drawing is then pulled together by the use of an olive-gray tint stone that lends substance to the architecture and atmosphere to the urban setting. In this respect Boys was indebted to the craftsmanship of Hullmandel, who had used tinted backgrounds in prints published as early as 1819 and who during the 1830s made numerous experiments in printing halftones, which led to the most important developments in the early history of tinted lithography (Twyman 1988, pp. 68–80).

Boys's relations with Hullmandel were not always cordial, however. Picturesque Architecture created a great sensation both in London and in Paris, where the French king, Louis-Philippe, recognized its importance with a letter and presented a diamond ring to the album's publisher rather than the artist. Hullmandel did not feel he received sufficient credit for the publication, however, and claimed in a letter to a London newspaper that he had invented color lithography. Boys replied in a letter to the same newspaper belittling Hullmandel's contributions and describing in detail his own methods of drawing on stones (Groschwitz 1962, p. 194). Regardless of who was primarily responsible for the beautiful and subtle coloristic effects of its prints, Picturesque Architecture stands as Boys's most important achievement in the art of lithography.

Samuel Palmer

Visionary landscape painter Samuel Palmer first exhibited at the Royal Academy in 1819, when he was just fourteen years old. His early pictures reveal the influence of J. M. W. Turner, David Cox, and his teacher William Wate. It was Palmer's contact with the art of William Blake, however, that would have the most decisive influence on his career.

From 1827 to 1835 Palmer lived in Shoreham, Kent, where he was the central figure among a small circle of Blake followers known as the Ancients, who, through discussions of art and literature, sought an artistic and commercial alternative to modern industrial society. There Palmer made landscape paintings and drawings that gave form to his pantheistic view of nature. His pastoral themes of harvest, shepherds, livestock, and moonlit cornfields extol the sanctity of rural life. It was not until 1850 that Palmer made his first etching, completing thirteen prints during the next thirty-one years. These etchings recall the mysticism and visionary intensity of his Shoreham period and show the influence of Blake's 1821 wood engravings for Virgil's Ecologues.

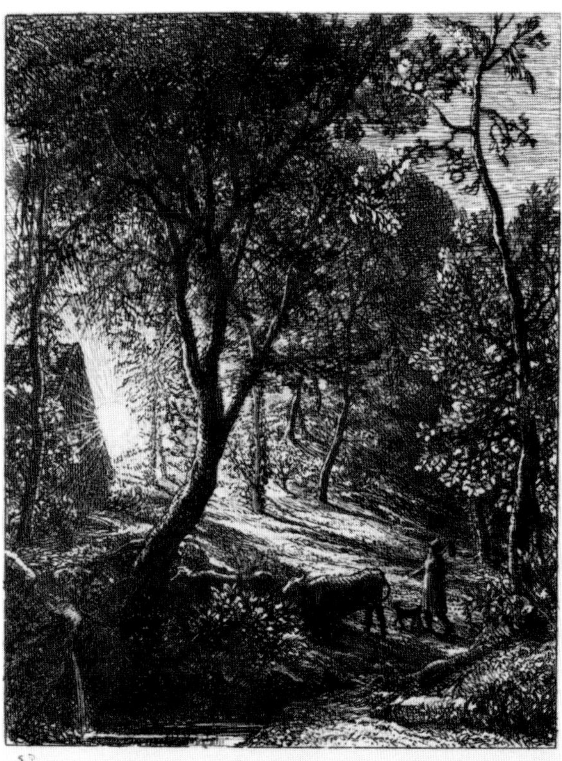

91

The Herdsman's Cottage or *Sunset* (1850)

SAMUEL PALMER
(London 1805–1881 Reigate)
Lister 3 ii/ii
Etching
98 x 77 mm
Provenance: Zeitlin and Ver Brugge, Los Angeles

Palmer's idyllic interpretation of nature and country life is exemplified by *The Herdsman's Cottage.* Accompanied by his dog, the herdsman drives home his cattle in the glowing light of sunset. The gleaming rays infuse the composition with a sense of wonder and poetic intensity. Palmer created these intense chiaroscuro effects through the use of minute lines and pinpoint touches, dramatically contrasting the white surface of the paper with rich black tones. To further heighten the luminosity of his images, Palmer often reworked the surface of his plates with multiple bitings, burnishing, and extensive use of stopping out and drypoint. Many of Palmer's themes have Christian overtones, and it is possible to associate this print with the theme of the Good Shepherd tending his flock. In Palmer's vision one attains peace and salvation through nature and the simple, bucolic life. Although based primarily on observation of nature, Palmer's landscapes are also a product of the artist's imagination.

In 1872 *The Herdsman's Cottage* was published by Seeley and Co. in the journal *The Portfolio* with the incorrect title *Sunrise.*

92

The Early Ploughman or *The Morning Spread upon the Mountains* (before 1861)

SAMUEL PALMER
(London 1805–1881 Reigate)
Lister 9 v/ix
Etching
133 x 198 mm
Provenance: Zeitlin and Ver Brugge, Los Angeles

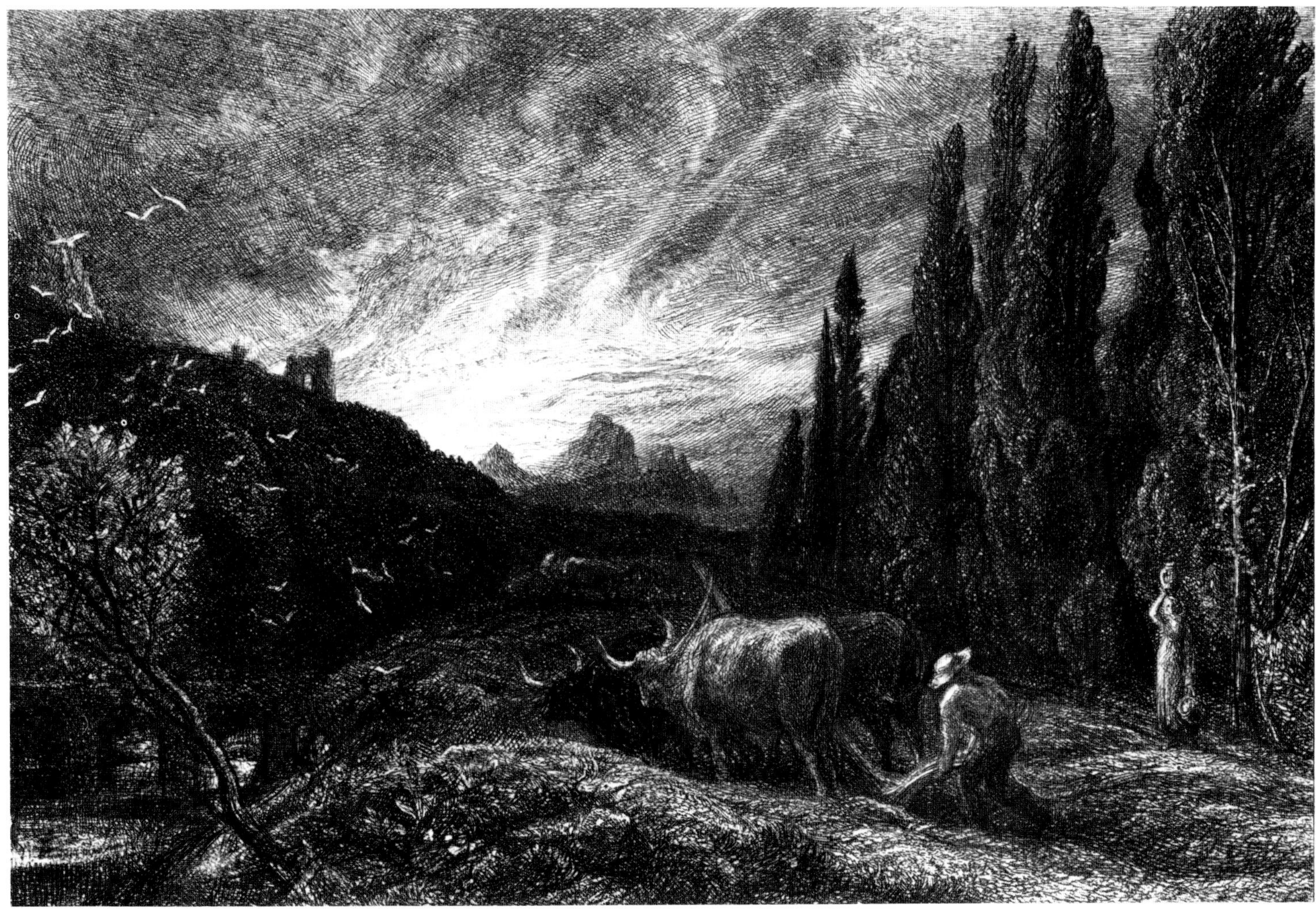

Beautifully conceived and finely rendered, *The Early Ploughman* is a remarkable example of Palmer's Shoreham style. A master of light effects, he rendered the rising sun on the horizon with sparkling luminosity. Through the use of multiple bitings and drypoint, Palmer endowed the landscape with a richness and wealth of tonal variations. In a series of nine states, he altered minor aspects of the composition, adding the plowman's cap, for example, and further intensified the image by rebiting. In harmony with the natural world, a plowman tills the soil near the riverbank while another works in the distance. A nearby woman carries pitchers of water, one on her head and another in her hand. The Alpine hills and cypress trees recall Palmer's honeymoon in Italy. Evocative and highly moving, Palmer's vision of nature is infused with a spiritual presence and the belief that one's labors will ultimately bring one closer to salvation.

EDWARD LEAR

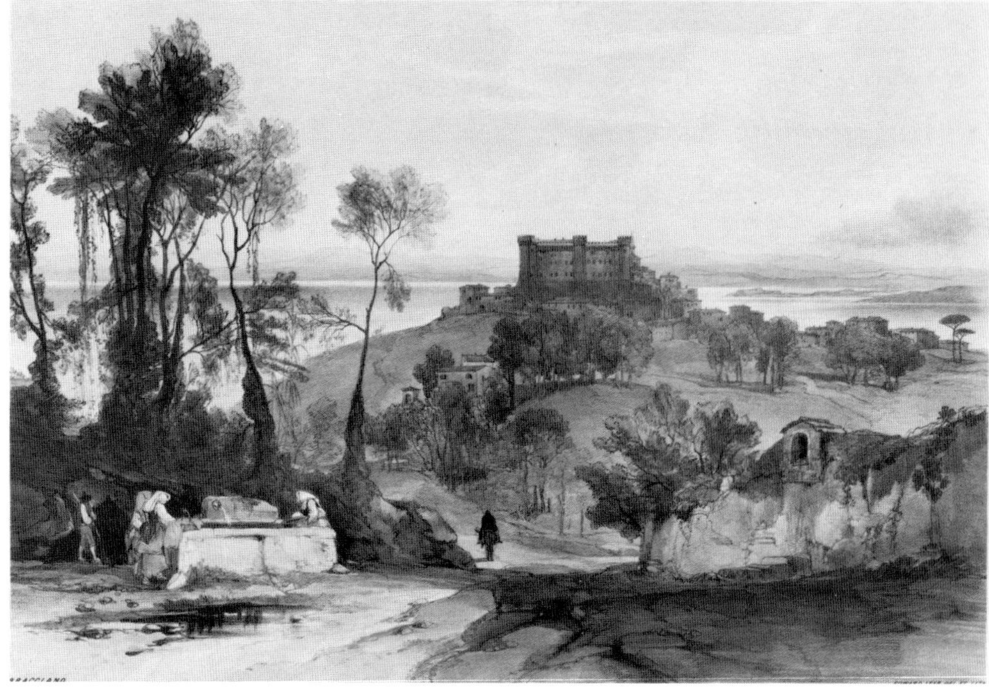

Known primarily as a writer of witty nonsense verse ("The Owl and the Pussycat"), Edward Lear was also a prolific draftsman and landscape artist, a late nineteenth-century practitioner of the eighteenth-century tradition of topographical watercolors. He began his artistic career early, drawing birds from books of natural history, and at nineteen he was employed as a draftsman by the Zoological Gardens. A year later (1832) he published Family of the Psittacidae, *one of England's earliest collections of colored ornithological drawings. Other zoological publications followed as a result of his acquaintance with Lord Derby of Knowsley and a number of other aristocratic patrons. Through his associations with the nobility, Lear was brought to the attention of Queen Victoria, to whom he gave drawing lessons in 1846.*

Lear began a series of extended travels around 1835 and 1836, when he journeyed to Ireland and the Lake District. From 1837 to 1864 he traveled through Italy, Malta, Greece, Egypt, and Switzerland, drawing and writing. Due to increasing ill health, he preferred a warm climate, wintering between 1864 and 1870 in Nice, Malta, Egypt, and Cannes, finally settling in San Remo, where he remained until his death in 1888.

Lear wrote and illustrated travel books and journals between 1841 and 1870, publishing his first Book of Nonsense *in 1846; he also taught drawing, sketched panoramic landscapes, and painted in oil. His paintings sold well to his many wealthy patrons, while his drawings and watercolors were far less successful in the marketplace.*

93

View of Bracciano (1841)

EDWARD LEAR
(Holloway 1812–1888 San Remo)
Plate 2 of *Views in Rome and Its Environs* (1841)
Lithograph with hand coloring
206 x 390 mm
Provenance: William Weston Gallery, London

View of Bracciano is the second of twenty-four full-page lithographs by Lear that were published by T. M'Lean as *Views in Rome and Its Environs* in 1841. The Grunwald Center impression is from one of the few copies of the book to be hand-colored, perhaps by Lear himself.[1] The first of seven travel books produced by Lear during his extensive journeys through Europe, the Middle East, and North Africa, *Views in Rome and Its Environs* includes examples of the kinds of views that attracted the artist throughout his life: long, panoramic vistas encompassing hills, bodies of water, silent ancient cities, overgrown walls, sparse vegetation, warmth, and stillness. Even the donkey in *View of Bracciano*, although moving toward the walled city in the middle distance, appears to be in a state of suspended animation.

A master of the quick, on-the-spot study expanded through copious notes as to tone, color, and atmospheric treatment, Lear would complete each pen-and-ink or graphite drawing at home, only then adding local color or pale washes following the eighteenth-century tradition of the tinted drawing. Although Lear always found picturesque scenery to sketch, his landscape drawings were topographical rather than idealized or fantastic. His strengths lay in his acute observation and fine draftsmanship, which he successfully transferred to the lithographic process. In *View of Bracciano* Lear has captured the contrasting textures and tonal qualities of exotic foliage, masonry and stucco structures, dusty earth, placid water, and hazy sky, all in modulated hues that further contrast with the brilliant coloring of the women's clothing, the sky reflected in the foreground puddle of water, and the whiteness of the stone well.

1. Philip Hofer, *Edward Lear as a Landscape Draughtsman* (Cambridge: Belknap Press of Harvard University Press, 1967), p. 72.

Francis Seymour Haden

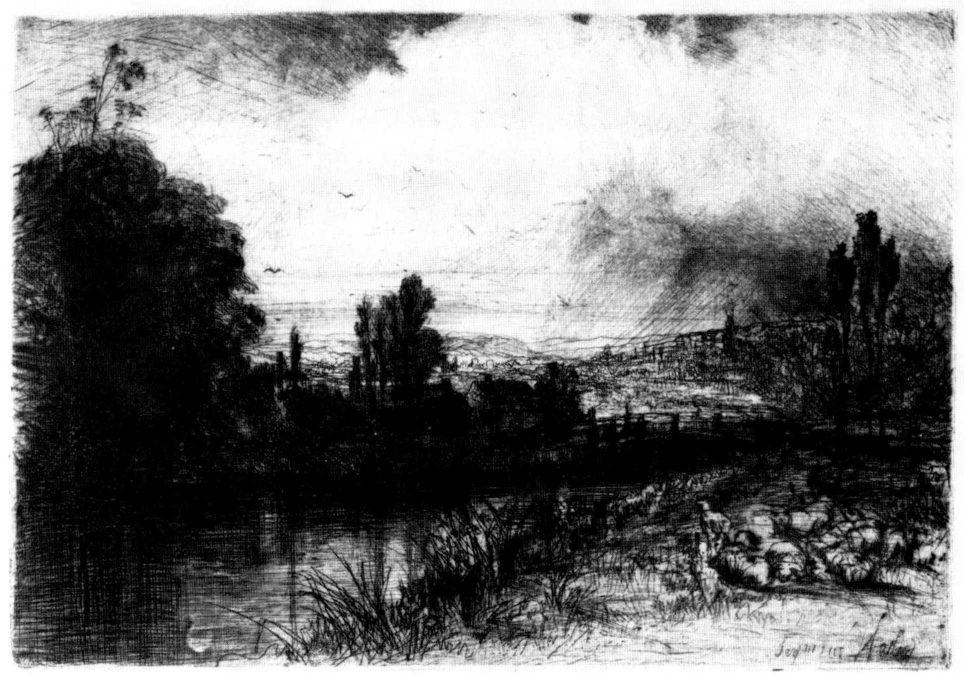

Francis Seymour Haden, a noted surgeon and brother-in-law of James McNeill Whistler, first took art lessons as a medical student in Paris in the early 1840s. It was not until the late 1850s, however, that he began in earnest to pursue his interest in etching, an avocation that developed into a second, parallel career.

The spontaneous quality of Haden's intimate landscapes, particularly of ponds and small wooded enclosures in the English countryside, received positive critical response at home and in Paris. As early as 1864 Philippe Burty wrote an extensive article praising Haden's work in the Gazette des beaux-arts, *and in 1865 the renowned French printer Auguste Delâtre produced a portfolio of twenty-five of Haden's etchings entitled Études à l'eau-forte.*

Haden was undoubtedly influenced by the example of his brother-in-law, and he and Whistler often traveled and sketched together outdoors, developing the art of drawing from nature directly onto a copper plate, often in drypoint. Gaining confidence in his art, Haden exhibited at the Royal Academy under the pseudonym H. Dean and then, from 1864 to 1886, under his own name.

In 1890 Haden founded the Society of Painter-Etchers in London, serving as its president until his death. Highly influential in the etching revival in both London and Paris, Haden was knighted in 1894 for his contributions to art.

94

On the Test (1859)

FRANCIS SEYMOUR HADEN
(London 1818–1910 Abersford)
Harrington 20 (trial proof d)
Etching and drypoint
150 x 225 mm
Signed lower right; inscribed *2* lower left
Provenance: Zeitlin and Ver Brugge, Los Angeles

Haden was well known for carrying small plates with him so that he could sketch directly onto them whenever a scene (usually a landscape or a view of the Thames) caught his attention. His etchings with drypoint are notable for their freshness and immediacy, giving the impression of having been printed with a minimum of reworking after the initial design was made. In fact, Haden's practice was to print a number of trial proofs prior to deciding on the actual state to be published. Often the changes were slight, however, and for *On the Test*, published in 1859, three of the four proofs involved changes in the inscription and signature only. The etching in the Grunwald Center is the fourth proof, or trial proof "d," indicated by the simple signature on the right side of the plate and the absence of any inscription. The differences between this final proof and the published state rest in the treatment of the clouds on the right, which were somewhat lightened prior to publication; the trees on the left, which were reworked to make branches and leaves more visible; and the sheep, which were more carefully defined.

Francis Seymour Haden

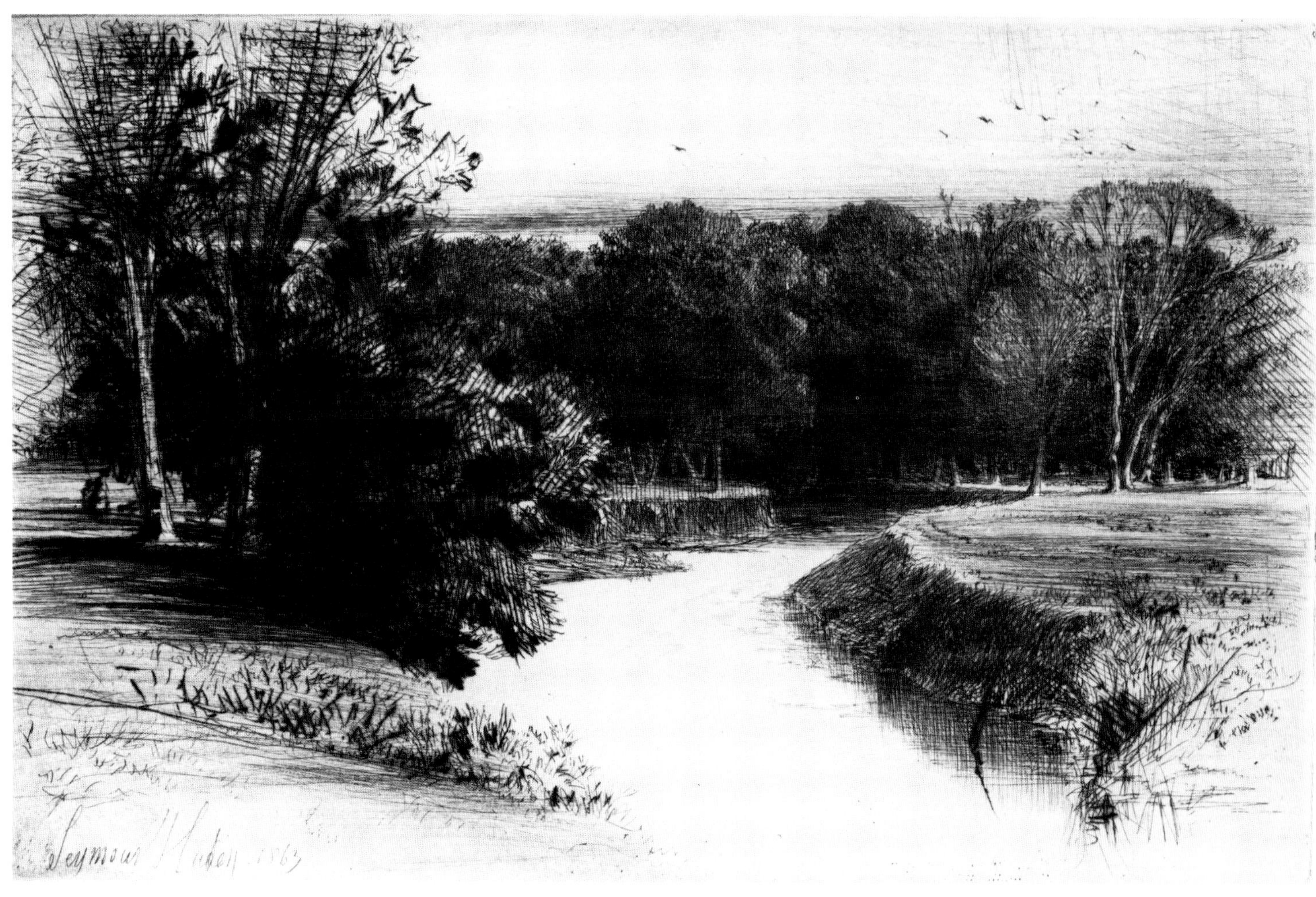

95

Sunset in Ireland (1863)

FRANCIS SEYMOUR HAYDEN
(London 1818–1910 Abersford)
Harrington 51 (trial proof e)
Drypoint
138 x 215 mm
Provenance: O. P. Reed, Los Angeles

Sunset in Ireland illustrates Haden's mastery of the etching technique, as he worked the various textures and tones of his composition. This version of the etching is trial proof "e," and the numerous changes, even after publication, when shadows in the middle distance were lengthened and the left bank was flooded, indicate that Haden was not entirely satisfied with his progress. The delicacy and care with which he drew his trees are readily apparent, however, particularly in the right background. The dark, velvety texture of the shrubbery on the left bank balances both the sharp branches of the tall trees on the far left and the more careful articulation of the trees in the background.

Haden frequently depicted ponds and streams banked by lush undergrowth and tall trees. These scenes are characteristic of his own artistic sensibilities and show less influence of his brother-in-law James McNeill Whistler than do his views of the Thames or the English seacoast.

WILLIAM WARD

After reading John Ruskin's Seven Lamps of Architecture, *William Ward enrolled in his drawing class at the London Working Men's College in 1854. Ruskin's influence over the younger man's career could not have been more complete. He became Ward's mentor, friend, and chief employer, commissioning him in 1858 to copy watercolors by the late J. M. W. Turner. Through his own talent as well as careful attention to materials used and techniques developed by Turner and taught him by Ruskin, Ward became the most accomplished of Turner's many copyists or imitators. Several of the smaller watercolor landscapes attributed to Turner over the years may in fact be by Ward. By 1869 Ruskin, aware of such real and potential difficulties, was signing and annotating Ward's watercolors, not only as a statement of the work's merit but also to ensure proper attribution by dealers and collectors.*

96

The Seine between Mantes and Vernon

WILLIAM WARD
(1829–1908)
Watercolor and body color
150 x 203 mm
Inscribed *Seen and entirely approved 5th July 77. John Ruskin* lower right
Provenance: Zeitlin and Ver Brugge, Los Angeles

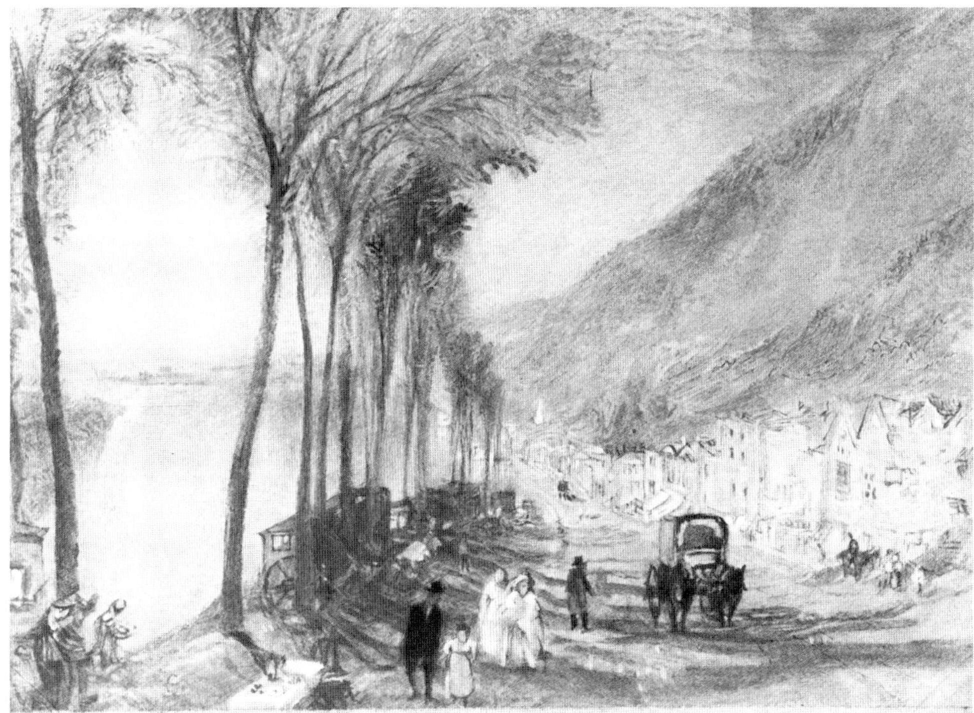

This drawing is a copy after J. M. W. Turner's view of the Seine between Mantes and Vernon in the Tate Gallery, London (Turner Bequest CCLIX–114), one of the drawings in Turner's French River series of around 1830. The Ward drawing was commissioned by John Ruskin and has an inscription indicating his approval of the drawing on July 5, 1877.

Turner's French River series was highly praised by Ruskin and may have provided models for other Ward copies as well.[1] In addition to making copies after Turner's vignettes, Ward particularly excelled in copying his drawings in body color and indeed provided Ruskin with an account of Turner's body color process.[2] The Grunwald Center drawing is particularly close in line quality to Ward's copy of Turner's *Luxembourg*, a body color drawing dated 1876 (Cambridge, Harvard University, Fogg Art Museum). Typically this betrays the somewhat stiff character of a copy.

1. In a letter to Ward of February 1883, Ruskin mentioned the receipt of eight *Rivers*, possibly a reference to Ward's copies after the French River series (*Letters from John Ruskin to William Ward*, ed. Thomas T. Wise, vol. 2 [1893], p. 84).
2. Ibid., p. 71.

DAVID YOUNG CAMERON

While still working as a clerk in the mercantile trade, David Young Cameron studied drawing at the Glasgow Art School. In 1885, however, he forsook commerce and enrolled full-time in the Edinburgh School of Art. There George Stevenson, an amateur etcher and friend of Seymour Haden, encouraged Cameron to take up etching. Four years later he was elected an associate of the Royal Society of Painter-Etchers. He contributed regularly to the society's exhibitions until 1902, when he resigned in protest over the introduction of a new rule admitting reproductive engravings. Nine years later he was elected to the Royal Academy as an associate engraver and, on the basis of his oil paintings, became a full academician in 1920.

Schooled in the etchings of Rembrandt van Rijn, Charles Méryon, and James McNeill Whistler, Cameron was highly sensitive to the color, texture, and absorbency of various handmade papers and modified the inking of his plates accordingly. Like his famous precursors, Cameron was attracted to the picturesque charms of rustic scenery and urban dwellings. His Venetian etchings of 1895–98 recall those of Whistler, while his London and Parisian etchings of 1899 and 1904, respectively, refer to Méryon's depiction of medieval Paris. Cameron is nevertheless perhaps best remembered for his evocative drypoints and etchings of the sweeping and barren landscapes of the Scottish moors and Highlands. He lived in Scotland and there executed most of his five hundred prints. With these, Cameron joined Muirhead Bone as one of the dominant British etchers of the first three decades of the twentieth century.

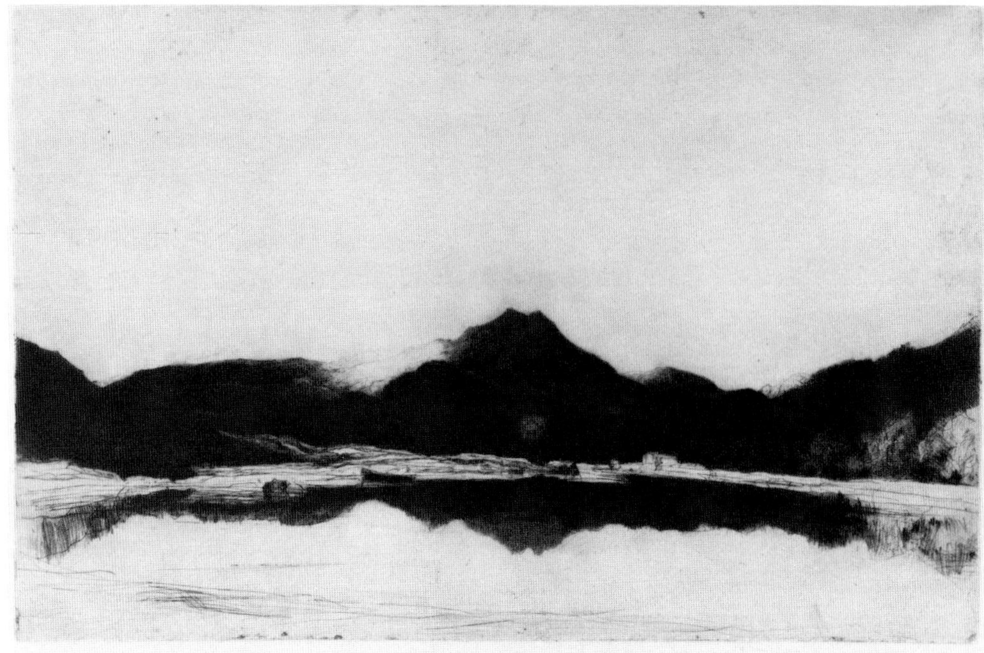

97

Ben Lomond (1923)

DAVID YOUNG CAMERON
(Glasgow 1865–1945)
Rinder 468
Etching and drypoint
Signed lower right
263 x 417 mm
Provenance: Kennedy Galleries, New York

Between 1917 and 1923 Cameron made no etchings. Instead he concentrated on oil paintings, submitting nineteen to the Royal Academy exhibitions during those years; in contrast he had submitted only one in the previous years. He returned to etching in 1923 with this print, which is among his most sublime landscape etchings.

Cameron's earliest landscape etchings, from 1888, were very much in the manner of Seymour Haden's prints, exploiting the wiry effect of freely drawn etched lines, only rarely retouched with drypoint. Toward the end of the century he began to emphasize large, dramatic tonal areas of deeply bitten and densely cross-hatched lines highlighted by selective plate wiping. Over the next decade he added drypoint to his repertory, often using it, as in this print, to strengthen areas within shadows and along riverbanks and lakeshores.

Typical of Cameron's mature landscape compositions, this print emphasizes the silent expanse of a Highland setting: a craggy mountain rising from the shadows of forested hills; a simple gabled house within the shadows; a boat house and fishing boat on the shore; and two figures, rail-thin and barely visible, along the water's edge. It is a contemplative scene in which outward appearances mirror an interior state, as in the romantic landscapes of Caspar David Friedrich. In this case the dominant emotion is a kind of sublime melancholy, in which one feels disembodied and suspended in time and space, at once distant from and drawn into the dark mystery of the towering mountain and its mirrored opposite.

The effect of this mirroring is compounded by our knowledge of the print process, as we recognize that the print itself is a mirror image of the design etched on the plate and thus that the vertical mirroring within the composition is a result of the lateral mirroring from the plate to the paper. What at first seemed to be a simple and faithful representation of Cameron's native landscape becomes a sophisticated meditation on printmaking itself.

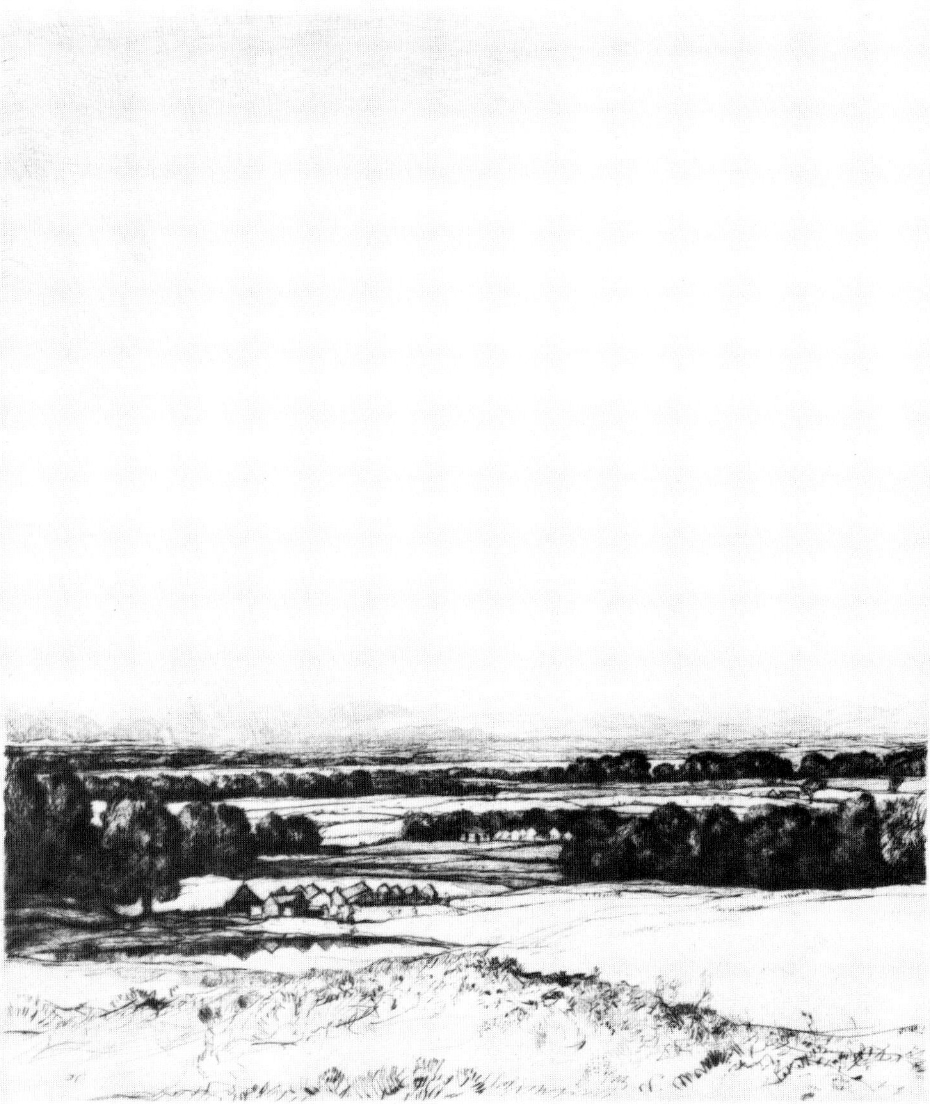

98

Valley of the Tay

DAVID YOUNG CAMERON
(Glasgow 1865–1945)
Rinder 493
Etching and drypoint
302 x 263 mm
Signed lower right
Provenance: Zeitlin and Ver Brugge, Los Angeles

Perhaps drawing upon the specific example of Jacob van Ruisdael's famous *View of Haarlem* of around 1670 (Amsterdam, Rijksmuseum), Cameron assumed a high vantage point in this print, forcing the receding ground plane deep into space and exaggerating the vertical sweep of sky. Like Ruisdael, Cameron focused on the articulation of a particular landscape; in this case the central valley of the Tay River. The valley is divided into discrete units of cultivated land separated by groves of trees or groups of houses and then set off dramatically by the great expanse of sky, across which a lightly etched and sun-filled rainstorm moves out of the distant hills to the left.

In contrast to the sublime *Ben Lomond* (cat. no. 97), *Valley of the Tay* is a domestic landscape illustrative of the fructifying effects of human labor. The gentle valley floor is marked off and measured and its bounty gathered, it would seem, without exceptional effort. It is a harmonious landscape in which the small country cottages sit comfortably within and are not dwarfed by the expansive space of the valley. As such, it represents one aspect of Cameron's landscape prints, offering the rustic counterpart to *Ben Lomond*.

MUIRHEAD BONE

Like Frederick Landseer Griggs, Muirhead Bone first studied architecture before turning to printmaking. He produced his first etchings in 1898. These prints and two series published in 1901 and 1904, when he had taken up printmaking as a full-time occupation, reveal his debt to the legacy of James McNeill Whistler, Seymour Haden, and Charles Méryon, just as his later drypoints reveal the influence of Rembrandt's landscape etchings. The delicate inking of his drypoints, the technique he favored in his later works, could be sustained only over very limited print runs. Thus the rarity of these impressions, along with their poetic compositions, have made the landscape drypoints the most prized of Bone's prints, although he is equally well known for his etchings of buildings or demolition areas, which depict architectural elements shrouded in evocative blackened scaffolding. Bone was also a prolific watercolorist and draftsman.

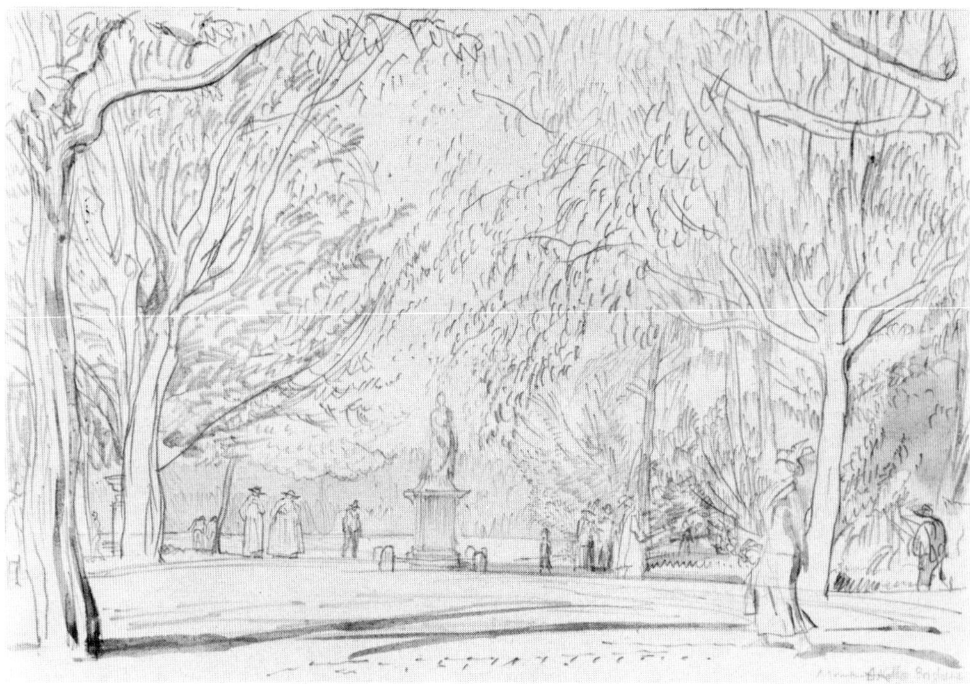

99

Garden of the Villa Borghese, Rome (c. 1913)

MUIRHEAD BONE
(Glasgow 1876–1953 Oxford)
Graphite with blue wash
155 x 232 mm
Signed and titled lower right
Provenance: Craddock and Barnard, London

In 1910 Bone went to Italy. There, despite his opinion that "every art cat in the world had been there and the plate had been licked clean" (Garton and Cooke 1984, p. 1), he was attracted to the modish life of the streets and gardens of Rome and depicted it in several prints and drawings.

In *Rainy Night in Rome*, a drypoint of 1913, for example, Bone described sheets of rain falling on smartly dressed pedestrians walking in and out of shadows cast by the streetlamp-lit facade of the Church of San Rocco. In this drawing, *Garden of the Villa Borghese, Rome*, quite probably of 1913 as well, a woman walks with her child along a path in the foreground. By the delicate foliage and bright light, it would appear to be early spring, and the woman is appropriately dressed in a fashionable suit and plumed hat. Along a path in the middle ground to the right, another woman walks wearing a long coat and wide-brimmed hat accompanied by similarly attired women and a young child. The costumes of these modern women are contrasted with the traditional dress worn by two priests walking in the left middle ground and with the more modest clothes of the workers who attend to the grounds.

The elegance of this rather simple view of urban leisure is suggested not only by the clothes of the figures but also by the quality of the graphite lines that describe with precision the flickering foliage of the trees and the sharply cut forms of the women's dress and postures. Blue-green watercolor was delicately brushed on to suggest both the color of the park's foliage and the coolness of the shadows cast by the late afternoon light of early spring. As far as we know, this drawing was not preparatory to a print but was executed as a work of art in its own right. As such, it is typical of Bone's interest in the striking juxtaposition of modern life and the architecture of old Rome.

FREDERICK LANDSEER GRIGGS

Frederick Landseer Griggs was first trained as an architect and architectural draftsman. At the age of twenty-two, however, he abandoned architecture and, on the advice of Joseph Pennell, studied drawing and illustration, earning his living as an illustrator for various architectural magazines and the popular topographical series of picturesque English architecture and scenery, Highways and Byways. He turned seriously to etching in 1912 and is now regarded as the finest etcher of English picturesque architectural subjects.

Griggs's serious interest in etching coincided with his conversion to Catholicism, which imbued his mature work with a nostalgia for pre-Reformation England. Initially Griggs recorded existing ecclesiastical buildings, but after 1915 he began to etch imaginative reconstructions of churches and towns as they might have looked before the Reformation. The delicate drawing of these prints and their glimmering light reflect his love for the etchings of Samuel Palmer. Indeed, with the assistance of Martin Hardie, then keeper of prints and drawings at the Victoria and Albert Museum, Griggs printed some of the finest impressions of Palmer's plates.

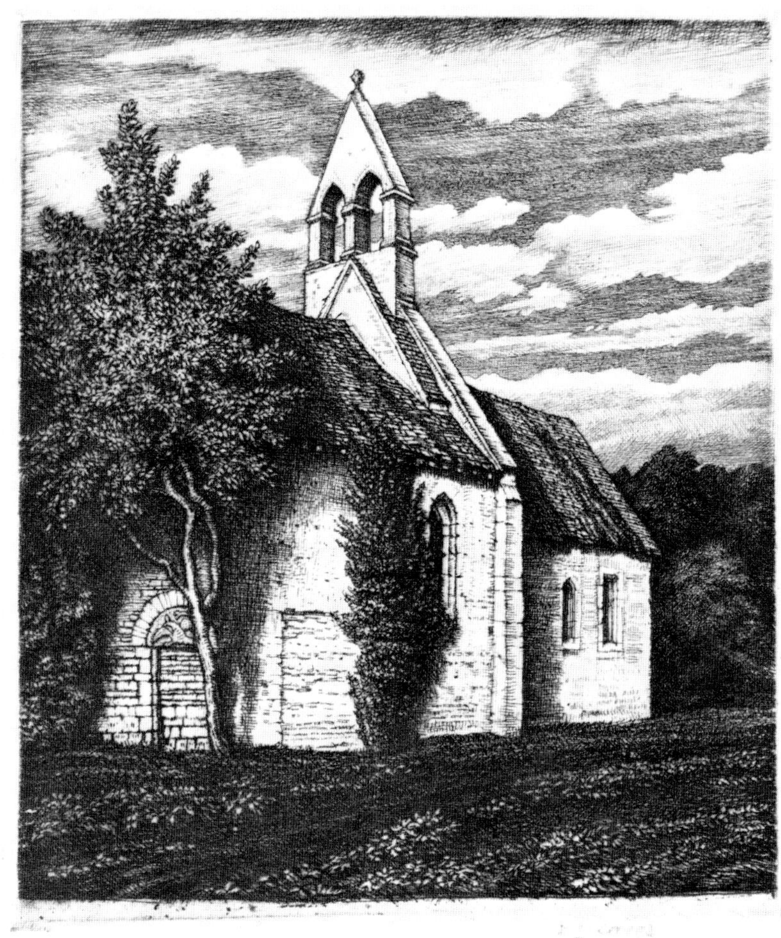

100

Netherton Chapel (1935)

FREDERICK LANDSEER GRIGGS
(Hitchin 1876–1938 Campden)
Dodgson 53 v/v
Etching
124 x 109 mm
Signed lower right
Provenance: Colnaghi, London

Typical of Griggs's most evocative works, this print exploits the tonal properties of etching. The modest country chapel is drawn in lightly etched lines that pattern its surface and describe the texture of its stones. The trees that grow alongside the chapel are drawn in more deeply etched lines densely gathered in webs of curling marks. The trees' shadows are defined by cross-hatchings that suggest light filtering through foliage. The sky consists of wiry lines more deeply etched than the pale lines scoring the clouds; together they convey the sense of clouds streaming rapidly past the quiet and stable chapel. All of these marks are then set off against the very deeply etched and variously drawn lines that form the ground plane of thick grass and rutted path.

The dramatic and rhythmic movement of light and dark suggests the very bright but transient lighting of the chapel. The resiliency of the religious edifice is thus underscored, and its ability to withstand the passage of time and encroaching nature is poetically celebrated. The chapel stands in all its modesty, like the print itself, as an emblem of the artist's desire to render permanent the old England that was rapidly disappearing.

ROBERT S. AUSTIN

Contemporary with the neoromantic landscape etchings of Frederick Landseer Griggs were the line engravings of Robert Austin. With these, Austin is credited with reviving one of the earliest techniques of printmaking, and his crisp engraved lines recall those of certain fifteenth-century masters, such as Martin Schongauer. Austin is most highly regarded for his depictions of rural scenes and religious figures, which suggest at once images of modern life and romanticized religious allegories.

Austin began his studies at the Royal College of Art in 1913, only to have them interrupted by four years of service in the army during World War I. He returned to the Royal College of Art in 1919 and published his first etching with the Twenty-one Gallery, which would continue to publish his prints throughout the 1920s. In 1921 he was elected an associate of the Royal Society of Painter-Etchers and the following year was awarded a scholarship in engraving at the British School in Rome. He lived and traveled in Italy from 1922 to 1926, when he returned to London to teach engraving at the Royal College of Art. There he taught and encouraged students to explore the qualities of early engraving that had inspired him. During World War II he produced war posters commissioned by the Ministry of Information and numerous drawings for the Women's Royal Naval Service and the Royal Nursing Service. These drawings were executed in a precise, deliberate style not unlike that of his better-known engravings. In 1949 he was elected a Royal Academician and in 1956, president of the Royal Watercolour Society.

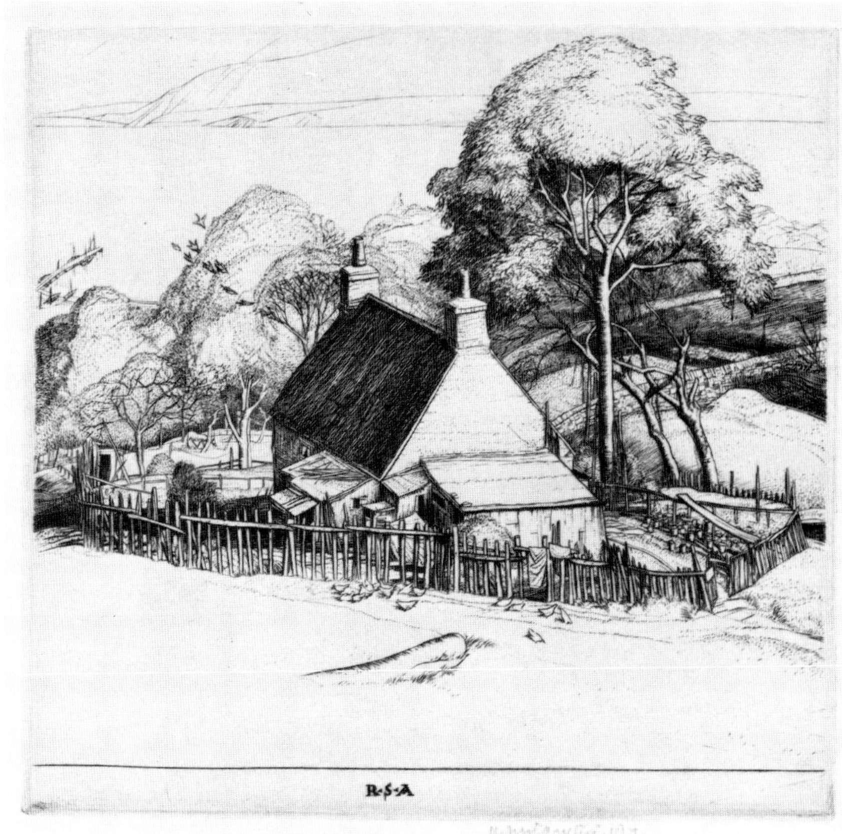

101

Plane Tree Cottage (1927)

ROBERT S. AUSTIN
(Leicester 1895–1973 Burnham Overy Staithe)
Dodgson 66
Engraving
138 x 147 mm
Signed and dated lower right
Provenance: Zeitlin and Ver Brugge, Los Angeles

In its rigorous simplicity, economy of line, and deliberate compositional order, this print recalls the landscape backgrounds of Martin Schongauer's engravings of the 1480s more than it does the landscape etchings of Rembrandt van Rijn, which, because of the prominence of cottages in them (see cat. no. 52), might otherwise come to mind. Indeed it is the precision of the engraved line and the delicacy of the marks giving texture to the foliage that characterize Austin's opposition to the Rembrandtesque landscape tradition best represented in England by Seymour Haden.

Haden emphasized the immediacy of the image and the suggestion of instantaneity in the description of landscape motifs. The trees seem capable of moving with the wind one feels to be blowing through the landscape, and the textures of the grass and underbrush seem moist and fresh. By contrast, the landscape motifs in Austin's print suggest permanence and its attendant qualities, including nobility. The trees do not seem capable of movement, of bending with the wind, but are impressive for the abstract rhythms of their forms, the crisscross of their branches, and the soft, rounded shapes of their foliage. Even the line of birds suggests a sweeping pattern of engraved marks more than movement through space.

Everything in this composition is deliberately placed and is not meant to suggest the innocent description of observed phenomena. Yet Austin includes just enough particular details of cottage life to arouse our sympathies for the place and what it represents of English culture. There is the jerry-built cottage itself, the outbuildings added to the main building as necessity dictates. There is the fence that leans in whatever direction the hills take. And there is the small garden to the right, beneath the precariously balanced plank, crowded with pots scattered in no particular order.

This is the beauty of Austin's otherwise quite modest prints: they are at once brilliant in their compositional control and technical execution and moving in the sympathetic way they offer detailed signs of human presence. They represent the artist's profound respect and nostalgic longing for the simple country life of old England, a life he saw rapidly declining in the decades following World War I.

GRAHAM SUTHERLAND

Following his apprenticeship as a railway engineer, in 1921 Graham Sutherland entered London's Goldsmiths' School of Art, where he learned the etcher's trade. During the 1920s and early 1930s he produced some thirty-five etchings in the tradition of William Blake and the English visionaries. His romantic, pastoral landscapes display a compelling degree of chiaroscuro and a love of texture and surface detail, endowing his prints with an almost mystical vitality. This appealing art earned him a fine reputation and a faculty position at the Chelsea School of Art, where he taught from 1928 to 1939. After 1934 Sutherland shifted his attention to oil and watercolor painting. His style also changed dramatically during this period, becoming more expressive and hallucinatory in character, reflecting his interest in the art of the surrealists. Vivid colors and strange, metamorphosizing forms from the hidden world of the unconscious dominate the art of much of Sutherland's later career.

During World War II Sutherland was employed as an official war artist from 1940 to 1945, recording the effects of bombing and strife. After 1947 he spent considerable time in southern France, where he derived most of his pictorial ideas from the sunlit landscape of the Riviera. In the last two decades of his life, Sutherland created a number of prints that reveal his earlier surrealist affinities, including a series of twenty-six color lithographs published in 1968 entitled Bestiary and a set of fourteen aquatints published in 1977 under the title Bees.

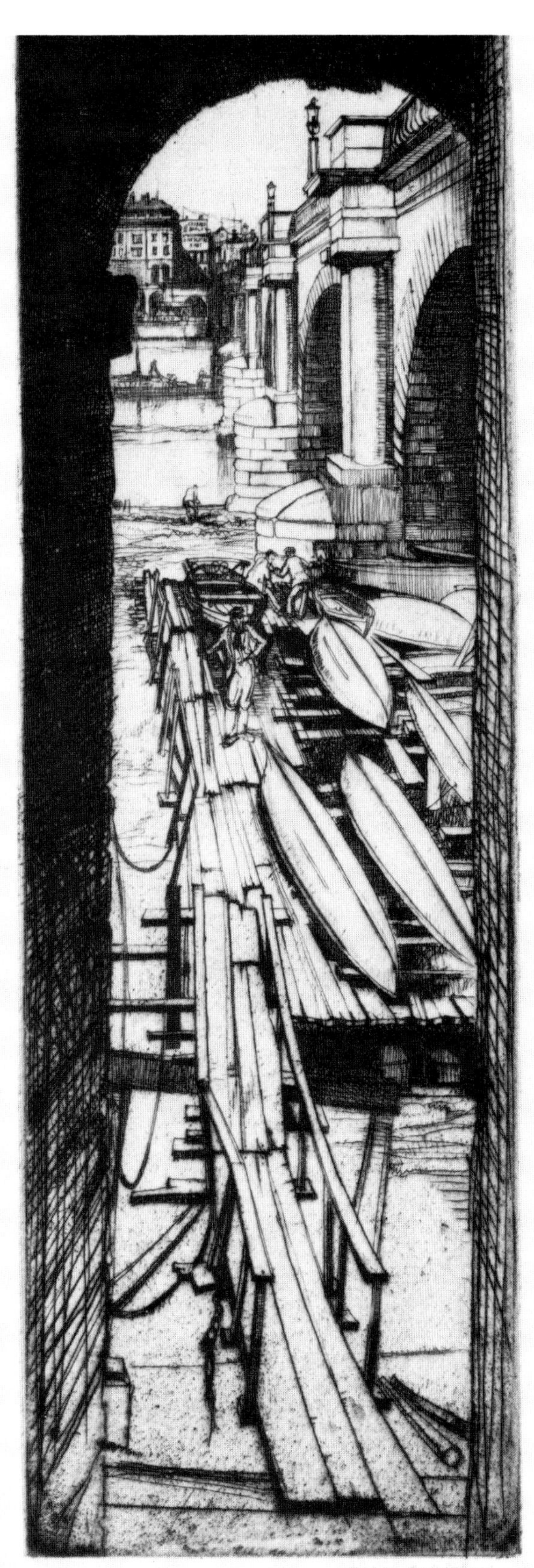

102

Waterloo Bridge (1923)

GRAHAM SUTHERLAND
(London 1903–1979 London)
Man 9 ii/ii; Tassi 5 ii/ii
Etching and drypoint
263 x 88 mm
Signed lower right; titled lower left
Provenance: Colnaghi, London

Sutherland first turned to the graphic arts in 1922, rendering views of London such as *Waterloo Bridge.* Reminiscent of Charles Méryon's Parisian vistas and James McNeill Whistler's 1859 Thames series, Sutherland's complex compositions closely record objects and forms. Through a constrained viewing access, one explores the riverbank, bridge, and distant skyline. Sutherland binds the diverse elements of the composition together with a network of intersecting lines and a racing perspective.

Graham Sutherland

103

The Village (c. 1925)

GRAHAM SUTHERLAND
(London 1903–1979 London)
Blue ink and blue wash over graphite
167 x 192 mm
Provenance: Shaunagh Fitzgerald, London

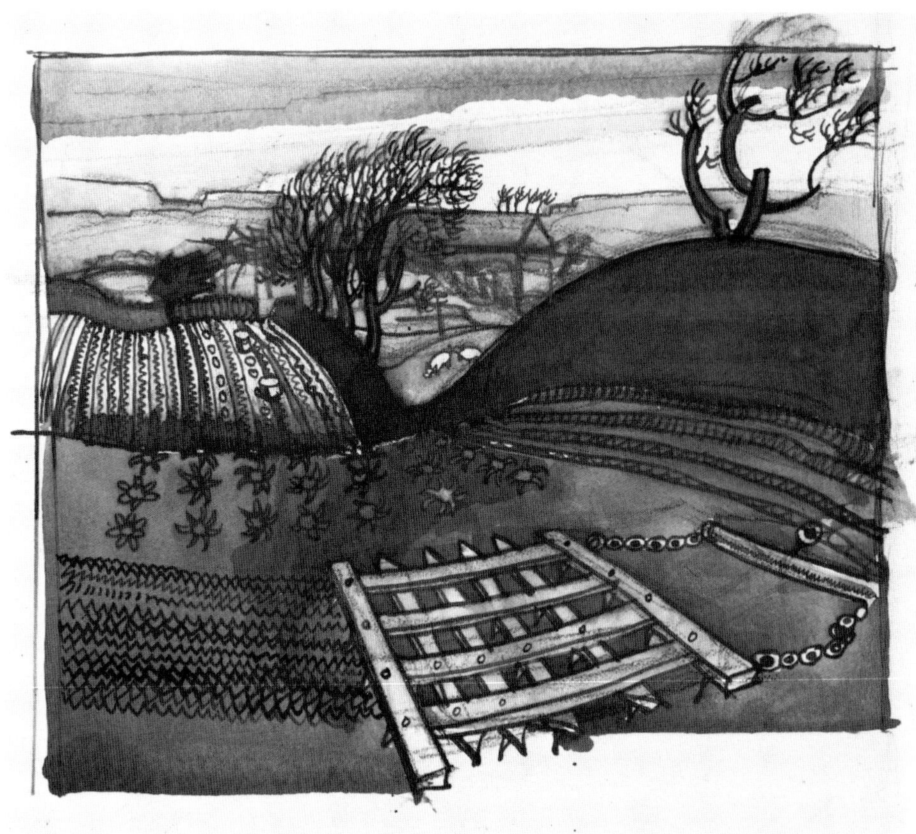

104

The Village (1925)

GRAHAM SUTHERLAND
(London 1903–1979 London)
Man 23 iii/iii; Tassi 20 iii/iii
Etching
172 x 224 mm
Signed and dated lower right
Provenance: Zeitlin and Ver Brugge, Los Angeles

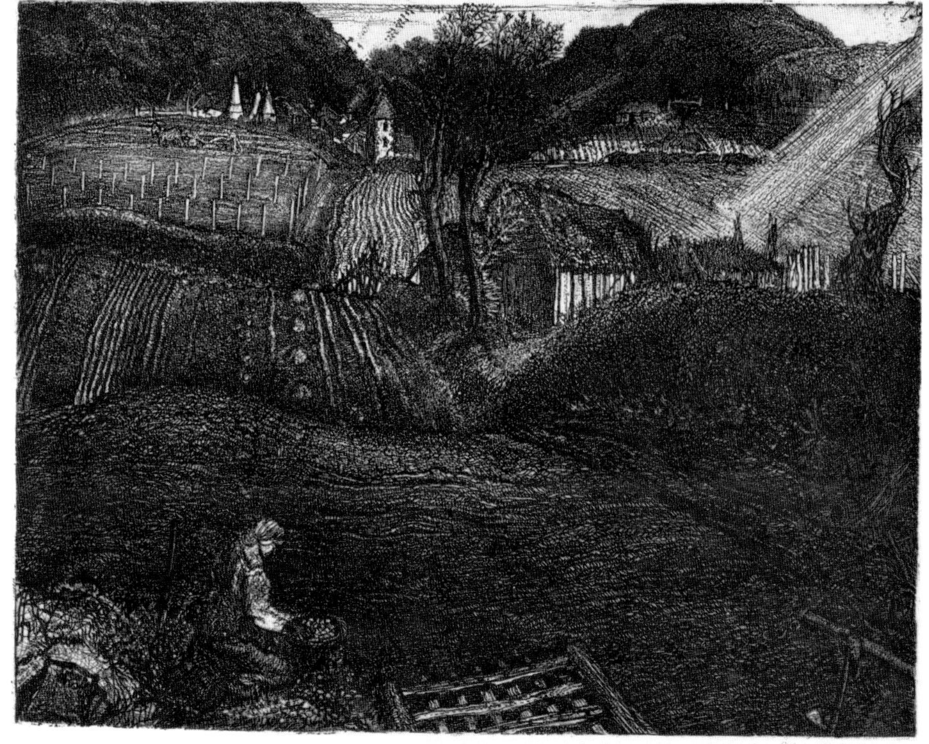

In 1923 Sutherland shifted his attention from urban views to pastoral landscape imagery. It was during this period that a sense of mysticism first appeared in his work. *Village* is one of three etchings Sutherland produced in 1925 while under the influence of the visionary style of Samuel Palmer's Shoreham period.

In this idyllic view of English country life, the fields have been harvested and a young woman sifts grain in the foreground. The earth is rich and abundant, and man's labors have brought him into harmony with nature. With a strong sense of patterning, multiple lines and overlapping planes blanket the earth and unite the composition. Rembrandt's influence on Sutherland's early career is apparent in the deep chiaroscuro effects that intensify the landscape while lending a compelling sense of mass and weight to the scene. In the preliminary drawing for this print, Sutherland mapped out the compositional arrangement with subtle tonal variations. The rolling hills are covered with highly schematic till marks, and a large plow dominates the foreground plane. Sutherland has yet to envision the thatched cottages and farm laborers that appear in the final printed image.

GRAHAM SUTHERLAND

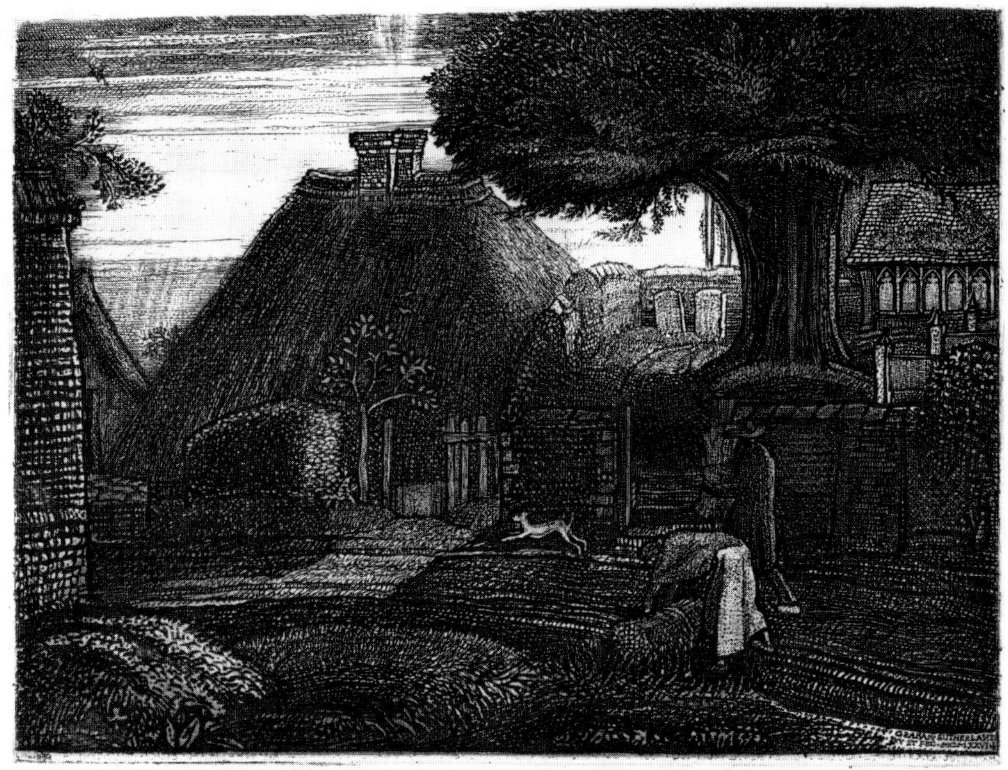

105

St. Mary's Hatch (1926)

GRAHAM SUTHERLAND
(London 1903–1979 London)
Man 26 i/v; Tassi 22 i/v
Etching
136 x 186 mm
Signed lower right
Provenance: Colnaghi, London

Highly resonant of the romantic qualities of light and mood in the etchings of Samuel Palmer, this print depicts a man and woman returning from the forest at the end of the day with bundles of firewood. The nobility of their drudging labor, repeated, it would seem, day after day, week after week, during the darkest of seasons, has religious overtones. As in Palmer's *The Early Ploughman* (cat. no. 92), this meaning is coincident with the symbolism commonly associated with the end the day and the final months of the year. It thus makes of an ordinary rustic scene a kind of memento mori evoking the transience of life, life's brevity and meaning. This is further underscored by the smoke that rises into the evening air from the chimney (a traditional symbol of transience) and by the two tombstones lit by the setting sun.

Indeed the figures seem to suggest by their postures, actions, and placement within the scene that they are in a moment of significant transition. They struggle under the weight of their bundles (the man steps carefully, while the woman has stopped to rest for a moment), they are just at the gate of the graveyard (as if the tombstones wait for them), and they are fully within the shadow of the large tree that rises vigorously, spreading its great, leafy branches like a natural equivalent of the cross of crucifixion.

In this respect the print is in the tradition of Sutherland's earlier *Adam and Eve (The Expulsion from Eden)* and *Cain and Abel* of 1924 (Man 1970, nos. 17–18), which represent religious subjects through scenes of contemporary rural life. Yet this print avoids a precise biblical reference and instead evokes the general biblical prophecy of eternal life through faith and faithful labor, not unlike the paintings of Jean-François Millet, such as *The Angelus* of 1858–59 (Paris, Musée du Louvre). Sutherland executed other prints with this theme, from *Pecken Wood* and *Cray Fields* of 1925 (Man 1970, nos. 24–25) to *Michaelmas* and *The Meadow Chapel* of 1928 (Man 1970, nos. 29–30), before ceasing to make prints, returning to the medium only in 1936 with a new pictorial vocabulary derived from surrealism.

One of a few known impressions of this state, this early proof bears an etched signature and date as well as an indecipherable Latin inscription with a cross, which disappears with the reduction of the plate in later states. Stamped on the print are two unidentified collection marks: S with a star and EEY.

French

Detail of cat. no. 111

CLAUDE GELLÉE, CALLED LE LORRAIN

In 1613 Claude traveled to Italy, where, with the exception of a brief return to Lorraine from 1625 to 1627, he would remain for the rest of his life. In Italy he studied with the Italian landscape and figure painter Agostino Tassi. He may also have studied with the Dutch landscape painter Godfredo Wals in Naples between 1628 and 1632.

The most significant developments in Claude's career began after his return to Rome from Lorraine, when he resolved to specialize in landscape painting and also to take up etching, probably inspired by another Lorrainese artist, Jacques Callot, whose etchings he copied. Though the genre was less valued than figure painting during the seicento, there were other well-established foreign artists in Rome at this time who concentrated on landscape painting, such as Paul Bril and Adam Elsheimer.

After abandoning fresco painting in 1630, Claude concentrated for the remainder of his career on easel paintings in addition to drawings and prints. By the early 1630s he was receiving numerous commissions for oil paintings from important patrons. He became a member of the Accademia di S. Luca in 1633 and received his first papal commission from Urban VIII in 1635. Inspired by classical literature, the art and architecture of ancient and Renaissance Rome, and the landscape of the Roman Campagna, Claude evolved a classical landscape style that by the late 1630s had earned him a reputation as the foremost landscape painter in Rome. He was also to become the most successful foreign artist in seicento Rome, and his patrons included numerous foreign collectors in addition to popes, cardinals, ambassadors, and prominent aristocrats, many of whom avidly collected his paintings and drawings.

Claude's etchings, which number around forty-four, constitute a relatively small part of his oeuvre and date primarily from the late 1620s and early 1630s. He resumed etching in 1651, though only five prints date from the 1650s and 1660s. There was a printing press in his house at the time of his death, suggesting the possibility of marketing prints, though no such editions are known. Claude's landscape art was particularly influential for later artists such as J. M. W. Turner and Camille Corot.

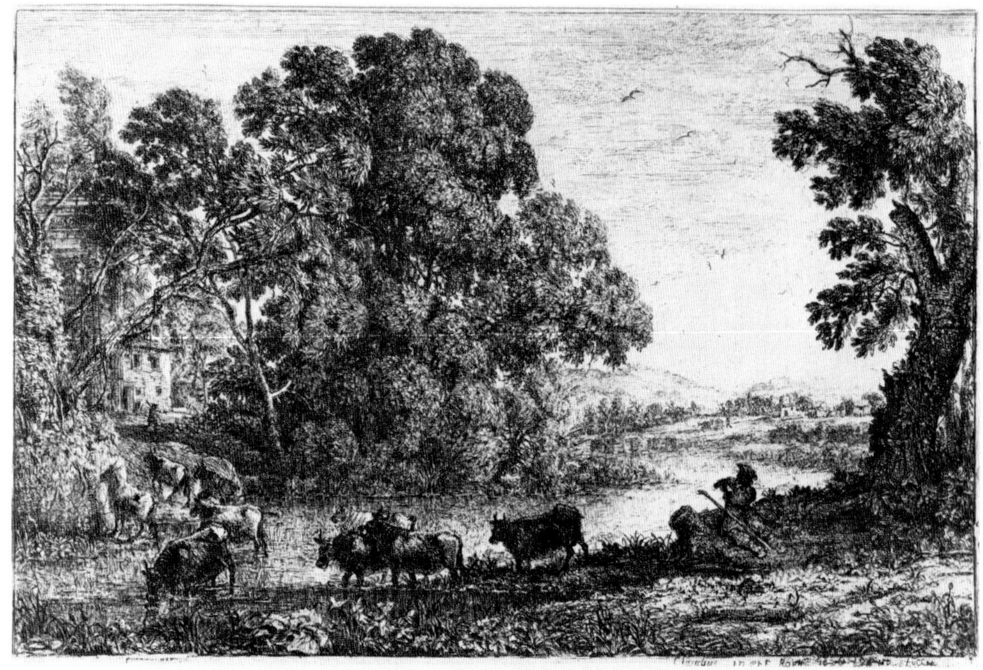

106

Le bouvier (1636)

(The Cowherd)

CLAUDE GELLÉE, called LE LORRAIN
(Champagne 1600–1682 Rome)
R.-D. 8 iii/iv; Russell 27 iii/iv; Mannocci 18 iii(A)/vi
Etching
125 x 194 mm
Provenance: William Schab, New York

Perhaps Claude's best-known print, *Le bouvier* dates to his first experiments with etching during the 1630s. Order and tranquillity prevail in this bucolic scene derived from the pastoral tradition of Petrarch's *De vita solitaria* and Angelo Poliziano's *Rusticus* (Russell 1982, p. 85). This print is typical of a kind of rustic landscape that dominated Claude's paintings of the 1630s. It suggests a retreat from the busy world and emphasizes the accord between man and nature.

Through skillful manipulation of the etching technique, Claude was able to capture the subtle effects of light and atmosphere, in this case a sultry summer evening sunset. Like his paintings, Claude's etchings rarely portray the turbulent conditions of nature, such as the storms and night scenes in the more romantic compositions of Gaspard Dughet (see cat. no. 109). The harmonious mood conveyed in this print reflects the artist's interest in the balance and harmony of nature rather than its dark or opposing forces.

Claude achieved different tonal effects by varying the inking of the plate (Russell 1982, pp. 385–86), and impressions range from darker, more somber effects to the more tranquil mood produced by a balance of dark and light, as in this impression.

Claude Gellée, called Le Lorrain

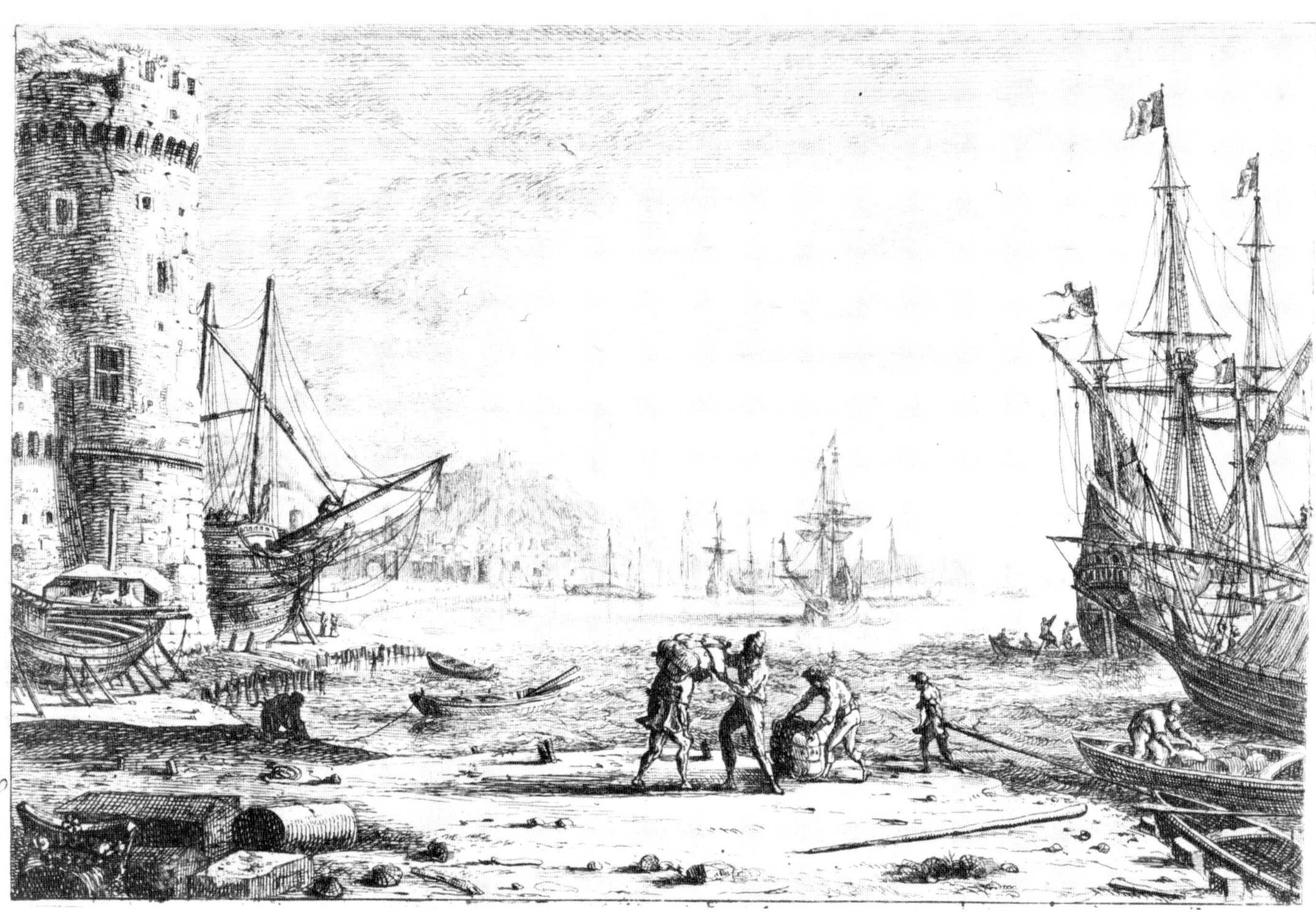

107

Le port de mer à la grosse tour (c. 1641)

(Harbor with Large Tower)

CLAUDE GELLÉE, called LE LORRAIN
(Champagne 1600–1682 Rome)
R.-D. 13 iii/v; Russell 29 iii/v; Mannocci 39 ii/vi
Etching
125 x 192 mm
Provenance: L'Art Ancien, Zurich

This etching depicts workmen at a seaport at sunset, a subject frequently depicted by Claude. The sun at the horizon, suggesting the unknown and the future, features prominently in Claude's paintings of travelers preparing to sail, and indeed the theme of journeying extends through the whole of his works (Russell 1982, p. 84). This motif often evokes a yearning for a golden age, expressed by a passage from a darkened foreground to a more tranquil, light-filled background. In the third state of this print, of which this impression is an example, Claude emphasized the light at the horizon by burnishing out the clouds around the mountains, which appeared in previous states, thereby opening up the sky and suggesting a more luminous atmosphere, while leaving the burnishing streaky to suggest rays of light (Reed and Wallace 1988, p. 173).

This etching reproduces in reverse a drawing in the Liber Veritatis number 17 (Russell 1982, p. 363) that served as a model for a painting. The painting is now lost but is datable by the position of the corresponding drawing in the Liber to 1637 (Roethlisberger 1961, vol. 1, pp. 133–34). A drawing in the Uffizi is probably a preparatory study for the etching (Roethlisberger 1968, vol. 1, p. 154).

Gabriel Perelle and Adam Perelle

The most productive publisher of landscape prints in Paris during the seventeenth century was the firm of Gabriel Perelle and his sons Adam and Nicholas. Their fifteen hundred landscape engravings and etchings, executed primarily in the French-Italian classical manner but incorporating Dutch landscape elements, remained extremely popular, and many were republished until the end of the century.

Most popular were their topographical prints, which include 300 plates of views of Paris and Versailles and 415 plates of Parisian monuments, both sets by Gabriel Perelle. Of their pure landscape prints, a suite of 150 engravings entitled Livres de divers paysages is attributed to Gabriel, while landscapes by Adam include the three-volume Leçons de paysages. Most of these prints include depictions of ruins, palaces, fortresses, and coastal views. Detailed preparatory drawings for their engravings exist in numerous collections. Most extant prints were published much later in Paris by Pierre Mariette (1694–1774). It is difficult to distinguish between the works of father and sons, as the same plates often appear with different names or simply with the name Perelle.

108
Landscape

GABRIEL PERELLE
(Vernon-sur-Seine c. 1603–1677 Paris)
or ADAM PERELLE
(Paris 1638–1695 Paris)
Engraving
Diameter: 182 mm
Provenance: R. E. Lewis, San Francisco

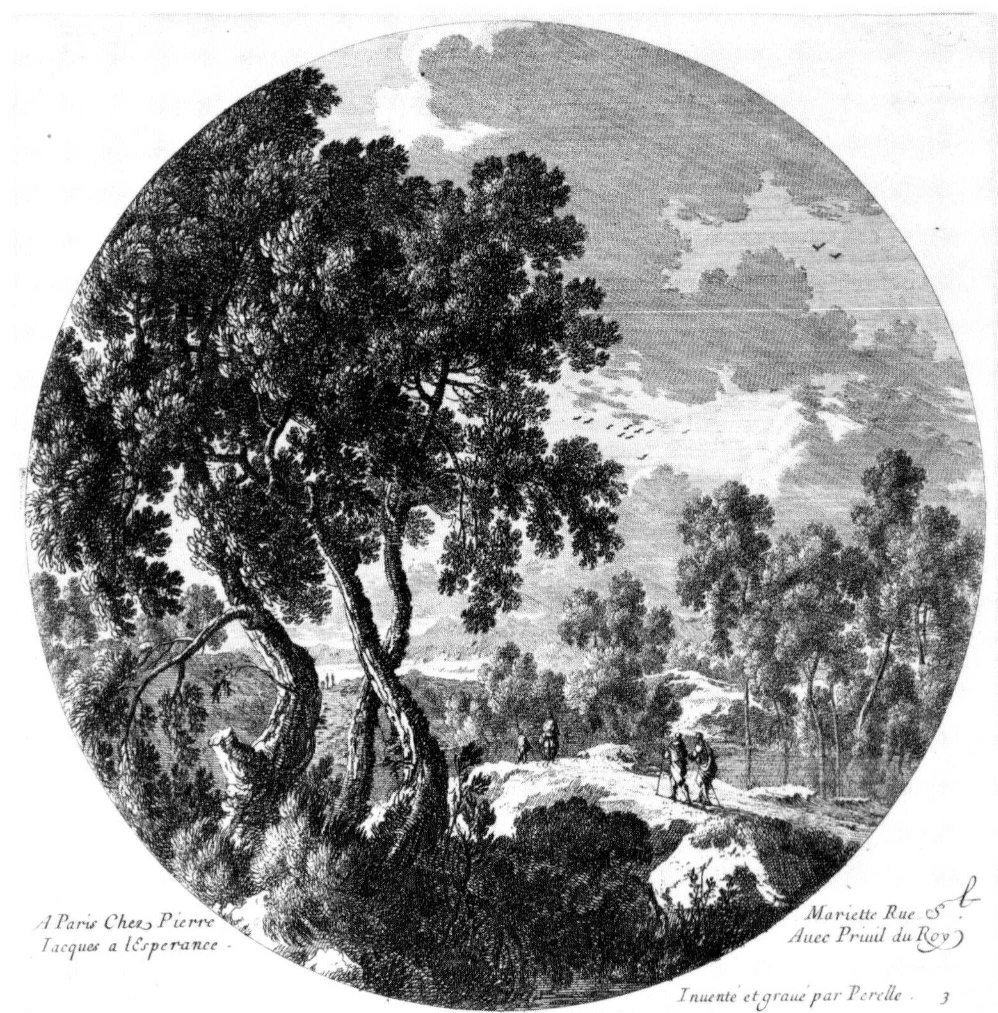

This print recalls the classical Roman landscape tradition exemplified by the art of Claude Lorrain and Nicolas Poussin. In contrast, however, to the etchings of Claude (see cat. nos. 106–7), which are characterized by a painterly concern for atmosphere, the Perelles' etchings have the technical clarity and systematic approach of engraving, in which "searching observation of nature is replaced by formulas" (Roethlisberger 1967, p. 284). The Perelles, along with Israel Silvestre and Sébastien Bourdon, are representative of a conservative strain of French printmaking during the mid-seventeenth century (Clark 1988, p. 55). It was at this time that the tradition of the *peintre-graveur,* as exemplified by the etchings of Claude, gave way to more controlled and systematic approaches to printmaking.

Gaspard Dughet

Born of French parents in Rome, landscape painter and etcher Gaspard Dughet remained in that city throughout his life. In 1630 his sister married Nicolas Poussin, and for at least the following three years Dughet studied painting with his brother-in-law, adopting his surname and painting pictures that reflect the order and structure of Poussin's compositions.

By 1635 Dughet was already a specialist in landscape, influenced by Dutch Italianates such as Jan Both and Herman van Swanevelt. Beginning in the 1630s he received numerous fresco commissions for private residences, including the Doria, Bernini, Muti, Costaguti, and Colonna palaces. During the 1640s Dughet painted a series of landscape frescoes in San Martino al Monti in Florence, which display a classical balance and clarity influenced by the contemporary works of Domenichino, Poussin, and Claude Lorrain. After the end of the 1640s Dughet remained in Rome and its surrounding areas, continuing to paint frescoes in Roman palaces as well as small landscape paintings for the balance of his career. His eight landscape etchings probably date to the 1640s and comprise the naturalistic views of rivers, trees, and mountains also characteristic of his paintings.

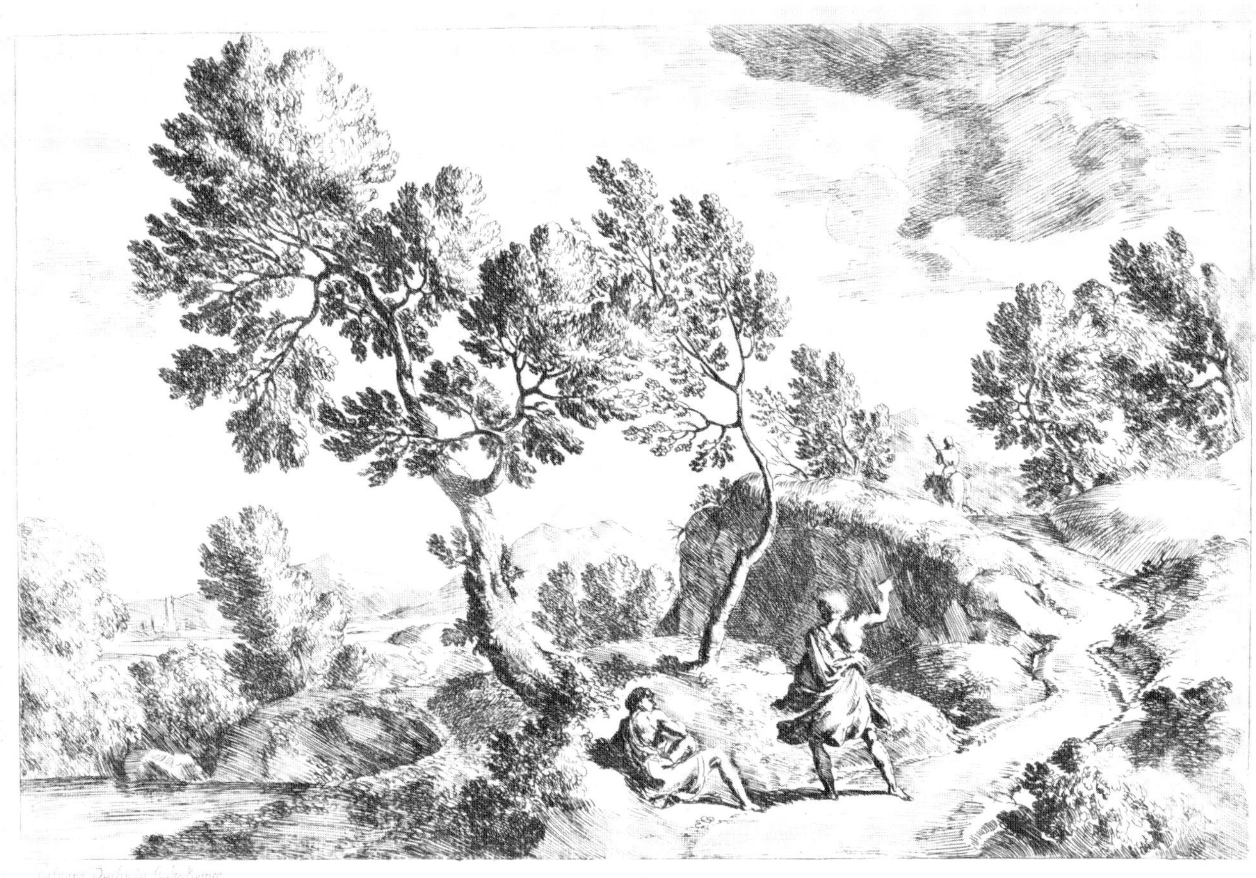

109
Landscape with Two Figures

GASPARD DUGHET
(Rome 1615–1675 Rome)
B. 6; R.-D. 6 i/ii
Etching
190 x 295 mm
Provenance: Colnaghi, London

Dughet's two sets of landscape prints, which consist of one with four rectangular etchings and another with four round etchings, can both be dated to the 1640s (Sutton 1962, p. 276). Like Dughet's paintings, all are scenes of figures in landscapes inspired by the Roman Campagna that have a restless, stormy quality reminiscent of the romantic landscape style of Salvator Rosa.

In this particular etching two figures gesture at each other across a windswept countryside. In contrast to the pastoral mood of the landscapes of Dughet's compatriot Claude Lorrain (see cat. no. 106), this landscape evokes a more unsettling dramatic tension. The two figures in ancient dress appear to be actors in some classical drama, although the nature of their relationship remains ambiguous. Dughet's primary interest was not clarity of narrative, but rather the potential drama between humankind and the forces of nature.

Israel Silvestre

A native of Lorraine, Israel Silvestre moved to Paris in 1631 to live with his uncle, Israel Henriet, painter and draftsman to Louis XIII. Around 1639 he went to Italy on the first of several visits and, while in Rome, published his first set of nine engravings. Influenced by Jacques Callot and Stefano della Bella, whose prints were published by his uncle in Paris, Silvestre earned a reputation for his topographical etchings. He had numerous collaborators on his prints, including della Bella and Gabriel Perelle, and his designs were published by his uncle and the well-known publisher Jean Le Blond, among others. In 1661 Silvestre inherited his uncle's collection of etched plates of Callot and della Bella and continued to publish their prints.

In 1663 Silvestre was appointed draftsman and engraver to Louis XIV, and his numerous commissions included two series of festivals as well as a suite of engravings of the royal châteaus. He was elected to the Académie Royale in 1670 and in 1673 was appointed drawing master to the dauphin. Silvestre lived at the Louvre from 1668 until his death. His printed oeuvre comprises more than one thousand topographical engravings and etchings as well as hundreds of drawings.

110–17

Eight Pages from a Sketchbook with Views of Châteaus and Fortresses

ISRAEL SILVESTRE
(Nancy 1621–1691 Paris)
Pen and brown ink
Each approximately 145 x 225 mm
Provenance: Hippolyte Destailleur (L. 1/740); Robert Schuman; William Schab, New York

These drawings form twenty-nine pages of a sketchbook formerly in the collection of the architect Hippolyte Destailleur. Each drawing has a number inscribed in brown ink in the upper right corner, and each varies slightly in size. The uniform border drawn around each composition suggests that they may have been designs for prints, though the drawings have not been linked to any of Silvestre's prints. It is also possible that they were executed for a patron who wanted an album of views or that the sketches served as a source of subjects for future use by the artist.

The scenes are primarily coastal landscapes, comprising various views of fortresses and castles, often on small islands. Soldiers are depicted in battle, riding on horseback, or merely engaged in conversation or leisurely activity. This kind of incidental activity is characteristic of Silvestre's otherwise primarily topographical scenes.

Silvestre traveled extensively and produced hundreds of topographical drawings and etchings. These sketches are similar in subject to a watercolor of the fortress of Jametz (Paris, Musée du Louvre, Cabinet des Dessins inv. no. 33,058), one of several views of fortresses in Champagne and Lorraine executed by Silvestre around 1665 (British Museum 1977, p. 20, no. 3). Though the scene depicted in the watercolor does not correspond exactly to any of the views in the Grunwald Center sketchbook, it bears a close resemblance to cat. no. 111 in its dramatic diagonal point of view and shading.

Israel Silvestre

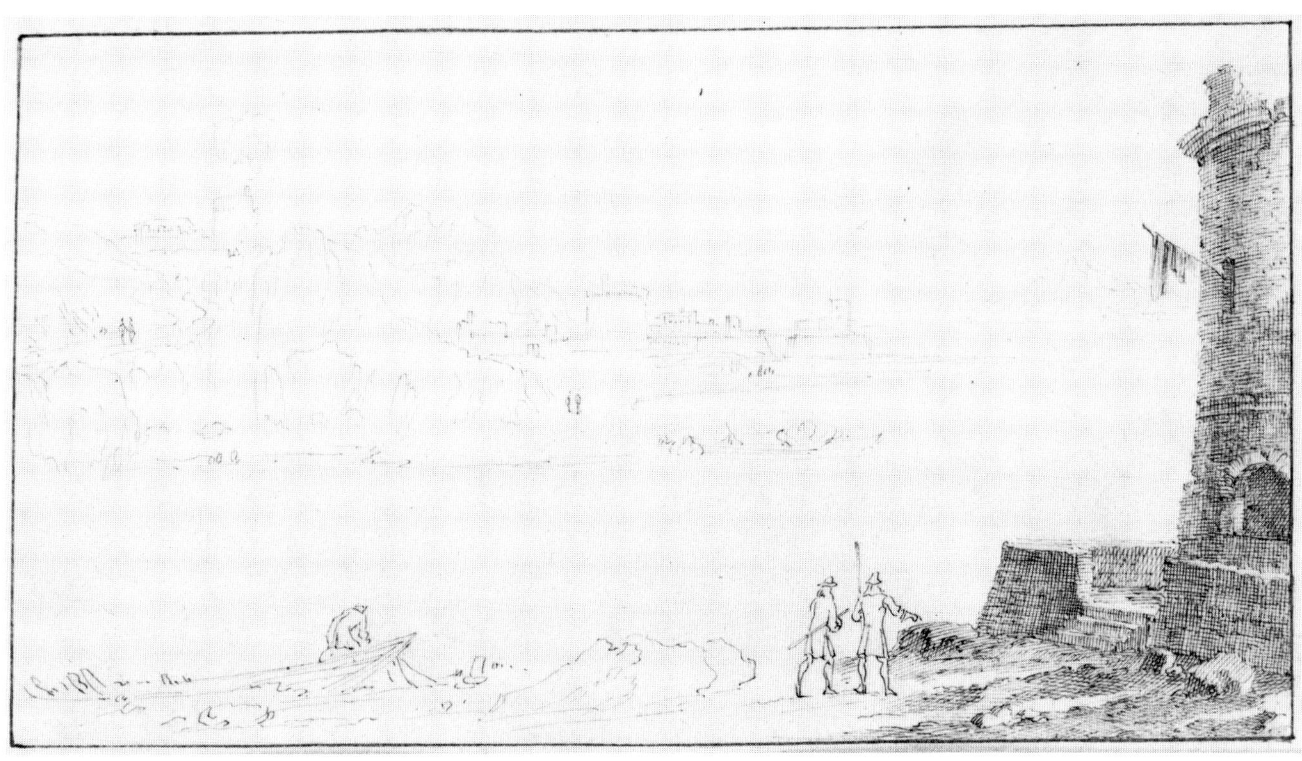

110

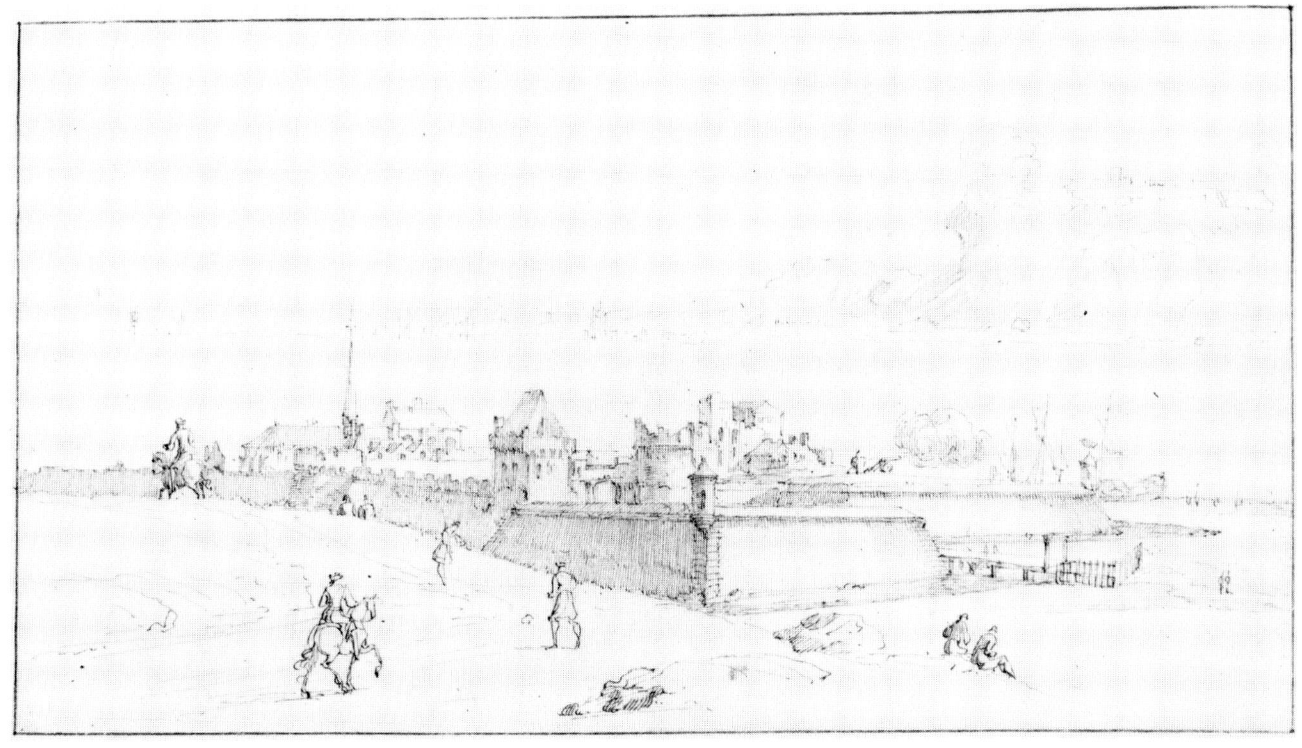

111

Israel Silvestre

112 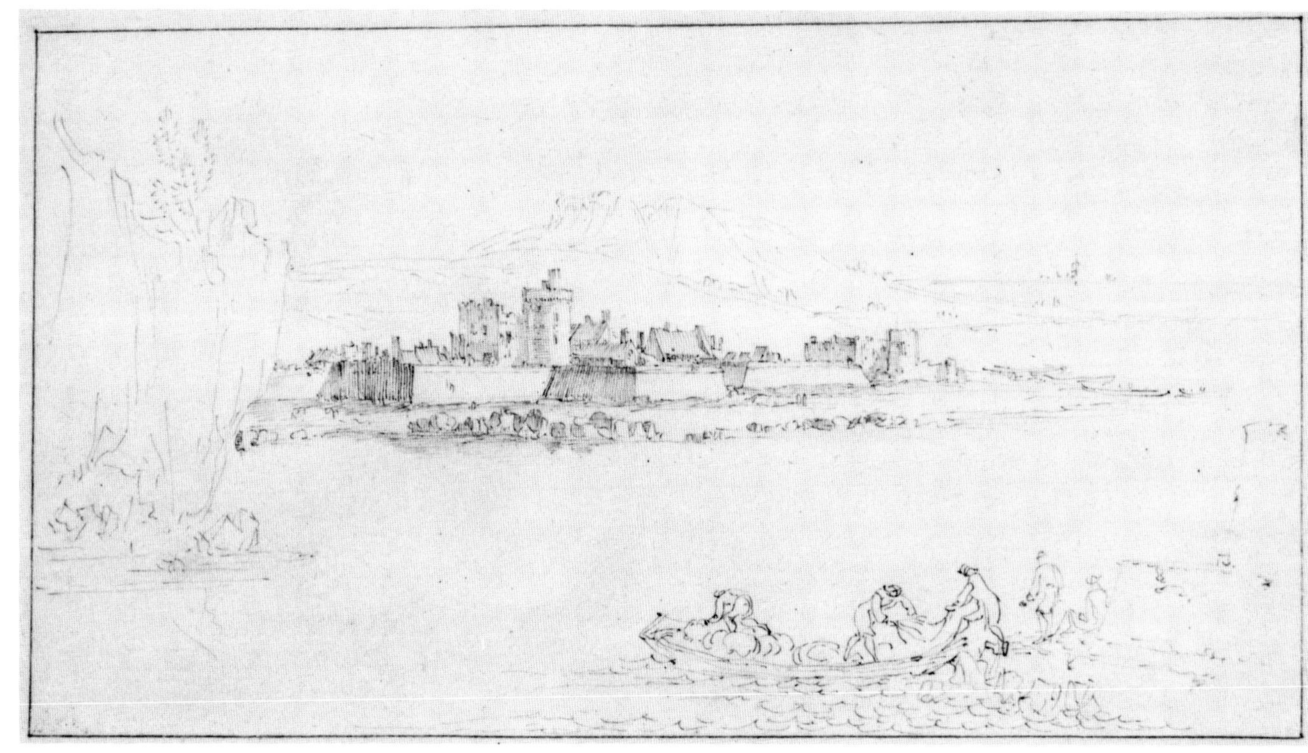

113 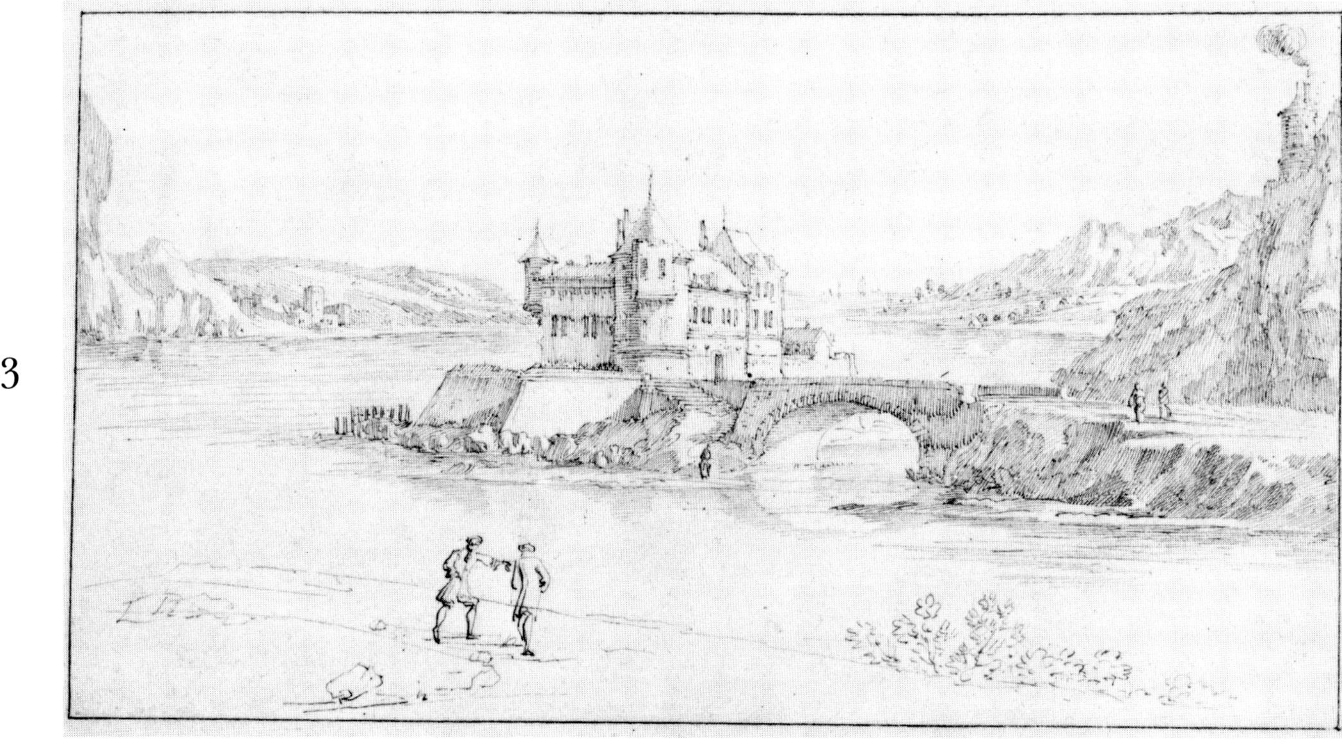

Israel Silvestre

114

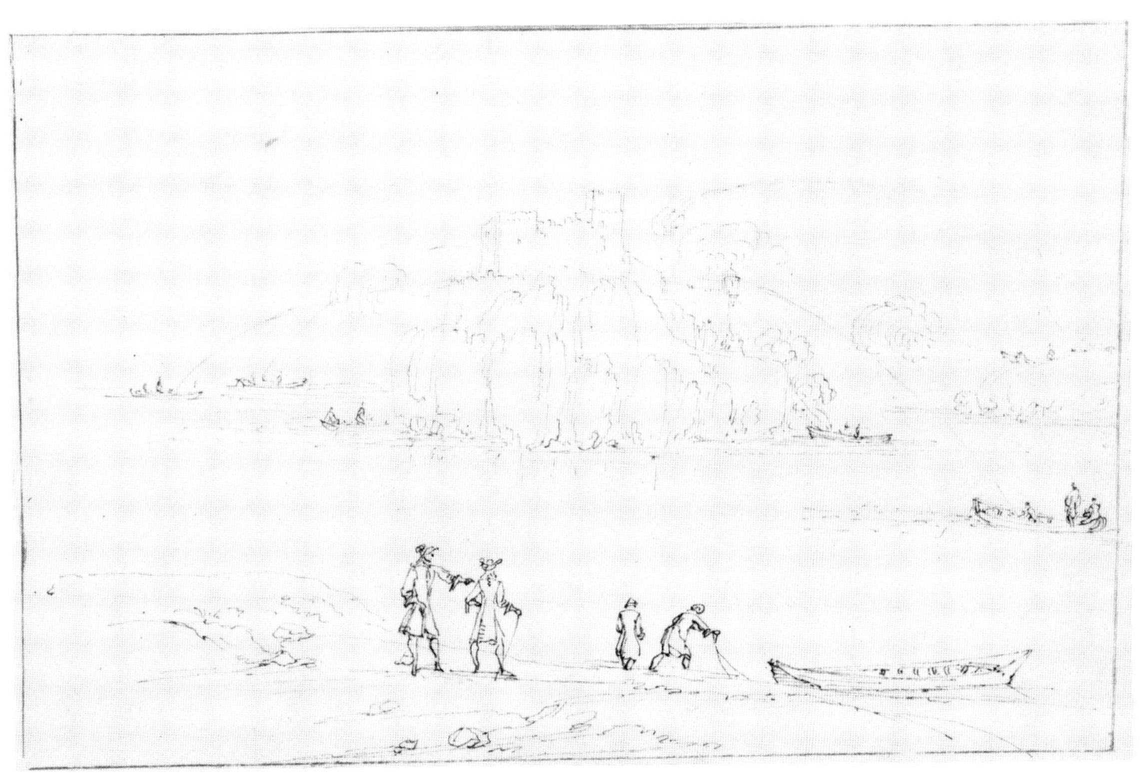

115

ISRAEL SILVESTRE

116

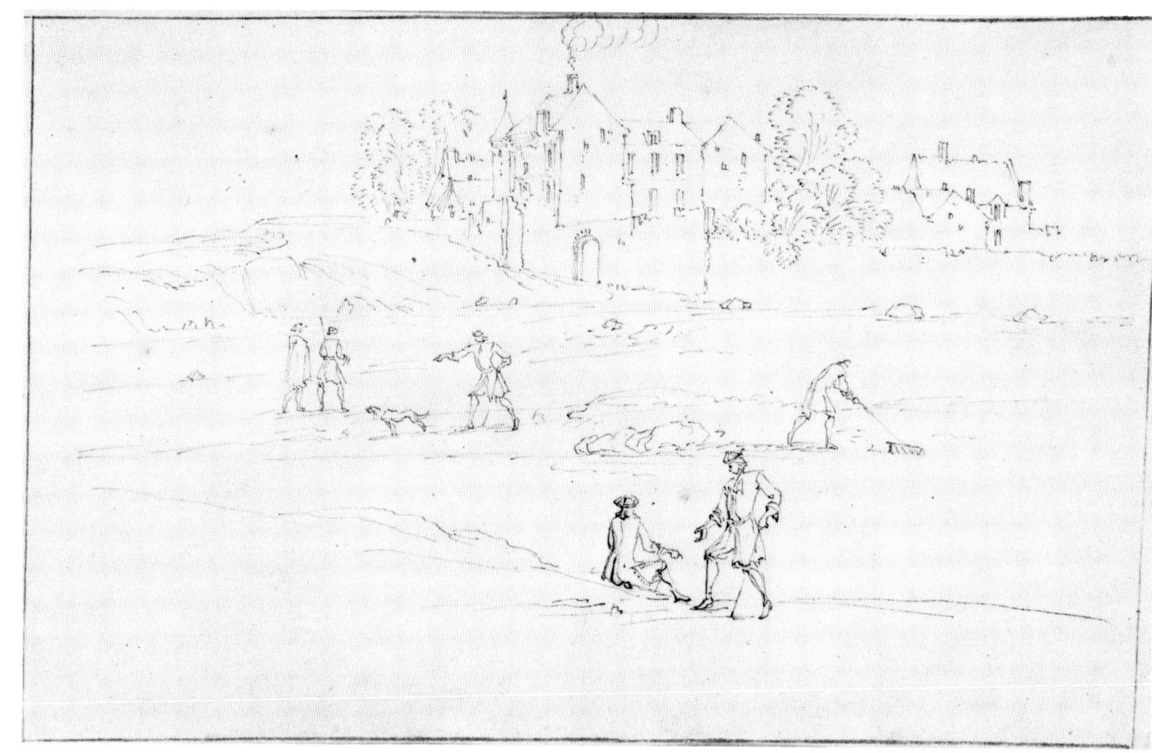

117

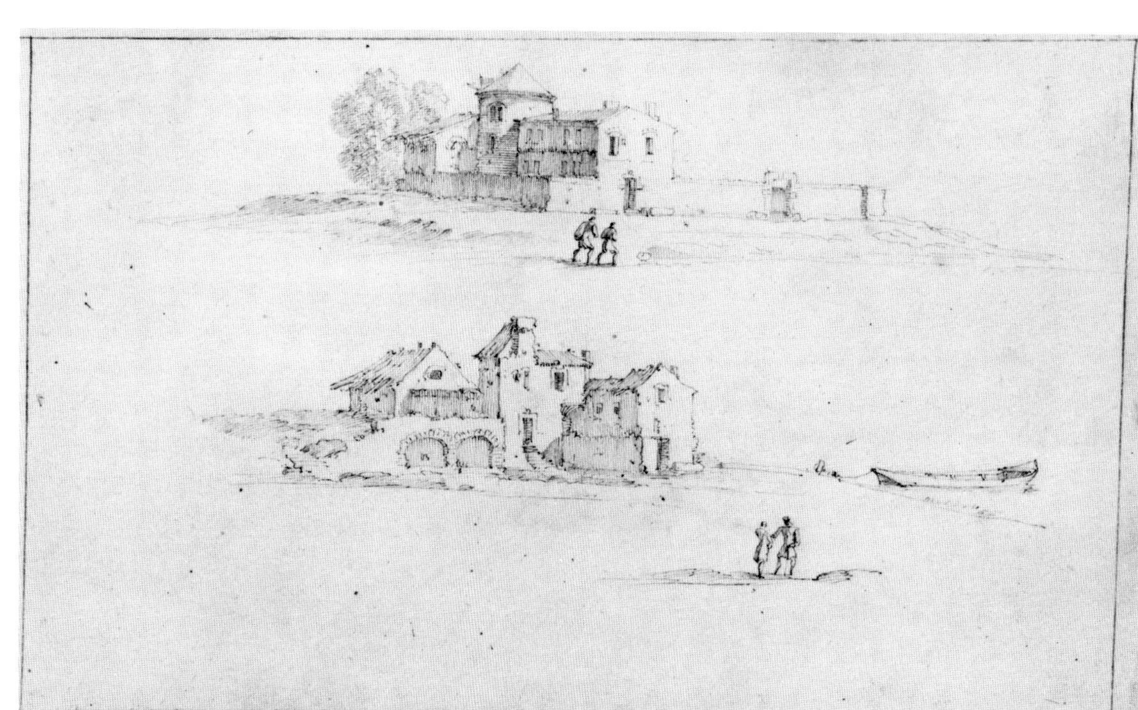

Camille Corot

At the age of twenty-eight Camille Corot began his artistic career in the studio of Achille-Etna Michallon, a leading classicizing landscape painter who nevertheless encouraged the young artist to work directly from nature with the utmost fidelity. Between 1822 and 1825 Corot painted primarily in Fontainebleau and Normandy; from 1825 to 1828, primarily in Italy; and from 1829 to 1834, throughout the French countryside, working in such areas as Fontainebleau, Normandy, Rouen, Chartres, and Burgundy. From 1831 he regularly exhibited at the Salon and was later elected to its selection and admission committees, becoming a member of the jury in 1870. In 1834 and again in 1843 Corot returned to Italy, where he recorded his travels in spontaneous, on-site sketches. He first experimented with the etching process in 1845. During the last decades of his life, Corot seldom journeyed outside France, preferring instead the environs of Paris and especially his family property in Ville-d'Avray.

Between 1850 and 1870 Corot abandoned the bright sunlight and stillness of his Italianate compositions in favor of windswept, twilight scenes in silvery, gray-green tones. His heightened interest in atmospheric effects may have resulted from his contact with the Barbizon artists as well as his investigation of photography. A close friend of Nadar, Corot began experimenting with the cliché verre *medium in 1853. In many ways the dreamlike evocations of his later period delicately balance the observation of nature with the creation of an imagined scene.*

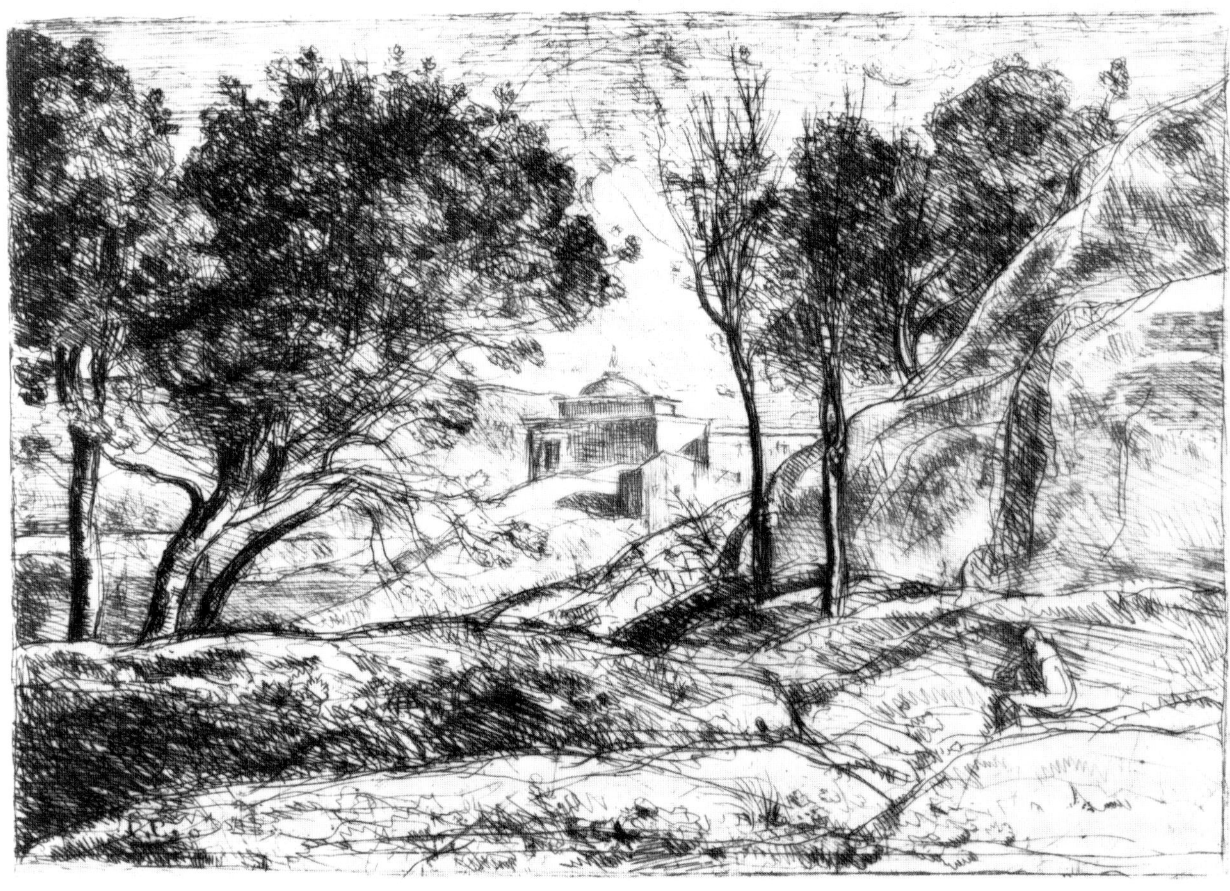

118

Souvenir de Toscane (c. 1865)

(Souvenir of Tuscany)

CAMILLE COROT
(Paris 1796–1875 Paris)
Delt. 1 ii/iv; Mel. 1 ii/iv
Etching
120 x 179 mm
Provenance: Lucien Goldschmidt, New York

Corot began *Souvenir de Toscane* in 1845, following his third trip to Italy, in 1843. In this view of the Italian countryside, a solitary figure sketches a classical monument in the distance. Corot lost interest in the etching, however, and abandoned the unbitten copper plate, which was retrieved some twenty years later by Félix Bracquemond. Thanks to Bracquemond's encouragement, the plate was printed. In this, the final state, Corot changed the image considerably, abandoning the clarity and brightly lit ambience of his first state, from which only three prints were pulled. This state is characteristic of his later works in that the forms are less distinguishable and a windswept atmosphere pervades the scene. *Souvenir de Toscane* summarizes Corot's aesthetic, combining elements from the classical tradition from which he evolved with the hazy, poetic character of his mature style. Appropriately, the print was used to illustrate the artist's obituary in the April 1, 1875, issue of the *Gazette des beaux-arts.*

[*French*]

EUGENE ISABEY

Son of the celebrated miniaturist and Napoleonic court painter, Jean-Baptiste Isabey, Eugène Isabey departed from his father's diminutive neoclassical style in favor of the more expansive and dramatic tenor of romanticism. Similarly, although his father was best known for portraits and costume pieces, Eugène preferred marine and landscape paintings. He traveled widely throughout France, making paintings of rustic scenes, which he exhibited to much acclaim in the Salons of 1824 and 1827. In 1830 Isabey and Eugène Delacroix were appointed to accompany the French expedition to Algeria, where they were to draw the sites and customs of North Africa. Unlike Delacroix, Isabey was not significantly impressed by the Mediterranean light or exoticism of Algeria, however, and his art was little affected. He returned to France and continued to paint in the dark tonalities characteristic of his earlier romantic views of the rugged Norman coast.

Isabey's earliest lithograph, drawn after a design by his father, dates from 1822 and is an architectural caprice of Venice in the manner of Giovanni Battista Piranesi. His next lithographs date from 1827 and are modest vignettes for six music sheets. Three years later, however, in the midst of his success at the Salons, Isabey developed a greater interest in lithography. In 1830 alone, he contributed thirteen lithographs to the series Croquis par divers artistes, six to a volume documenting the French expedition to Algeria, and five to Voyages pittoresques. The following year he contributed further to Voyages pittoresques, and in 1832 and 1833 he published two series of his own, Souvenirs d'Eugène Isabey and Six marines. (The latter prints show most clearly Isabey's sensitivity to the rich coloristic effects of the soft lithographic crayon. These depictions of the storm-tossed seaside towns of northern France are marked by a fluidity of line and varied shading.) Although Isabey continued to make lithographs through the 1830s and 1840s, he did so with less rigor, concentrating instead on painting, for which he was awarded a first-place medal at the Universal Exposition of 1855.

119
Vue de Rouen (1832)

(View of Rouen)

EUGENE ISABEY
(Paris 1803–1886 Paris)
Plate 3 of Souvenirs d'Eugène Isabey
Curtis 60 i/iii; Hédiard 3 i/iii
Lithograph
292 x 191 mm
Provenance: R. E. Lewis, San Francisco

Published as part of a suite of lithographs depicting views of Normandy and Brittany, this print is typical of Isabey's affection for the picturesque architecture of old France, especially that of its river and coastal areas.

Two years earlier Isabey began contributing lithographs to Voyages pittoresques; he would contribute seventeen to the two volumes on Auvergne published between 1830 and 1832. There he emphasized the romance of old châteaus dramatically sited in rocky landscapes swept by storm clouds. During this period he also published five lithographs of marine views in the series Croquis par divers artistes. In these he concentrated on the rugged nobility of shipping boats aground at low tide, their sails lowered and riggings and gear draped over their sides.

After first exhibiting in the Salon of 1824, Isabey became widely known as a painter of marine subjects, especially Norman port cities and fishing villages. He continued to explore these subjects in Six marines. These prints, which were later reissued with those of Souvenirs d'Eugène Isabey, bring the river view of Rouen into context with its seaside complement, as in the famous *Intérieur d'un port* of 1833 (Curtis 68), which shows fishing boats docked beside picturesque Norman buildings.

The delicate details of the stone walls and wooden roofs of the houses in *Vue de Rouen* are typical of Isabey's draftsmanship and handling of the lithographic crayon. The crayon is scribbled lightly across the building facades and then scraped away in places to suggest the wear of age. Similarly, the low vantage point that exaggerates the vertical rise of the buildings and elevates the facade of the light building in the rear is typical of Isabey's lithographs of this period. It first appeared in his view of the château at Polignac in the second Auvergne volume of Voyages pittoresques. There it rendered majestic the lone surviving tower of the ruined château, making it stand witness to the glory of old France surviving still in the modern age. In *Vue de Rouen* it functions similarly, giving dignity to the small but charming buildings of the old river city and endowing them with a hopeful nostalgia for a simpler, more truthful age.

[*French*]

Eugene Isabey

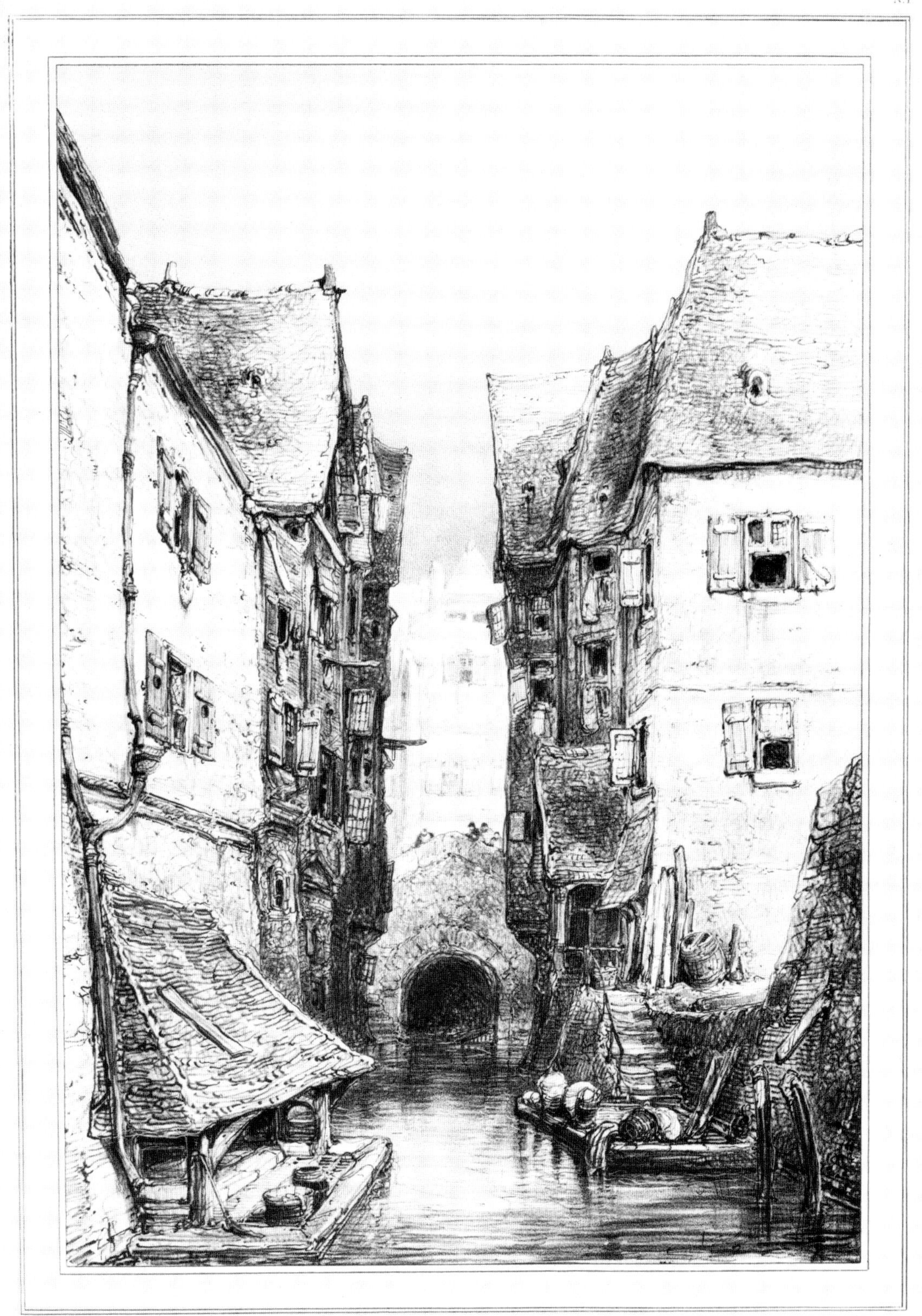

Eug Isabey lith

Lith de Lemercier

VUE DE ROUEN.

THÉODORE ROUSSEAU

Théodore Rousseau briefly studied under landscape artist Jean Rémond and the neoclassical painter Guillon Lethière during the 1820s. His artistic temperament, however, was shaped more by his enthusiasm for plein-air painting and his appreciation for the works of Claude and the Dutch masters. During the 1830s Rousseau toured the French countryside, painting the forests of Fontainebleau, Normandy, and the Auvergne region. He first exhibited his landscapes at the Salon in 1831 but was excluded from 1837 to 1847.

After 1837 Rousseau settled in Barbizon. There, along with Jules Dupré, Charles-François Daubigny, Jean-François Millet, Constant Troyon, and Narcisse-Virgile Diaz de La Peña, he pioneered the art of landscape painting directly from nature and is considered a central figure of the Barbizon school. The primary themes of Rousseau's art were trees silhouetted against the sky and the forest interior, as opposed to the meadows and harbor scenes of Camille Corot and Daubigny. Captivated by unspoiled, rustic nature, Rousseau based his works on close scrutiny and analysis of natural forms. His almost scientific curiosity about the environment led him to study geology, meteorology, and botany. Rousseau had little interest in carefully contrived academic landscapes, portraying instead the expressive power and sublime energy of nature. The somber intensity of his earlier romantic phase gave way during the 1840s to a more objective view of nature. His expansive vistas of this period reflect his sensitivity to light and subtle climatic conditions.

Rousseau seldom left the countryside around Barbizon after 1848. His later landscapes range from luminous panoramas of the changing atmosphere to expressive, melancholic forest scenes. By 1849 he was again exhibiting at the Salon and was awarded a first-class medal and the Légion d'honneur. Although Rousseau had difficulty selling his works, he was internationally recognized in 1855 at the Universal Exposition, and in 1867, the year of his death, he was elected president of the jury for the Universal Exposition and received a medal of honor.

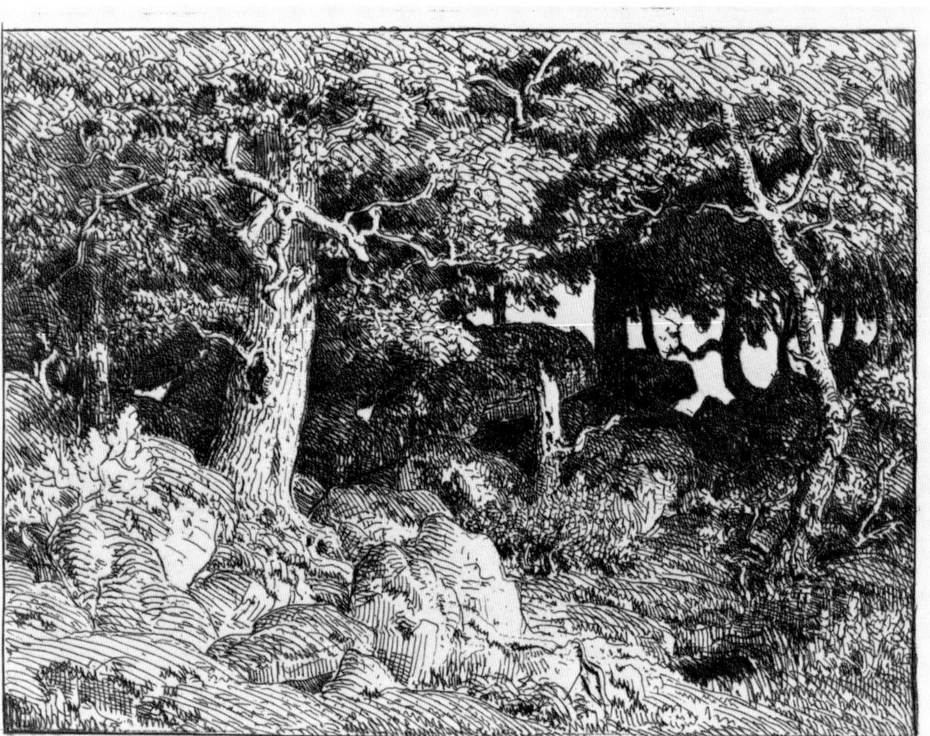

120

Chênes de roche (1861)

(Oak Trees Growing among Rocks)

THÉODORE ROUSSEAU
(Paris 1812–1867 Barbizon)
Delt. 4 ii/iii; Mel. 4 ii/iii
Etching
125 x 168 mm
Provenance: R. E. Lewis, San Francisco

Though he produced very few prints, only six in all, Rousseau was an admirer of the graphic arts, collecting prints by Albrecht Dürer, Lucas van Leyden, Adriaen van Ostade, Rembrandt van Rijn, and a number of Japanese artists. Rousseau etched *Chênes de roche* after a painting he exhibited in the Salon of 1861. The print appeared in the August 1, 1861, issue of the *Gazette des beaux-arts* and was to be his only published etching.

Rousseau's preference for untouched forest interiors is apparent in this Fontainebleau scene. An oak tree growing among rocks is depicted from a vantage point deep inside the forest looking out toward the clearing. For Rousseau such rugged, age-worn oaks were emblems of permanence, representing continuity from generation to generation (Weisberg 1985, p. 142). His vigorous handling of line, shade, and texture recalls the art of the seventeenth-century Dutch master Jacob van Ruisdael, whose landscape paintings, which often capture the rugged, dramatic character of forest trees, were very popular in France at this time.

Charles-François Daubigny

Charles-François Daubigny was born into a family of artists who encouraged his early interest in painting and drawing. At age eighteen he traveled to Italy for six months and settled in the Roman countryside, where his fascination with landscape flourished. There he prepared for the Prix de Rome in the category of historical landscape, and although he did not win the competition, he was accepted in the Salon in 1838 and regularly exhibited his landscapes throughout his career.

Closely associated with the Barbizon artists and sharing their interest in painting directly from nature, Daubigny worked primarily in the forest of Fontainebleau during 1843. His preferred sites, however, were along the Oise and Seine rivers and the Channel coast, where he traveled each summer after 1854. Daubigny's contact with Camille Corot in the summer of 1852 led him to place greater emphasis on painting landscapes directly from nature. In 1857 he launched his "botin," the studio boat that fostered the development of his plein-air aesthetic by enabling him to paint while traveling the French waterways. Many of his landscapes from this period approach the Dutch tradition in their sensitivity to light and atmosphere.

Daubigny received considerable recognition for his landscape prints after the publication of two albums of etchings in 1850 and 1851. Throughout his career printmaking was the basis of his livelihood; he created numerous book and magazine illustrations as well as independent landscape etchings.

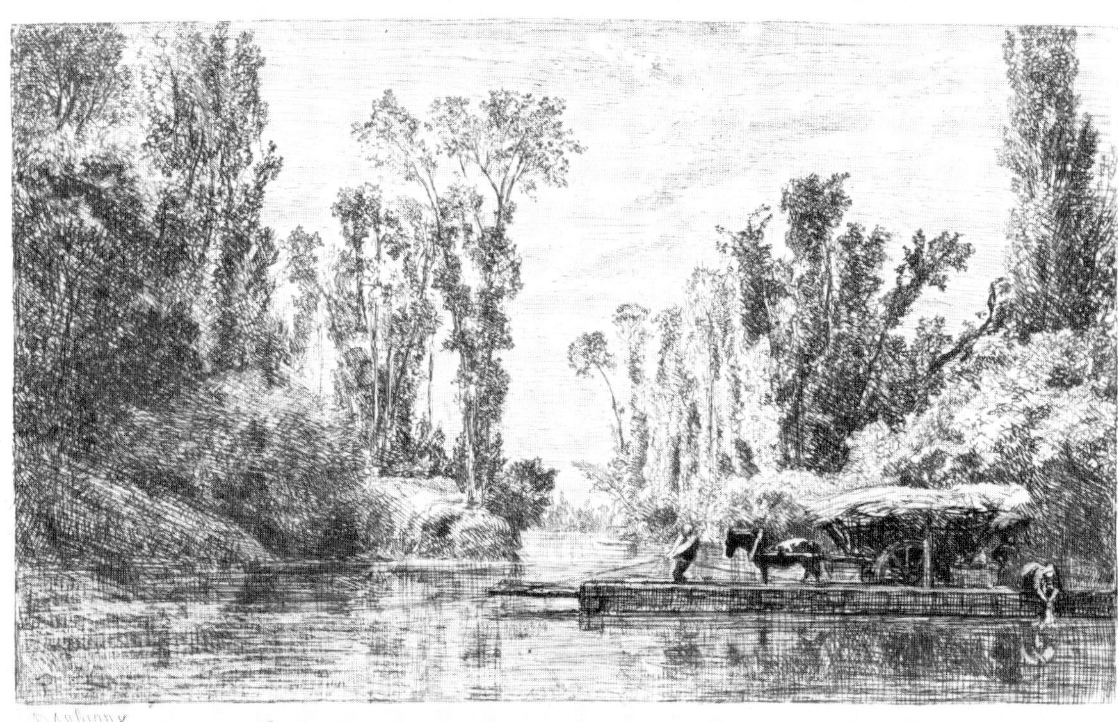

121

Le bac de Bezons (1850)

(The Ferry at Bezons)

CHARLES-FRANÇOIS DAUBIGNY
(Paris 1817–1878 Paris)
Delt. 81 i/v; Mel. 81 i/v; Henriet 74 i/v
Etching
97 x 161 mm
Provenance: L. Delteil (L. I/773); J. F. Gautier (L. II/1463a); William Weston Gallery, London

Daubigny's love of water scenes led him to portray innumerable sites along the banks of the Oise, Marne, and Seine rivers. *Le bac de Bezons* was part of one of his albums of etchings published during the 1850s, marking the high point of his printmaking career. Republished several times during his lifetime, Daubigny's landscape prints were well received and played an important role in the etching revival that occurred in France and England at midcentury. In this rare first-state impression Daubigny has not yet added the ferryman's skullcap and the additional branches and foliage that appear at the upper left in later states. The finely rendered lines reveal his sensitivity to the subtle effects of light reflecting on the surface of the water and his delicate handling of foliage. Daubigny's low vantage point encourages the viewer to experience the setting as if from a boat on the water. The artist was to adopt this vantage point himself in 1857, when he launched a studio boat on which he frequently painted while traveling the French rivers.

HENRI-JOSEPH HARPIGNIES

In 1846 Henri-Joseph Harpignies entered the atelier of the landscape painter Jean Achard, who encouraged the young artist's interest in outdoor painting. With his teacher, Harpignies traveled to Brussels, Flanders, and Holland, where he became familiar with the seventeenth-century Dutch landscape tradition. While in Belgium, Harpignies began a series of thirteen etchings that he completed upon his return to France in 1849. During the same year he went to Italy, where he first experimented with the watercolor medium. Harpignies remained a prolific watercolorist throughout his career and was instrumental in reviving this art form in France. In 1852 he returned to Paris and was introduced to Camille Corot at the popular Café Fleurus. Corot's use of silvery tonalities and his interest in the changing effects of light were to have a lasting influence on Harpignies. During the late 1850s Harpignies's interest in outdoor painting led him to explore the French countryside, visiting Nièvre, Mars-sur-Allier, Plagny, and the Fontainebleau Forest region in search of new areas to paint. He returned to Italy in 1863 for two years and then settled in Paris, where he exhibited his Italianate landscapes at the Salon.

In 1869 Harpignies discovered the village of Hérisson, where he would spend each summer for the next ten years. It was there that many young landscapists congregated around Harpignies, forming a group known as the École d'Hérisson. Harpignies later returned to Paris, where he taught art at his studio on the rue de l'Abbaye. In his later years he was especially highly regarded. His works sold well, and he received numerous awards, including the Légion d'honneur and the grand prize at the Universal Exposition of 1900.

122

House at the Top of a Rocky Hill

HENRI-JOSEPH HARPIGNIES
(Valenciennes 1819–1916 Paris)
Etching on blue paper
76 x 114 mm
Provenance: A. Beurdeley (L. I/421); R. E. Lewis, San Francisco

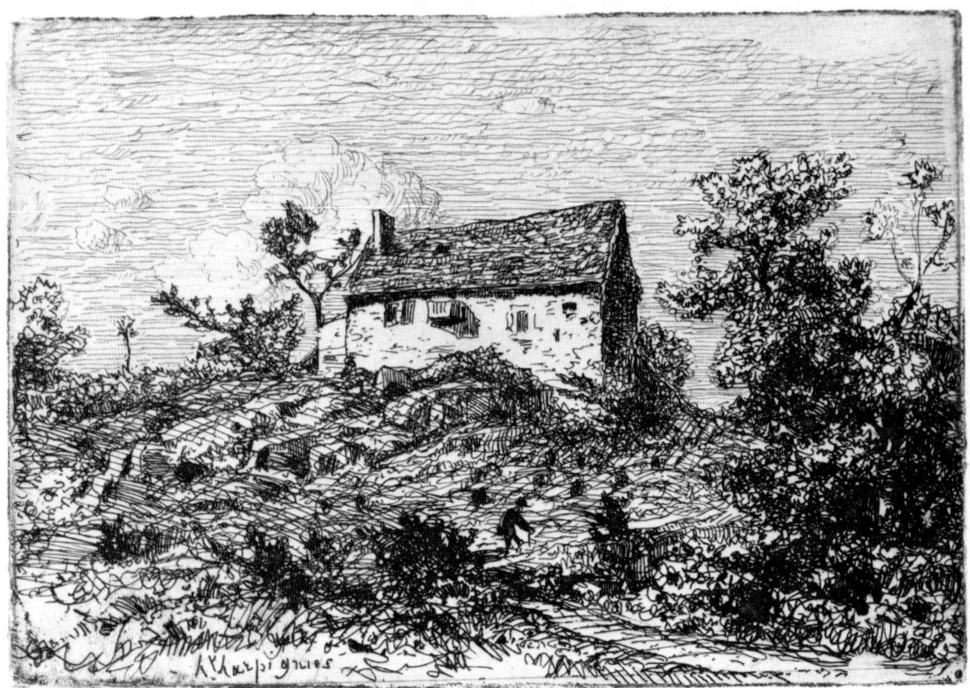

Not recorded by Beraldi, this charming print depicts a rustic cottage atop a rocky hill. A man, barely visible in the lower center, walks up a path toward the house. In its diminutive scale and scratchy lines, the print gives every indication of being a quick, freely drawn sketch, tinted by the blue paper to suggest the late afternoon or early evening light. In this respect it reveals the influence of Charles Jacque's etchings of peasant cottages published between 1843 and 1845, in the years just preceding the probable date of this print. Jacque's etchings were extremely popular at this time and were often compared to those of the Dutch masters, particularly Adriaen van Ostade. Harpignies was undoubtedly influenced by these early masters, and here he uses a coarse, quick line not unlike that of Jacob van Ruisdael. Similar effects are seen in the etchings of Harpignies's contemporary Charles-François Daubigny, who was also influenced by the paintings and prints of Ruisdael and who, in such prints as *Le bac de Bezons* (cat. no. 121), drew manifestly unromantic views of marshy flatlands. While Harpignies's *House at the Top of a Rocky Hill* is not unromantic, neither is it as brooding and dramatic as Rousseau's typically romantic view of rocks and gnarled tress (cat. no. 120). It lies somewhere between the romantic and the realistic landscape modes, looking forward to the impressionism of Camille Pissarro and back to the rustic conventions of Hendrik Goltzius's *Landscape with Farmhouse* (cat. no. 24).

Despite their beauty and eccentricity, Harpignies's etchings remain little known and poorly catalogued. This is due in part to the fact that his early prints often remained unpublished or uneditioned or were issued only in very small editions. This etching appears to be among his early prints and may be ascribed to the years following the 1849 etching *Landscape at Bouquet d'Arbes, Roisin,* also unrecorded by Beraldi.

HENRI-JOSEPH HARPIGNIES

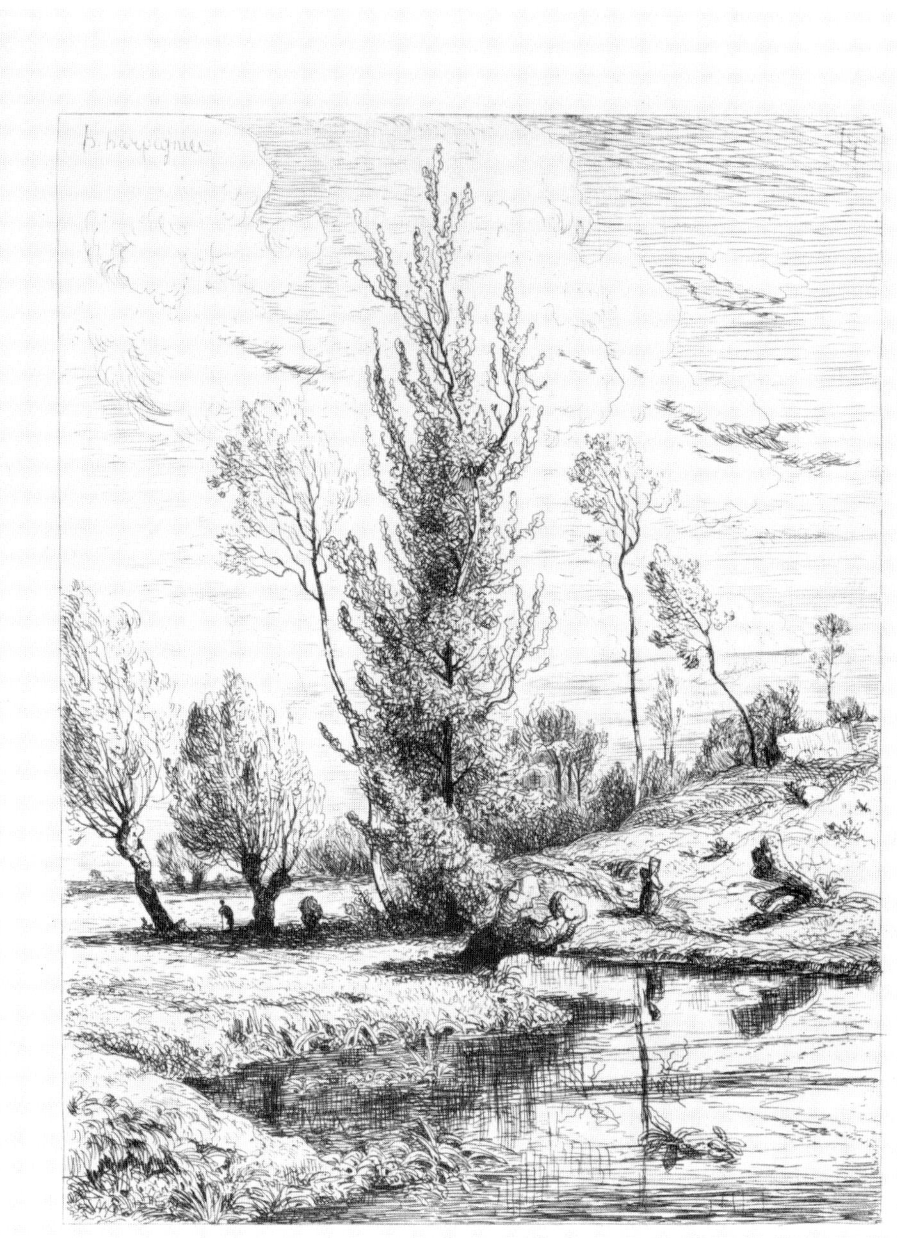

123
Marécage
(Marsh)

HENRI-JOSEPH HARPIGNIES
(Valenciennes 1819–1916 Paris)
Beraldi 26 (dedicated proof before all letters)
Etching
182 x 142 mm
Signed with dedication lower right
Provenance: R. E. Lewis, San Francisco

Even more than *House at the Top of a Rocky Hill* (cat. no. 122), this print reveals the similarities between Harpignies's early etchings and those of his better-known contemporary Charles-François Daubigny. The lightness of touch in the lines, which are wiry and scratchy yet descriptively accurate, and the suggestion of a warm, light-filled space within a simple composition free of romantic conventions recall Daubigny's *Le bac de Bezons* of 1853 (cat. no. 121). The two prints are typically realistic and, in their emphasis on the transience of light, are prototypically impressionist. Although listed in Beraldi, this print is not dated, yet one can be confident that it is a work of the mid-1850s, more advanced in its realism than the earlier *House at the Top of a Rocky Hill.*

Henri-Joseph Harpignies

124

River Estuary (1890)

HENRI-JOSEPH HARPIGNIES
(Valenciennes 1819–1916 Paris)
Watercolor
143 x 250 mm
Signed and dated lower left
Provenance: Zeitlin and Ver Brugge, Los Angeles

Watercolor was a favorite medium of Harpignies; with ease and spontaneity he worked directly from nature, recording sites throughout the French countryside. In this river landscape he revealed his interest in the subtle nuances of light and atmosphere as he rendered a specific time of day. Less detailed than his landscapes of the 1870s and 1880s, Harpignies's later watercolors are characterized by broad, summary brushwork and an increased emphasis on patterning. With subtle washes of color, he silhouetted a clump of densely foliated trees against a bright, sunlit sky, a characteristic motif. Boats and a picturesque riverside town fill the distant vista. Harpignies added highlights and luminosity to the scene by allowing the white paper to become an integral part of the composition. His freshness, immediacy, and delicate, transparent colors made him one of the master watercolorists of his time.

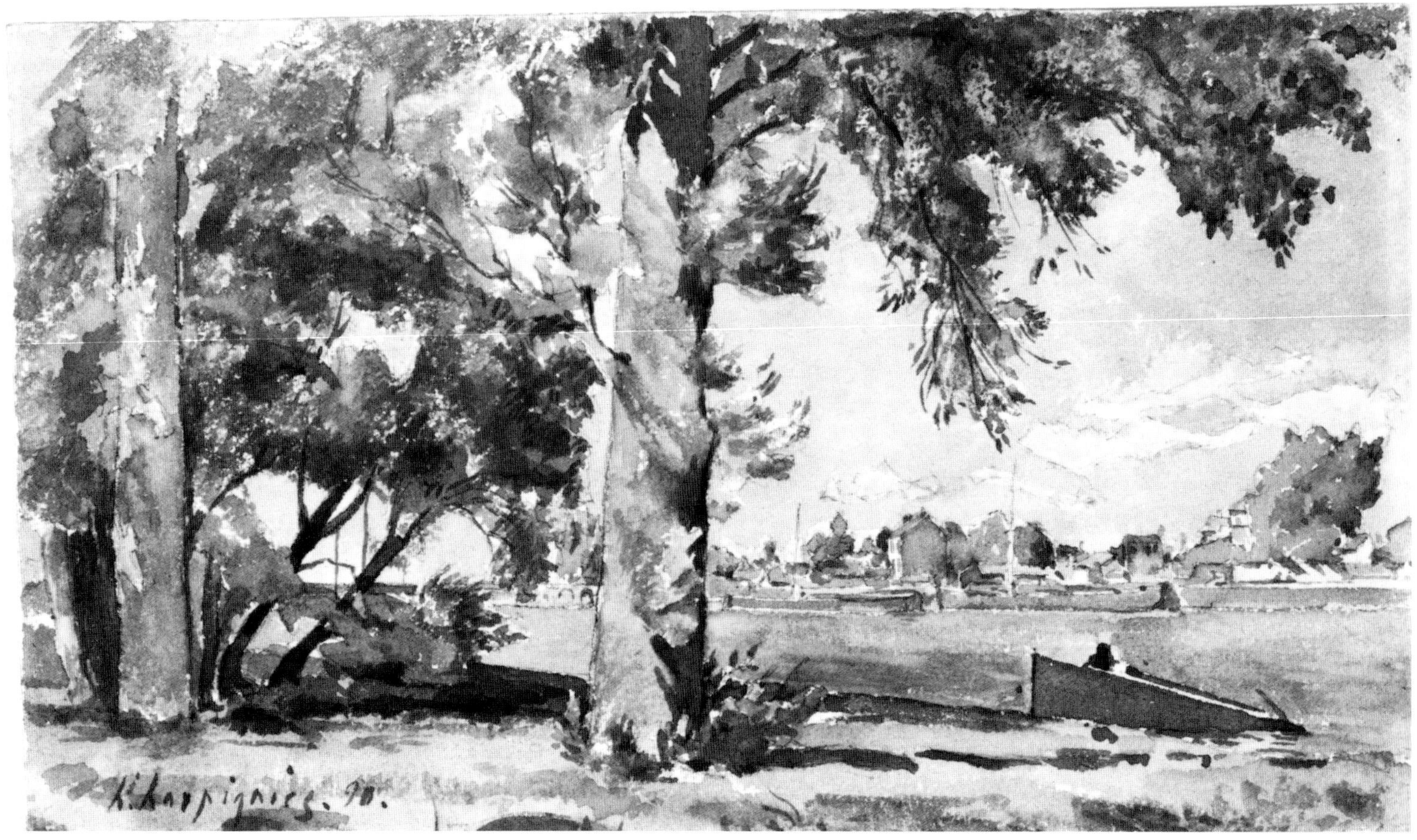

JOHAN BARTHOLD JONGKIND

Johan Barthold Jongkind received his initial training at The Hague Drawing Academy, where he studied under the landscape artist Andreas Schelfhout. In 1846 he went to Paris to join the atelier of French marine painter Eugène Isabey, who encouraged the young artist to paint the Normandy and Brittany coasts. In 1855, due to financial misfortune, Jongkind was forced to leave Paris for Rotterdam. Three years later he sent several paintings of Dutch subjects to the Parisian art dealer Pierre Firmin Martin, but they did not sell well. In 1860 Camille Corot, Théodore Rousseau, Jean-François Millet, Adolphe-Félix Cals, Narcisse-Virgile Diaz de La Peña, Henri-Joseph Harpignies, Charles-François Daubigny, Constant Troyon, and many others contributed works to an exhibition organized by Martin to raise funds to bring Jongkind back to Paris. Jongkind's fortunes finally changed when he met Josephine Fesser-Borrhée, a Dutch expatriate who became his devoted sponsor and companion.

Early in 1862 Jongkind produced his first album of etchings, Views of Holland. During the mid-1860s he was highly prolific, rendering many of his finest paintings and watercolors of the Normandy coast, Paris and its environs, and his native Holland. In the late 1860s Jongkind returned to Holland for several years but encountered a less than enthusiastic reception from Dutch artists and critics. Late in his career Jongkind settled in Côte-Saint André and visited Paris intermittently. He participated in several Salon exhibitions, but after his works were rejected in 1873 he decided never again to submit work to official exhibitions.

125

La nourrice (1862)

(The Nurse)

JOHAN BARTHOLD JONGKIND
(Lattrop 1819–1891 Côte-Saint André)
Mel. 4 i/ii (dedicated proof)
Etching
165 x 205 mm
Signed with dedication lower right
Provenance: R. E. Lewis, San Francisco

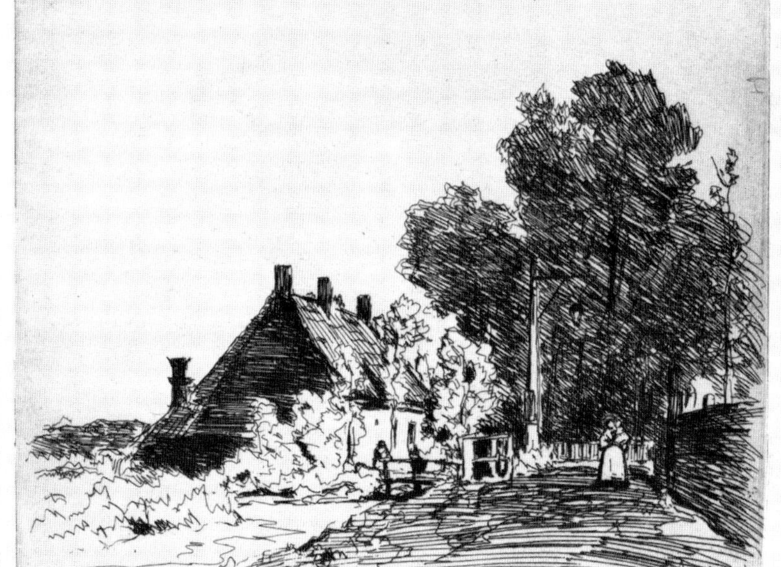

Jongkind produced only twenty-two etchings during his career, publishing his first album in 1862. One of his earliest prints, *La nourrice* was part of this first publication, which included six views of Holland. Although not as prolific a printmaker as many of his Dutch predecessors, Jongkind did not forsake his heritage in this landscape. Indeed, with its fluid, sketchy lines, *La nourrice* is reminiscent of Rembrandt van Rijn's etching *Landscape with Three Gabled Cottages beside a Road* (cat. no. 52), which features a similar compositional arrangement. Characteristically Jongkind rendered a drawing of this same subject and an oil painting of the same title in 1862.

Johan Barthold Jongkind

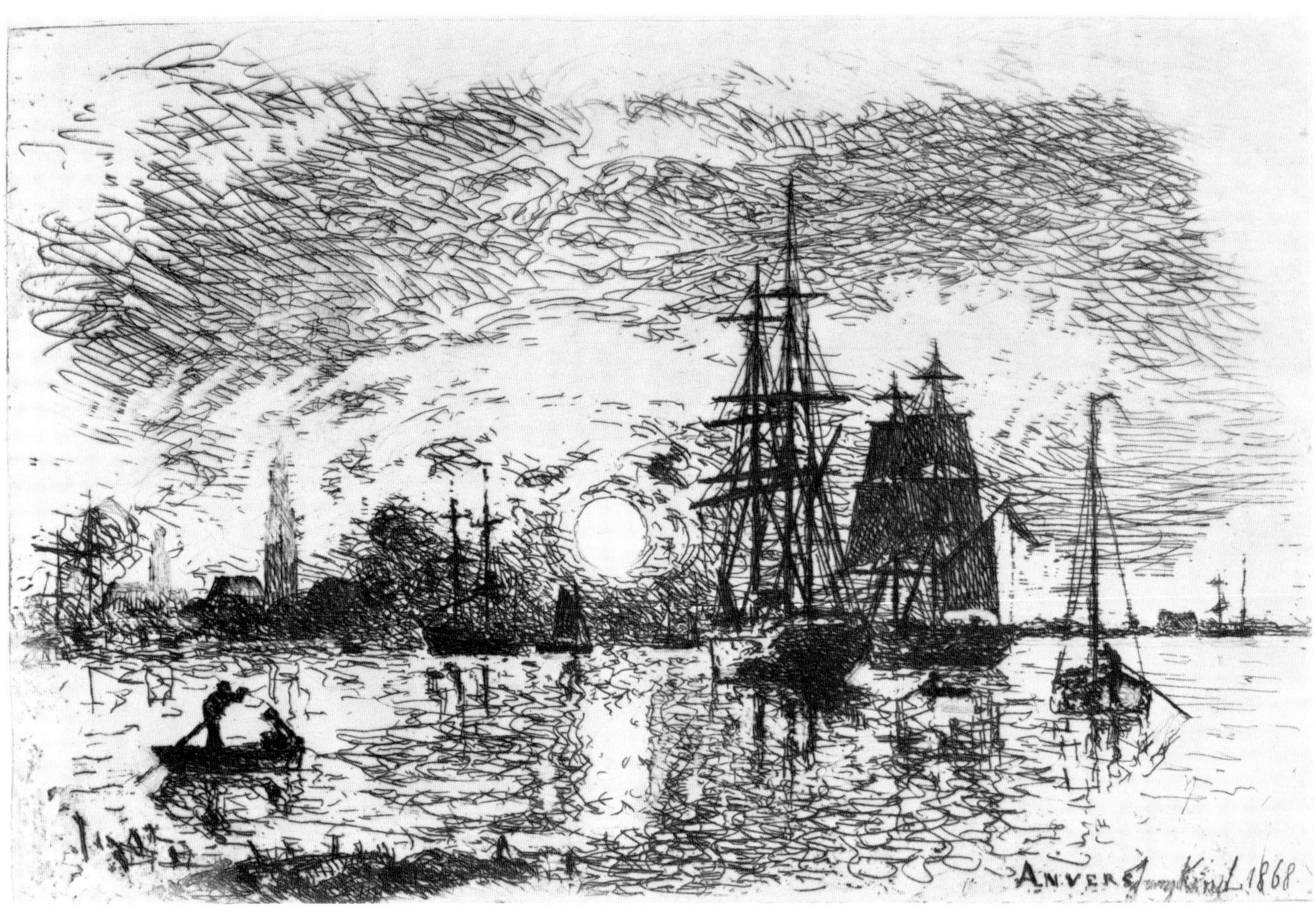

126

Soleil couchant, Port d'Anvers (1868)

(Setting Sun, Port of Antwerp)

JOHAN BARTHOLD JONGKIND
(Lattrop 1819–1891 Côte-Saint André)
Mel. 15 i/iv
Etching
151 x 282 mm
Provenance: Zeitlin and Ver Brugge, Los Angeles

In *Soleil couchant, Port d'Anvers,* a view of Antwerp harbor, Jongkind captured the fugitive quality of nature by suggesting a late afternoon sky filled with glowing light, an effect he achieved by printing from a heavily burnished copper plate. Based on a preparatory drawing of two years earlier, this impressionistic seaport view was published in four states that vary only in their annotations. Using a freely etched tangle of lines and cross-hatching, Jongkind captured the moment just before sunset. The shimmering reflections and rippling water of this twilight scene foreshadow Claude Monet's celebrated painting of 1872, *Impression: Sunrise.* Indeed Jongkind paid tribute to the precocious art of Monet by claiming that he owed the final training of his eye to the artist. As with the majority of Jongkind's etchings, this print was first published by Cadart, and it appeared in volume 1 of *L'illustration nouvelle* in 1868.

Charles Méryon

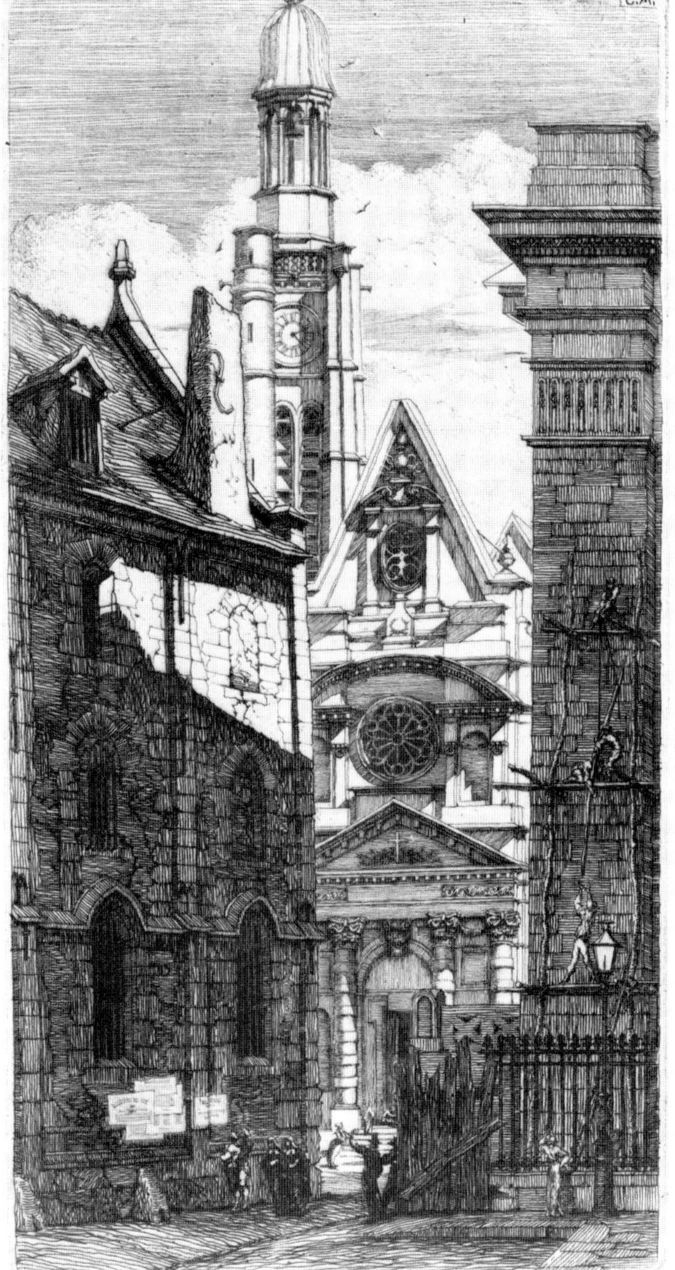

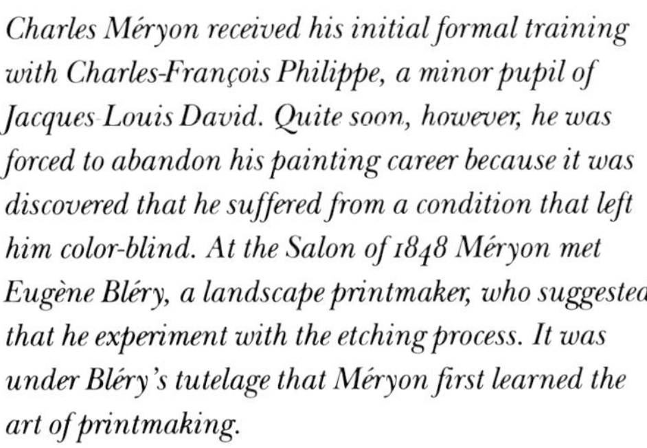

Charles Méryon received his initial formal training with Charles-François Philippe, a minor pupil of Jacques Louis David. Quite soon, however, he was forced to abandon his painting career because it was discovered that he suffered from a condition that left him color-blind. At the Salon of 1848 Méryon met Eugène Bléry, a landscape printmaker, who suggested that he experiment with the etching process. It was under Bléry's tutelage that Méryon first learned the art of printmaking.

Méryon's earliest prints were copies after etchings by old masters such as Karel Dujardin, Salvator Rosa, Adriaen van de Velde, and especially Reynier Nooms, called Zeeman, whose clarity and precision of detail greatly impressed Méryon. These were followed by numerous etchings of the city of Paris, the most famous of which were published between 1850 and 1854 as the series Eaux-fortes sur Paris. Méryon received several important commissions during the late 1850s, and his works were exhibited at the Salon, but he was increasingly plagued by financial hardship and mental instability. In 1859 he met Charles Baudelaire, who greatly admired his prints and tried to foster his artistic career by arranging for the reprinting of Eaux-fortes sur Paris. Méryon's etchings were exhibited at the Salons of 1863 to 1867, and in 1863 a catalogue of his works was published in the prestigious Gazette des beaux-arts.

127

Saint-Etienne-du-Mont (1852)

CHARLES MÉRYON
(Paris 1821–1868 Paris)
Delt. 30 iv/viii
Etching
245 x 128 mm
Provenance: R. E. Lewis, San Francisco

In *Saint-Etienne-du-Mont* three monumental buildings vie for dominance on the city street: the church facade in the center, the Collège de Montaigu on the left, and a corner of the Panthéon on the right. The confined space and the sharp contrast of light and shade heighten the tension and dramatic intensity of this urban view. With great precision Méryon recorded the minute details of the church's facade.

Méryon's preoccupation with Paris coincided with the city's mid-nineteenth-century rebuilding by Baron Georges-Eugène Haussmann and Louis-Napoléon. It was during this period that Paris came to be regarded as a sophisticated urban center and a fitting subject for artists and writers. Awareness of the city's cultural heritage also increased, and churches such as Saint-Etienne-du-Mont began to be considered important national treasures.

Charles Méryon

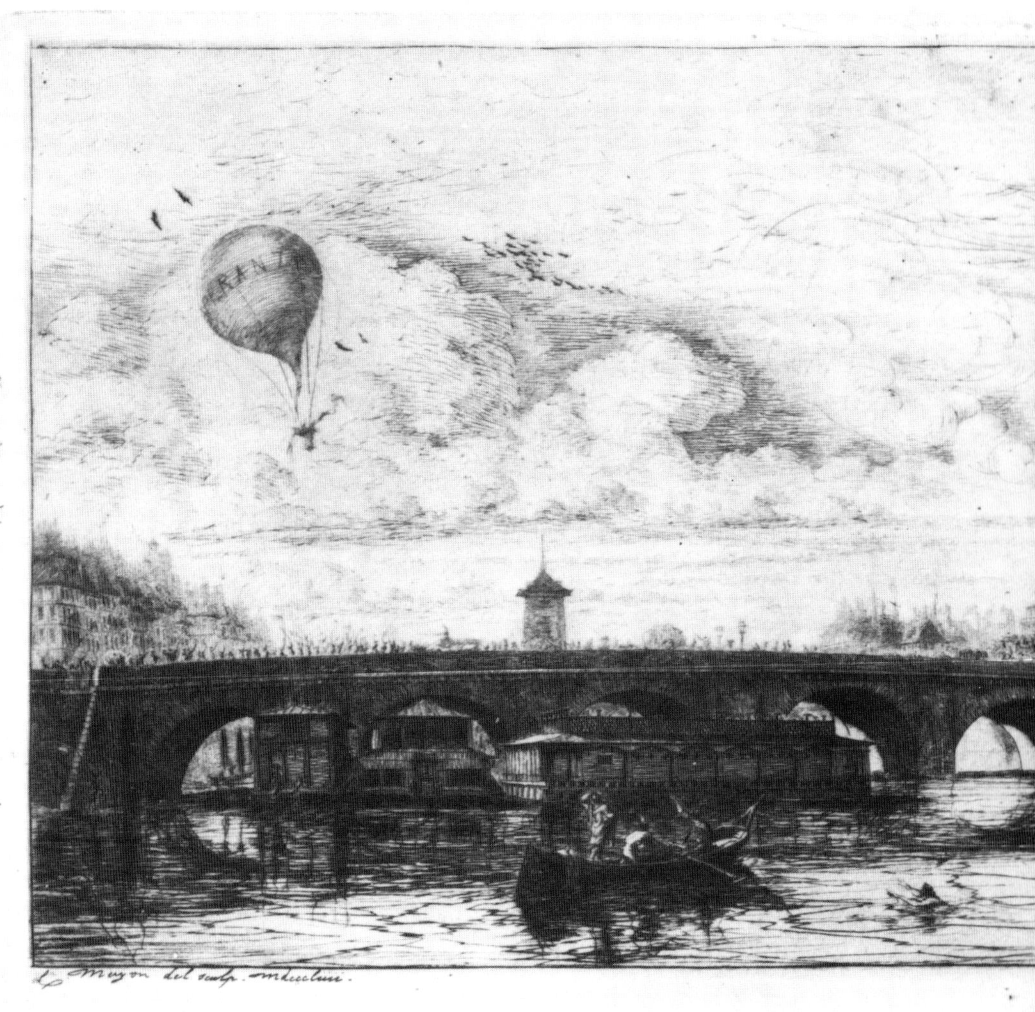

128

Le Pont-au-Change (1854)

CHARLES MÉRYON
(Paris 1821–1868 Paris)
Delt. 34 v/xii
Etching
157 x 335 mm
Provenance: William Schab, New York

129

L'espérance (1854)

(Hope)

CHARLES MÉRYON
(Paris 1821–1868 Paris)
Delt. 35 ii/iii
Etching
62 x 127 mm
Provenance: William Schab, New York

The expansive, panoramic view of Paris in *Le Pont-au-Change* is somewhat unusual for Méryon, whose cityscapes were generally more limited in scope (see cat. no. 127). Just beyond the Pont-au-Change, one sees the tower of the Pompe Notre-Dame, and to the right, on the Ile de la Cité, are the Palais de Justice and the Tour de l'Horloge. In various states Méryon reworked the fantastic imagery that appears in the sky, each time altering the meaning of the print. The fifth state was the first published edition of the print. The balloon in the sky bears the word *SPERANZA* (Italian for "hope"), as if to comment on the man floundering in the river near a small boat, ignored by the boaters as they watch the balloon. In the seventh state Méryon penciled reclining females, a snake, and a chariot in the clouds, although these changes were never rendered on the copper plate. The next major revision of the print occurred in the tenth state, when Méryon added a crescent moon and a large flock of birds that circle the city in a predatory manner. It has been suggested that Edgar Allen Poe's "The Raven" may have inspired this alteration (Burke 1974, p. 63). The eleventh state underwent a dramatic change; the menacing birds were removed, and a series of small balloons were added, endowing the print with a more lighthearted, whimsical character. In 1854 Méryon wrote the poem "L'espérance" to accompany the print and metaphorically parallel the image.

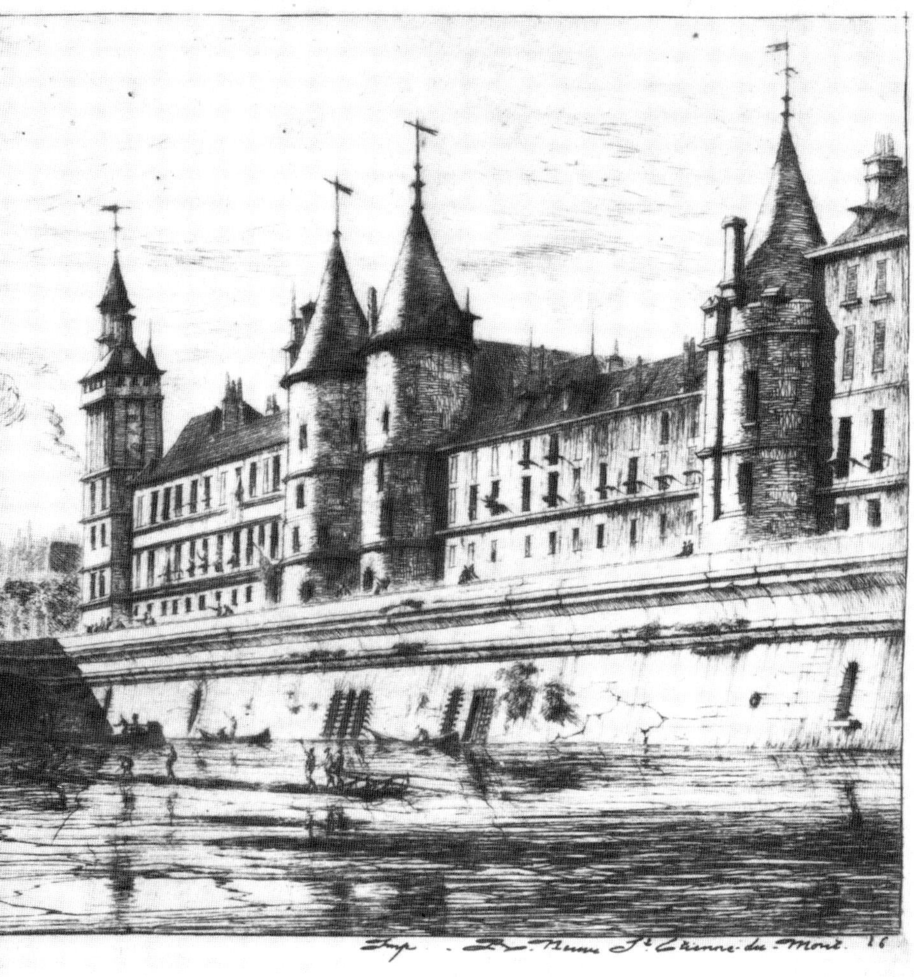

– L'Espérance –

Léger Aérostat, ô Divine Espérance,
Comme le frêle esquif que la houle balance,
Au souffle nonchalant des paisibles Autans
Vas-tu, dans les vapeurs que promènent les vents,
Découvre toi parfois à nos regards avides,
Sur le fond bleu du Ciel, dans les régions placides,
Où d'un riche soleil les rayons fécondants,
Tracent en lignes d'or tous les rêves brillants
D'un douteux Avenir, viens rendre le courage
Au rude matelot qu'a fatigué l'orage,
Au valeureux guerrier qui pour un sort meilleur,
De tous coups ennemis sait braver la douleur;
Au pauvre cœur blessé, qui cherche en vain sur terre,
Le bonheur inconnu qu'il sent et qu'il espère!
(Du bas de la Xme des Eaux-fortes sur Paris)

Mais ô triste rêveur, pourquoi dans les nuages,
Te promener ainsi quand il s'agit d'images?
Reviens, reviens à terre et laisse là le soin,
D'escalader du Ciel le trop rude chemin;
Crains de tenter du sort le caprice bizarre:
Toujours de ses faveurs pour nous il est avare.
Puisqu'un Destin nouveau t'a mis la pointe en main,
T'a fait pauvre graveur de trop frêle marin;
Vas! que sur l'enduit noir qui recouvre ton cuivre,
Ta main laisse après toi le renom qui doit suivre,
Tout esquif passager sur l'orageuse mer,
Qu'on appelle "la Vie", Océan dur, amer,
Où trop souvent hélas! fallacieux mirage,
L'espoir qui nous leurrait, va mourir au rivage!
C. M. Ms ans MDCCCLVII

à Monsieur C. Sabatier
son bien dévoué
C. Meryon

Rodolphe Bresdin

Although admired in Parisian literary circles, Rodolphe Bresdin was virtually ignored by fellow artists and critics. As a young man he read James Fenimore Cooper's adventure story The Last of the Mohicans *and identified with the novel's Indian hero, Chingachgook, prompting his friends to nickname him Chien-Caillou, a mispronounced version of the name. Bresdin's bohemian life-style inspired Champfleury's first novel,* Chien-Caillou *(1847), which brought fame to the author but did little to further Bresdin's artistic career.*

Largely self-taught, Bresdin drew his early inspiration from Rembrandt van Rijn, Albrecht Dürer, and the Barbizon painters. He was initially recognized for his drawings, which were first exhibited at the Salon of 1848, and later turned to etching and lithography. Bresdin left Paris on several occasions for Tulle, Toulouse, and Bordeaux, where he lived in extreme poverty. Bresdin's fortunes improved in 1861, when he returned to Paris and had thirteen etchings published in Revue fantaisiste. *His prints were also exhibited at the Salon. In 1871 Bresdin apparently entered a contest to design an American banknote and won, enabling him to fulfill his lifelong dream of visiting North America. He settled in Montreal with the hope of finding a commercial outlet for his work. He was unsuccessful, however, and in 1876 Bresdin and his family returned penniless to France, where he remained primarily in solitude until his death in 1885.*

With the exception of one small painting, Bresdin's oeuvre consists entirely of drawings, etchings, and lithographs in which nature played a predominant role. Macabre fantasies, biblical stories, landscapes, and themes of solitude are among his recurrent subjects. Possessing an extraordinary imagination and poetic insight, Bresdin created highly personal and enigmatic images.

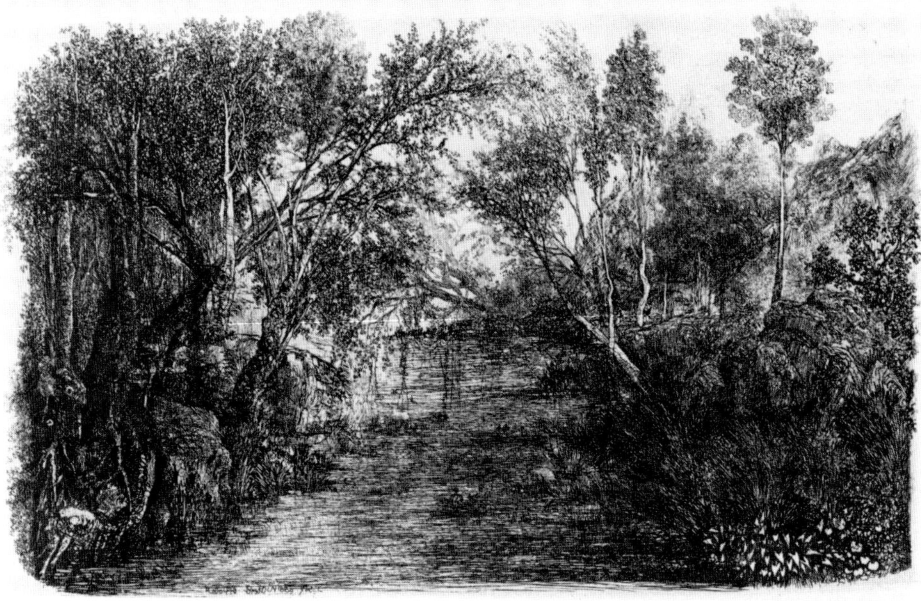

130
Le cours d'eau (1880)

(The Stream)

RODOLPHE BRESDIN
(La Fresne 1822–1885 Sèvres)
Neumann 37; Van Gelder 144
Etching
136 x 210 mm
Provenance: Sabersky, Los Angeles

Le cours d'eau was published in the June 1882 issue of *L'artiste* under the title *Paysage.* This particular impression is one of those described by Van Gelder as printed on yellowish laid Van Gelder Zonen paper. The blurring of the image at the tops of the trees in the upper right and left is also characteristic of this group and occurred during the wiping of the plate.

This print includes motifs from Bresdin's etching *La cité lointaine* (1868–71), particularly the ducks and the rocks at the left of the composition (Van Gelder 1976, p. 142). It is also similar to *Le ruisseau sous bois,* an etching of the same year.

Le cours d'eau is characteristic of prints executed during the artist's later years, when he no longer included any human activity or the bizarre and macabre subject matter of his early prints. In this respect it is one of Bresdin's most intimate landscape prints, reminiscent of Charles-François Daubigny's etchings.

CAMILLE PISSARRO

Camille Pissarro began his formal artistic training in 1855 at the École des Beaux-Arts and the Académie Suisse, although he was soon drawn to the more naturalistic, less conventional works of Camille Corot, Jean-François Millet, and Gustave Courbet. Following rejection by the Salon jury in 1863, Pissarro exhibited in the newly established Salon des Refusés and later allied himself with the impressionist group, participating in all eight of its exhibitions (1874–86). From 1866 to 1869 he worked at Pontoise, but following the outbreak of the Franco-Prussian War in 1870, he joined Monet in London and, influenced by the works of J. M. W. Turner and John Constable, painted highly atmospheric views of the English countryside.

Returning in 1872 to Pontoise, where he would remain until 1883, Pissarro experimented with printmaking, especially the aquatint and mixed intaglio processes. During the late 1880s he experimented with the pointillist technique, under the influence of Georges Seurat, but found this methodical approach contrary to his artistic temperament, preferring instead a freer, plein-air style. During the early 1890s he increasingly devoted his attention to printmaking, and in 1891 his etchings were jointly exhibited with those of Mary Cassatt. After a major retrospective show in 1892, organized by art dealer Durand-Ruel, Pissarro's artistic achievements were internationally recognized.

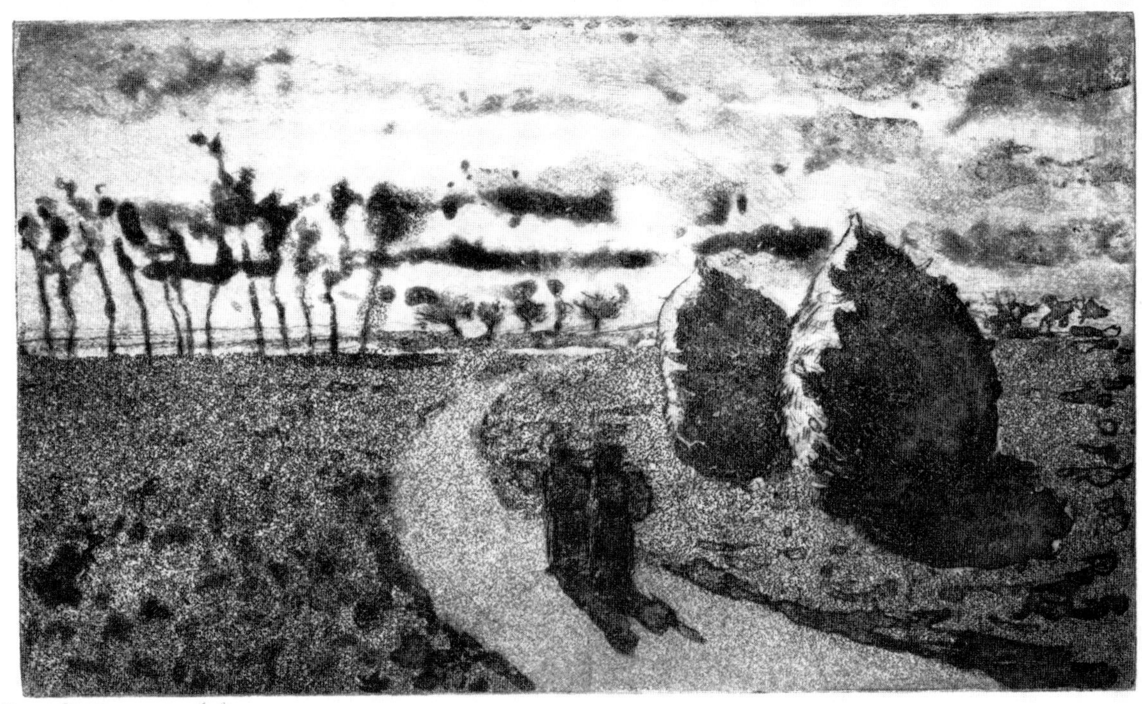

131
Crépuscule avec meules (1879)

(Twilight with Haystacks)

CAMILLE PISSARRO
(Saint Thomas 1830–1903 Paris)
Delt. 23 iii/iii; Mel. 22 iii/iii (no. 1 of 15 numbered and annotated trial proofs)
Aquatint and drypoint
104 x 179 mm
Provenance: R. E. Lewis, San Francisco

While at Pontoise, Pissarro experimented with the aquatint process, creating finely textured and highly painterly images such as this one. With its luminosity, subtle tonality, and lack of harsh contours, *Crépuscule avec meules* can be considered the graphic equivalent of an impressionist painting.

It was after 1879 that Pissarro began collaborating with Edgar Degas, sharing printmaking techniques and exploring the creative possibilities of the etching process. *Crépuscule* was produced in three states as well as fifteen trial proofs. Pissarro annotated and signed the prints as they were pulled, thereby giving credence to each progressive phase of the process. The second and third states were printed on colored paper with different colored inks to create a sequence of images that vary in terms of light and atmospheric effects, much like Claude Monet's 1891 series of painted haystacks (Melot 1974, p. 16).

Paul Signac

Almost entirely self-taught, Paul Signac met Georges Seurat in 1884, an encounter that had a decisive and lasting influence on his artistic sensibility. Signac adopted Seurat's methodical divisionist technique and later became an ardent exponent of the neo-impressionist movement. Along with Seurat, he participated in the founding of the Société des Artistes Indépendants in 1884 and contributed to all nine of the group's exhibitions between 1884 and 1893. Based on contemporary theories of optics and color perception, divisionism was a systematic method of applying small dabs of pure color that would combine in the eye of the beholder to achieve the highest degree of brilliance. Signac employed this technique in numerous marine and seaport views as well as scenes of the industrial suburbs of Paris. In 1887 he accompanied Seurat to an exhibition at the Salon des Vingt in Brussels and in the following year was invited to contribute to their next show.

During the mid-1890s Signac began experimenting with watercolor and printmaking techniques and soon liberated himself from strict adherence to the divisionist method. Although his work of this period exhibited a sense of freedom and spontaneity not in tune with the scientific divisionist premise, he became the leader of the neo-impressionist movement after Seurat's death in 1891. In 1899 Signac published De Delacroix au néo-impressionnisme, *a theoretical treatise that became the movement's manifesto. After the turn of the century, he worked primarily in watercolor, choosing his subjects from the Channel, Atlantic, and Mediterranean coastal regions. During his last years Signac traveled extensively, visiting Holland, Venice, Istanbul, and Corsica, and devoted more of his time to writing than painting.*

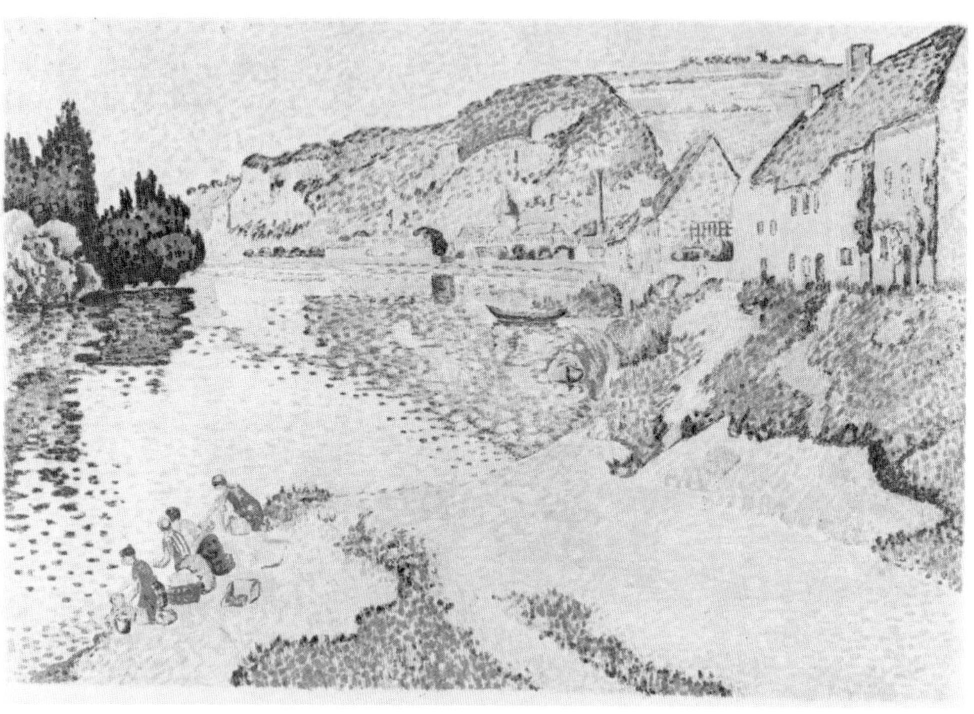

132
Les Andelys (1895)

PAUL SIGNAC
(Paris 1863–1935 Paris)
Kornfeld and Wick 10
Lithograph
300 x 453 mm
Provenance: William Schab, New York

Interested in contemporary life, Signac favored industrial suburbs and commercial riverbank scenes such as this view of the tower of Les Andelys on the Seine near Rouen. The smokestack in the distance and women washing on the riverbank reflect the artist's interest in portraying the working world and the effects of industrialization on late nineteenth-century society. Water also figures in much of Signac's work; he was a passionate sailor, owning some thirty-two boats during his lifetime.

A strong sense of compositional order, characteristic of Signac's divisionist style, dominates this landscape. Like other neo-impressionists, Signac sought to reveal the essence of form by ridding his pictures of the accidental or transitory elements of nature. This pursuit of the underlying structure of things did not, however, result in a static, petrified view of reality. As the eye struggles to fuse the small dabs of pure color, an optical vibration takes place, duplicating the shimmering effect of light reflecting on natural surfaces.

During the mid-1890s Signac completed a series of six color lithographs for the publisher Gustave Pellet, basing his prints primarily on his paintings and watercolors. The separation of color inherent in the lithographic process allowed him to control the distribution of colored ink. Using only seven colors, Signac achieved a full spectrum of tonal variations in *Les Andelys.* His painting of the same subject, dated 1886, is in a private collection in Paris.

Paul Signac

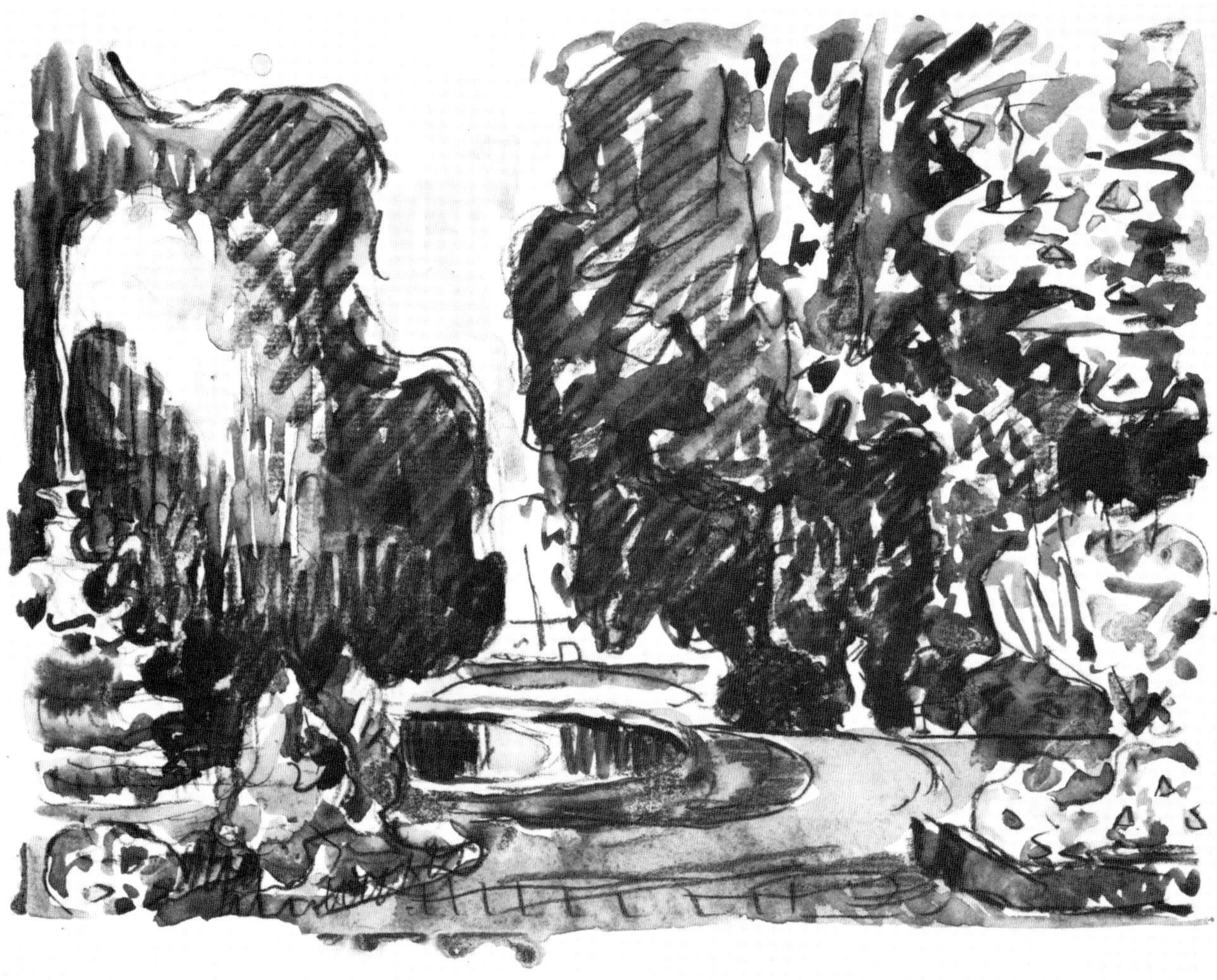

133

Garden at Saint-Tropez (c. 1910)[1]

PAUL SIGNAC
(Paris 1863–1935 Paris)
Watercolor over black crayon
205 x 278 mm
Provenance: Françoise Cachin; William Schab, New York

Enchanted by the Saint-Tropez peninsula, Signac moved to this region in 1892 after discovering it on one of his sailing trips. The city's harbor and lush Mediterranean countryside became the focus of his work.

During the mid-1890s Signac increasingly turned to watercolor, favoring the freedom and spontaneity the medium offered while working outdoors, directly from nature. With only a restless evocation of form and a high regard for the expressive properties of color, Signac created a garden setting with flowers and thick foliage bathed in sunlight. A dominant color contrast of orange and blue often appears in Signac's watercolors of the early twentieth century; the correlation between color and object described diminished as his work became increasingly abstract. The energetic brushwork and looser, more decorative patterning evident in this landscape recall a drawing of a similar subject that dates to 1909, now in a private collection (Cachin 1971, p. 89). As Signac abandoned verisimilitude, he adopted brilliant colors and impetuous forms that were highly influential for Henri Matisse and the Fauves, who frequently visited him in Saint-Tropez.

1. We would like to thank Françoise Cachin for her suggestion regarding the date of this watercolor.

Ker-Xavier Roussel

Ker-Xavier Roussel began his artistic training in 1885 in the studio of Diogène Maillart, a minor history painter. There he prepared for the École des Beaux-Arts, which he entered three years later and where he studied with Tony Robert-Fleury. At the same time he frequented the Académie Julian, where he met Paul Sérusier, who worked at the Académie as a proctor and who had come under the influence of Paul Gauguin. Gauguin's ideas informed the work and ambitions of a small group of young painters, including Roussel, Sérusier, Maurice Denis, Édouard Vuillard, and Pierre Bonnard, who called themselves the Nabis. Their name, derived from the Hebrew word for prophets, is indicative of the mystical and oracular nature of their work.

The Nabis exhibited together semiannually throughout the 1890s and presented, until the emergence of Paul Cézanne at the end of the century, the most progressive art in Paris. Roussel exhibited infrequently with the group, however, identifying more closely with the decorative art of Vuillard, whose sister he married in 1893. Following Vuillard's suggestion, Roussel turned to color lithography and, with Vuillard, Bonnard, and Henri de Toulouse-Lautrec, contributed to the first album of L'estampe originale, a quarterly series dedicated to reviving interest in original prints, that is, prints of original designs of the highest quality in technique and printing. While the series was a critical success, Roussel contributed only to the first album, concentrating instead on his paintings, which, inspired by the 1895 Galerie Vollard exhibition of 150 paintings by Cézanne, were increasingly concerned with classical mythological subjects set in delicate landscapes. Roussel was praised by Denis for making pictures that were like Poussin's in their depiction of large-scale, noble figures in light-filled settings. Roussel's high regard for decorative effects and his sure sense of composition led to numerous commissions for public and private murals, including the decoration of the Théâtre de Chaillot. Such projects brought great praise to Roussel, who, with Vuillard, is ranked among the great decorative painters of the modern era.

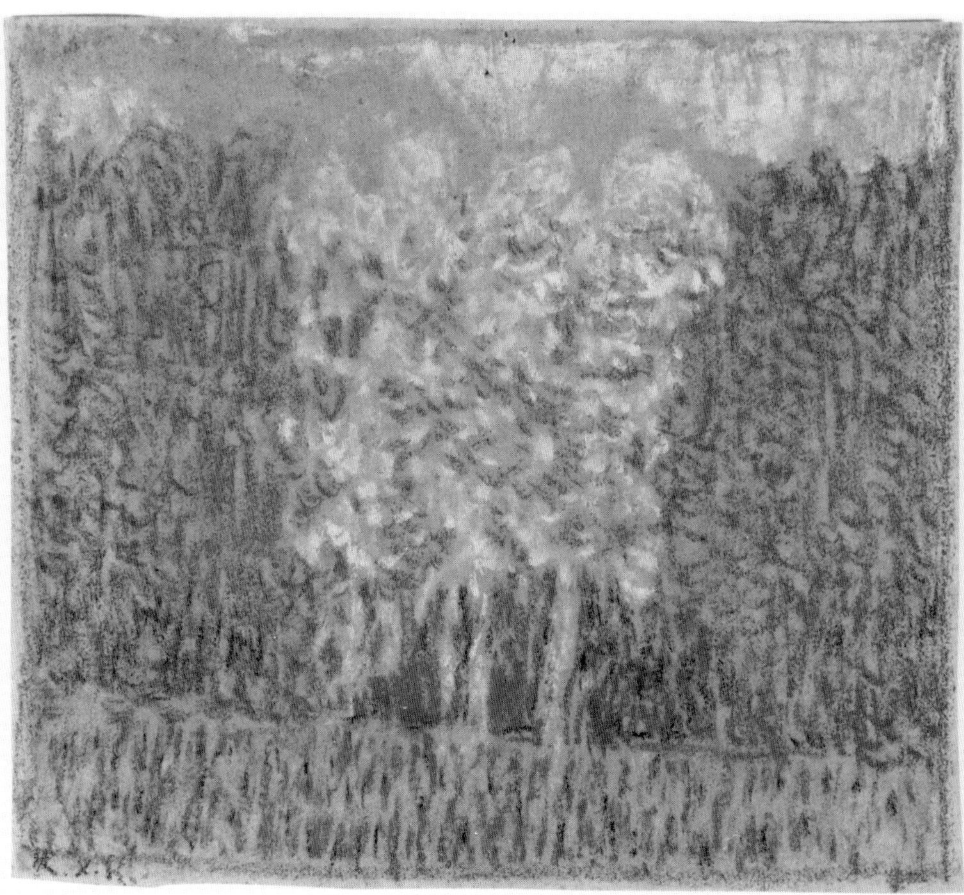

134

Three Tall Trees (c. 1892–98)

KER-XAVIER ROUSSEL
(Lorry-les-Metz 1867–1944 L'Étang-la-Ville)
Pastel
160 x 183 mm
Initialed lower left corner
Provenance: Jacques Solomon; Lucien Goldschmidt, New York

With its emphasis on pattern and a composition that barely distinguishes between foreground and background, this diminutive drawing probably dates from the second half of the 1890s, when Roussel was twice engaged in painting mural decorations for public buildings and when he drew the landscape lithographs *La femme en rouge dans un paysage* and *Femme en robe à rayures* (see entry for cat. no. 135). In each instance Roussel merged figures with ground to present a unified field of color and atomized form. Here the trees are drawn as if on the same plane as the hills behind and the field before them. Each element is distinguished from the others by its color and by the character of the crayon marks that define it: a yellow-green field by short, vertical marks; a dark green hill by loosely drawn, angled marks; the blue and white sky by vigorous strokes rubbed together; and the trees by small white dashes depicting blossoms. It is a charming drawing, quite rare in Roussel's oeuvre; his published drawings are almost all of figures in landscapes, although, like this drawing, they are most frequently executed in pastel. Yet there is no doubt as to its attribution: it is initialed at lower left and was once in the collection of Jacques Solomon, the author of numerous books and exhibition catalogues on Roussel, Édouard Vuillard, and others among the Nabis.

135

La femme en rouge dans un paysage (1899)

(Woman in Red in a Landscape)

KER-XAVIER ROUSSEL
(Lorry-les-Metz 1867–1944 L'Étang-la-Ville)
Alain and Solomon 15 (only state)
Color lithograph
233 x 352 mm
Provenance: Zeitlin and Ver Brugge, Los Angeles

Barely distinguishable from the patterned background, a woman in red walks with a parasol along a park path before blossoming trees. As in his contemporary lithograph *Femme en robe à rayures* (1898; Alain and Solomon 16), Roussel here explores a kind of decorative abstraction that blends figure and ground into a common field of color. In this respect the print is closer to the paintings of Édouard Vuillard—especially his interiors of the early 1890s, in which figures are fused with their environment—than to any of Roussel's own paintings. For at that time Roussel was painting either patterned pictures with larger color areas or more freely drawn pictures that resembled those of the mature Eugène Delacroix. Only in *Femme en robe à rayures* did Roussel explore the atomization of form with such delicacy.

Both *La femme en rouge dans un paysage* and *Femme en robe à rayures* are from the lithographic album Paysages, commissioned by the art dealer Ambroise Vollard and printed by Auguste Clot, the incomparable lithographer who had drawn the color stones of Édouard Manet's *Polichinelle* in 1874 and who had printed numerous lithographs for Henri Fantin-Latour, Odilon Redon, and Henri de Toulouse-Lautrec, most notably Lautrec's masterful portfolio of 1896, Elles (Gilmour 1988, pp. 129–82). Comprising twelve color lithographs and a cover, Roussel's album was left unfinished, however. He released only six prints to Vollard, each in an edition of 100; *La femme en rouge dans un paysage* and *Femme en robe à rayures* were among them.

The Grunwald Center also has a proof of *La femme en rouge dans un paysage* from the Baumfeld bequest. It prints only the landscape and in lighter colors: the foliage to the right is gray rather than blue, and the grass is a lighter green. The woman and the blossoms on the trees are not printed but are drawn in orange crayon, and the grass is heightened with yellow to suggest a carpet of flowers. The impression is clearly a working proof, as its margins are covered with color tests and printing errors.

In its precocious abstraction *La femme en rouge dans un paysage* is more advanced than Vuillard's later landscape lithographs, also printed by Clot and published in the 1899 portfolio Paysages et intérieurs. Indeed this eccentric print by Roussel is comparable only to Edgar Degas's extraordinary landscape monotypes of the early 1890s. Roussel never pursued the implications of the print but quickly turned to the depiction of nymphs and fauns cavorting in pastoral landscapes much like those of Paul Cézanne of the 1870s. It remains, with *Femme en robe à rayures,* an isolated experiment.

Jacques Villon

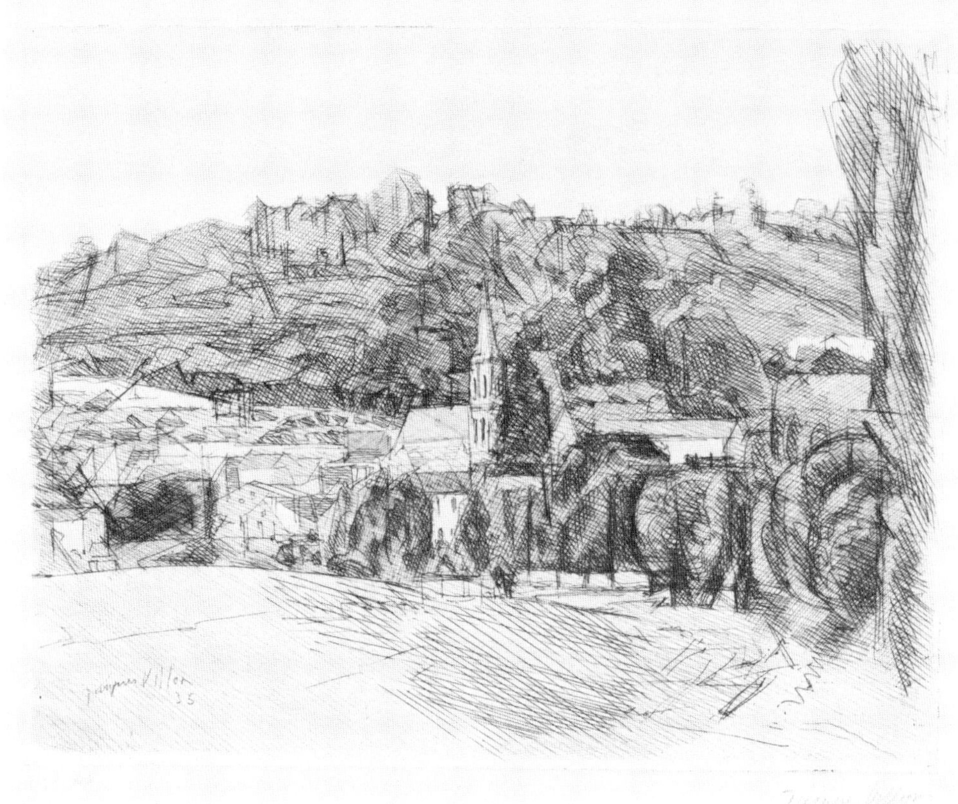

Born Gaston Duchamp, Jacques Villon took up etching in 1891 at the urging of his maternal grandfather, Émile-Frédéric Nicolle, who specialized in architectural views. Villon produced numerous lithographs, etchings, and aquatints between 1891 and 1921. In 1894 he left for Paris, where he found employment as a newspaper illustrator and cartoonist. As his artistic career progressed, he renounced his family name, which he felt did not suit his sophisticated life-style, and adopted the name Villon from the poet François Villon and the name Jacques from Alphonse Daudet's novel Jack.

Early in his career Villon was influenced by the impressionists, Henri de Toulouse-Lautrec, and the Fauves, but between 1911 and 1914 he became interested in analytical cubism, which would prove to have a significant impact on his subsequent career. Villon is best remembered for the numerous prints and paintings he created working within the cubist idiom. He believed that artists should strive for objectivity in art and developed a highly structured style based on mathematical proportions. In 1912 Villon was instrumental in forming a group of artists that advocated the same approach, including Fernand Léger, Albert Gleizes, Jean Metzinger, and his half-brothers, Marcel Duchamp and Raymond Duchamp-Villon. They were known as the Section d'Or after a treatise by Leonardo da Vinci containing the principle of "pyramidal vision," which was adopted by the group.

During the 1920s Villon's style became more abstract as he sought to portray the essence of objects, rather than their outward appearances. It was only after a vacation in southern France in 1934 that landscape became a major theme of his paintings and etchings.

136

Chevreuse (1935)

JACQUES VILLON
(Damville 1875–1963 Puteaux)
Auberty and Perussaux 272 xviii/xxv
Etching
210 x 269 mm
Numbered lower left; signed lower right
Provenance: R. G. Michel, Paris

This view of the city of Chevreuse, located just outside Paris, is a fine example of Villon's landscape prints of the mid-1930s. The Tour de France, a famous bicycle race, travels through this city, and in another state of this print Villon added cyclists to the foreground. Characteristic of the artist's somewhat cubist approach to nature, overlapping planes and geometric shapes structure the composition. Villon achieved a subtle balance between observation of nature and his pursuit of the essence of form. A finely rendered grid of systematically arranged lines unifies the diverse elements of the composition and endows the landscape with a sense of light and texture. Villon used dense cross-hatchings to create shadow and contour, achieving a quality of line similar to that of a fine pen drawing. The architectonic manner in which he structured the natural world not only reflects his cubist proclivities but also serves to emphasize the enduring qualities of nature and modern life.

Jacques Villon

137

The Vegetable Garden at La Brunié (1940)

JACQUES VILLON
(Damville 1875–1963 Puteaux)
Pen and ink
230 x 300 mm
Signed and dated lower right
Provenance: Lucien Goldschmidt, New York

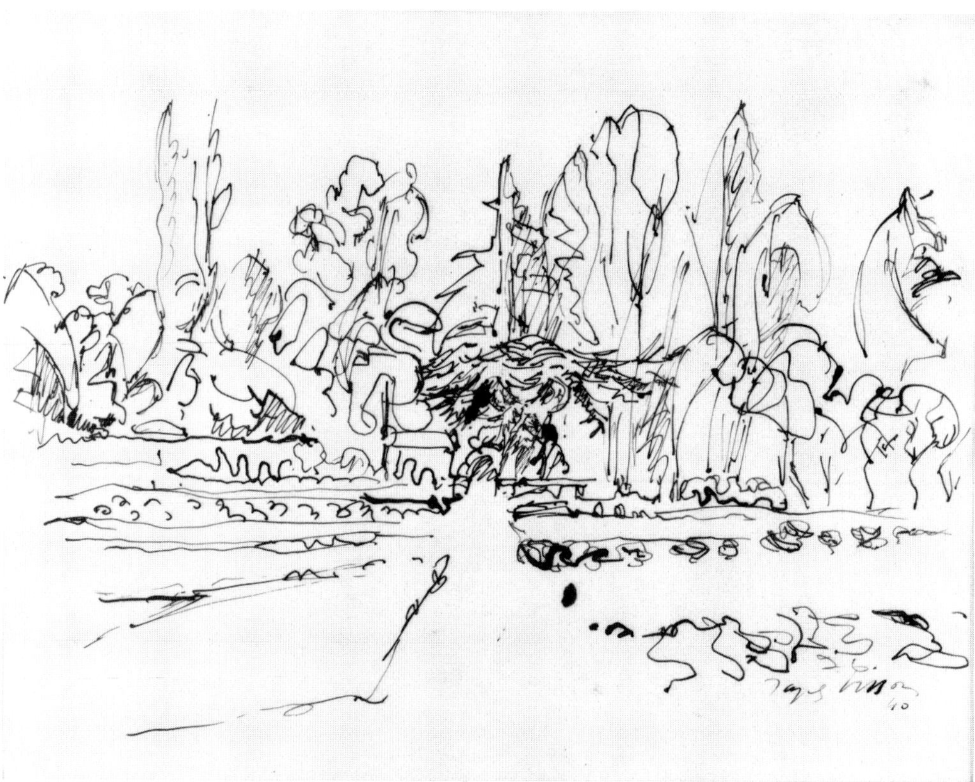

Quickly sketched on tracing paper, this drawing records the eastern view from the vegetable garden of the home of Villon's friends the architect Marc Vène and his wife, Anne-Françoise Mare.[1] The country house was located in the south of France at La Brunié in Tarn. Villon had fled occupied Paris for La Brunié in the summer of 1940. There he made numerous sketches that he would use over the next two years in painting his first important series of landscape pictures.

In a letter of September 16, 1940, addressed to the American writer Francis Steegmuller, whose wife, Béatrice Stein, was his student, Villon described the peace of the countryside in contrast to the troubles of Paris. On two of the four pages of that letter, he sketched the southern, northern, eastern, and western views from the house's vegetable garden. The northern view corresponds very closely to the Grunwald Center drawing, with a path receding deeply into space and gardens extending to the left and right and with a barrier of trees across the background. Next to the drawing Villon describes the view as "the north side, the side by which one arrives at the garden opposite its lower border." A painting of this view is in a New York private collection.[2] A painting of the western view, in the collection of the Cleveland Museum of Art, is dated 1941 and entitled *Le potager à La Brunié,* while a painting of the eastern view, now in the Art Institute of Chicago, is entitled *Le potager aux citrouilles.*

The western and northern views were also etched in 1942, although there is some confusion over the titling of the prints. The catalogue of Villon's prints identifies the etching after the Grunwald Center drawing as the eastern view and the etching of the western view as the northern view.[3] The letter of September 16, 1940, however, is quite clear in its depiction and description of the four views, leaving no doubt that the Grunwald Center drawing is of the eastern view. Further, as the Grunwald Center drawing is on tracing paper and is squared off with graphite in proportions quite close to those of the published etching, one can assume that the drawing was the preliminary sketch for the print; the two are very close in their drawing of the view, although the etching is more detailed and less spontaneous in character.

The liveliness of the drawing accurately suggests Villon's feelings about La Brunié, where he wrote that he had rediscovered nature, confessing that "[t]he superiority for me of landscapes over still lifes is that I find in landscapes the movement of life."[4]

1. Anne-Françoise Mare was Villon's goddaughter and the daughter of André Mare, who, with Villon, was an original member of the Section d'Or.
2. The letter is in a New York private collection but is reproduced in Daniel Robbins, ed., *Jacques Villon,* exh. cat. (Cambridge, Mass.: Fogg Art Museum, 1976), no. 132, and *Jacques Villon,* exh. cat. (Rouen: Musée des Beaux-Arts, 1975), no. 127. A painting of the northern view is reproduced in Robbins, *Jacques Villon,* no. 133a. It includes workers hoeing in the foreground.
3. See Auberty and Perussaux 1950, nos. 440–42
4. Rouen, *Jacques Villon,* no. 127.

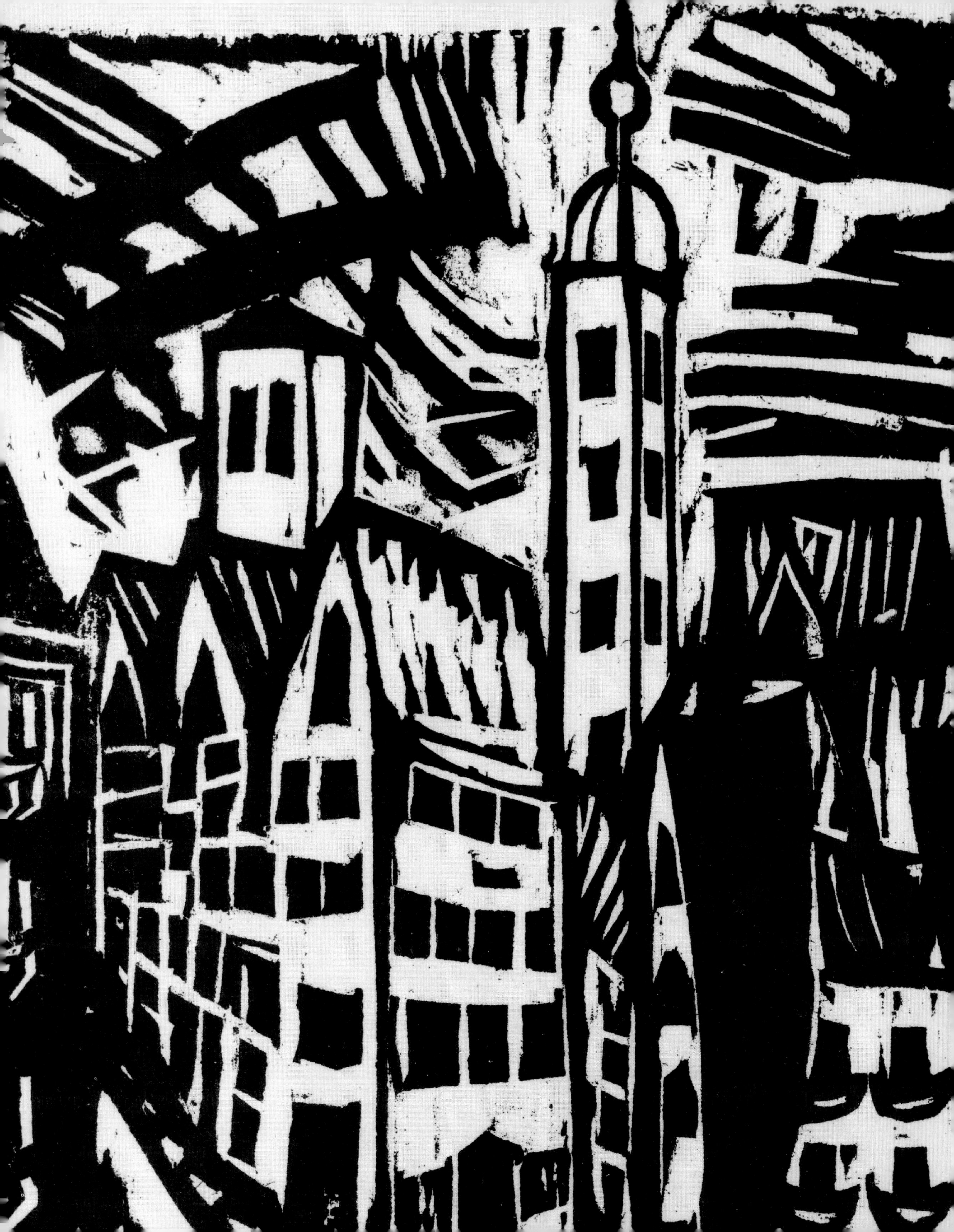

German

Detail of cat. no. 145

Wolf Huber

Wolf Huber probably apprenticed in Feldkirch, in the Austrian province of Vorarlberg. Although he was formerly thought to have been a pupil of Albrecht Altdorfer, it is now believed more likely that the relationship was one of friendship, possibly initiated during an early trip to Vienna. By 1515 Huber was the head of a workshop in Passau, where until his death he was court painter to Wolfgang von Salm, bishop of Passau. The latter commissioned his most important painting, the Saint Anne Altarpiece *(Bregenz, Landesmuseum, and Feldkirch, St. Nikolaus).*

A number of Huber's drawings of specific places document trips up the Danube to Germany in 1513–14 and down the Danube to Vienna in 1529–31. Around 1541 he became city architect of Passau. Although he designed woodcuts, he was not as active a printmaker as Altdorfer and never produced etchings. Huber is best known for his independent landscape drawings, which are executed in pen, or occasionally watercolor, on white paper. Huber and Altdorfer are the principal artists of the Danube school, a stylistic trend in German Renaissance art distinguished by its emphasis on landscape and the transcendent dynamism of nature.

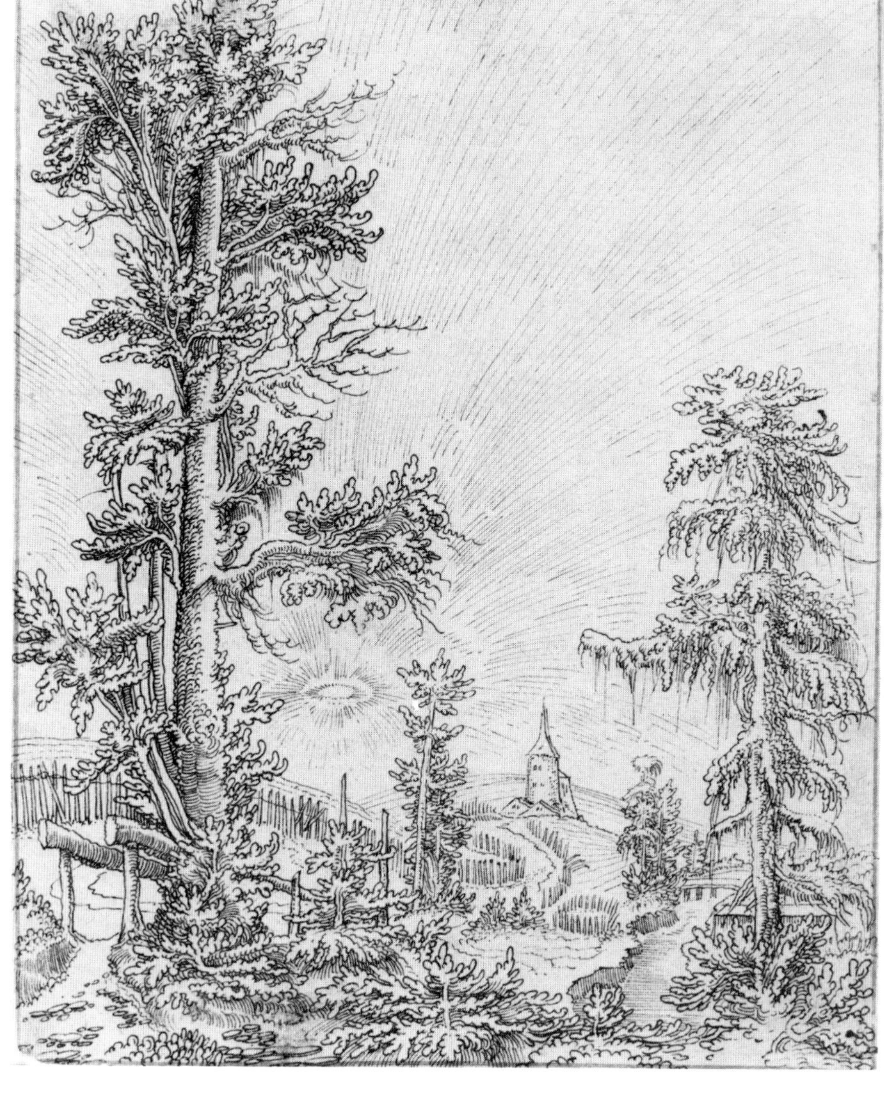

138

The Path to the Church (c. 1530)

Circle of WOLF HUBER
(Feldkirch c. 1480–1553 Passau)
Pen and black ink, framing line in light brown ink
193 x 153 mm
Provenance: Prince Liechtenstein (sold, Klipstein and Kornfeld, Bern, 19 June 1960, lot 115); Lucien Goldschmidt, New York

As noted by Halm and subsequent authors, this is one of several versions of a lost drawing by Huber.[1] The spare, linear style of the present drawing, as well as the tendency to focus upon the vertical elements of the landscape, such as the trees and the distant church steeple, become evident when it is compared with the Göttingen version (see Winzinger 1979, vol. 2, pl. 181), which emphasizes the articulation of dense, curling vegetation. Talbot and Shestack propose that these drawings are based on a Huber model of around 1515–25; Winzinger believes this model would have been slightly later, however, adducing comparisons to drawings by Huber of around 1530.[2]

Huber's more naturalistic depiction of a road to a church in an earlier drawing in Dresden (Kupferstichkabinett; Winzinger 1979, no. 66, dated c. 1518–20) here gives way to a visionary approach to the theme, conveyed most explicitly through the presence of the radiant sun (*Sonnengestirn*), a recurrent motif in the landscape imagery of the Danube school, expressing God's vital presence in nature.[3] Such pantheism is clearly evident in the present drawing, in which the diminutive church appears to serve as an emblem of the divine energy coursing through the trees and furrowed hills that surround it. A similar juxtaposition of the radiant sun and a church steeple occurs in Albrecht Altdorfer's earlier engraving of Saint Christopher of around 1515–20 (B. 19).

1. Peter Halm, "Die Landschaftszeichnungen des Wolfgang Huber," *Münchner Jahrbuch der bildenden Kunst*, n.s., 7 (1930): 104, no. 133, and 98, under no. 90; Talbot and Shestack 1969–70, no. 80, pl. 45; Winzinger 1979, vol. 1, p. 144, no. 181b. Others in Göttingen, Kunstsammlung der Universität; formerly Rotterdam, Museum Boymans, Koenigs collection (Winzinger 1979, nos. 181, 181a).

2. Talbot and Shestack 1969–70, p. 79, no. 80; Winzinger 1979, p. 143, under no. 181. Most comparable, according to Winzinger, are *Forest Landscape* (Kiel, Kunsthalle, Kupferstichkabinett) and *Landscape with a Tree with a Double Trunk* (Erlangen, Graphische Sammlung der Universität; Winzinger 1979, nos. 88, 89).

3. Dieter Koepplin, "Das Sonnengestirn der Donaumeister," in *Werden und Wandlung: Studien zur Kunst der Donauschule* (Linz, 1967), pp. 78–114; Talbot and Shestack 1969–70, p. 83, under no. 86.

Augustin Hirschvogel

Born in Nuremberg, Augustin Hirschvogel was trained in the atelier of his father, Veit, a prominent designer of stained-glass windows. He appears to have received an education beyond that normally granted craftsmen, as reflected in his later activities as a mathematician and cartographer. By 1536 he had left Nuremberg and settled in Laibach, in modern Yugoslavia, where he appears to have been active as a maiolica manufacturer. In 1539 he delivered a map of the Turkish borders to the city council of Nuremberg, the first in a series of mapping projects. The most important of these was a group of views of Vienna, completed in 1547, in which he was the first cartographer to employ triangulation as a standard of measurement. In 1543 he moved permanently to Vienna, where he began his career as an etcher. Although he produced a large number of biblical illustrations and portraits, his hunting scenes, ornamental designs, and landscapes best exemplify the refinement of his graphic style. His fanciful, panoramic landscape vistas are indebted to the precedent of the Danube school masters, Albrecht Altdorfer and Wolf Huber.

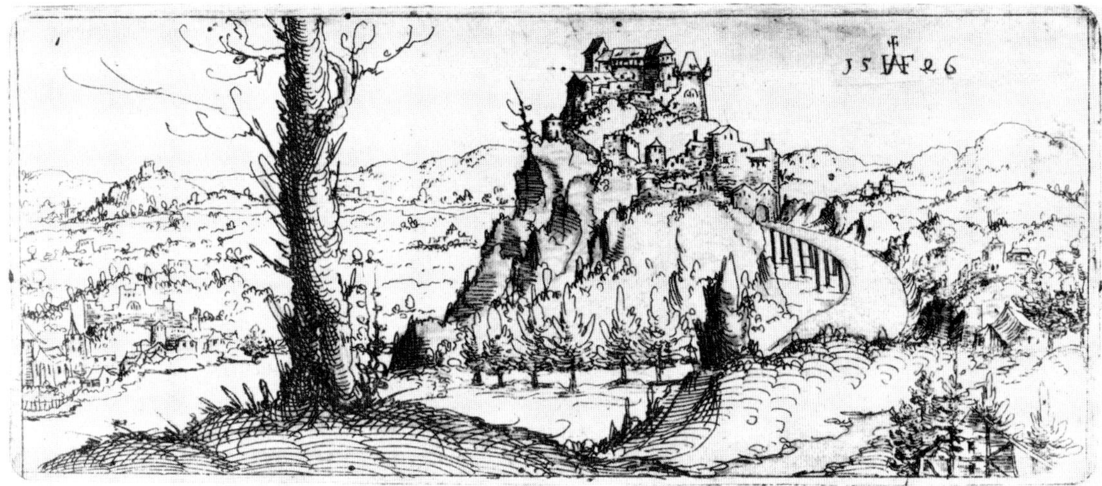

139

Landscape with a Rocky Mountain and a Castle (1546)

AUGUSTIN HIRSCHVOGEL
(Nuremberg 1503–1553 Vienna)
B. 52; Schwarz 52
Etching
63 x 149 mm
Provenance: William Schab, New York

Although Hirschvogel's graphic work is diverse in subject matter, he is best known for the thirty-six landscape etchings that he produced between 1545 and 1549.[1] The present scene, with its vast, panoramic vista and use of motifs such as the rocky fortress and dynamically curving bridge, demonstrates Hirschvogel's overarching stylistic debt to Wolf Huber. This is especially evident in the Huberesque placement of a single cropped tree in the foreground, which gives way to a distant landscape, a compositional schema occurring commonly in Hirschvogel's etchings. Preferring landscapes of a low, horizontal format, Hirschvogel tended to place his trees off to one side, where they balance the expansiveness of the landscape by echoing the vertical margins of the print. They also enhance the effect of spatial recession through the contrast between the shadowed tree trunk and the brightly illuminated landscape beyond.[2] This small-scale, emphatically horizontal format was new to German landscape art.[3] Both intimate and precious, it evidences an aesthetic similar to that found in contemporary ornamental engravings as well as in the diminutive prints of the so-called *Kleinmeister*.[4]

Such preciosity also extends to Hirschvogel's style of etching. While the example of Altdorfer's landscape etchings no doubt prompted Hirschvogel to take up the medium, he eschewed the broken, scintillating line of his predecessor in favor of a more draftsmanlike, calligraphic approach. Developing a highly stylized linear vocabulary, seen most clearly in his love of looping, bowlike forms, Hirschvogel exploited the decorative potential of etched line to a degree unequaled by other printmakers of the period.

---

1. Schwarz 1917, nos. 45–S.142. See also the discussion in Talbot and Shestack 1969–70, pp. 88–93.
2. See Schwarz 1917, p. 85.
3. Ibid.
4. Konrad Oberhuber, *Die Kunst der Graphik IV: Zwischen Renaissance und Barock: Das Zeitalter von Bruegel und Bellange*, exh. cat. (Vienna: Graphische Sammlung Albertina, 1967–68), p. 134, under no. 167.

Hanns Lautensack

Born in Bamberg, the son of a painter and musician, Hanns Lautensack moved with his family to Nuremberg in 1527. His name first appears in the Nuremberg city registry in 1552, the year he became an independent artist. It is likely that he received his training with a goldsmith. Lautensack's two earliest landscape etchings, which date to 1554 (B. 44; Schmitt 45, 46), evidence his direct study of the works of Albrecht Altdorfer and Wolf Huber. His monumental views of Nuremberg from the east and west of 1552 (B. 58, 59; Schmitt 51, 50) mark the high point of his early career. During this period he also began to produce portrait engravings of members of Nuremberg's aristocracy, into which he incorporated detailed landscape backgrounds. In 1553–54 Lautensack made his first series of landscape etchings (Schmitt 52–67), which was strongly influenced by the works of Altdorfer and Huber. In 1554 Emperor Ferdinand I summoned him to Vienna to publish the imperial coin collection. Lautensack's later cycles of landscape etchings, dated 1554–55 and 1558–59, are panoramic in scope and frequently incorporate figural staffage (Schmitt 68–73, 74–81). His few surviving drawings are rarely as finished as his prints. Although some documents refer to him as a painter, his extant works indicate that Lautensack was active primarily as a graphic artist.

140

River Landscape with a Church (1553)

HANNS LAUTENSACK
(Bamberg c. 1520–c. 1564–66 Vienna)
B. 42; Schmitt 52
Etching
102 x 170 mm
Provenance: William Schab, New York

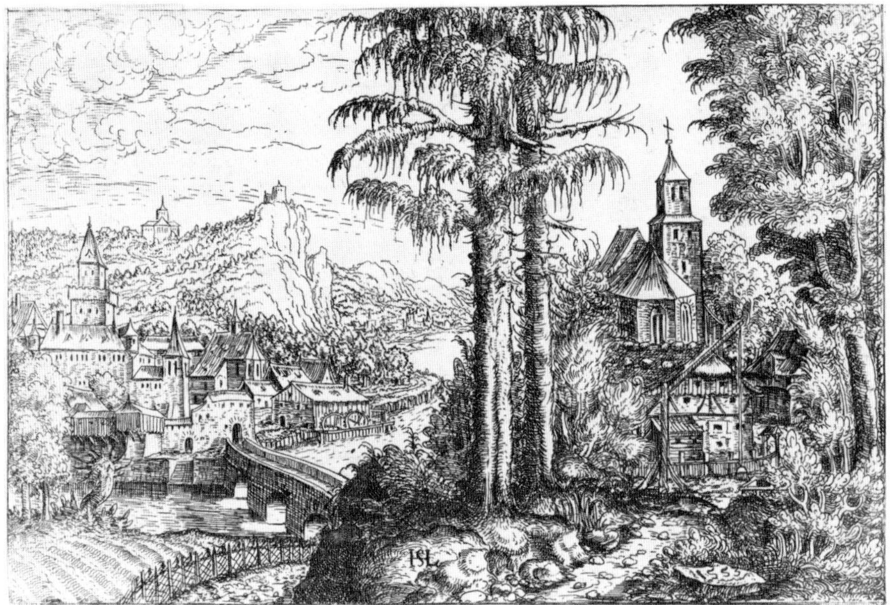

Together with Augustin Hirschvogel, Lautensack was the principal artist to take up the production of pure landscape prints initiated by Albrecht Altdorfer in his pioneering etchings of around 1517–22.[1] The present example is one of a series of sixteen intimately scaled landscape etchings dating from 1553 and 1554 which represents Lautensack's finest effort in this genre.[2] In this print Lautensack closely follows the composition of his own etching of 1551 (B. 32, 33; Schmitt 49), which itself echoes Altdorfer's etching *Landscape with a Double Pine* (B. 70).[3] In the latter, a soaring fir, cropped at the top of the page, occupies the center foreground of a centrifugally expanding mountain valley.[4] In contrast to Altdorfer's pine, which dominates the landscape as an expression of the superhuman power of nature, those of Lautensack link the hill with a chapel and cottages at the right foreground with the vista of a river village and distant peaks at the left. Lautensack's linear technique, consisting for the most part of short lines, flicks, and stipples, is also ultimately derived from Altdorfer's etchings. Compared with the spareness and ethereality of Altdorfer's line work, however, it is more densely packed, varied in tone, and intended to evoke effects of texture and atmosphere.

Architecture, which in the work of Altdorfer and Wolf Huber is portrayed as a vibrant extension of the natural environment, is here harmoniously integrated into a picturesque natural setting. Lautensack particularizes each of his landscapes by introducing a few distinguishing features, such as the double pines and river village in the present example.[5] In so doing, he moves away from the transcendent symbolism of Altdorfer and Huber toward a more topographical approach; indeed, at least one print in this series depicts a specific city.[6] The prints produce a greater effect as a group than they do singly; by comparing one to another, one appreciates their variety and the artist's skill at combining disparate topographical and architectural elements to form a plausible whole. The creation of a series of pleasing landscape vistas was a new development in German art; predating similar trends in seventeenth-century Dutch printmaking, it owes its genesis to the efforts of Lautensack and Hirschvogel.

---

1. For Altdorfer's landscape etchings, see esp. Hans Mielke, *Albrecht Altdorfer: Zeichnungen, Deckfarbenmalerei, Druckgraphik*, exh. cat. (Berlin: Staatliche Museen Preussischer Kulturbesitz, Kupferstichkabinett, 1988), pp. 227–36.
2. For this print, see Schmitt 1957, pp. 22–24, no. 52, p. 86 under no. 49; for the series as a whole, see pp. 24–26, nos. 52–67.
3. As noted by Schmitt, ibid., pp. 23–24.
4. Talbot and Shestack 1969–70, no. 59, p. 58 (entry by H. Manner).
5. As pointed out by Jeffrey Chipps Smith in his discussion of another print in this series (Schmitt 54); see Jeffrey Chipps Smith, *Nuremberg: A Renaissance City, 1500–1618*, exh. cat. (Austin: Archer M. Huntington Art Gallery, University of Texas, 1983), p. 258, under no. 165.
6. Schmitt 67; the city depicted is Steyr.

HANNS LAUTENSACK

141

Landscape with Combat between Balaam and His Ass

(c. 1558–59)

HANNS LAUTENSACK
(Bamberg c. 1520–c. 1564–66)
B. 55; Schmitt 80
Etching
192 x 291 mm
Provenance: Zeitlin and Ver Brugge, Los Angeles

This print belongs to Lautensack's final series of landscape etchings, which he made around 1558–59.[1] The series is characterized by a dramatic increase in the scale of the images, accompanied by a heightened monumentality of form.[2] This and most of the other scenes in the series each contain a few figures, for the most part taken from the Bible, whose diminutive size further enhances the grandeur of the natural surroundings.

Lautensack's tendency to use the same motif repeatedly is in evidence here; the natural arch framing a view toward a stream and mountains to the left and offering a glimpse into the distance through its passageway echoes a print from the 1553–54 series (B. 30, Schmitt 66) as well as an etching of 1544, one of his two earliest dated landscape prints (Schmitt 46).[3] Caves and rocky archways commonly occur in biblical scenes by Wolf Huber and Altdorfer, such as the latter's woodcut *Saint Jerome in a Cave* (B. 57), in which the vaulted rocky hideaway is treated as a natural cathedral.[4] Lautensack transformed the natural arch into an independent motif, however, and in so doing, he largely dissociated it from such religious implications.[5] Compared with his previous depictions of natural arches, the one here is more massive, contorted, and dramatic. The emphasis upon contrasts of light and dark in this print, while evident throughout Lautensack's graphic work, here produces a nuance of tone and corresponding three-dimensionality of form that is unequaled in his earlier prints. Schmitt has also noted a more integrated spatial conception in this series, which she attributes to Lautensack's study of prints by Netherlandish masters such as Hieronymus Cock.[6]

---

1. Schmitt 1957, pp. 28–31, nos. 74–81, and pp. 94–97; Konrad Oberhuber, *Die Kunst der Graphik IV: Zwischen Renaissance und Barock: Das Zeitalter von Bruegel und Bellange*, exh. cat. (Vienna: Graphische Sammlung Albertina, 1967–68), p. 139, no. 184.
2. Schmitt 1957, p. 29.
3. Ibid., p. 19.
4. See Talbot and Shestack 1969–70, no. 43 (entry by J. Bailey).
5. Schmitt 1957, p. 19; ibid., no. 107 (entry by A. Gyongy).
6. Schmitt 1957, p. 28. For example, the series of landscapes with biblical and mythological scenes after Matthys Cock (see cat. no. 15; Riggs 1977, pp. 273–79, nos. 38–50).

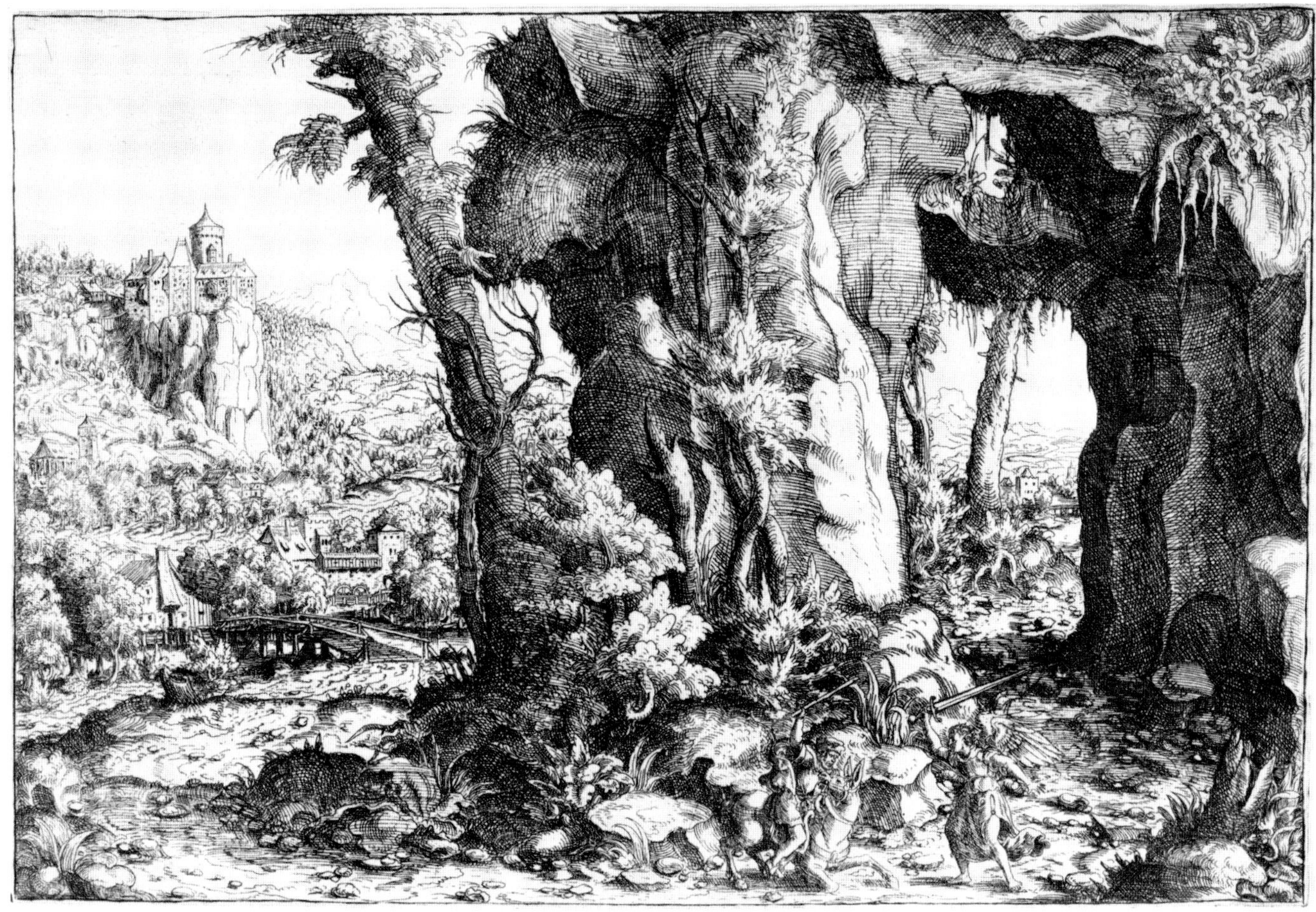

[*German*]

EMIL NOLDE

Born Emil Hansen, Nolde took the name of his northern Schleswig birthplace sometime between 1901 and 1904. He spent several years as a furniture designer (1884–91), then served as a drawing master in a school for the applied arts in Saint Gall, Switzerland. From 1898 to 1901 he studied art in Munich, Paris, and Copenhagen, embarking on a career as an artist in 1902, at the age of thirty-five. One of the first German expressionist artists, he developed a passionate style of painting and printmaking, using strident colors applied with strong brush strokes thick with color, deliberately producing distorted shapes and a sense of violent motion. His early landscapes, whether of the garden at his northern island retreat of Als or harbor scenes in Hamburg, although saturated with vivid color, were often gentler than his other work.

In January 1906 Nolde exhibited a body of his most recent paintings at the Galerie Arnold in Dresden and was subsequently invited to join the artists' group the Brücke. He moved to Dresden and worked with the group for about eighteen months. It was during this time that Nolde began experimenting with woodcut, quickly mastering the technique and producing a number of landscapes, harbor scenes, and biblical images. Like the other Brücke artists, he also worked in etching and lithography and is usually considered the finest etcher among the expressionists. Nolde, an older, more developed artist than Ernst Ludwig Kirchner and the others, left the group in 1907, preferring to work alone on artistic problems of his own choosing. He exhibited frequently during these years: with the Berlin Secession in 1905, with the Brücke in 1906 and 1907, with the Neue Sezession in 1912, at the Blaue Reiter exhibition in Munich in 1912, and at the Sonderbund exhibition in Cologne, also in 1912.

In 1913–14 he joined an anthropological expedition to the South Seas, which traveled east by way of Russia, China, and Japan. He painted little but made quantities of drawings and watercolor sketches, which he reworked from memory after his return to Germany. Ironically, although he bemoaned the destruction of "primitive" cultures through European colonialism, he was a strong believer in racial superiority and an early member of the National Socialist party in Germany.

In 1937 the Nazis presented their exhibition of "degenerate art" and prohibited Nolde and many others from working, despite his membership in the party. After the war he continued to paint, expressing his lifelong belief in a primordial instinct shared by all humanity and nature.

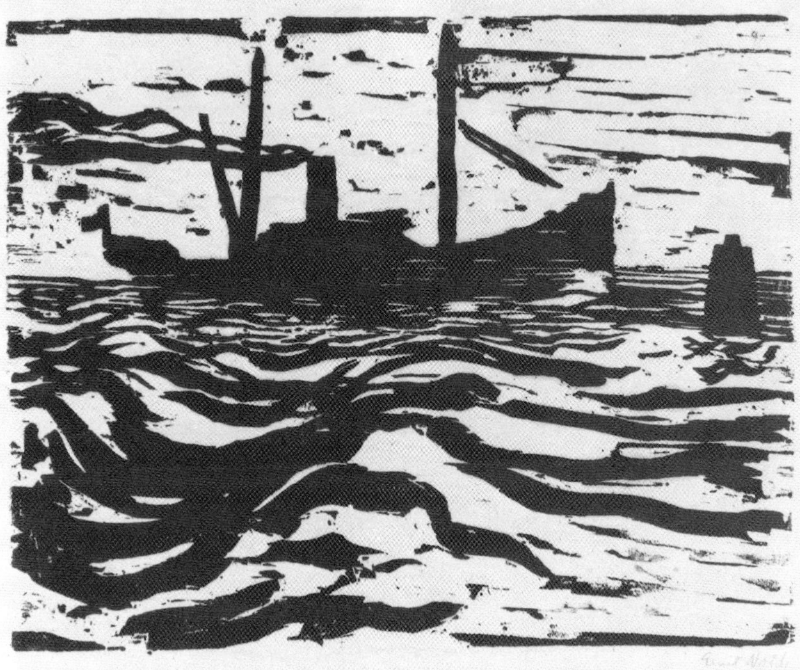

142

Fischdampfer (1910)

(Steam Trawler)

EMIL NOLDE
(Schleswig 1867–1956 Seebüll)
Schiefler and Mosel 34 ii/ii
Woodcut
302 x 390 mm
Signed lower right; numbered lower left
Provenance: L'Art Ancien, Zurich

In 1910 Nolde created a series of etchings devoted to the activities of the Hamburg harbor and the different vessels working its waters. *Fischdampfer,* also of 1910, continues that theme using a different print technique, woodcut. Nolde exploits the patterning and sharp contrasts between large forms and areas of black and white that are characteristic of the woodcut, particularly as practiced by members of the Brücke. He contrasts the undulating foreground waves with the straight, almost ruled lines of the water as it approaches the horizon line. This juxtaposition is repeated on a smaller scale in the sky by the wavy trail of steam originating in the smokestack, which contrasts with the straight, parallel lines representing clouds on the right. The motion of the waves, indeed the entire composition, is balanced by the solid profile of the tall-rigged trawler.

The curved elements forming the waves resemble the brushwork and line found in Nolde's work in other media, for example, his harbor watercolors (see cat. no. 142) or the grass skirts and even the legs of his famous South Seas dancers.[1] Such repetitions in the articulation of natural forms can be read as visual representations of Nolde's belief in and search for the primordial, instinctual, and mystical connections between humanity and nature.

1. Los Angeles County Museum of Art, *German Expressionist Prints and Drawings: The Robert Gore Rifkind Center for German Expressionist Studies,* vol. 1 (Los Angeles: Los Angeles County Museum of Art; Munich: Prestel Verlag, 1989), p. 44, fig. 63.

Emil Nolde

143

Harbor (c. 1913)

EMIL NOLDE
(Schleswig 1867–1956 Seebüll)
Watercolor
235 x 325 mm
Signed lower left
Provenance: Zeitlin and Ver Brugge, Los Angeles

This watercolor bears a close resemblance to many of Nolde's studies of tug steamers in Hamburg harbor, a subject that preoccupied the artist throughout the year 1910. It is sparser and more summary than many of the Hamburg watercolors, however, and in this respect is closer to Nolde's harbor scenes painted in 1913–14, when he joined a German anthropological expedition whose destination was the Bismarck Archipelago in the South Pacific. During his six-week stay in China and Japan, the artist made numerous drawings of the people and their harbors. His fascination with Chinese junks resulted in several watercolor and charcoal studies of these vessels, with their distinctive sails. The boat on the extreme right in the Grunwald Center watercolor appears closely related to some of these studies, and the composition is typical of the harbor scenes painted during Nolde's yearlong journey.[1] The significant elements of sky and water are indicated by broad washes of unusual colors, the boats are rapidly sketched in black, and much of the paper is left untouched by color.

Upon the expedition's hurried return to Germany after the August 1914 declaration of war, Nolde's sketches, along with the rest of the baggage, were confiscated by the British at Suez, to be returned to him in 1921 (Selz 1957, p. 290).

1. Compare, for example, brush drawings of Chinese junks in *Emil Nolde: Aquarelle aus den Jahren 1894–1956*, exh. cat. (Hamburg: Kunstverein, 1967), no. 33.

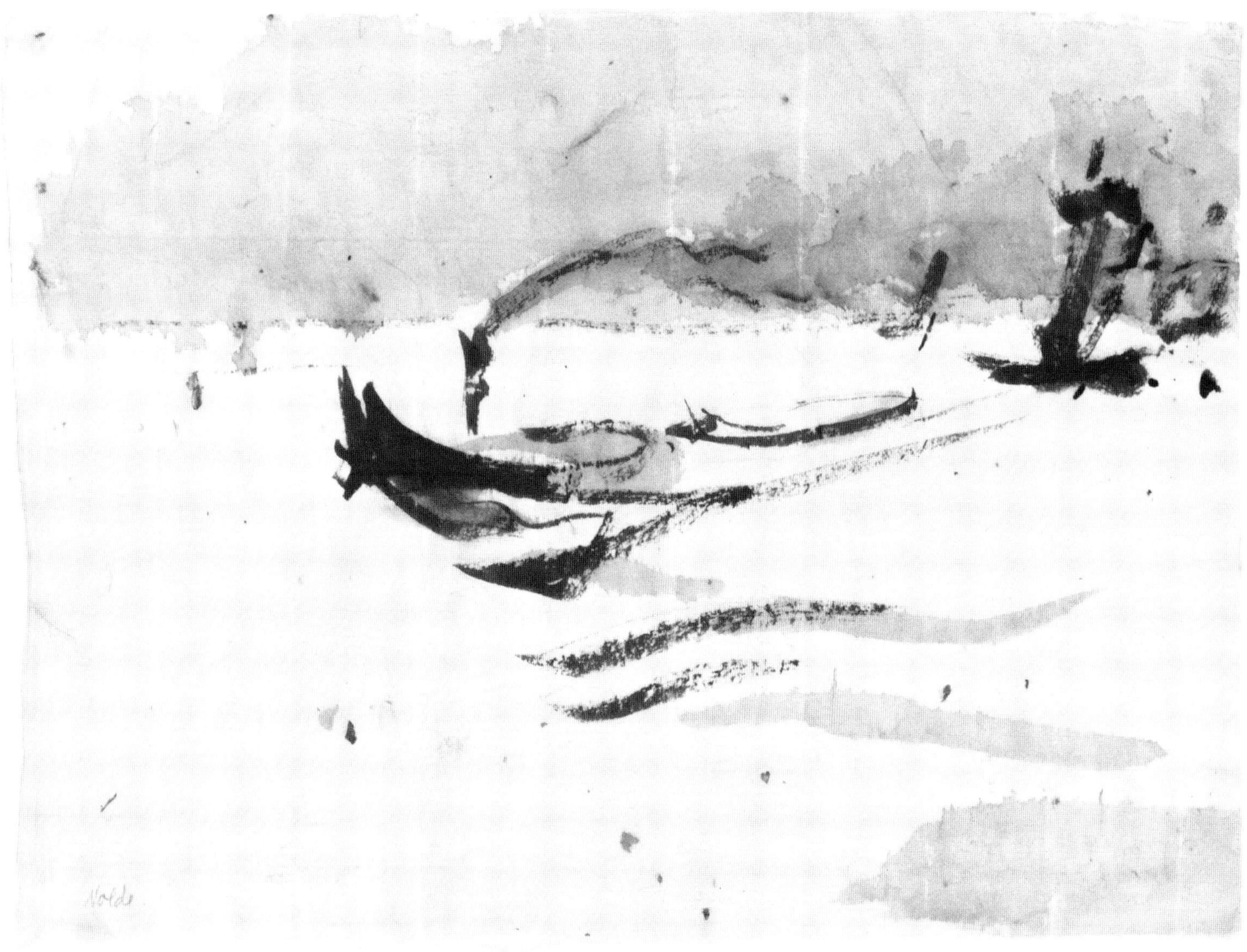

Ernst Ludwig Kirchner

An innovative artist of great versatility, the German expressionist Ernst Ludwig Kirchner was a master of painting, drawing, and several printmaking techniques, producing landscapes, cityscapes, and figural compositions with equal enthusiasm throughout his life. He first studied drawing in high school, then continued his artistic studies after graduation, enrolling in an architectural program at the Technische Hochschule in Dresden in 1901.

Kirchner experimented with the woodcut medium early (around 1900), and his later efforts in drawing and painting display a simplicity of line and form first developed in this medium. He was influenced by early German masters, particularly Albrecht Dürer, whose woodcuts he saw on a visit to Nuremberg in 1898. Later he was attracted to the woodcuts of Edvard Munch and Félix Vallotton and to the simplicity and power of Rembrandt's line, as seen in drawings and etchings. The color of Vincent van Gogh, the Fauves, and James Ensor as well as the forms and textures of African and Oceanian sculpture contributed to his artistic development.

In 1905 he joined with three other artists in Dresden—Fritz Bleyl, Erich Heckel, and Karl Schmidt-Rottluff—to found the Brücke, one of the earliest and most important German expressionist artists' groups. Kirchner functioned as its spokesman and chronicler, often using the pen name L. de Marsalle. For years the expanding group collaborated, publishing annual portfolios and exhibiting together in Dresden and elsewhere in Germany and Switzerland. By 1911 most of the Brücke artists, including Kirchner, had moved to Berlin, attracted by the city's cultural vitality and the prospect of finding greater acceptance there. The group disbanded in 1913.

In 1914 Kirchner was inducted into the armed services, and shortly afterward he suffered a complete mental and physical collapse. Ultimately he was sent to Switzerland by friends, where from 1917 until his suicide in 1938 he produced his greatest body of work, including landscapes, portraits, and figural compositions, leaving some two thousand woodcuts, lithographs, and etchings as well as a large number of canvases.

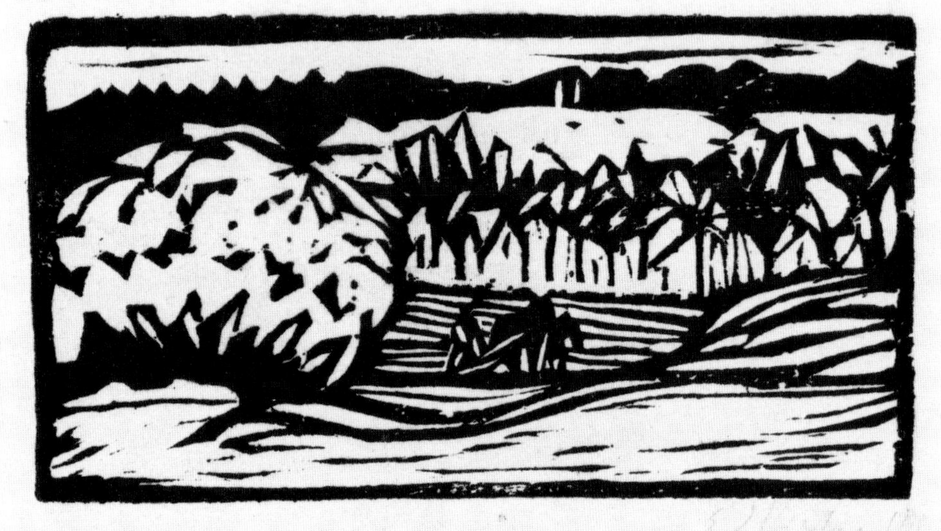

144

Landschaft mit pflügendem Bauer (1908)

(Landscape with Plowing Farmer)

ERNST LUDWIG KIRCHNER
(Aschaffenburg 1880–1938 Frauenkirch)
Schiefler 54 ii/ii; Dube 78
Woodcut
97 x 158 mm
Signed and dated lower right
Provenance: L'Art Ancien, Zurich

By far the most prolific and arguably the greatest printmaker of the Brücke, Kirchner produced the woodcut *Landschaft mit pflügendem Bauer* a few years after the group's founding in 1905. Kirchner's early woodcut technique drew heavily on the curving lines of the Jugendstil (the German version of art nouveau), particularly after 1903, when he studied for two semesters in Munich with the Swiss Jugendstil artist Hermann Obrist. The heightened decorative and expressive qualities of this print are characteristic of his Brücke period. It is signed and appears to be dated 1908 in the lower right-hand corner. This is also the date given in Schiefler's catalogue of Kirchner's graphic work.[1] Dating Kirchner's work is often problematic, however, due chiefly to the artist's practice of antedating drawings, prints, and paintings by three to six years, and it was Kirchner himself who provided Schiefler with his dates.[2] The composition is formally comparable to other work exhibited or published around 1908, although Dube's catalogue of Kirchner's graphic oeuvre places *Landschaft mit pflügendem Bauer* in 1906.[3]

A stamp that reads "Nachlass, E. L. Kirchner" on the verso of this and many other Kirchner prints was placed there by the Kunstmuseum in Basel, which was given the responsibility of overseeing Kirchner's estate when he died intestate as a German citizen in Switzerland in 1938.[4]

1. Gustav Schiefler, *Die Graphik Ernst Ludwig Kirchners*, 2 vols. (Berlin: Euphorion Verlag, 1926 and 1931), no. 54.
2. Frances Carey and Antony Griffiths, *The Print in Germany, 1880–1933: The Age of Expressionism*, exh. cat. (New York: Harper and Row, 1984), p. 107.
3. Annemarie Dube and Wolf-Dieter Dube, *E. L. Kirchner: Das graphische Werk*, 2d ed., 2 vols. (Munich: Prestel Verlag, 1980), no. 78.
4. Carey and Griffiths, *The Print in Germany*, p. 111.

[*German*]

ERICH HECKEL

A self-taught artist, Erich Heckel came from a well-educated middle-class family in Döbeln, near Chemnitz, where he was a boyhood friend of the artist Karl Schmidt-Rottluff. By the time he began his architectural studies at the Technische Hochschule in Dresden in 1904, Heckel already possessed a well-developed interest in poetry and the visual arts.

In 1904 Heckel began to experiment in earnest with painting, wood sculpture, and woodcuts, and it was during this period that he met the slightly older artist Ernst Ludwig Kirchner. In 1904 they, along with Karl Schmidt-Rottluff and Fritz Bleyl (a friend of Kirchner's), founded the Brücke, an important early avant-garde German expressionist artists' group, in order to create a new, vital, distinctly German art in opposition to the dominant artistic tendencies of the period, among them impressionism and the Jugendstil, which they perceived as stultifyingly academic, superficial, and overly decorative. During the first years of the group's existence, the artists' work developed similar formal properties as they examined man's relationship to the dynamism and alienation of the city as well as the intensity of nature, as seen in their many urban scenes and landscapes. In 1912 Heckel and Kirchner decorated the chapel for the Sonderbund exhibition in Cologne. By 1913 the Brücke had disbanded, having moved to Berlin two years earlier, and Heckel had his first solo exhibition.

From 1915 to 1918 Heckel served in the medical corps in Belgium, where he befriended Max Beckmann and James Ensor. After the war Heckel lived and worked in Berlin, producing landscapes as well as figure studies and portraits. He fled to Switzerland in 1944, after hundreds of his paintings, prints, and drawings had been removed from German museums as part of the National Socialists' "degenerate art" campaign. From 1949 to 1956 he taught art in Karlsruhe. After his retirement he returned to Switzerland, where he died in 1949.

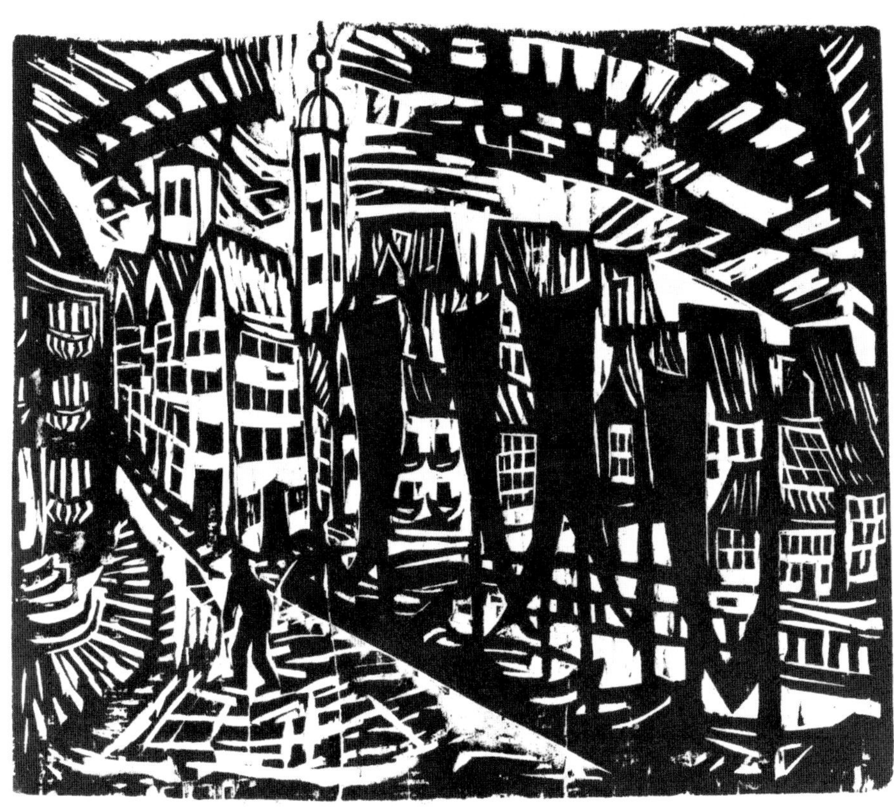

145

Stralsund (1912)

ERICH HECKEL
(Döbeln 1883–1970 Radolfzell)
Dube 243 iia/iib (second state A of iib before 1921 edition of 40)
Woodcut
300 x 356 mm
Provenance: David Tunick, New York

This woodcut of a northern European city and harbor filled with small sailboats is typical of Heckel's graphic work of 1912–13, toward the end of his association with the Brücke. The overwhelming quantity of sharply pointed squares, rectangles, and triangles is intensified by the juxtaposition of black and white areas that define both positive and negative shapes and space, causing the entire image, from the sky above to the street and harbor below, to vibrate. Because of these formal properties, the otherwise static scene (in which the only overt activity is that of a solitary figure walking down the street) is filled with motion. Heckel, along with Ernst Ludwig Kirchner and other members of the Brücke, had explored ways to flatten the composition and emphasize the picture plane without losing the pictorial coherence of the image.

By 1912 Heckel had met the artists Franz Marc, Robert Delaunay, and Lyonel Feininger. The philosophical premises and formal properties of these artists' work influenced Heckel's further development, particularly his use of crystalline light as a unifying element.

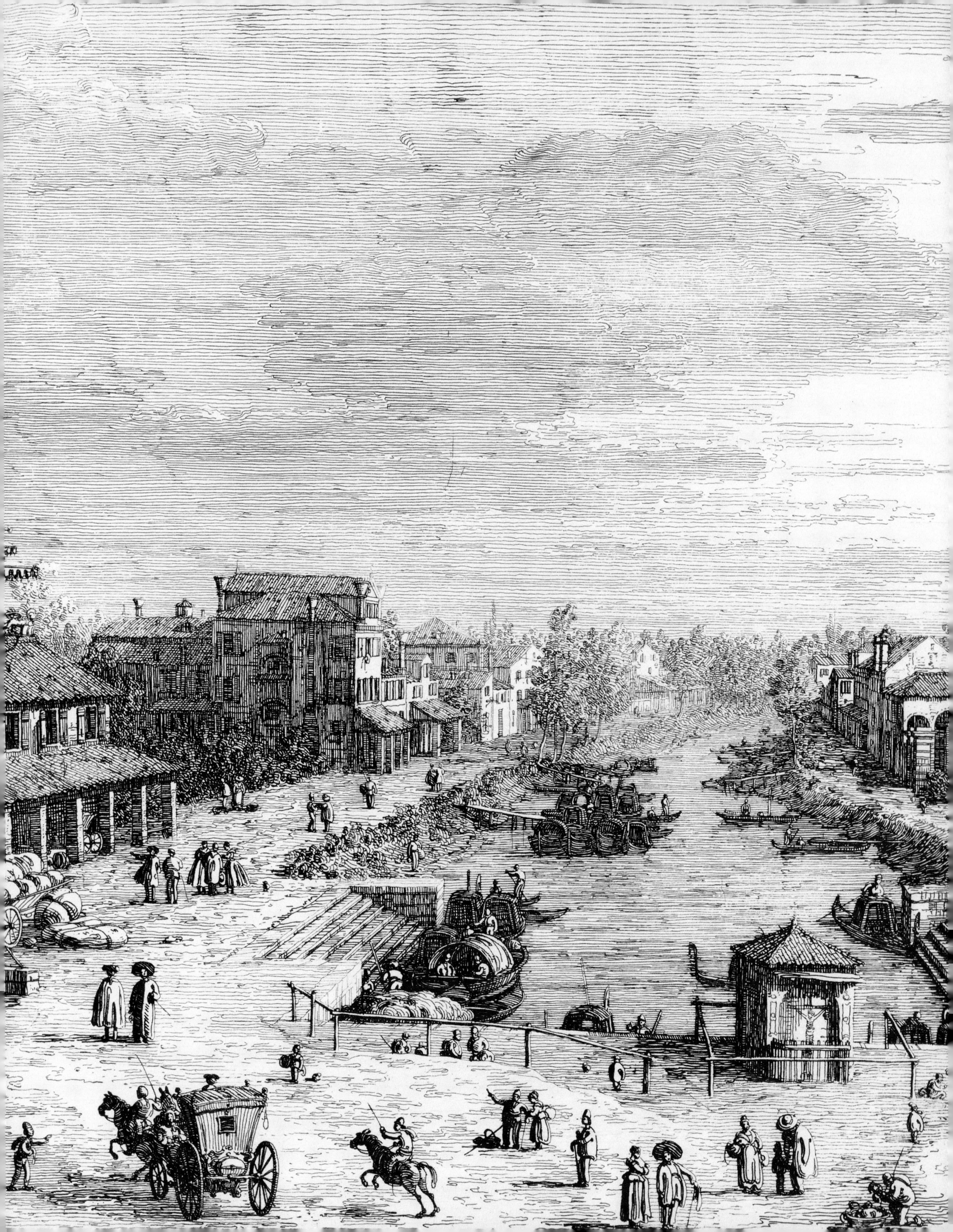

ITALIAN

Detail of cat. no. 150

Remigio Cantagallina

146
Rocky Landscape

REMIGIO CANTAGALLINA
(Borgo San Sepolcro c. 1582–c. 1656 Florence)
Pen and brown ink on tan paper, laid down
222 x 342 mm
Inscribed *RG* lower left
Provenance: Zeitlin and Ver Brugge, Los Angeles

Remigio Cantagallina began his career as a painter in Borgo San Sepolcro but soon went to Florence, where he received training in engraving and drawing at the school of Giulio Parigi, an architect and pageant designer at the Medici court. In Parigi's circle Cantagallina collaborated with a variety of architects, engineers, and artists working under the patronage of Grand Duke Ferdinand I de' Medici and his son Cosimo II. His earliest dated works, a series of seven landscape etchings from 1603, reveal the influence of his training in their treatment of landscape elements as stage decoration. In 1608 Cantagallina collaborated with Parigi on opera decorations for the marriage celebration of Cosimo II, which were later reproduced in engravings by the two artists.

Cantagallina's travels to the Low Countries in 1612–13 are documented by a book of fifty sketches (Brussels, Bibliothèque Royale), which in their stiff and somewhat mechanical quality of execution reveal the influence of Flemish landscape prints and drawings, particularly those of Paul Bril. A suite of twelve landscape etchings dated 1627, however, reveals a more direct observation of nature, a quality that would become increasingly apparent in his later drawings. His last etching is dated 1635, after which he seems to have devoted himself exclusively to drawing. Though he was a relatively minor artist, Cantagallina's landscape etchings and drawings served to popularize the genre, thus allowing for future innovations by artists such as Jacques Callot and Stefano della Bella.

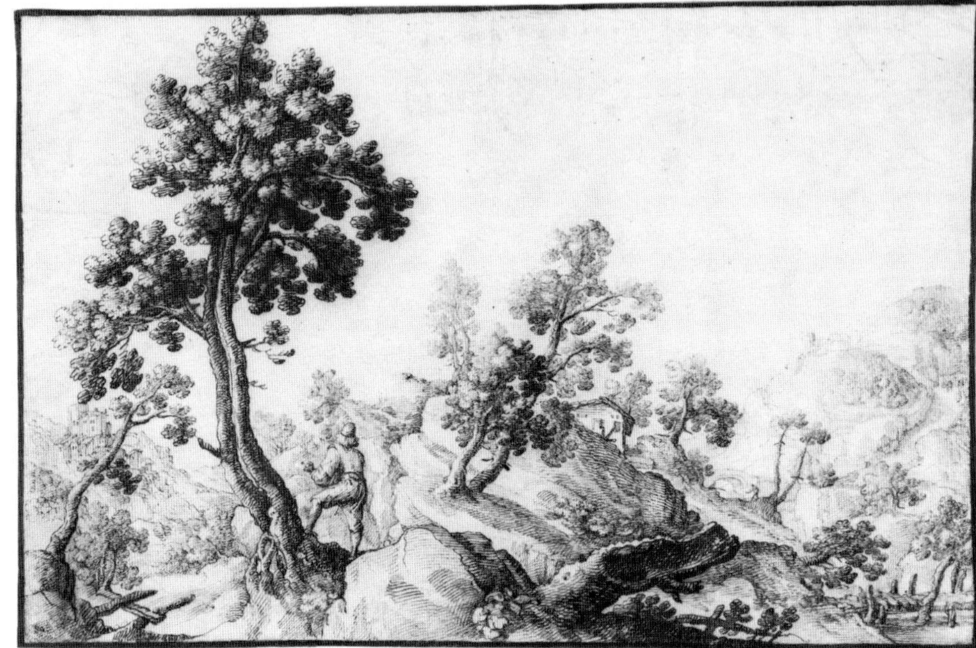

In its depiction of a rocky landscape, knotted trees with bare roots, thatched huts, and rustic bridges, this drawing is typical of the late Florentine mannerist style of Cantagallina and other artists in the circle of Giulio Parigi. Yet the subtle alteration of light and dark across the foreground evokes a sense of atmosphere and creates a more integrated space than one finds in Cantagallina's earlier drawings, which emphasize a dark repoussoir of trees (Roli 1969, no. 97). This suggests a date for this drawing during the latter part of his career, when his direct observations of landscape led to a modification of his earlier mannerist conventions.[1]

The drawing bears a monogram that is a conflation of the letters *RCG*, one of the numerous monograms used by Cantagallina throughout his career. It is similar to the monograms on a drawing in Paris (Musée du Louvre inv. no. 14992; see Louvre 1981, p. 117, no. 70) and on one in the Los Angeles County Museum of Art (inv. no. 60.13; see Schulz 1968, no. 31).

1. Compare this drawing with a similar one in the Louvre indistinctly dated 1641 (inv. no. 875; see Louvre 1981, p. 116, no. 68).

REMIGIO CANTAGALLINA

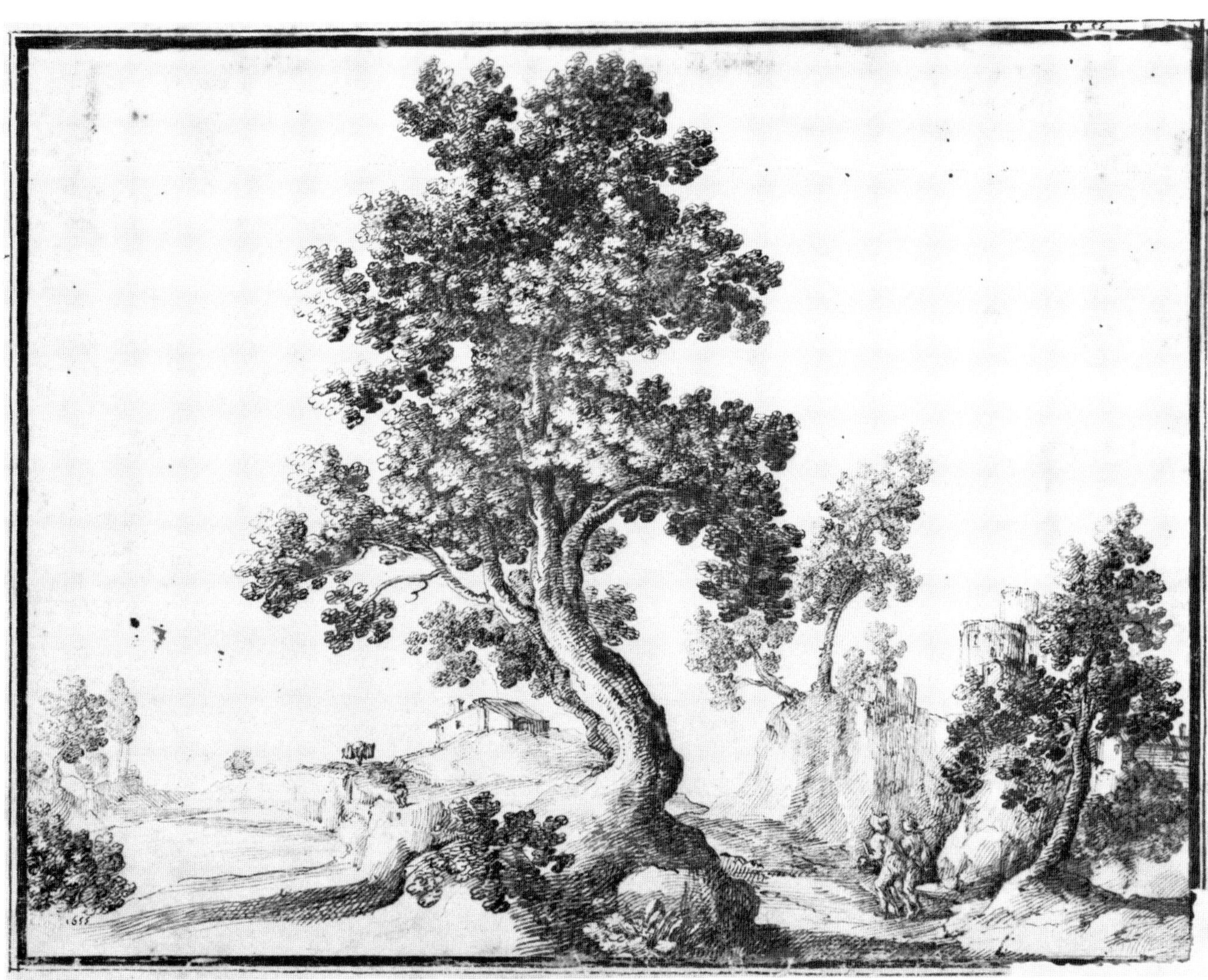

147

Landscape with a Large Tree (1655)

Attributed to
REMIGIO CANTAGALLINA
(Borgo San Sepolcro c. 1582–c. 1656 Florence)
Pen and brown ink
208 x 277 mm
Dated upper right
Provenance: William Schab, New York

Formerly attributed to Ercole Bazicaluva, this drawing was recently given to Cantagallina, who may have been originally excluded from consideration because the 1655 date on the drawing places it after that traditionally given for Cantagallina's death, 1635.[1] Based on the evidence of two drawings attributed to him dated 1654 and 1655 (Florence, Uffizi inv. nos. 167, 168 P), Cantagallina is now believed to have died in 1656, a date recorded by one of his original biographers.[2] In addition, the drawing is very similar in style and composition to a drawing in Boston also attributed to Cantagallina (Museum of Fine Arts inv. no. 1894.100; see Macandrew 1983, no. 130), and comparison with an earlier drawing by Cantagallina also in the Grunwald Center (cat. no. 146) suggests that both are by the same hand.

1. We would like to thank Marco Chiarini for suggesting the attribution to Cantagallina.
2. See Chiarini 1975, p. 230.

Giovanni Francesco Grimaldi

Though Giovanni Francesco Grimaldi's early training is not documented, on the basis of his classical style it can be assumed that he was apprenticed to a follower of the Carracci, probably in Bologna. Soon after he arrived in Rome in 1627, he was engaged in collaboration with Alessandro Algardi, his lifelong friend, on two commissions, Santa Maria della Vittoria and Santa Maria dell'Anima. The date of Grimaldi's arrival in Rome can be estimated from his letter of July 8, 1651, to Cardinal Mazarin, in which the artist stated that he had resided in Rome for twenty-four years (Paris, Archives Nationales, Affaires étrangères, Correspondence politique, Rome, 118, fol. 164v). Grimaldi's talents as a decorator, either architectural or theatrical, and a painter of vast fresco projects and easel landscapes were soon recognized. Among his patrons were the most important Roman families—the Pamphili, Borghese, Colonna, Falconieri, and Santacroce—and Popes Alexander VII and Clement IX. His most notable fresco decorations are in the Quirinal Palace, the casino of the Villa Doria Pamphili, and the Villa Falconieri at Frascati. Grimaldi spent brief periods at Frascati and Tivoli but worked primarily in Rome. In 1648 Mazarin called him to Paris to decorate the gallery in his palace, today the Bibliothèque Nationale, and the queen's rooms in the Louvre. Grimaldi owed his renown in Europe to his easel landscapes, which were considered the equal of Gaspard Dughet's, after those of Claude Lorrain. He has left a vast corpus of drawings, of both decorative projects and landscapes, and fifty-seven etchings, predominantly landscapes.

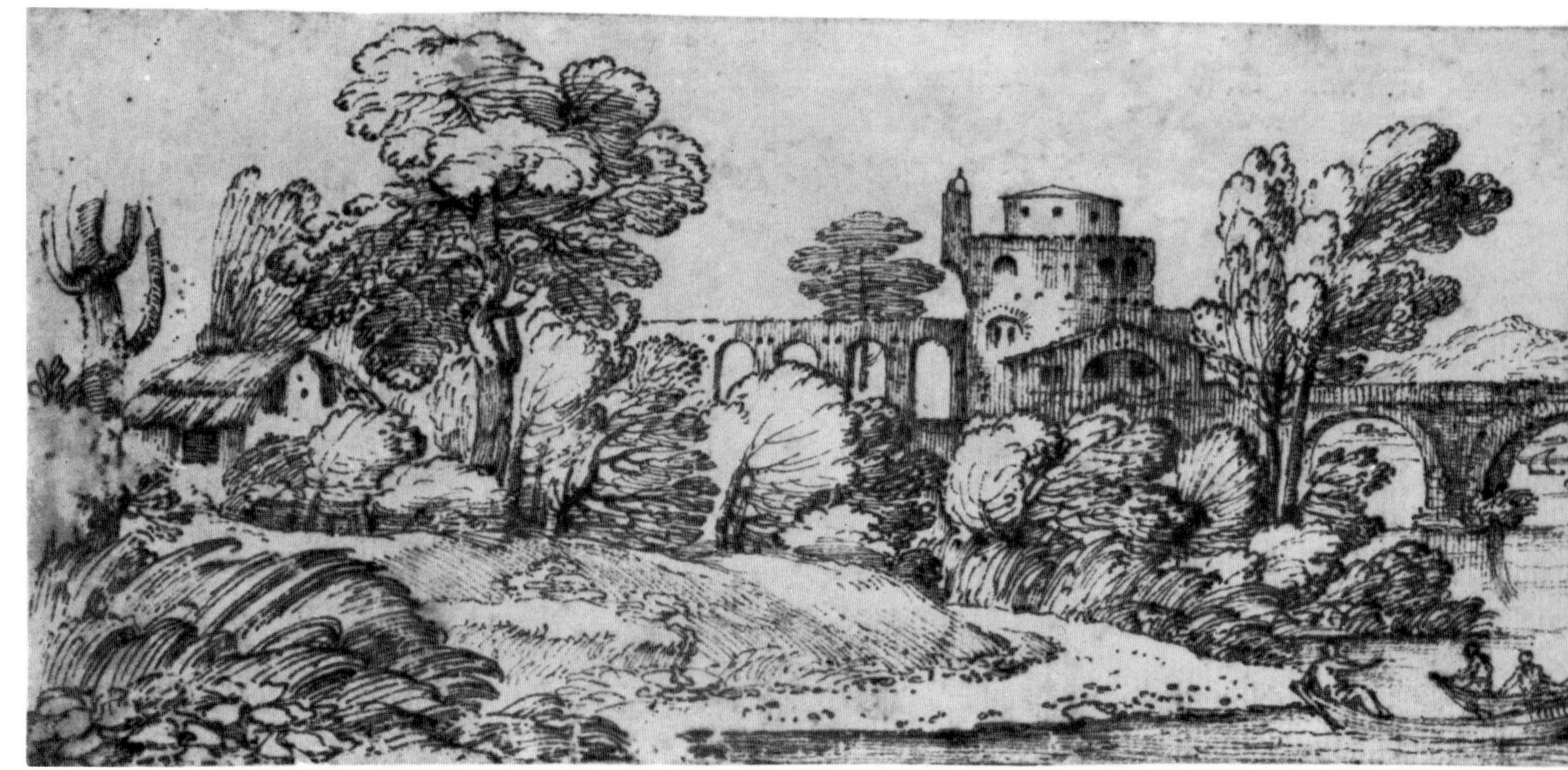

148

Landscape with a Castle and a Bridge over a River (c. 1667–69)

GIOVANNI FRANCESCO GRIMALDI
(Bologna 1605–1680 Rome)[1]
Pen and brown ink on brown prepared paper
135 x 497 mm
Provenance: J. Richardson (L. I/2184); William Mayor (L. I/2799); William Schab, New York

The drawing depicts the Roman Campagna with a river in its center flowing under a bridge in the middle ground. To the left of the bridge stand a tower and an aqueduct and, further to the left and closer to the foreground, a simple hut. On the right side of the river a town straddles a distant mountaintop, and beyond it rise mountains on the horizon. Lush vegetation covers both banks of the tranquil river, its surface punctuated by boats ferrying cargo and passengers. It is an ideal classical landscape in the tradition of Annibale Carracci and Domenichino, both of whom influenced Grimaldi. The composition is replete with motifs from Carracci's landscapes, yet these are fully integrated into a Grimaldesque landscape.

The careful execution of the sketch suggests it was done in a studio, most likely as a study for one of the landscape frescoes in the larger of the two Sale Rosse in the Quirinal Palace.[2] Except for a few minor changes—the careful elaboration of vegetation on the right and left of the foreground, which creates a repoussoir framing the vast space; the relocation of the town from the mountaintop to the right of the bridge; and a softening of the rugged outlines of mountains and riverbanks—the composition is essentially the same. Only its classicism has been heightened, and each area has been clearly defined. In view of the above, it can be assumed that the date of the drawing corresponds to that of the decorative project, sometime between June 20, 1667, and December 2, 1669.

At a somewhat later date, in the 1670s, Grimaldi used a similar layout of landscape, changing only the motifs on both sides of the river, for two landscapes in the Galleria Muti-Papazzurri.[3] This was not an unusual working method for the artist, who freely interchanged landscape motifs within similar layouts. Despite this practice, his landscapes are sensitively executed in the best classical tradition.

The high quality of the drawing corresponds to Grimaldi's sketches in the British Museum, London, which formed part of Vincenzo Vittoria's sketchbook.[4] The British Museum's corpus of Grimaldi's drawings is the best source for authentication of his numerous sketches, as no other sheets can be as securely dated or attributed to him. In the present drawing, as in the sketchbook, the artist used a broken line to describe atmosphere, motion, and volume and to abbreviate human figures. By close application of parallel lines, he created darks to heighten volume, and by varying the direction of lines, he insinuated motion. It is a sketch by a master draftsman possibly intended to be a finished work of art, as was the practice in the seventeenth century.

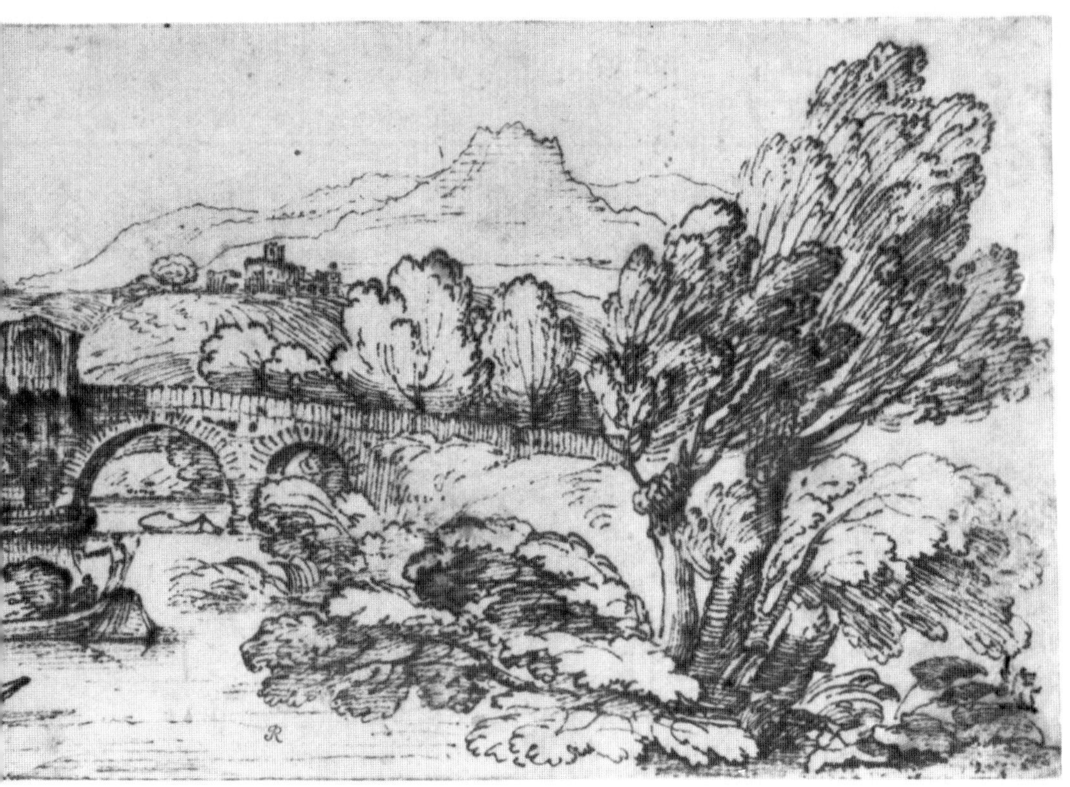

1. For documentation of Grimaldi's death and its effects on his birth date, see Danuta Batorska, "Grimaldi at Frascati," *Master Drawings* 10, no. 2 (1972): 145, 149.
2. As proposed by Cynthia Burlingham; see Danuta Batorska, "Grimaldi's Frescoes in the Palazzo del Quirinale," *Paragone*, no. 387 (1982): 3, fig. 3.
3. Danuta Batorska, "Grimaldi and the Galleria Muti-Papazzurri," *Antologia di belli arti* 7–8 (1978): 204, figs. 1, 5.
4. Batorska, "Grimaldi at Frascati," p. 148.

Marco Ricci

Marco Ricci was probably instructed in the art of landscape painting by his uncle, history painter Sebastiano Ricci, in Florence from 1706 to 1707. From 1708 to 1712 he worked in London as a scenographer, probably returning to Italy in 1710. In 1712 he moved again to London with his uncle, remaining there until 1716, when he returned permanently to Venice, where he continued to collaborate with his uncle, executing landscapes in Sebastiano's large religious paintings. Marco Ricci initiated a new landscape style influenced by the landscapes of Titian, Salvator Rosa, and Alessandro Magnasco, and his paintings soon enjoyed great international success. He began etching in 1723, seven years before his death, and twenty etchings were compiled and published posthumously in 1730. An additional thirteen etchings have subsequently been discovered, as well as numerous proofs with the artist's inked corrections.

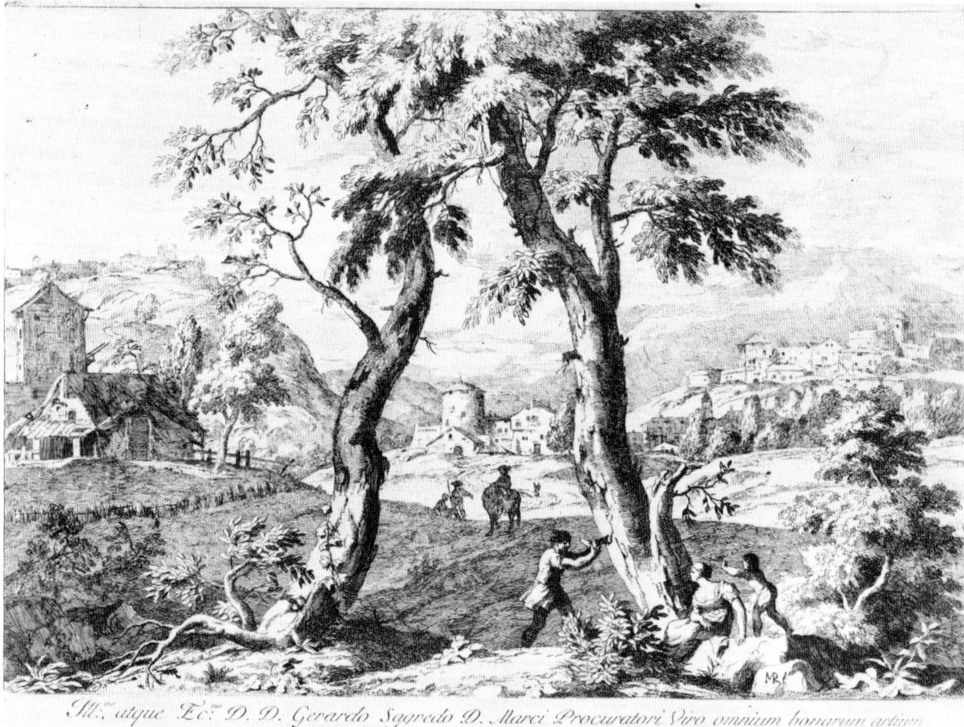

149

Paesaggio con contadini e villagio nello sfondo

(Landscape with Peasants and a Village in the Distance)

MARCO RICCI
(Belluno 1676–1730 Venice)
B. 6; Pilo 203
Etching
288 x 420 mm
Provenance: R. M. Light, Boston

This print is part of a set of twenty landscapes published after Ricci's death in 1730 by the printmaker and publisher Carlo Orsolini. Orsolini engraved the frontispiece for the set after a design by Visentini and added a dedication to an important Venetian at the bottom of each print. The etchings are generally considered to date from the period between 1723 and Ricci's death in 1730 (Pilo 1963, p. 84).

The Orsolini series comprises a range of landscape types, including pastoral scenes, fantastic views of ancient ruins, and mountain vistas, all typical subjects of Ricci's landscape paintings. Though many of Ricci's etchings depict more dramatic ruins or romantic landscapes reminiscent of those of Salvator Rosa, the artist frequently returned to the more pastoral sixteenth-century landscape tradition of Titian and his followers, as exemplified by this print. Like all Ricci's landscape etchings, this print, with its widely spaced parallel lines, is similar in technique to his pen drawings, which also recall the drawings and woodcuts of Titian and Giulio Campagnola. By leaving large areas of sky untouched by the etching needle, thereby allowing the luminous white paper to show through, the artist conveys the impression of sun-drenched atmosphere, much as Canaletto would portray the Venetian sunshine decades later.

GIOVANNI ANTONIO CANAL, CALLED CANALETTO

Canaletto began his career in the studio of his father, who drew and painted theatrical designs for stage sets. He spent a year in Rome in 1719, returning to Venice to take up a career painting views of the city. During the early 1620s he met Joseph Smith, the British consul in Venice and an art collector, who would become Canaletto's lifelong patron and his link to the great English collectors. Smith's patronage of Canaletto began in 1630, and from that time on virtually all the artist's paintings were bought by English collectors, evidently through Smith's connections.

In response to tourists' demand for prints recording their Venetian sojourns, Canaletto published a set of thirty-one vedute, *dedicated to and probably financed by Smith, in 1744. These etchings, along with three other unique examples, constitute his entire graphic production.*

In 1746 Canaletto left for England, where he would remain, painting English views, for almost ten years before returning to Venice for the balance of his career. Though his views of Venice were renowned throughout Europe, view painting was not highly esteemed in settecento Venice, and Canaletto was elected to the Venetian Academy only in 1763, five years before his death.

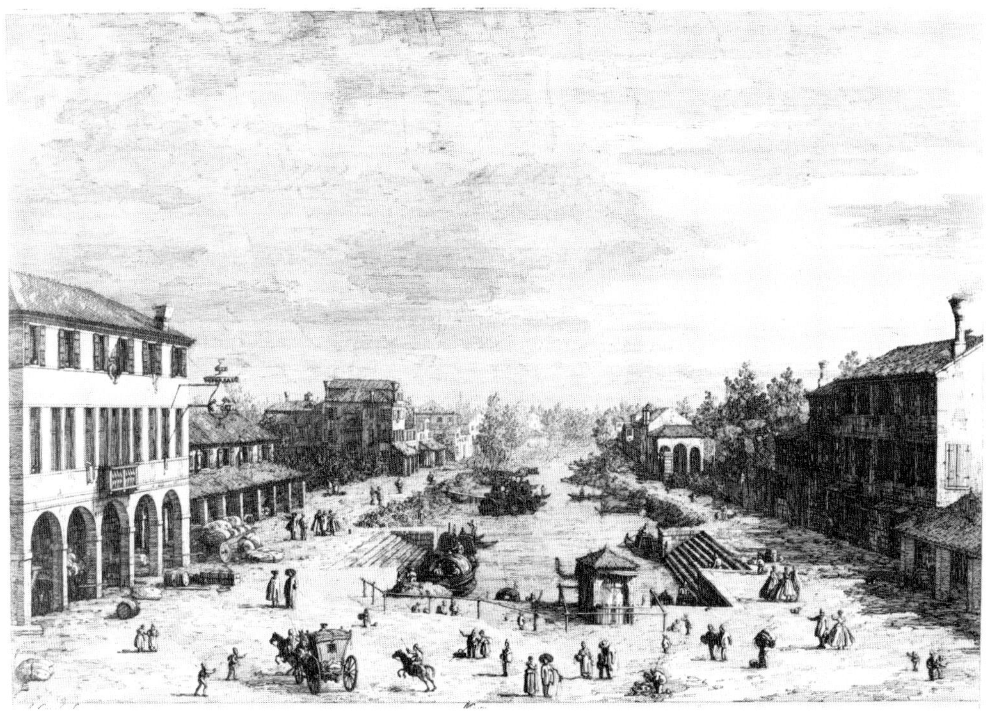

150
Mestre

GIOVANNI ANTONIO CANAL,
called CANALETTO
(Venice 1697–1768 Venice)
de V. 3 i/ii; P.G. i/ii; Br. 3 ii/ii
Etching
294 x 428 mm
Provenance: William Schab, New York

Mestre is part of an unnumbered series of thirty-one prints comprising both actual and imaginary views of Venice and the surrounding countryside. Venice had been an active tourist center since the time of the Crusades, when ships embarked for the Holy Land from its port. During the eighteenth century Venice attracted thousands of visitors to its annual civic pageants and processions and served as an essential stop on the grand tour of Europe. As these visitors longed to take home visual mementos of Venice, many purchased Canaletto's detailed impressions of the city.

Mestre is a harbor just outside Venice. Characteristically Canaletto presents a highly detailed rendition of this locale enlivened with people and activity. The tree-lined canal in the center carries ships off into the distance, beyond the boundaries of the composition. Canaletto's careful choice of a viewpoint from above, looking down the canal, heightens the impression of spaciousness. People and carriages populate the foreground area. There is a small shrine with a crucifix at the end of the canal, an inn on the left, and a stable and coach house beneath the arched portico. Although the composition is highly structured, the print appears to be an eyewitness view of a particular place, and Canaletto's broken etched lines on white unworked paper create the informal, atmospheric effect of sunlight sparkling on water. There is an undated painting of this same scene attributed to Canaletto (John Y. Sangster collection; see Constable 1976, p. 380, no. 370).

151

Al Dolo

GIOVANNI ANTONIO CANAL, called CANALETTO
(Venice 1697–1768 Venice)
de V. 4 i/ii; P.G. 4 i/ii; Br. 4 ii/iii
Etching
295 x 427 mm
Provenance: William Schab, New York

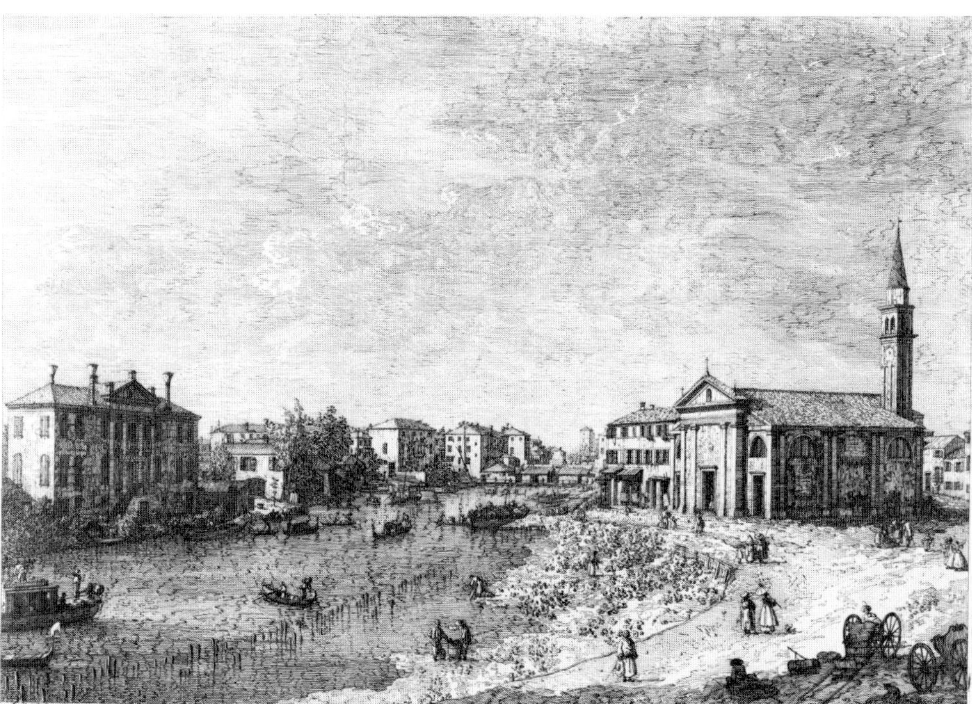

This print depicts a scene on the banks of the Brenta Canal in the village of Dolo, outside Venice, with the church of San Rocco at right and the Palladian Villa Zanon-Bon, formerly the Villa Andruzzi, at left.

Most of Canaletto's etchings were published as part of an undated and unnumbered series, within which his etching style varies considerably. Bromberg (1974, p. 27) has divided the series into five different stylistic groups. She places both *Al Dolo* and *Mestre* (cat. no. 150) in the fifth and latest group, which she dates between 1741 and 1744, the date of publication of the entire series. In these later prints Canaletto's mastery of the etching medium allowed him to achieve a luminous quality contrasted by shadow, conveyed through a seemingly infinite variety of line.

The etchings actually comprise few views of the city of Venice but rather depict sites along Canaletto's journey to Padua and the Brenta Canal around 1740, at which time the artist had abandoned the views of Venice that had made him the most celebrated view painter of his day. It has been suggested that his departure was occasioned by a decline in the number of foreign visitors to Venice, who had formed his principal clientele. He may also have simply grown tired of painting Venetian scenes (Links 1977, p. 49).

Both *Mestre* and *Al Dolo* are examples of the ten prints depicting *prese da i luoghi* (actual places) mentioned on the title page and titled by Canaletto himself. The remaining prints were untitled and are largely of unidentifiable views and imaginary places (*altre ideate*). The series was probably intended for patrons and friends of the artist and Consul John Smith, primarily foreign travelers who probably would not have distinguished between their memories of an actual site and Canaletto's imaginary evocations.

There is a drawing related to the print in London, but it is uncertain whether it is a preparatory drawing (see Bromberg 1974, p. 58). An undated painting (Venice, private collection; see Constable 1976, p. 381, no. 372) is close to the etching and drawing in composition, but it is not known whether it predates the etching (see Constable 1976, p. 650).

Giovanni Battista Piranesi

As a young man, Giovanni Battista Piranesi pursued a career as an architect and was apprenticed to his uncle, Matteo Lucchesi, in Venice. His older brother, a Carthusian monk, taught him Latin and Roman history, instilling in Piranesi a great love of Roman antiquity that would shape the rest of his career. Although much of his early training is not well documented, Piranesi reportedly studied stage design and set painting at the school of Ferdinando Bibiena in Bologna. In 1740 he left for Rome, where he probably first studied perspective and stage design with Domenico and Giuseppe Valeriano and then studied etching under Giuseppe Vasi, a Sicilian architect and the foremost engraver of Roman views. After the publication of his first work, the Prima parte di architteture e prospettive, in 1743, Piranesi went briefly to Venice before returning to Rome.

Most of Piranesi's subsequent career was spent in Rome etching, writing, publishing, and directing a workshop that restored and sold antiquities. He published numerous suites of prints, celebrating the grandeur of Rome in archaeologically precise views of existing monuments or in imaginary scenes combining real and invented elements. Among his most renowned publications are the Vedute di Roma (1748–78), the Carceri d'invenzione (first edition, 1749–60), and Le antichità romane (1756). Piranesi had numerous patrons among the papacy, clergy, and aristocrats of Rome and others throughout Europe, especially in England, and sets of his prints were frequently purchased by connoisseurs and collectors who visited Rome.

152
Arco di Costantino (1748)

(Arch of Constantine)

GIOVANNI BATTISTA PIRANESI
(Venice 1720–1778 Rome)
Number 9 from Antichità romane de' tempi della repubblica (1748)
F. 50
Etching
133 x 260 mm
Provenance: Zeitlin and Ver Brugge, Los Angeles

153
Sepolcro della famiglia di Sipioni (1748)

(Tomb of the Sipioni Family)

GIOVANNI BATTISTA PIRANESI
(Venice 1720–1778 Rome)
Number 19 from Antichità romane de' tempi della repubblica (1748)
F. 60
Etching
133 x 260 mm
Provenance: Zeitlin and Ver Brugge, Los Angeles

These two prints are part of a series of thirty-two views of the principal monuments in and around the city of Rome entitled Antichità romane de' tempi della repubblica. The series was published in 1748 and dedicated to Piranesi's friend Giovanni Bottari, a librarian at the Vatican. It was expanded and reissued in 1765 under the title Alcuni vedute di archi trionfali ed altri monumenti, in order to avoid confusion with Piranesi's four-volume Le antichità romane, published in 1756.

One of Piranesi's earliest series of *vedute*, Antichità romane de' tempi della repubblica combines the fantasy of Piranesi's *grotteschi* with the topographical accuracy of his vedute. The fantastic element is exemplified by the ground-level vantage point, which exaggerates the height of the monuments and throws deep shadows across their shapes. This contrasts with the more conventional topographical views of Piranesi's former teacher Giuseppe Vasi and other engravers, which depict the architectural monuments of the city in a more straightforward manner, with little sense of atmosphere. For example, in *Sepolcro della famiglia di Sipioni*, Piranesi presents the effects of time and decay on the vine-covered ruin, while the addition of figures contributes to the more picturesque quality of the image. His sense of drama, however, never compromises the communication of fact; in prints such as the one of the Arch of Constantine, the monument is seen through an arch of the neighboring Colosseum, thus indicating the actual proximity of the two buildings (Wilton-Ely 1978, p. 29).

Giovanni Battista Piranesi

152

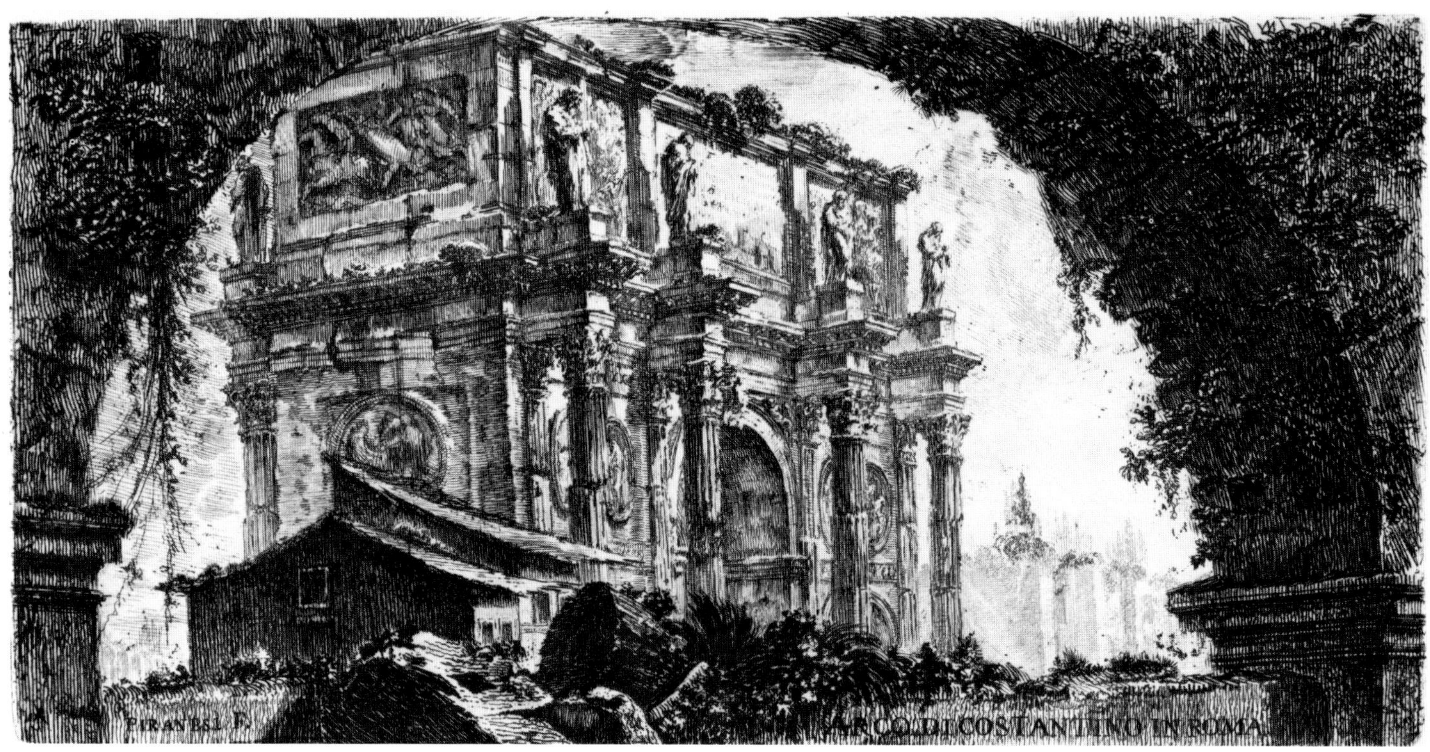

153

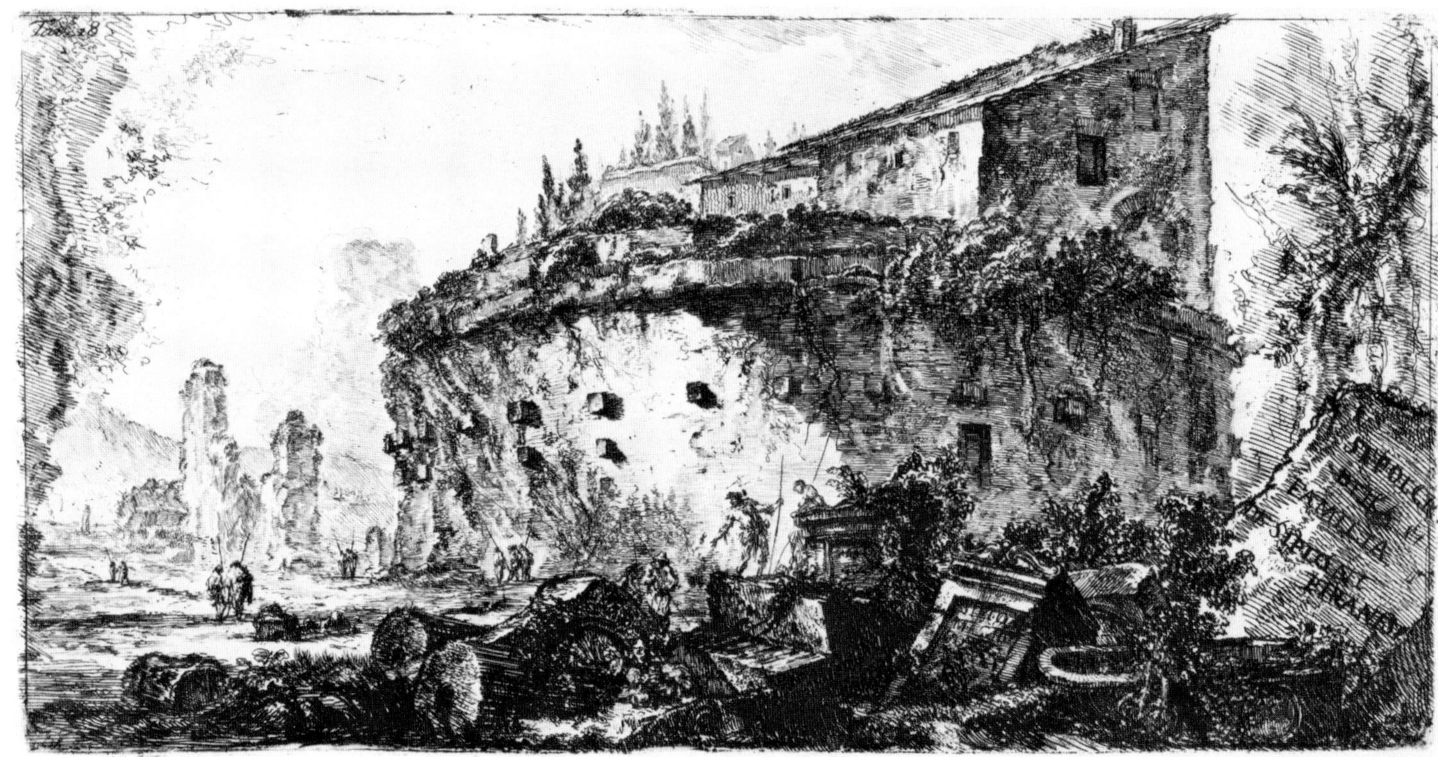

GIOVANNI BATTISTA PIRANESI

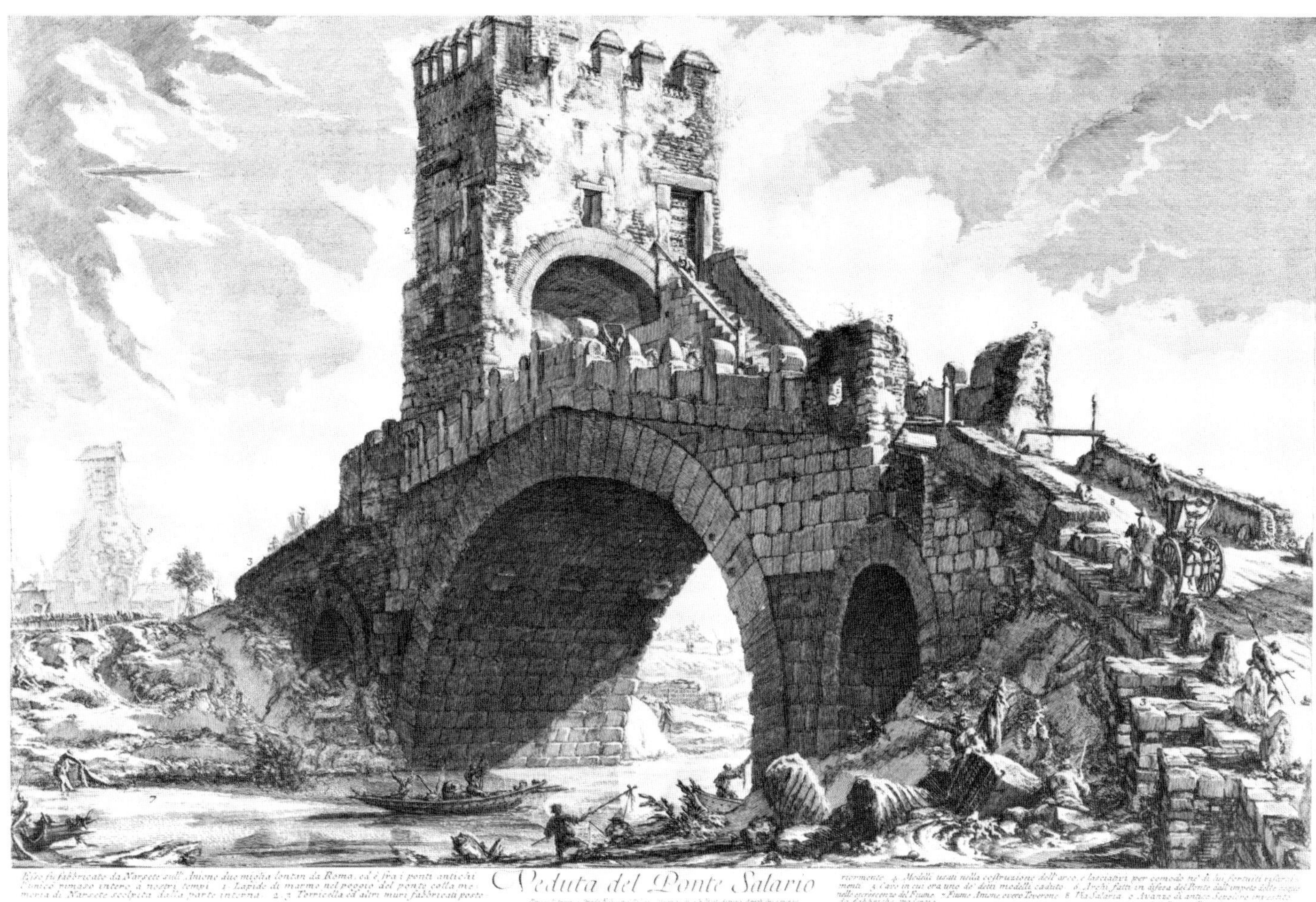

154

Veduta del Ponte Salario

(View of the Ponte Salario)

GIOVANNI BATTISTA PIRANESI
(Venice 1720–1778 Rome)
From Vedute di Roma (1748–78)
Hind 31 ii/v; F. 744
Etching
403 x 615 mm
Provenance: Zeitlin and Ver Brugge, Los Angeles

Ponte Salario was part of the Vedute di Roma series, which featured 135 views of the main tourist sights of Rome and a few views outside the city. The series, begun in 1748, occupied Piranesi until his death in 1778 and in many ways documents the evolution of his artistic career. In the first phase of the project, from 1748 to 1754, Piranesi issued prints exclusively of contemporary Rome and of well-known sights such as the great basilicas and piazzas. In the second phase (1754–60), however, he focused on individual monuments of ancient Rome.

Ponte Salario is characteristic of the second phase of the series and takes as its subject the ancient Roman bridge that crosses the Aniene River near its confluence with the Tiber. In contrast to the smaller, more impressionistic portrayals of ancient monuments in Piranesi's Antichità romane de' tempi della repubblica (see cat. nos. 152–53) series, the Ponte Salario is rendered on a large scale, with striking contrasts of light and shade that heighten the dramatic impact of the monument. To further enhance its grandeur, Piranesi rendered the bridge from an oblique angle, thereby showing the monument in its entirety.

Selected Bibliography

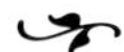

Ackley 1981
Ackley, Clifford S. *Printmaking in the Age of Rembrandt.* Exhibition catalogue. Boston: Museum of Fine Arts, 1981.

Alain and Solomon
Alain and Jacques Solomon. *Introduction à l'oeuvre gravé de K. X. Roussel.* Paris: Mercure de France, 1968.

Auberty and Perussaux, Auberty and Perussaux 1950
Auberty, Jacqueline, and Charles Perussaux. *Jacques Villon: Catalogue de son oeuvre gravé.* Paris: Paul Prouté et ses fils, 1950.

B.
Bartsch, Adam von. *Le peintre-graveur.* 21 vols. Vienna: Degen, 1803–21.

Bast.
Bastelaer, Rene van. *Les estampes de Pieter Bruegel l'Ancien.* Brussels: G. van Oest, 1908.

Bauer 1984
Bauer, George, and Linda Bauer. "*The Winter Landscape with Skates and Bird-Trap* by Pieter Bruegel the Elder." *Art Bulletin* 66 (1984): 145–50.

Beck, Beck 1972
Beck, Hans-Ulrich. *Jan van Goyen.* 3 vols. Amsterdam: Van Gendt, 1972–87.

Benesch, Benesch 1973
Benesch, Otto. *The Drawings of Rembrandt.* London: Phaidon, 1973.

Beraldi
Beraldi, Henri. *Les graveurs du XIXe siècle: Guide de l'amateur d'estampes modernes.* 12 vols. Paris: L. Conquet, 1885–92.

Bermingham 1986
Bermingham, Ann. *Landscape and Ideology: The English Rustic Tradition, 1740–1860.* Berkeley and Los Angeles: University of California Press, 1986.

Bernt 1958
Bernt, Walter. *Die niederländischen Zeichner des 17. Jahrhunderts.* 2 vols. Munich: F. Bruckman, 1958.

Bierens de Haan, Bierens de Haan 1948
Bierens de Haan, J. C. *L'oeuvre gravé de Cornelis Cort.* The Hague: Martinus Nijhoff, 1948.

Biörklund and Barnard
Biörklund, George, and Osbert H. Barnard. *Rembrandt's Etchings: True and False.* Stockholm: Esselte Aktiebolog, 1968; distributed in the U.S. by Museum Books.

Bredius 1969
Bredius, Abraham. *The Complete Edition of the Paintings of Rembrandt.* 3d ed., revised by Horst Gerson. London: Phaidon, 1969.

Breitbarth-van der Stok 1969
Breitbarth-van der Stok, M. H. "Josua de Grave, Valentinus Klotz en Barnardus Klotz." *Bulletin van de Koninklijke Nederlandse Oudheidkundige Bond* 68 (1969): 93–115.

British Museum 1977
British Museum. *French Landscape Drawings and Sketches of the Eighteenth Century.* London: British Museum Publications, 1977.

Br., Bromberg 1974
Bromberg, Ruth. *Canaletto's Etchings: A Catalogue and Study. . . .* London and New York: Sotheby Parke Bernet, 1974.

Brussels 1968–69
Dessins de paysagistes hollandais du XVIIe siècle de la collection particulière conservée a l'Institut Néerlandais de Paris. Exhibition catalogue. Brussels: Bibliothèque Royale Albert 1 er, 1968–69.

Brussels 1980
Brussels, Palais des Beaux-Arts. *Bruegel: Une dynastie de peintres.* Exhibition catalogue. Brussels: Europalia 80, 1980.

Burchard 1917
Burchard, Ludwig. *Die holländische Radierer vor Rembrandt.* Berlin: Paul Cassirer, 1917.

Burke 1974
Burke, James. *Charles Meryon: Prints and Drawings.* New Haven, Conn.: Yale University Art Gallery, 1974.

Burke, Burke 1976
Burke, James D. "Jan Both: Paintings, Drawings, and Prints." Ph.D. diss., Harvard University, 1972. New York: Garland Publishers, 1976.

Cachin 1971
Cachin, Françoise. *Paul Signac.* Translated by Michael Bullock. Greenwich, Conn.: New York Graphic Society, 1971.

Chiarini 1975
Chiarini, Marco. "Remigio Cantagallina." In *Dizionario biografico degli italiani.* Rome: Società Grafica Romana, 1960–.

Clark 1988
Clark, Alvin L. *From Mannerism to Classicism: Printmaking in France, 1600–1660.* Exhibition catalogue. New Haven, Conn.: Yale University Art Gallery, 1988.

Constable 1976

Constable, W. G. *Canaletto.* 2d ed., revised by J. G. Links. Oxford and New York: Clarendon Press, 1976.

Cortissoz

Cortissoz, Royal. *Catalogue of the Etchings and Dry-Points of Childe Hassam, N.A.* New York and London: Charles Scribner's Sons, 1975.

Curtis

Curtis, Atherton. *Catalogue de l'oeuvre lithographié et gravé de Eugène Isabey.* Paris: Paul Prouté, 1939.

Delt.

Delteil, Loys. *Le peintre-graveur illustré.* 31 vols. Paris: 1906–26.

De V., de Vesme 1906

De Vesme, Alexandre. *Le peintre-graveur italien: Ouvrage faisant suite au Peintre-graveur de Bartsch.* Milan: U. Hoepli, 1906.

Dodgson

Dodgson, Campbell. "The Etchings of F. L. Griggs." *Print Collector's Quarterly* 11 (February 1924): 93–124.

Dodgson, Campbell. *A Catalogue of Etchings and Engravings by Robert Austin, R.E., 1913–29.* London: Twenty-one Gallery, 1930.

Drugulin

Drugulin, W. *Allart van Everdingen: Catalogue raisonné de toutes les estampes qui forment son oeuvre gravé.* Leipzig: W. Drugulin, 1873.

Dube

Dube, Anne Marie, and Wolf-Dieter Dube. *Erich Heckel: Das graphische Werk.* 2 vols. New York: Ernest Rathenau; Berlin: Euphorion Verlag, 1964.

Dube, Anne Marie, and Wolf-Dieter Dube. *E. L. Kirchner: Das graphische Werk.* 2d ed. 2 vols. Munich: Prestel Verlag, 1980.

Dut.

Dutuit, Eugène. *Manuel de l'amateur d'estampes.* 6 vols. Paris: A. Lévy, 1884–85.

Florence 1966

Florence, Istituto Universitario Olandese di Storia dell'Arte. *Artisti olandesi e fiamminghi in Italia,* by Carlos van Hasselt and Albert Blankert. Florence: L. S. Olschki, 1966.

F., Focillon 1918

Focillon, H. *Giovanni Battista Piranesi, 1720–1778.* Paris: Laurens, 1918.

Franken

Franken, Daniel. *L'oeuvre de Jan van de Velde.* Amstdam: F. Muller and Co., 1883.

Freedberg 1980

Freedberg, David. *Dutch Landscape Prints.* London: British Museum Publications, 1980.

Garton and Cook 1984

Muirhead Bone, 1876–1953. Sale catalogue. London: Garton and Cook, 1984.

Gerszi 1976

Gerszi, Terez. "Bruegels Nachwirkung auf die niederländischen Landschaftsmaler um 1600." *Oud-Holland* 90 (1976): 201–29.

Gerszi 1982

Gerszi, Terez. "Pieter Bruegels Einfluss auf die Herausbildung der niederländischen See- und Kustenlandschaftsdarstellung." *Jahrbuch der Berliner Museen* 24 (1982): 143–48.

Getscher and Staley 1977

Getscher, Robert, and Allen Staley. *The Stamp of Whistler.* Exhibition catalogue. Oberlin, Ohio: Allen Memorial Art Museum, 1977.

Gilmour 1988

Gilmour, Pat, ed. *Lasting Impressions: Lithography as Art.* Philadelphia: University of Pennsylvania Press, 1988.

Gluck 1963

Gluck, G. *Das grosse Bruegel-Werk.* Vienna: A. Schroll, 1963.

Grad and Riggs 1982

Grad, Bonnie L., and Timothy A. Riggs. *Visions of City and Country: Prints and Photographs of Nineteenth-Century France.* Worcester, Mass.: Worcester Art Museum, 1982.

Groesbeek 1966

Groesbeek, J. W. *Amstelveen: Acht eeuwen geschiedenis.* Amsterdam, 1966.

Groschwitz, Groschwitz 1962

Groschwitz, Gustave von. "The Prints of Thomas Shotter Boys." In *Prints,* edited by Carl Zigrosser, pp. 191–216. New York: Holt, Rinehart and Winston, 1962.

Harrington

Harrington, H. Nazeby. *The Engraved Work of Sir Francis Seymour Haden, P.R.E.: An Illustrated and Descriptive Catalogue.* Liverpool: Henry Young and Sons, 1910.

Haverkamp-Begemann 1975

Haverkamp-Begemann, Egbert. "Joos van Liere." Paper presented at colloquium, "Pieter Bruegel und seine Welt." Kunsthistorischen Institut der Freien Universität, Berlin, and Kupferstichkabinett der Staatlichen Museen Preussischer Kulturbesitz, 13–14 November 1975. Edited by Otto von Simson and Matthias Winner, pp. 17–28. Berlin, 1979.

Hayes 1965

Hayes, John. *The Drawings of Thomas Gainsborough.* 2 vols. New Haven, Conn., and London: Yale University Press, 1971.

Hédiard

Hédiard, Germain. *Eugène Isabey: Étude suivie du catalogue de son oeuvre.* Paris: L. Delteil, 1906.

Henriet

Henriet, Frédéric. *C. Daubigny et son oeuvre gravé.* Paris: A. Lévy, 1875.

Hind

Hind, Arthur M. *Giovanni Battista Piranesi: A Critical Study with a List of His Published Works and Detailed Catalogues of the Prisons and Views of Rome.* London: Cotswold Gallery, 1922.

Hind, Arthur M. *A Catalogue of Rembrandt's Etchings.* 2d ed. 2 vols. London: Methuen, 1923.

Hind 1938–48

Hind, Arthur M. *Early Italian Engravings: A Critical Catalogue. . . .* 7 vols. London: B. Quaritch, 1938–48.

HIRSCHMANN, HIRSCHMANN 1921

Hirschmann, Otto. *Verzeichnis des graphischen Werks von Hendrick Goltzius, 1558–1617.* Leipzig: Klinkhardt and Biermann, 1921.

HOLL.

Hollstein, F. W. H. *Dutch and Flemish Etchings, Engravings, and Woodcuts, ca. 1450–1700.* Amsterdam: Menno Hertzberger, 1949–.

Hollstein, F. W. H. *German Engravings, Etchings, and Woodcuts.* Amsterdam: Menno Hertzberger, 1954–.

KAUFFMANN 1984

Kauffmann, C. M. *John Varley, 1778–1842.* London: B. T. Batsford in association with the Victoria and Albert Museum, 1984.

K.

Kennedy, Edward G. *The Etched Work of Whistler.* New York: Grolier Club, 1910.

KEYES, KEYES 1977

Keyes, George. "Les eaux-fortes de Ruisdael." *Nouvelles de l'estampe* 36 (November–December 1977): 7–20.

KORENY

Koreny, Fritz. *Franz von Zülow: Frühe Graphik, 1904–1915.* Vienna: Christian Brandstätter Edition, 1983.

KORNFELD AND WICK

Kornfeld, E. W., and P. A. Wick. *Catalogue raisonné de l'oeuvre gravé et lithographié de Paul Signac.* Bern: Kornfeld and Klipstein, 1974.

LARKIN 1980

Larkin, Susan G. "The Cos Cob Clapboard School." In *Connecticut and American Impressionism.* Exhibition catalogue. Storrs, Conn.: William Benton Museum of Art, 1980.

LAWRENCE 1983

Spencer Museum of Art. *Dutch Prints of Daily Life.* Essay and catalogue by Linda Stone-Ferrier. Lawrence, Kans.: Spencer Museum of Art, 1983.

LEBEER, LEBEER 1969

Lebeer, Louis. *Catalogue raisonné des estampes de Bruegel l'ancien.* Brussels: Bibliothèque Royale Albert 1er, 1969.

LEHRS 1908–34

Lehrs, Max. *Geschichte und kritischer Katalog des deutschen, niederländischen und französischen Kupferstichs im XV Jahrhundert.* 9 vols. Vienna: Gesellschaft für vervielfältigende Kunst, 1908–34.

LEVY

Levy, Mervyn. *Whistler's Lithographs: A Catalogue Raisonné.* London: Jupiter Books, 1975.

LIESS 1979–82

Liess, Reinhard. "Die kleinen Landschaften Pieter Bruegels d. A. im Lichte seines Gesamtwerks." Parts 1–3. *Kunsthistorisches Jahrbuch Graz* 15–18 (1979–82): 1–117, 35–150, 79–165.

LINKS 1977

Links, J. G. *Canaletto and His Patrons.* New York: New York University Press, 1977.

LISTER, LISTER 1988

Lister, Raymond. *Catalogue Raisonné of the Works of Samuel Palmer.* Cambridge: Cambridge University Press, 1988.

LOUVRE 1981

Paris, Musée du Louvre. *Dessins baroques florentins du Musée du Louvre.* Exhibition catalogue. Paris: Éditions de la Réunion des Musées Nationaux, 1981.

LUGT 1915

Lugt, Frits. *Wandelingen met Rembrandt in en om Amsterdam.* Amsterdam, 1915.

L.

Lugt, Frits. *Les marques de collections de dessins et d'estampes.* Amsterdam: Vereenigde Drukkerijen, 1921. *Supplement.* The Hague: Martinus Nijhoff, 1956.

MACANDREW 1983

Macandrew, Hugh. *Italian Drawings in the Museum of Fine Arts, Boston.* Boston: Museum of Fine Arts, 1983.

MAN

Man, Felix H. "Lithography in England (1801–1810)." In *Prints,* edited by Carl Zigrosser, pp. 97–130. New York: Holt, Rinehart and Winston, 1962.

MAN, MAN 1970

Man, Felix H. *Graham Sutherland: Das graphische Werk, 1922–1970.* Munich: Verlag Galerie Wolfgang Ketterer, 1970.

MANNOCCI

Mannocci, Lino. *The Etchings of Claude Lorrain.* New Haven and London: Yale University Press, 1988.

MEDER 1922

Meder, J. *Handzeichnungen alter Meister in der Albertina.* Vienna, 1922.

MEL., MELOT 1974

Melot, Michel. *L'estampe impressioniste.* Paris: Bibliothèque Nationale, 1974.

MEL., MELOT 1980

Melot, Michel. *Graphic Art of the Pre-Impressionists.* New York: Harry N. Abrams, 1980.

MRAZEK 1981

Mrazek, Wilhelm. *Leopold Forstner: Ein Maler und Material-Künstler des Wiener Jugendstils.* Vienna: Belvedere Verlag A. Hadwiger, 1981.

MÜNZ

Münz, Ludwig. *A Critical Catalogue of Rembrandt's Etchings.* 2 vols. London, 1952.

Münz, Ludwig. *Pieter Breugel: The Drawings.* London: Phaidon, 1961.

NEUMANN

Neumann, J. B. *Rodolphe Bresdin.* New York: Artlover Library, 1929.

OBERHUBER 1968

Oberhuber, Konrad. "Hieronymus Cock, Battista Pittoni und Paolo Veronese in Villa Maser." In *Munuscula Discipulorum: Kunsthistorische Studien Hans Kauffmann zum 70. Geburtstag, 1966,* pp. 207–24. Berlin: Verlag Bruno Hessling, 1968.

P.G.

Pallucchini, Rodolfo, and G. F. Guarnati. *Le acqueforti di Canaletto.* Venice: Edizioni Daria Guarnati, 1945.

PARTHEY, PARTHEY 1853

Parthey, Gustav. *Wenzel Hollar: Beschreibendes Verzeichnis seiner Kupferstiche.* Berlin: Verlag der Nicolaischen Buchhandlung, 1853.

Pilo, Pilo 1963

Pilo, Giuseppe Maria. *Marco Ricci: Catalogo della mostra.* Venice: Edizione Alfieri, 1963.

Popham 1949

Popham, A. E. "Two Landscape Drawings by Pieter Bruegel the Elder." *Burlington Magazine* 91 (1949): 319–20.

Posner 1971

Posner, Donald. *Annibale Carracci: A Study in the Reform of Italian Painting around 1590.* 2 vols. London: Phaidon, 1971.

Reed and Wallace 1989

Reed, Sue Welsh, and Richard Wallace. *Italian Etchers of the Renaissance and Baroque.* Exhibition catalogue. Boston: Museum of Fine Arts, 1989.

Reznicek 1961

Reznicek, Emil Karel Josef. *Die Zeichnungen von Hendrick Goltzius.* Utrecht: Haentjens Dekker and Gumbert, 1961.

Riggs, Riggs 1977

Riggs, Timothy A. *Hieronymus Cock, Printmaker and Publisher.* New York: Garland Publishers, 1977.

Rinder

Rinder, Frank. *D. Y. Cameron: An Illustrated Catalogue of His Etched Work.* Glasgow: James Maclehose and Sons, 1912.

R.-D.

Robert-Dumesnil, Alexandre Pierre. *Le peintre-graveur français: Catalogue raisonné des estampes gravés par les peintres et les dessinateurs de l'école française.* 11 vols. Paris: G. Waree, 1835–71.

Roethlisberger 1961

Roethlisberger, Marcel. *Claude Lorrain: The Paintings.* 2 vols. New Haven: Yale University Press, 1961.

Roethlisberger 1967

Roethlisberger, Marcel. "The Pérelles." *Master Drawings* 5, no. 3 (1967): 283–86.

Roethlisberger 1968

Roethlisberger, Marcel. *Claude Lorrain: The Drawings.* 2 vols. Berkeley and Los Angeles: University of California Press, 1968.

Roethlisberger 1969

Roethlisberger, Marcel. *Bartholomeus Breenbergh: Handzeichnungen,* Berlin: De Gruyter, 1969.

Roli 1969

Roli, R. *I disegni italiani del seicento: Scuole emiliana, toscana, romana, marchigiana e umbra.* Treviso: Libreria editrice Canova, 1969.

Romdahl 1905

Romdahl, Axel Ludwig. *Peter Brueghel der Aeltere und sein Kunstschaffen.* Vienna: F. Tempsky, 1905.

Rotterdam 1988

Museum Boymans-van Beuningen. *Italianisanten en Bamboccianten.* Rotterdam: Museum Boymans-van Beuningen, 1988.

D. Russell 1975

Russell, H. Diane. *Jacques Callot: Prints and Related Drawings.* Exhibition catalogue. Washington, D.C.: National Gallery of Art, 1975.

Russell, Russell 1982

Russell, H. Diane. *Claude Lorrain, 1600–1682.* New York: George Braziller; Washington, D.C.: National Gallery of Art, 1982.

Russell 1975

Russell, Margarita. *Jan van Capelle 1624/6–1679.* Leigh-on-Sea: F. Lewis, 1975.

Schepers 1976

Schepers, Josef. *Haus and Hof westfälischer Bauern.* 3d ed. Munster, 1976.

Schiefler

Schiefler, Gustav. *Die Graphik Ernst Ludwig Kirchners.* 2 vols. Berlin: Euphorion Verlag, 1926 and 1931.

Schiefler and Mosel

Schiefler, Gustav. *Emil Nolde: Das graphische Werk.* Rev. ed., edited by Christel Mosel. 2 vols. Cologne: DuMont Schauberg, 1966.

Schmitt, Schmitt 1957

Schmitt, Annegrit. *Hanns Lautensack: Nürnberger Forschungen.* Nuremberg: M. Edelmann, 1957.

Schneider and Ekkart 1973

Schneider, H. *Jan Lievens: Sein Leben und seine Werke.* Supplement by R. E. O. Ekkart. Amsterdam, 1973 (first edition, Haarlem, 1932).

Schulz 1968

Schulz, Juergen, ed. *Master Drawings from California Collections.* Exhibition catalogue. Berkeley: University of California, 1968.

Schwarz, Schwarz 1917

Schwarz, Karl. *Augustin Hirschvogel: Ein deutscher Meister der Renaissance.* Berlin: J. Bard, 1917.

Scrase 1979

Scrase, David. *Drawings and Watercolours by Peter De Wint.* Exhibition catalogue. Cambridge: Cambridge University Press, 1979.

Selz 1957

Selz, Peter. *German Expressionist Painting.* Berkeley and Los Angeles: University of California Press, 1957.

Six 1909

Six, Jan. "Gersaints lijst van Rembrandts prenten." *Oud-Holland* 27 (1909): 65–110.

Slive 1982

Slive, Seymour, and H. R. Hoetink. *Jacob van Ruisdael.* Exhibition catalogue. New York: Abbeville Press, 1982.

Smith 1982

Smith, Hammond. *Peter De Wint, 1784–1849.* London: F. Lewis Publishers, 1982.

Stoddard 1972

Stoddard, Whitney S. *Art and Architecture in Medieval France.* New York: Harper and Row, 1972.

Strauss, Strauss 1977

Strauss, Walter. *Hendrik Goltzius, 1558–1617: The Complete Engravings and Woodcuts.* 2 vols. New York: Abaris Books, 1977.

SUMOWSKI 1980
Sumowski, Werner. "Observations on Jan Lievens' Landscape Drawings." *Master Drawings* 18, no. 4 (1980): 370–72.

SUTTON 1962
Sutton, Denys. "Gaspard Dughet: Some Aspects of His Art." *Gazette des beaux-arts* 104 (July–August 1962): 269–312.

TALBOT AND SHESTACK 1969–70
Talbot, Charles, and Alan Shestack, eds. *Prints and Drawings of the Danube School.* Exhibition catalogue. New Haven, Conn.: Yale University Art Gallery, 1969–70.

TASSI
Tassi, Roberto. *Graham Sutherland: Complete Graphic Work.* New York: Rizzoli, 1978.

THEOBALD, THEOBALD 1906
Theobald, Henry Studdy. *Crome's Etchings: A Catalogue and an Appreciation with Some Account of His Paintings.* London: Macmillan and Co., 1906.

TISSINK AND DE WIT 1987
Tissink, Fieke, and H. F. de Wit. *Gorcumse schilders in de gouden eeuw.* Gorinchem, 1987.

TOLNAY
De Tolnay, Charles. *The Drawings of Pieter Bruegel the Elder.* Translated by Charles R. Sleeth. New York: Twin Editions, 1952.

TR., TRAUTSCHOLDT 1973
Trautscholdt, Eduard. "Johannes Ruischer alias Jonge Hercules: Die Radierungen." Supplement to *Hercules Segers: The Complete Etchings,* by E. Haverkamp-Begemann, pp. [113]–36. Amsterdam, 1973.

TWYMAN 1970
Twyman, Michael. *Lithography, 1800–1850.* London: Oxford University Press, 1970.

TWYMAN 1988
Twyman, Michael. "Charles Joseph Hullmandel: Lithographic Printer Extraordinary." In Gilmour 1988, pp. 42–90.

VAN GELDER, VAN GELDER 1976
Van Gelder, Dirk. *Rodolfe Bresdin: Catalogue raisonné de l'oeuvre gravé.* 2 vols. The Hague: Martinus Nijhoff, 1976.

VAN HASSELT 1965
Van Hasselt, R. J. "Drie topografische tekenaars der XVIIe eeuw." *Jaarboek Oudheidkundige Kring de Ghulden Roos* (1965).

VAN HASSELT 1967
Van Hasselt, R. J. "Supplement bijgewerkt tot 1. September 1967." Typescript supplement B to van Hasselt 1965.

VAN REGTEREN ALTENA 1983
Van Regteren Altena, I. Q. *Jacques de Gheyn: Three Generations.* 3 vols. The Hague, 1983.

WATROUS 1984
Watrous, James. *A Century of American Printmaking, 1880–1980.* Madison: University of Wisconsin Press, 1984.

WAY, WAY 1914
The Lithographs of Whistler: Arranged according to the Catalogue by Thomas R. Way. Edited by Edward G. Kennedy. New York: Kennedy and Co., 1914.

WEIGEL 1843
Weigel, Rudolph. *Suppléments au Peintre-graveur de Adam Bartsch. . . .* Leipzig: R. Weigel, 1843.

WEISBERG 1985
Weisberg, Gabriel. *Millet and His Barbizon Contemporaries.* Tokyo: Art Life, 1985.

WHITE 1969
White, Christopher. *Rembrandt as an Etcher.* University Park: Pennsylvania State University Press, 1969.

WHITE 1977
White, Christopher. *English Landscape, 1630–1850: Drawings, Prints, and Books from the Paul Mellon Collection.* New Haven, Conn.: Yale Center for British Art, 1977.

WILCOX 1985
Wilcox, Scott. *British Watercolors: Drawings of the Eighteenth and Nineteenth Centuries from the Yale Center for British Art.* New York: Hudson Hills Press, 1985.

WILTON 1980
Wilton, Andrew. *The Art of Alexander and John Robert Cozens.* New Haven, Conn.: Yale Center for British Art, 1980.

WILTON-ELY 1978
Wilton-Ely, John. *The Mind and Art of Giovanni Battista Piranesi.* London: Thames and Hudson, 1978.

WINZINGER 1979
Winzinger, Franz. *Wolf Huber: Das Gesamtwerk.* 2 vols. Munich, 1979.

WUERTH
Wuerth, Louis A. *Catalogue of the Etchings of Joseph Pennell.* Introduction by Elizabeth Robins Pennell. Boston: Little, Brown, 1928.

WURZ., WURZBACH 1910
Wurzbach, Alfred von. *Niederländisches Künstler-Lexikon.* 3 vols. Vienna: Verlag von Halm and Goldmann, 1906–11.

ZIGROSSER, ZIGROSSER 1969
Zigrosser, Carl. *The Complete Etchings of John Marin.* Philadelphia: Philadelphia Museum of Art, 1969.

ZUMTHOR 1962
Zumthor, Paul. *Daily Life in Rembrandt's Holland.* Translated by Simon Watson Taylor. Daily Life Series. London: Weidenfeld and Nicolson, 1962.

ZWOLLO 1985
Zwollo, An. "Enkele nieuwe tekeningen van Gillis Mostaert." In *Rubens and His World: Bijdragen Opgedragen aan Prof. Dr. Ir. R.-A. d'Hulst,* pp. 61–69. Antwerp, 1985.

Index of Artists

Numbers refer to catalogue entries.

Austin, Robert S., 101
Bloemaert, Abraham, 25–29
Bol, Hans, 18
Bolswert, Boetius Adam, 26–29
Bone, Muirhead, 99
Bonington, Richard Parkes, 89
Both, Jan, 56
Boys, Thomas Shotter, 90
Breenbergh, Bartholomeus, 46–47
Bresdin, Rodolphe, 130
Bril, Paul, 23
Bruegel, Pieter, the Elder, 16–17
Cameron, David Young, 97–98
Canal, Giovanni Antonio (Canaletto), 150–51
Cantagallina, Remigio, 146–47
Claude Lorrain. *See* Gellée, Claude
Cock, Hieronymus, 14–15
Cock, Matthys, 15
Cooper, Richard, II, 75
Corot, Camille, 118
Cox, David, 85
Cozens, John Robert, 76
Crome, John, 80–82
Daubigny, Charles-François, 121
Delamotte, William, 83
De Wint, Peter, 86
Dughet, Gaspard, 109
Dujardin, Karel, 63–64
Dupont, Gainsborough, 77
Englemann, Godefrey, 89
Everdingen, Allart van, 60–61
Forstner, Leopold, 10
Gellée, Claude (Claude Lorrain), 106–7
Goltzius, Hendrik, 24
Goyen, Jan van, 44–45
Grave, Josua de, 71
Griggs, Frederick Landseer, 100
Grimaldi, Giovanni Francesco, 148
Haden, Francis Seymour, 94–95
Haghe, Louis, 87
Harpignies, Henri-Joseph, 122–24
Hassam, Childe, 5
Heckel, Erich, 145
Hirschvogel, Augustin, 139
Hollar, Wenzel, 72–73
Huber, Wolf, 138
Huys, Frans, 17
Isabey, Eugène, 119
Jongkind, Johan Barthold, 125–26
Kirchner, Ernst Ludwig, 144
Koller-Pinnell, Broncia, 9
Lautensack, Hanns, 140–41
Lear, Edward, 93
Lievens, Jan, 54
Marin, John, 6–7
Master of the Small Landscapes, 12–13
Méryon, Charles, 127–29
Moll, Carl, 8
Monro, Thomas, 79
Mostaert, Gillis, 19–22
Naiwincx, Herman, 65
Nolde, Emil, 142–43
Palmer, Samuel, 91–92
Pennell, Joseph, 4
Perelle, Adam, 108
Perelle, Gabriel, 108
Piranesi, Giovanni Battista, 152–54
Pissarro, Camille, 131
Rembrandt Harmensz. van Rijn, 50–53
Ricci, Marco, 149
Roberts, David, 87
Roghman, Roeland, 57–59
Rousseau, Théodore, 120
Roussel, Ker-Xavier, 134–35
Rowlandson, Thomas, 78
Ruisdael, Jacob van, 67–68
Ruisscher, Johannes, 66
Sadeler, Johannes, I, 19–22
Sandby, Paul, 74
Signac, Paul, 132–33
Silvestre, Israel, 110–17
Stannard, Joseph, 88
Sutherland, Graham, 102–5
Ulft, Jacob van der, 62
Varley, John, 84
Velde, Jan van de, II, 39–43
Verboom, Adriaen, 69–70
Villon, Jacques, 136–37
Visscher, Claes Jansz., 30–38
Ward, William, 96
Waterloo, Anthonie, 55
Whistler, James McNeill, 1–3
Zülow, Franz von, 11

Composed and formatted with
Pagemaker 3.02 program on a
Macintosh IIx computer with a Laserview screen.
Typeface: ITC Baskerville.
Both roman and italic old-style figures were
drawn expressly for this book by the designer
with Fontographer 2.0 program.
Based on John Baskerville's
1757 Grand Primer type.

Imaging by Electric Pencil
Los Angeles, California.
Printed on 80-pound Lustro dull book with
120-pound Brilliant Art Gloss Cover C1S
by Typecraft, Inc.
Pasadena, California.

DESIGNED BY DOYALD YOUNG